SUSPENSE

Conceptualizations,
Theoretical Analyses,
and Empirical Explorations

SUSPENSE

Conceptualizations, Theoretical Analyses, and Empirical Explorations

Edited by

Peter Vorderer
University of Music and Theater, Hannover

Hans J. Wulff
Mike Friedrichsen
Free University of Berlin

Routledge
Taylor & Francis Group
New York London

Copyright © 1996, by Lawrence Erlbaum Associates, Inc.

First published by
Lawrence Erlbaum Associates, Inc., Publishers
10 Industrial Avenue
Mahwah, New Jersey 07430

Transferred to Digital Printing 2009 by Routledge

Routledge
Taylor & Francis Group
270 Madison Avenue
New York, NY 10016

Routledge
Taylor & Francis Group
2 Park Square
Milton Park, Abingdon
Oxon OX14 4RN

Cover design by Gail Silverman

Library of Congress Cataloging-in-Publication Data

Suspense : conceptualizations, theoretical analyses, and empirical
    explorations / edited by Peter Vorderer, Hans Jürgen Wulff, Mike
    Friedrichsen.
        p.   cm.
    Includes bibliographical references and index.
    ISBN 0-8058-1965-7 (cloth). — ISBN 0-8058-1966-5 (paper)
    1. Suspense in motion pictures. 2. Suspense in literature.
I. Vorderer, Peter. II. Wulff, Hans Jürgen. III. Friedrichsen,
Mike.
PN1995.9.S87S87   1996
791.43′653—dc20   95-39720
                                                                CIP

Contents

Preface

This book begins with the general assumption that suspense is a major criterion for both an audience's selection and evaluation of entertaining media offerings. This assumption is supported not only by the popularity of suspenseful narratives, but also by the reasons users give for their actual choice of media contents. At the same time, we have to admit that psychology, film theory, and communication research have not provided a satisfying theory to describe and explain what suspense actually is, how exactly it is caused by films or books, and what kind of effect it has on audiences. The main objective of our book is to provide this theory. We do not do so by proposing a single theoretical or methodological approach, but by bringing together scholars from different disciplines who are working on this issue. Our goal is to reflect the "state of the art" as much as it is to highlight and encourage further developments in this area.

There are basically two different ways to approach the problem of describing and explaining suspense. One begins with an analysis of suspenseful texts (books, films, etc.), whereas the other focuses on the reception process. Researchers who follow the more text-oriented method identify the uncertainty of the narrative's outcome, the threat or danger for a protagonist, the play with time delays, and so on, as important and necessary for the production of suspense. The more reception-oriented scholar, on the other hand, focuses on the cognitive activities of audiences, the expectations of readers, the curiosity of onlookers, their emotions (fear, hope, etc.), and their relationships with the protagonists. None of the researchers would deny the importance of aspects investigated by their colleagues, but it is obvious that every individual scholar concentrates primarily on either

the text or the viewer. The focus on the text itself and on audience's comprehension of it mark the two opposite ends within the research field that deals with
suspense. A correspondence between the two seems to be quite difficult, although
necessary, to determine. This is because concentration on the text implies the
danger of underestimating viewers' activities and might support the assumption
that the text determines its understanding. An exclusive analysis of the understanding, on the other hand, overlooks the importance of the text and fails to
explain the cause of the specific reception. It is obvious that both perspectives
are important to describe and explain suspense. Our starting point, therefore, is
the thesis that suspense is an activity of the audience (reader, onlooker, etc.) that
is related to specific features and characteristics of the text (books, films, etc.).
The question is: What kind of relation is this? We will have to find out how,
why, and which elements of the text cause effects that are experienced as suspense.

   Scholars in semiotics, literary criticism, cultural studies, and film theory look
at this problem from a more text-oriented point of view. That means that they
deal primarily with the how and which. According to Hans J. Wulff, the dramaturgy of suspense refers to the activity of anticipating; it provides the material
from which viewers can extrapolate future developments. *Cataphora* are functional elements that inform and pilot hypotheses and expectations that viewers
form on seeing a film. The Lacanian theory of film viewing, on the other hand,
suggests a complex mirror relation between the viewer's experience and the
activity of watching a film. A fictional text incorporates a subject position that
is constructed for viewers. The subject is a construct, produced and controlled
by the cinematic apparatus itself. Suspense is—as Garry Leonard shows—a
strategy by which the mirroring identification of the viewer and the textual subject
is broken, and the subject's mastery of events seems to be problematic. Also
using psychodynamic concepts as a base, Lothar Mikos sees suspense as an
experience between fear and pleasure. Peter Wuss identifies "passive control" as
a receptive goal that reduces uncertainty of events. Given the uncertainty of the
course of events, viewers may try to orient themselves using the few regularities
that appear in these events (i.e., they look intuitively in the plot for invariant
moments on the perceptual level). Suspense in Antonioni's films is, as Wuss
shows, not based mainly on narrative, but on a text's topical structure. Noël
Carroll shows how the structure of a film elicits specific hypotheses from viewers
and deals with the question of how it can be rational for people to review or
reread suspense stories with which they are already familiar. Richard Gerrig is
concerned with the same question and tries to explain anomalous suspense from
a cognitive point of view. Still another contribution that deals with this so-called
"paradox of suspense" comes from William Brewer, who looks at the specific
relationship between event structure and discourse structure of literary texts and
their effect on curiosity, surprise, and suspense.

   Although most of the authors already mentioned imply assumptions and
hypotheses about the reading and viewing of suspenseful material, the following

chapters take the psychological perspective explicitly and focus on the cognitive and emotional processes that underlie viewers' experiences of suspense. This means that reception theory tries to answer the question of why suspenseful texts may be experienced as they are. Peter Ohler and Gerhild Nieding apply schema theory to explain suspense in cognitive terms. They hold that it is the specific processing of information that is responsible for this experience. Ed Tan and Gijsbert Diteweg exemplify this by showing, in detail, which predictive inferences are made by viewers on the basis of which textual information. As a byproduct of their study, it becomes clear that other cognitive and emotional processes like curiosity, mystery, surprise, and irony go along with the experience of suspense. This is also important to Gerry Cupchik, who distinguishes and differentiates between those processes by using an emotion and motivation psychological perspective. For him, it is basically a question of how much cognitive activity (accommodation) a text affords. Dolf Zillmann gives a most extensive conception of suspense, both in terms of theoretical hypotheses and empirical confirmations. He demonstrates the usefulness of his theory, based on the assumption that viewers participate in films by feeling empathetic with positive protagonists. Peter Vorderer tries to elaborate and differentiate the given reception theories by looking at the differences between texts, viewers, and reception situations.

In the background of these theoretical considerations remains the open question of how we can and how we should conduct research in this field. Because there is quite a controversy surrounding the methods and methodologies in suspense research, we decided to dedicate part of the book to this problem. Minet de Wied and Dolf Zillmann give an overview of the different possibilities and show their respective advantages and disadvantages. Axel Mattenklott begins with Zillmann's empathy theory and shows how empathetic distress can be measured. Gerhild Nieding, Peter Ohler, and Claudia Thußbas show what a time series analysis can do in that field. Mike Friedrichsen suggests possibilities for integrating different methods in future research.

We are most grateful to our contributors and translators, the Friends of Communication Research, and the Office of International Affairs at the Free University of Berlin. We would also like to thank those who, in various ways, helped us to make this volume possible: Corinna Kastner and Ines Deppe in Hannover, Stefan Jenzowsky in Berlin, and Kirstin Gunther in Toronto. They all invested a lot of time studying or helping us to study suspense and its conceptualizations, theoretical analyses, and empirical explorations.

Peter Vorderer
Hans J. Wulff
Mike Friedrichsen

1

▼▼▼▼▼▼▼

Suspense and the Influence of Cataphora on Viewers' Expectations

Hans J. Wulff
Free University of Berlin

The experience of suspense essentially lies in equally calculating, expecting, and evaluating a coming event. I call this activity *anticipation*. It consists of several different acts:

1. Given information should not only be understood as such, but should also be regarded as the starting point for future developments in a story, social situation, or course of events.
2. It is necessary to draw up a scenario of what is coming from what the text has informed viewers and what viewers know outside of the text—about life, physics, and psychology in general, but also about genres and modes of narrative.
3. The future situations in the plot are an ensemble of alternative possibilities that are more or less probable—and it is in the acts of anticipation that the degree of probability with which the story can develop in one or another direction can be calculated.
4. Finally, the individual possibilities can be evaluated and possible counter-actions by the protagonist conceived. Only this scenario will create the conditions for the feeling of suspense: There is no experience of suspense without anticipation!

The *dramaturgy* of suspense refers to the activity of anticipating; it provides the material from which viewers can extrapolate future developments. The *textual theory* of suspense describes operational aspects of the staging. It is charged with describing elements of the text in their function, role, and status. This starting point holds true for the examination of processes of suspense in all medias and genres.

CATAPHORIC TEXT ELEMENTS

It is of absolute importance for the dramaturgy of suspense to be informed about the place of suspense—for suspense is not in the text, but rather in what the text triggers. Viewers cannot make any extrapolations from what they are told if regularities and legalities did not bring a given situation together with a forth-coming development, so that knowledge of rules and conventions is always incorporated into the prognostic work of the experience of suspense. Such pieces of information are "pre-information" (Borringo, 1980, p. 53), references to future developments in the plot. Chatman (1978), who spoke of *foreshadowing*, brought this together with an evaluation of scenes and episodes regarding the narration: Narrative *kernels* are those scenes that propel the narrative forward; *satellites*, though, where the announcement function is characteristically bundled, are the kind of scenes that prepare the way for the kernels. Satellites can be removed from a narrative without causing any major damage—although the text would then lose any suspense it had.

Chatman's distinction makes an important point: In the examination of proc-esses of suspense, the issue is not the recording of narrative structures as they are realized in the text itself. Rather, it is about possible and probable develop-ments in the plot, which often cannot even be proven on the surface of the film. At issue are hypotheses and expectations that viewers form on seeing a film. A certain task that the text must fulfill can be defined here: All the advance references and all the anticipation of future events undertaken by the text are attempts to influence the area where the anticipation of the following event can happen. Thus, one should inquire less about how the plot is represented in the text than how readers are guided through the plot: It is instruction, rather than representation, that is the basic textual semantic function.

It seems appropriate to determine classes of textual elements that serve the purpose, within the framework of textual reception, of evoking or indicating possible future courses of events. Semantically, these elements of suspense construction can be taken as *cataphora*, as textual references pointing to sub-sequent information in the text.[1] They help to shape the viewers' scope of expectation. The cataphora are not used primarily for the representation or the exposition of the narrative course of events, but rather for the manipulation of the anticipated course, the modulation of the area for problem solutions in which viewers move and orientate themselves. The cataphora include viewers' cognitive operations; it is only these that result in any meaning.

---

[1]On the one hand, *anaphor* is used as a complementary term to *cataphor* (in the sense of reference back); on the other hand, it is the generic term for all kinds of inert textual reference.

Such cataphoric elements operate, naturally, in the textual process in an "open" textual field of reference where further developments have not yet become manifest and where they can only be forecast with more or less probability from the respective place of reading. The analysis of suspense constructions is thus only useful and possible as an analysis of textual processes and not of synoptic textual structures. The advance reference takes place in a still undefined information process and is targeting a specific element in the text. It is characteristic for cataphoric elements in suspense constructions to stay "unfulfilled" here and to show themselves to be an advance reference for a course of events that does not happen.

When subsequent information in the cataphor is only indicated but not exposed, the cataphora are constructions of attention (although it may remain to be seen whether the cataphorically aroused attention is satisfied or disappointed by the actual following text). Brugmann (cit. from Bühler, 1965) spoke of a "preparatory" function of the advance reference and thereby gave a name to this aspect of the manipulation of the textual scenario that is so central to the understanding and processing of a text: Viewers are prepared for possible future courses of events, they are put into the mood for the web of possible events, the probability of future events and intrigues are altered, and so on. In other words, cataphoric advance references are a central means of developing a field of anticipation in viewers.

The possibility of using cataphoric advance references is closely linked with the fact that word processing systems are regulated by schematized stores of knowledge that are activated and applied in the processing (compare Ohler, 1990, as well as Ohler & Nieding, chap. 8, this volume). Bühler (1965) wrote in his *Sprachtheorie*, about the understanding of sentences: "The 'anticipating' of something that has not yet been said is, psychologically, quite understandable now that we know how often our as yet unrealised thoughts are preempted by a more or less 'empty' sentence schema. The advance reference follows on from places in this schema" (p. 121). This observation can be applied fully to the function of cataphoric information in suspense constructions, but must be modified in one respect: The nature of a story's development is quite an open number of possibilities, moving either toward a good or bad ending, always open to enlargement through the introduction of new informational elements. The "schema" in which the advance reference is possible is a productive calculation of alternative textual developments.

In the linguistic study of cataphora, it is said that advance references are cohesive relationships of one sign to a subsequent one. Cohesion results there, above all, from coreference: such as when a proform stands in front of the coreferring expression ("Das Glück der Frau, die *er* liebt, ist eine Tortur für *den Eifersüchtigen*") or when reference is made to a following line of text ("*These* were the verses the White Rabbit read: . . ."). The coreferring expression can be deduced even when it does not actually appear in the text; it is connoted by the cataphoric term.

In semiotic terms, cataphoric information has its own particular position, but then the factor of showing (*Zeigemoment*), which is always present in cinematic speech, can be identified particularly clearly in them. At the same time, the cataphor is a manifestation of a textual instance, an authority that controls the action in such a way that it points to future developments. If one so wishes, this is a paradox: the advance reference aimed to a still open situative development. It is one of the conventions of storytelling that one only foreshadows things that actually happen, and that actually become a subject of the situation. The following course of events must, therefore, already be known before a cataphor can be installed.

Let us refer to Bühler (1965) on anaphoric expression as he wrote in general about textual references: "There is a showing in the form of the anaphora; and whoever looks for the field of showing ('Zeigfeld') where it is happening, will find the ribbon of emergent speech itself being treated as a 'Zeigfeld.' The context is the anaphoric 'Zeigfeld,' the emergent speech becomes retrospective and prognostic in places, becomes *reflexive*" (p. 258). In two respects, this concept is important and puts in a nutshell the juxtaposition of a work's structure and the activity of reception that is so difficult to convey:

1. The staging of this field of reference, and thus of the movement of reception, is absolutely essential for the dramaturgy of suspense.
2. The experience of suspense follows a strategy of referential showing and is thus always orientated to the text. Viewers cannot free themselves completely from the text—despite the importance that the workings of the imagination have for the experience of suspense. In fact, the viewers are always being led back into that domain of controlled information.

NARRATIVE, THEMATIC, AND ATMOSPHERIC FRAMEWORKS

Every narratively eventful storyline opens up a series of possible connections that each person who has mastered the laws of the genre or the rules of everyday life can calculate. Someone, for example, who steals some money, commits an offense, is sought after by the police (and possibly others). Another person, who finds some incriminating material that can send the highest echelons of a crime syndicate to prison, must be conscious of the fact that there will be an attempt to get the material back at any price. One can dispense with further examples here—it is clear that the way someone gets caught up in a story is almost identical to the way that one gets further into a field of complications, antagonisms, and the like. When the story gets going, the further developments can be extrapolated, at least in part, from what has already happened.

Let us stay with the first example. The connections are there at the point when someone commits an offense. An interpretative framework is thereby created in which viewers may be able to transform accidental, coincidental, and perhaps peripheral things into a scenario of future events. An example of this very simple, initial constellation comes from Hitchcock's *Psycho*, in which one can see that we are dealing with conclusions when one attempts to pass from the given situation to what is to come: The action centers on a chance meeting of Marion Crane with her boss. Marion is on the run to her lover with the $40,000 that she had been entrusted to bank. She has to wait at a traffic light in the town, where pedestrians jostle over the crossing in front of the cars. One of them is Marion's boss, who is under the impression that she is ill and at home, because she had left with a migraine a few hours before. He recognizes her and stops in confusion and in thought, but is then pushed on by the other passersby. The reception of a film is also a comparison of what one knows with possible outcomes for the film characters. What do we know about the boss? We were told that $40,000 is a lot of money for him, too. What could he do? We do not know whether the chance meeting has aroused his suspicion. If he really had become suspicious and had called the bank, Marion's robbery would have been discovered and the police would already be on her trail. The meeting with her boss thus forms a possible element of uncertainty for the protagonist: Perhaps her situation has been aggravated, perhaps she is no longer on the run by herself, but pursued by others. Then the police would be involved. Hitchcock clearly picks up on this in *Psycho*: Marion has slept in the car after the terrible journey through the night. A policeman wakes her up, a dramatic idea that once more stresses the heroine's possible uncertainty. He is, however, unsuspecting. The diversion that the meeting with the boss had made possible does not come about.

A theory of filmic or filmic-textual referential structures is still to be formulated. A first attempt at this would be to elaborate on the distinction made between *narrative, thematic*, and *atmospheric* advance references. Korte (1987) wrote, in his analysis of *Jaws*, about "advance references" (p. 111) and meant by this those elements of the props or the staging that can be brought together with the action in the broadest sense—skeleton fish heads are characteristics of Quint's passion for hunting; on several occasions, a jawbone frames the picture, and so on. We are dealing here, though, with details of a film's staging that serve the purpose in the further functional framework of attuning the narrated world to the problem of being treated in the narration. I only want to speak more closely about narrative cataphors when they have immediate relevance to the textual or dramatic narration, when they have the function of being more specific about a problem or problem-solving area, or when they install them to start with. The elements that Korte listed are part of the film's thematic strategy and can be classed as the principle of redundance, which takes many forms in Hollywood cinema. When, in *Jaws*, for example, the issues of the sharks, the fishing hunt, or the big game hunt at sea are dealt with, the intense description of Quint as an obsessive shark hunter is part of the thematic structure. The framing mentioned already is also a reference to this subject as well as to an atmospherically effective detail that underscores the fundamental nature of the battle being fought here. On the other hand, the particular emphasis on the oxygen tanks that Brody will use to kill the shark in the end is an advance reference that can be effective after all. Let us note Korte (1987) on this particular scene:

> Even the most important detail for the solution of the "shark problem" [!] is presented beforehand almost in passing: Brody mistakenly undoes the wrong knot. The oxygen tanks roll overboard. He has almost caused a catastrophe, as Hooper angrily declares. The observer now knows that they are explosive, but doesn't attach any further importance to all of this at this stage. Quint mocks: "I just wonder what this bastard of a shark would do with them. Perhaps he'll swallow them. I once saw how one of them ate up a rocking chair." (p. 112)

In fact, such narrative long-range references play a significant role in many suspense films, because objects of the narrated world, which can be functionalized in the final problem solving, are being presented in the film's exposition strategy (Hartmann, 1992). When we learn that someone loses their self-control when they drink, this knowledge infiltrates through the reception into the development of the scenario (a comic example is Blake Edwards' *Blind Date*). Of major significance here are the rules and laws, taboos, and bans that apply in the narrated world (Wulff, 1985). Lüthi (1975) rightly drew attention to the fact that bans are also anticipations, and generalized:

> [Bans] say negatively what will later happen positively, the later event is, in this respect, a repetition of what has been expressed in the ban. Every outline, whether it be an announcement, an instruction of how to act or a ban, creates expectation, suspense is created. Every anticipation, even those with a minus sign, and especially those ones, are straining to be realised. (p. 105)

Because the disregard of taboos and bans is one of the most elementary approaches of narration, viewers can always reckon, in their anticipatory activity, on the infringement of the law, the breaking of the rules, and the consequences of such a deed. At the same time, they operate in conventional territory, for infringements of laws result in other actions that are implicit. If someone steals money from the mafia, a whole structure of roles can be created—something that works very closely with one's knowledge of genre and is part of the viewers' genre competence.

Lüthi's ideas are also central because, on closer observation, the depicted moral of a story (regarded by Carroll as a separate defining element of suspense) lets it be referred to as the functional aspect of the predefinition of actions and outcomes. The moral correctness of an outcome does not only play a role in the evaluation of possible courses of events but also in the estimation of the characters' outcome. How well the narrated figure fits into the story becomes really tangible only when the rules are broken: A protagonist, who is falsely accused and is almost executed by hanging (as in *Under Suspicion*, 1991), is perceived using the hypothesis that he will do everything to clear his name; when he turns out, in the end, to have been the real culprit, who organized the evidence against himself so that he could then accuse another person of the crime, viewers are forced to revise their hypothesis about the hero's motives—and the outcome of the story becomes ambivalent. The protagonist has cleared himself; in that respect, the good outcome that is formally expected of the protagonist role has been reached; but, in the moral sense, it has turned out to be a bad outcome. The interesting thing about this is that the potential of intentions and actions that viewers think the hero capable of are rigorously restricted once the protagonist is regarded as a framed person.

DRAMATIC DANGER AREA

A whole series of cataphoric advance references that occur in the dramatic-situative close-range area already begin below the narrative level. This has very much to do with the fact that, over and above the narrative intricacy, the execution of actions and the existence of situations are the textual instances that focus viewers' registering and creative activities. The entity of scene, situation, or sequence is, moreover, a separate, integral space of orientation, in respect to both the cinematic structures and the unities of treatment.

A scene is often not fully developed, but only realized to the extent necessary to give an impression of the relevant information that a protagonist must respond to, which the protagonists or antagonists themselves do not even have to be aware of. It is important to give viewers a picture of the situation so they can see a field of dangers, resistances, and obstacles. It is not necessary for a possibly dangerous situation actually to come about. Complications in actions are, for example, often only hinted at. A typical case is the following: The protagonist is hanging from a rope that is scraping against a cliff edge and could snap. The rope often does not snap, but that is not what it is about. The important thing is that viewers can visualize the possibility of an unhappy course of events. The danger indicator remains as an anticipatory reference to a possible complication (or here, even, to the mortal danger the protagonist is in).

Dangers are brought into play as possibilities but not as actual developments. The danger is the "not yet" of a catastrophe or injury. The activity of anticipation reaches out to this state of "not yet" and tries to give it a more precise definition. What is the target for a given course of events? Which rule or law extends a given situation into other possible situations? What probability do the various alternatives have for the course of events? A given situation, thus, is located in a field of possible developments. The action of reception covers the transition between the real and what is coming about. An intermediate area is established between the modes of being and a given situation is compared with what might happen. The viewers and the work are equally involved in this process: Viewers themselves must create the possibilities in which the situation can be developed. It is the job of the film to give hints about which possibilities, in the respective case, are nearer than others.

The characteristics of objects play an important role in these deliberations. In this respect, moreover, understanding film is often not much different from the planning of actions and calculations of risk in everyday life. In one of the Laurel and Hardy shorts, the idea is that a piano will be heaved up on to a balcony. A block and tackle is tied to a blind that cannot possibly take the weight. Laurel is on the balcony and makes a great effort to pull the rope up. Hardy, who has put a ladder against the balcony, is supporting the piano from below. One can extrapolate from everyday knowledge about the stability of objects that the awning must tear and the weight of the piano will be come down fair and square on the fat man. However, the film disappoints our expectation, and the piano arrives above in one piece. Hardy only comes to harm when Laurel undoes the block and tackle and carelessly throws it down. It lands on Hardy's head.

The dramaturgical conceptions of suspense scenes are intended to show the "not yet" of the scene or to evoke this in the viewer. It is evident that the indication of danger forms a central starting point for receptive activities. Dramaturgy of the scene and processes of anticipation are closely interrelated: Clearly, the resolution of the scene is arranged in such a way that the individual elements—from which the picture of the situation must be composed—have the primary function of depicting the danger of the situation and the actors' corresponding actions.

In the James Bond film *A View to a Kill* (1984), there is a short sequence that illustrates the forementioned principle:

1. Bond and the girl are trapped in a lift stuck between two floors. The villain has thrown a Molotov cocktail onto the lift and then escaped. We see Bond and the girl in the cabin. Bond tries to kick one of the steel trap doors off from the lift ceiling.

2. We see the burning mountings of the lift. The pressure of heat causes some of the cords to break.

3. The girl is terrified.

4. As in 1, Bond manages to break open one of the trap doors.

5. As in 2, the mountings burn.

6. As in 4, Bond disappears through the gap.

7. In the shaft, Bond tries to reach out to the girl to pull her out of the cabin.

8. As in 5, the mountings burn.

9. As in 6, the girl climbs out of the cabin.

10. The lift shaft is burning.

11. As in 7, Bond.

12. The girl, almost from Bond's perspective, tries desperately to reach out for Bond's hand.
13. As in 11, Bond is still reaching out to the girl. The camera follows the outstretched hand.
14. As in 8, a burning mounting.
15. As in 12, the girl tries to get hold of the hand.
16. As in 14, the mounting breaks away.
17. We see the girl's foot and the lift falling away into the depths below. The girl does not fall.

In this short scene, whose structure also appears in countless other films, the elements that make the situation exciting are the very center of attention. The situation is almost a classical one: The protagonist is trapped, he is in the greatest of danger, and escape seems impossible.[2]

There are two kinds of danger here and an awful end seems unavoidable: The fire, which has spread like a wall of flame above the cabin in the lift shaft, has cut off the way upward, and the lift's cables, whose mountings are burning one by one, threaten to give, leaving the lift to crash into the depths. The protagonists are threatened by a double tragedy: They are in danger of being burned alive and of falling to their deaths. Bond does the absurd thing: He tries to make a run for it above the lift despite the danger from the fire. The first danger proves to be surmountable. The second danger now has to be shown so that it will stay in the viewer's consciousness, especially as the events are coming to a head. This is the reason that the shots of the mountings are so important for the montage. In fact, they chiefly make us aware that Bond is working under pressure. Therefore, it is also a last-minute rescue that we have at the end. The cramped space corresponds with the restricted amount of time left for the protagonist to act.

This example is about constructing a particularly dramatic field that can be analyzed specifically as a suspenseful situation. The breakdown of scenes is based on scene-by-scene analysis. In the suspense scenes, dangers, conditions of actions, complications, and counteractions form a referential network of situative-dramatic entities, which must be obtained by a breakdown of scenes and be orchestrated in the film's staging. It may be that this idea is methodically very significant. If so, one would then be able to come up with a hypothesis about how viewers are located between the components of a situation. The partial situations gained in this way should be regarded as descriptions of situations, namely *danger situations*.

The dramaturgy of suspense—particularly when it is a question of the staging and depiction of scenes—is the dramaturgy of danger on all levels of the staging through to the process of framing. An almost classic example for the use of indicators close up is Spielberg's *Jaws* (1975). Spielberg not only used classic, indirect danger indicators, but also played, sometimes in a stylish way, with

---

[2]On the restriction of space as a characteristic of the dramaturgy of suspense, see Borringo (1980).

filmmaking techniques. Interestingly, the shark, for example, is shown via the subjective camera. Right at the beginning, the film passes between shots from above and below the water line: The underwater pictures are filmed with a moving camera that is clearly observing the girl. Earlier, I had assumed that the viewer develops the hypotheses from this material. The inference[3] offered by *Jaws* is as simple as it is effective: First, it is assumed that there is an intention steering the camera movement. If an intention is there, then a protagonist capable of some intent can and must be assumed—an underwater protagonist could be the shark announced in the title. Second, an interaction will be assumed between the protagonist who is only shown via the camera angle and the girl depicted. The intentional framework for the image is quite different depending on whether the protagonist is a bloodthirsty shark or a pubescent voyeur.

Another example is the showdown of the same film, beginning with the shark attacking the boat. Here, Spielberg started by showing the movement of the drum(s) on the water as an indicator of the shark's movements under the water; then he showed from within the boat's interior the planks breaking and the water beginning to seep through the cracks into the boat. The depiction of the shark's activities is given an implicit perspective—we only see those things that the protagonists could also see. The shark itself stays hidden underwater, an element of the action that must be synthesized and pieced together by the viewer from circumstantial evidence.

Getting the perspective in scenes of suspense is very ambivalent. The only fundamental thing appears to be the separation of the world into protagonists and antagonists. Whereas the activity of the antagonists may be shown through their influence on the environment of the protagonists (i.e., the events are perceived by protagonists) in another case, here it will be depicted as if the antagonist was observing the activities of the protagonist. Here, it is mainly the means by which one creates a subjectivizing of the perspective that also serves to indicate an absent "actor." Whereas in the case of *Jaws*, it is the obviously intentional movement of the underwater camera that leads one to conclude the existence of an underwater protagonist, in Clément's *Le Passager de la Pluie* (1969), it is the height of the camera in several scenes that leads one to suspect that the camera is here representing a secret observer (the female protagonist has just thrown the body of the rapist, whom she had killed in self-defense, over the cliff). Here the camera exactly copies the viewpoint of an as-yet-unidentified opponent who could possibly pose a new threat to the girl—an observer who watches her doing a forbidden act.[4] The example may, in addition, stand for

---

[3]Wuss (1993) pointed out that such conclusions can be regarded as abductions—a point that is highly significant.

[4]It has since become standard practice to show the antagonist through the camera. A film like *Platoon* indicates, in the position of the camera and in the framing, the view of the Vietcong, an unsettling moment that pervades the whole of the film. In some of the more recent horror films (Dika called them, significantly, *stalker* films), the subjective camera of the murderer is even the basis of the film's staging (Dika, 1990).

viewers, who have to transform themselves into a "foxhound" for the purpose of the act of anticipating (Wuss, 1993), making use of generic patterns like the role model of protagonist and antagonist to propel the story forward into that area of narrative "not yet," which is the center of the actual attention.

Representing the antagonists directly may be deduced from the fact that the orientation of the viewer occurs by means of the orientation of the protagonist's actions. When one does not directly present protagonists' opponents or the source of the danger threatening them, but only shows its effect on the protagonists' world, then antagonists become uncontrollable, pure calculation, and the product of the workings of the viewers' imagination—for what is only documented in traces can, on the one hand, be calculated, but then proves, of course, to be a free projection surface for the workings of one's imagination. Indexically represented antagonists are structurally defined, can be deduced from the material, and are not empty; but they are only definable as a *functor*, and are not presented in all plasticity. One hears that the indirect representation of antagonists makes the working of the viewers' imaginations inevitable. Because fantasizing about evil is pleasurable, the monster is consequently disappointing and scarcely terrifying when it finally does materialize and is shown to viewers. The best monsters only appear in the imagination of the viewer—they are not shown, just indicated and established as opportunities for the imagination to work.

Another thing results from the indexical representation of the antagonist, because every event that is interspersed with such indexes is immediately a suspenseful scene on which the protagonists and antagonists both exert their influence. Portraying one of the suspense roles indirectly opens the events, at any rate, into the area of the action (Comisky & Bryant, 1982).

It is easy to find plenty of examples. A simple one occurs in the Bond film *A View to a Kill*. There is an establishing shot opening a scene in which a dark figure, an armed man who evidently has the house under observation, moves in the foreground at the end. The dramatic space is immediately broken and a moment of danger changes the subsequent events when a further figure is introduced. With each moment, viewers are certain that the scene is under observation. It is only when Bond and the girl are attacked that the danger indicator presented at the beginning of the scene disappears, possibility becomes reality, and the suspense (coming from the uncertainty as to who the observer is and what he or she plans to do, etc.) dies down. Appearances by villains are often prepared using a designatory and anonymous technique such as indicating figures as shadows. In *The Ladykillers* (1955), Professor Marcus (Alec Guinness) appears at the beginning of the film only as a shadow that seems to chase the old lady and encircle the house. John Badham's *Stakeout* (1987) provides a very good example that articulates both dramatic and narratively relevant information with the same iconographic trick: The violent criminal, who had been hunted by the police throughout the whole land, has crashed into an icy river while on the run. He has, apparently, drowned—at least, that is what the police firmly believe.

The fact that he is still alive is made clear by a brief shot showing him secretly emerging from the water, unnoticed by all the others who we see searching the river in the background.

NARRATIVIZATION OF OBJECTS

In the dramaturgy of suspense, all the elements of the text should be examined to see how one can use them to exert influence on the viewer's expectations. In particular, the world of objects is used to present the viewer with a world that is interspersed potentially with meanings and dangers. The fact that the world of objects cannot be left neutral, but is incorporated into the film's discourse and strategies to establish meanings, is perhaps one of the most elementary principles of cinematic signification and communication. No landscape is serene, one might agree with Eisenstein. The landscape loses its innocence in cinematic narrative, turns out to be full of threats and profound thoughts, and is filled with meaning because people act in line with the environments. In his often very direct manner of addressing basic elements of filmic narrative, Hitchcock said, in talks with Truffaut (1968): "We use lakes for drownings and the Alps to have our characters fall into crevasses" (p. 85). The world of objects is presented in the actions of the protagonists and thereby given functions that can be different in every story. What remains the same, though, is how the world of the material outer is occupied in the story by the action's outer layer. The most elementary rules are combined with this basic movement of how the story can be brought forward: In Kusturica's film *Arizona Dream* (1993), one of the protagonists says very aptly: "If a gun is shown in the first half of the film, you can be sure that it will be used at some time during the film."

It is the communicative frame of the narration that ensures that objects are used in such a way as to cast light on and be specific about the actual subjects of the narration. The principle of the (thematic) relevance ensures that the framework of meaning for the story does not get lost. Pudovkin (1961) described a little scene in which the images of a tramp, a down-at-heel, rough fellow, are juxtaposed with a little, plump kitten dozing in the sun. The tramp picks up a stone, with the obvious intention of smashing the sleeping little animal, and only a coincidence prevents him from actually carrying out his evil plan. Pudovkin wrote:

> In this small scene there isn't a single explanatory title. The impression is clear and vivid in spite of this. Why? Because it was the correct and appropriate vivid material that was selected. The dozing kitten is the perfect expression of pure innocence and carefreeness and the heavy stone in the hand of the enormous man is an apt symbol for brutal, senseless cruelty. (p. 53)

Vivid material is one of cinema's basic means of expression, and it is no surprise that it also occupies an important place in the strategies of the generation of suspense.

A popular term for suspense-related aspects of objects or uses of objects is Hitchcock's *MacGuffin* (Truffaut, 1968). Hitchcock included here objects around which a story can be developed, but which, formally, can be neutral. If one follows Wuss' (1992) arguments, then:

> [It seems] to be enough if the action of the figures has a goal[5] which the viewer accepts as being important for them without them having to know any more about it or to accept as something particularly valuable. The problem solving can then be undertaken within the prescribed sphere of investigation so that the field of reference is not altered during the game by pragmatic information. (pp. IV-18–19)

On closer examination, the MacGuffin proves to be a particular kind of strategy that Hitchcock made use of in many different variations and that one could label *narrativization* of objects. It is a question of giving meaning to objects that are legible or open to interpretation for viewers with regard to the situation, possible threats, and the intentions of the protagonists and antagonists. In the deployment of objects in a film's action, Hitchcock provided items of *evidence*, whose subjective or objective meaning must be read for the course of the action. The indexical value assigned to the objects connects them with actions and scenes. An interesting example is the ties in *Frenzy*:

> During the confusion surrounding the dead body [at the beginning of the film] the speaker says in the cool, "British" way: "I say—this is not my club tie, is it?", and the tie is given a *colossal importance* when the camera picks it out in close-up around the dead woman's neck. It becomes a *sign of recognition* in the film. Its use, though, immediately takes the audience on a ride. We are thrown into the next information-packed scene . . . without any kind of leisurely transition like a fade-out or fade-in. We see *Richard Blaney*, alias Jon Finch, standing in front of a mirror as cool as a cucumber, carefully putting on his *tie*. (Frevel, 1993, p. 25)

The tie is used to suggest an ending that would make the "murderer" comprehensible within the murder schema. The viewer becomes a criminological *bricoleur*. Objects are elements forming the hypothesis; they have the status of circumstantial evidence.[6]

The situativity of the filmic scene is closely connected with the fact that the way people deal with a danger also—and even in particular—covers the adapting of the people to the facts of the situation. This requires one to instrumentalize the object's surroundings for the purpose of showing resistance. Objects are

---

[5]Vale (1987) identified suspense completely from this vantage point. He wrote: "Suspense is the doubt of the spectator as to the outcome of an intention of an actor in the story. Therefore the first necessity in order to achieve suspense is the intention. A story without intentions cannot possibly cause suspense" (p. 174).

[6]One only has to think of the cigarette lighter in *Strangers on a Train*. Spoto (1977) wrote "The whole story in a single early image" (p. 210).

newly defined as weapons, and so on. In a given framework, the situation will be newly constituted as a scenario for the story. By being able to define objects anew for the purpose of analysis, one sees, on the one hand, that the hero has left his impotence, paralysis, and helplessness behind; on the other hand, it shows that his intelligence, alertness, and craftiness can also be a match for a seemingly powerful antagonist.[7] In *Torn Curtain* (1966), the protagonist and the peasant woman have to kill the Stasi agent, Gromek, in a long and desperate fight. The fight must not be noisy, however, or it will attract the attention of the taxi driver, who is waiting in the farmyard. Thus, the peasant woman puts Gromek's pistol in a drawer. Among all the other household items, there is a big meat knife, which looks as if it could be used even against an enemy who fights like a lion. The knife almost proves irresistible as a weapon. It has a cataphoric impulse that is oriented to the mortal struggle. A similar, microsituative reinterpretation of a knife as a murder weapon can be seen in Hitchcock's *Sabotage* (1936). It falls, by chance, into the hands of a woman who will kill her husband because he was responsible for the death of her young brother (Truffaut, 1968).

The way Hitchcock approaches the narrativization of objects becomes particularly apparent when he drops a narrated object for no reason. A famous and oft-mentioned example is a bundle of money in *Psycho* that represents a new life for the protagonist as well as a break with the bourgeois existence. It is reason enough for viewers to draw conclusions about intricacies specific to the plot—a report to the police, a chase, a new burglary, and so on—that have a major influence on the sphere of information in which viewers are orientating themselves. The fascination of this film comes, in part, from the fact that this bundle of money, which has been exposed beforehand in numerous acts of emphasis and underscoring, is not given as much attention after the murder of the protagonist. Its narrative significance is greatly reduced. Hitchcock called the bundle of money a *red herring* and said:

> [T]hat was deliberate, you see, to detract the viewer's attention in order to heighten the murder. We purposely made that beginning on the long side, with the bit about the theft and her escape, in order to get the audience absorbed with the question of whether she would or would not be caught. Even that business about the forty thousand dollars was milked to the very end so that the public might wonder what's going to happen to the money. (Truffaut, 1968, p. 228)

Such strategies of staging can be directly referred to the processes where viewers construct the problem-solving area in which they can interpret the course of the plot, evidence, and other exhibits, and so produce their own plot scenarios.

The fact, though, that these strategies are so prominent in Hitchcock, that they can also be ironically alluded to, can be demonstrated by the final reference to the

---

[7]A wonderful example is *Wait Until Dark* (1967), in which the situation is fundamentally altered with every action by the protagonist and antagonist. With each move, the old ingredients in the situation are evaluated and functionalized anew.

bundle of money in *Psycho*. After the murder of the protagonist, the camera travels and pans once more through the apartment to end in a close-up on the newspaper where she had hidden her booty. This final underscoring at the end of what appeared to be an aimless search by the camera is also a sly reference to the strategy by which the film had guided viewers thus far—the unmotivated emphasis of the object that was part of the narration until now and had no importance whatsoever for the murder. We are confronted here with a *reflexive retroreference*, a metadramatur-gical anaphor. Of course, the robbery is still important for the story. It motivates the investigation of the detective, the second victim. But the narrative compactness developed to this point, which had covered a dense network of actions with the motives of robbery/embezzlement and escape/pursuit, is abandoned, and the money is marginalized and presented in an ironic light.

INDICATIVENESS

Indirect portrayals of danger indicate to viewers that they should interpret them to complete the presented pieces of evidence and arrange them as dramatic partial information. We are dealing here with the expansion of information into the area of future, the possible and probable developments of the drama. According to Bruner, one must go "behind" the given information (Bordwell, 1992). There is a close correlation between the productivity connected with the formulation of given information and the intensity of subjective experience. This seems to be closely allied to a finding in research on pornography, which says that the sub-jectively experienced stimuli are all the more intense the more the imagination works on comprehending a text (Byrne & Lambeth, 1970). The more indirect a depiction is, the more viewer activity is drawn to it and the greater the increase in the experienced involvement.

A given description of a situation provided by a film will be processed by viewers into an ensemble of possible extrapolations of the situation, into the open horizon of the "not yet" of the situation. I call this work *anticipation*. Now, the viewers are not left to their own devices, and not every film simply refers back to the competence of the everyday calculation of risks. Rather, film offers a whole series of conventional and film-specific techniques that allow it to influence viewers' development of a storyline. These are, to start with, advance references (cataphora) with which references are made to the forthcoming text, regardless of whether the reference comes about or not. Then there are the principles of the breakdown of scenes in which the situation is analyzed for its moments of danger (so that a cataphoric power is present even in the cinematic forms of representation). Third, there are the techniques by which objects as plot elements are developed into their own carriers of meaning so that the viewer can read the object level as carriers of evidence referring to other strata of meaning of the work.

16 WULFF

The experience of suspense does not come from something exciting being shown in a film. Rather, it results from the extrapolation of possible events from a given situation; it is the result, or concomitant, of the anticipating activity. It is not what the film shows, but what it discloses, that is the subject of the analysis of suspense.

REFERENCES

Bordwell, D. (1992). Kognition und Verstehen. Sehen und Vergessen in *Mildred Pierce* [Cognition and understanding. Seeing and forgetting in *Mildred Pierce*]. *Montage/AV*, *1*(1), 5–24.

Borringo, H.-L. (1980). *Spannung in Text und Film. Spannung und Suspense als Textverarbeitungskategorien* [Suspense in text and film. Tension and suspense as categories of text processing]. Düsseldorf, Germany: Schwann.

Bühler, K. (1965). *Sprachtheorie. Die Darstellungsfunktion der Sprache* [Theory of language. The function of representation in language]. Stuttgart, Germany: Gustav Fischer.

Byrne, D., & Lambeth, J. (1970). *The effect of erotic stimuli on sex arousal evaluative responses, and subsequent behavior* (Commission on Obscenity and Pornography, Tech. Rep. No. 8). Washington, DC: U.S. Government Printing Office.

Chatman, S. (1978). *Story and discourse. Narrative structure in fiction and film.* Ithaca, NY: Cornell University Press.

Comisky, P., & Bryant, J. (1982). Factors involved in generating suspense. *Human Communication Research*, *9*(1), 49–58.

Dika, V. (1990). *Games of terror.* Halloween, Friday the 13th *and the films of the stalker cycle.* Rutherford, NJ: The Fairleigh Dickinson University Press.

Frevel, S. (1993). *Das "Spiel zu dritt." Grundlagen der Erzeugung von Suspense beim Filmrezipienten* [The "game for three persons": Basic principles of the production of suspense in viewing films]. Unpublished manuscript, Institut für Semiotik und Kommunikationstheorie, Berlin.

Hartmann, B. (1992). *Zur Texttheorie des Filmanfangs. Überlegungen zur filmischen Exposition und exemplarische Analyse* [Text theory of film beginnings. Considerations about exposition in film and exemplaric analysis]. Unpublished master's thesis, Freie Universität, Institut für Semiotik und Kommunikationstheorie, Berlin.

Korte, H. (1987). *Der weisse Hai* (1975). Das lustvolle Spiel mit der Angst [Jaws. The game with pleasure and fear]. In H. Korte & W. Faulstich (Eds.), *Action und Erzählkunst. Die Filme von Steven Spielberg* (pp. 89–114). Frankfurt: Fischer Taschenbuch Verlag.

Lüthi, M. (1975). *Das Volksmärchen als Dichtung. Ästhetik und Anthropologie* [The folktale as poetic work: Aesthetics and anthropology]. Düsseldorf, Germany: Diederichs.

Ohler, P. (1990). Kognitive Theorie der Filmwahrnehmung: der Informationsverarbeitungsansatz [Cognitive theory of film perception: The information processing approach]. In K. Hickethier & H. Winkler (Eds.), *Filmwahrnehmung* (pp. 43–57). Berlin: Edition Sigma.

Pudovkin, W. I. (1961). *Filmtechnik. Filmmanuskript und Filmregie* [Film technique. Film manuscript and film direction]. Zürich: Die Arche.

Spoto, D. (1977). *The art of Alfred Hitchcock.* New York: Hopkinson & Blake.

Truffaut, F. (1968). *Hitchcock* [with the collaboration of H. G. Scott]. London: Secker & Warburg.

Vale, E. (1987). *Die Technik des Drehbuchschreibens für Film und Fernsehen* [The technique of screen and television writing]. München, Germany: TR-Verlagsunion.

Wulff, H. J. (1985). *Die Erzählung der Gewalt. Untersuchungen zu den Konventionen der Darstellung gewalttätiger Interaktion* [The narration of violence. Investigations in the representation of violent interaction]. Münster, Germany: MAkS Publikationen.

Wuss, P. (1992). *Filmanalyse und Psychologie. Kognitionspsychologisch orientierte Einführung in die Theorie des Films* [Film analysis and psychology. Introduction to a cognitivistic theory of film]. Unpublished manuscript.
Wuss, P. (1993). Grundformen filmischer Spannung [Basic forms of film tension]. *Montage/AV, 2*(2), 101–116.

2

▼▼▼▼▼▼▼

Keeping Our Selves in Suspense: The Imagined Gaze and Fictional Constructions of the Self in Alfred Hitchcock and Edgar Allan Poe

Garry Leonard
University of Toronto

> *Observe how healthily—how calmly I can tell you the whole story.*
> —The Tell-Tale Heart

> *I know they are watching me.*
> —Norman Bates, in *Psycho*

I wish to discuss the phenonemon of suspense from a Freudian and Lacanian perspective. My purpose is not to assess the best way to determine whether or not a subject is reacting to suspense, but rather to suggest the nature of human subjectivity is such that it predisposes us not only to the experience of suspense, but, in the case of reading and cinema, actually causes us to seek it out, and, in a manner that is both instructive and problematic, actually enjoy it, despite the level of anxiety and discomfort normally associated with this experience. For Lacan, the ego and identity are fictional constructions.[1] What Lacan calls *the*

---

[1]Lacan (1988a) wrote, "the ego is structured exactly like a symptom. At the heart of the subject it is only a privileged symptom, the human symptom par excellence, the mental illness of man" (p. 16). In reading or viewing suspense, the subject puts this symptom into play. The ego and identity, normally experienced as at the base of reality, are put into doubt. In a vicarious position, the subject watches as apparent presentations of reality turn out to be illusion. Such a conflict is represented in every subject's conscious experience of reality. He also argued in Lacan (1988b) that, "the ego is never just the subject . . . it is essentially a relation to the other . . . it finds its point of departure and its fulcrum in the other" (p. 177). In Lacanian film theory, this supplies the basis for talking about how the gaze constitutes identity for the subject. The movie screen is like the mirror; it offers the subject a way to organize the fiction of identity: "The human being only sees his form materialised,

mirror stage is a process whereby an infant develops a sense of self through observing how he or she appears to other people (how he or she imagines the reflection of his or her self, via his or her gaze). The resulting subjective structure grants the child an illusion of coherence, stability, and unification, but the authentification of this self requires the gaze of something Other in order for the subject to imagine this coherency. It is this authenticating gaze, not anything inherent in the subject, that confirms the (apparent) unification of the figure in the mirror. From this reflection, the subject deduces a (mythical) unity of self. Subjects are henceforth dependent on the gaze of the Other to stave off an uneasy sense that the apparent unity of their consciousness is a construction built on top of a void of incertitude (best understood as the fragmented and chaotic unconscious, always threatening to subvert the apparent order of conscious reality).[2]

Thus, even as we live our life with an illusion of autonomy, we are in a constant state of suspense in case something in our myth of the self should be undermined or subverted by something unexpected that intrudes on our conscious life. The bad dream, or nightmare, which typically involves a feeling of intolerable suspense, is a reminder that more is going on in our conscious life than we can afford to understand. This is like the character in a suspense novel or film who misses clues because the truth they point to is at odds with what he or she regards as the truth about his or her self. But although the clue can be misread or ignored, it can not be vanquished, and its refusal to go away, even though it doesn't make any sense to the character's view of reality, serves to generate an atmosphere of suspense, often described as "nightmarish." A Lacanian analysis of suspense suggests we willingly read a suspenseful book, or attend a suspenseful film, because we derive vicarious pleasure from watching a character stumble on, endure, and transcend a feeling of suspense already at the base of identity construction in the human subject.

The subject immerses himself or herself in what Lacan calls the Symbolic Order, which includes language and all the other available symbols in a given

---

whole, the mirage of himself, outside of himself ... It is through the exchange of symbols that we locate our different selves in relation to one another" (Lacan, 1988a, p. 140). In short, subjectivity is not an essence but a set of relationships. Suspense begins by offering a symbolic system that appears to be natural, in relation to which readers or viewers are invited to constitute their identity, and then this natural order begins to crumble, galvanizing an identity crisis that is unacknowledged by the subject, but not entirely unknown. For an extended discussion of this and other Lacanian terms, see Leonard (1993) entitled, *Reading "Dubliners" Again: A Lacanian Perspective.*

[2]The primary role of confirmation played by the gaze of the Other is later repressed in the subject's mental economy because he or she must see identity as self-originating in order to preserve the illusion that he or she controls (rather than is controlled by) this Other. Another way to describe suspense, then, would be to call it the return of the repressed gaze of the Other, now shown to be the external source of an internalized gaze, mistaken by an individual as the authenticator of an essence of subjectivity. Crucial to a Lacanian notion of suspense is Lacan's theoretical premise that subjectivity is not an essence, but rather the effect of a set of relationships.

culture.[3] The subject is split between an original incoherency (the Imaginary Order, akin to Freud's unconscious) and the fictional construction of a supposedly unified ego.[4] The conscious subject is constantly looking to the Symbolic Order for reasurrance of a wholeness that is, in fact, fundamentally lacking. Lacan's central thesis, then, is that identity is based on a permanent sense of deficiency, and the fragmentation the ego wishes to deny is always threatening to break through and reveal the myth of the self as a fiction. We obscure this deficiency (Lacan uses the term "lack") and compensate for it by understanding our selves through symbols and language. For Lacan, we gain the word but lose the world, which is to say that language powerfully constructs an apparent reality within which we feel like autonomous, individual subjects, capable of formulating our own destiny based on what we consciously know. Lacanian theory challenges our common sense notions of knowledge, insisting that what we know is a compromise formation negotiating between what we are afraid of and what we wish to understand. This is similar to the situation in a suspenseful book or film, where an inexplicable event, letter, or discovery puts in doubt facts previously considered too obvious to even question.

In other words, through the creative perception and rearrangement of all types of symbols, we construct a myth of the self. Such a myth compensates and organizes the primal sense of lack, but can never eliminate it. In terms of what we desire, Lacan maintains that, for the human subject, the object of desire is not the actual thing we desire, but it is what causes us to desire. In other words, objects of desire promise to compensate for a deficiency that can never be fulfilled

---

[3]Kaja Silverman (1983) offered a succinct summary of the Symbolic Order, describing it as a sort of factory that produces the individual subject: "The subject not only learns to desire within the symbolic order; it learns what to desire. It is there taught to value only those objects which are culturally designated as full and complete.... Lacan indicates that the subject's desires are manufactured for it. The factory—the site of production—is the symbolic" (p. 177). Once having left the factory, subjects forget they have been produced by the Symbolic Order, and henceforth celebrate their sense of self as original and autonomous. Suspense, in this sense, returns us to the factory, to the site of our production. The result is both fascination, as we glimpse something we have dimly suspected, and terror as we reflect on what it means. For this reason, perhaps, uncovering conspiracies are a constant in works of suspense (as they are the staple of the recent highly successful books and movies by John Grisham—*The Client, The Firm, The Pelican Brief*). The discovery that what poses as the truth has been manufactured corresponds to the uneasy relationship between an individual subject and a hidden, conspiratorial, Symbolic Order. The destruction of a conspiracy at the resolution of a suspense story serves to reactivate the myth that the Symbolic Order can be vanquished as evil.

[4]Christian Metz (1977) postulated that the cinema affords a return to the Imaginary Order; the movie screen, like the mirror, offers the viewer an apparent seamless reality (the narrative of the film), which is actually a sequence of fragmentary cuts, produced by the effect of editing: "that other mirror, the cinema screen, [is] in this respect a veritable psychical substitute, a prosthesis for our primally dislocated limbs" (p. 4). Suspense encourages us to use this prosthesis, and then threatens to take it away, after we have put all the weight of our identity on it.

and inevitably remind us of that deficiency when they fail to satisfy it.[5] Attaining the object, or anticipating the attainment of it, appeases the insatiable deficiency, but can never absolve it. In particular, sexual desire involves a fantasy of completion. The desired person is perceived to be, mythically and exclusively, someone who could satisfy and complete the other. For Lacan, love is the result of a mutual misrecognition of the other as a bearer of the gaze that authenticates his or her identity. The point I wish to make that relates to suspense is that for Lacan, the construction of ego, and, by extension, a conscious identity, are both constructs that are already in suspense. The subject is dependent on a Symbolic Order that must neither shift, nor reveal itself to be what it in fact is: a representation of reality, and not the whole of reality. Lacan insists the process of understanding the world and our experience of it through symbols, always leaves something out because no signifier can perfectly embody what is understood. The individual subject tries to act like a signified—something coherent and whole prior to language—but he or she is, in fact, a floating signifier forever masquerading as a signified. This something that is left out is what Lacan calls the Real—some reminder of the Imaginary Order that escapes representation within the Symbolic Order, and so remains a threat to the fictional unity of identity.

   This, I would argue, is a basic ingredient of the suspenseful plot: Someone receives information, they try to make sense of it, to incorporate it into their belief of what is real, but there still remains something incontrovertible about the information. The suspense builds because the Symbolic Order that the protagonist has come to depend on begins to shift, revealing apparent reality as a fictional construction. In this sense, the villain of a suspenseful plot brings unwelcome evidence of something beyond the protagonist's reality that calls that reality into question, at which point, the protagonist, as the saying goes, doesn't know who to trust—least of all whomever he or she formerly regarded as himself or herself. For the viewer of the film or reader of the book, witnessing the protagonist's dilemma is both frightening and a relief. It is frightening because feelings of sudden dissolution and panic are all too well known to the subject, and yet reassuring because the movie or story makes it clear the protagonist has an identifiable danger to contend with—a monster, an assassin, a treacherous friend—and watching the protagonist deal with this threat—killing it, outwitting it, or unmasking it—allows a vicarious sense of triumph over a similar tension, within one's self, which can only be resolved, in a temporary manner, through the sort of fantasy safely enacted by suspenseful movies and books.

---

[5]We are, in a sense, creatures of contingency. We search for substitute objects in our world that will complete us and return us once again to the Edenic mirror stage where we first imagined our unity. Desire is a crucial element in suspense. The objects that are desired become desirable to the viewer or reader, and the disappointment that takes place when the object is revealed as a fake is an important minor chord in the sensation of suspense. But, once again, we derive pleasure from seeing a character survive a disappointment that is an unavoidable reality in our own lives: Objects of desire always disappoint, because they promise to complete us, but they can only mark the site of a permanent deficiency.

Psychoanalytic film theory, at least the kind that draws on the work of Lacan, sees the experience of the spectator watching the film equivalent to the individual regarding his or her own reflection in a mirror. In both cases, the subject misrecognizes the image as proof of his or her completeness and coherence (his or her identity). But the image—both in the mirror and on the screen—can only symbolize completeness; it cannot actualize it. In the cinema, through the process of directing and editing, a subject position is constructed for the viewer. It appears to be a position of mastery in that we see everything the camera sees, but what does the camera fail to show us, or refuse to look at? The paradox of editing is that it provides viewers with a sense of omniscience, but the process by which this feeling of omniscience is produced (editing), also indicates what the viewers see is not all that can be shown. This tension between imaginary plenitude and demonstrable deficiency is a form of suspense already known to the human subject. Indeed, in a very similar manner, the subject constructs reality through an editing process that creates a sense of continuity through a process-constitution of the self by the Symbolic Order—that is fundamentally fragmented. Lacanian film theory sees the viewer not as someone with individual autonomy, but—during the course of the film, at least—as an artificial construct, produced and activated by the cinematic apparatus. The spectator is a part of this machine, even at its center, but by no means in control of it. The name given to the techniques that cinematic texts confer subjectivity on viewers is *suture*. This is a complex concept, but, relative to the issue of suspense and the film viewer, we might define it as the process by which the subject "inserts" himself or herself into the symbolic register of the film as a signifier in search of a signified, much like the infant enters the Symbolic Order in search of a coherent identity.

The result, as Silverman (1983) noted, is an increase in signification, at the cost of decentering one's being (the need to authenticate the self via the gaze of the Other, produces a self-alienation).[6] Suspense activates the potentially soothing process of *suture*, but only in order to generate a situation where the suturing effect

---

[6]The process of *suture* is a complex one, and it has relevance beyond cinema. Basically, it is the process through which a subject constitutes himself or herself through available symbols, narratives, and genres. Advertisements, for example, wish to provide their product as the reason for the suturing effect, because this makes their product special and builds brand loyalty. Silverman (1983) offered a concise definition: "Suture can be understood as the process whereby the inadequacy of the subject's position is exposed in order to facilitate (i.e., create the desire for) new insertions into a cultural discourse which promises to make good that lack. Since the promised compensation involves an ever greater subordination to already existing scenarios, the viewing subject's position is a supremely passive one, a fact which is carefully concealed through cinematic sleight-of-hand" (pp. 231–232). Understood primarily as a cinematic affect, I also use it, in the case of suspense, equally as a force in the reading process. Silverman (1983) gestured in this direction: "The theory of suture has yet to be extended to literary discourse, although it has obvious relevance to that discourse. First-person narration and other indicators of point-of-view would seem to be the equivalents for novels and poems of the shot/reverse shot formation in cinema, and like the latter would seem both to conceal all signs of actual production, and to invite identification" (p. 236).

might be ripped open. To put this another way, a movie or story about love might be very careful to preserve the suturing effect from beginning to end (i.e., *Sleepless in Seattle*); conversely, a suspense film or story will, in a subtle but unsettling manner, suggest the possibility of the sutured reality splitting open again. Perhaps the most famous example of this is provided by the narrator of Poe's (1976) "The Fall of the House of Usher." Just before entering the ancient stone edifice, the narrator casually remarks: "Perhaps the eye of a scrutinizing observer might have discovered a barely perceptible fissure, which, extending from the roof of the building in front, made its way down the wall in a zigzag direction, until it became lost in the sullen waters of the tarn" (p. 90). The crack may be barely perceptible, but its range is extensive, threatening the stability of the entire fortress. In the final moment of the story, it is this crack that becomes real, and the apparent solidity of the fortress is completely exploded: "[T]hat once barely discernible fissure . . . this fissure rapidly widened . . . my brain reeled as I saw the mighty walls rushing asunder . . . and the deep and dank tarn at my feet closed sullenly and silently over the fragments of the 'House of Usher' " (p. 98). In this story, Poe makes it explicit the house is a metaphor for identity. To argue through analogy, let me suggest the most effective suspense builds the most elaborate fortress, with the least discernible fissure, thus maximizing the sense of the brain reeling when the structure is split apart. The devastation is so complete even the fragments sink out of sight into the deep and dank tarn. In Lacanian terms, the carefully constructed and mighty fortress of the ego cracks and tumbles into rubble when the treacherous ground of the unconscious suddenly shifts.

The phenomenon of suturing, although appearing to offer stability, actually predisposes the subject to terror because the viewer, at the outset, agrees to accept the reality presented in the film as the whole of reality. As a result of this act of faith, the viewer experiences what the camera shows as an imaginary plenitude. And yet, from the outset this is demonstrably false because the image onscreen must be shot from some perspective offscreen. The viewing subject enjoys the onmniscient sense of gazing on all there is to see, but this feeling of mastery can be easily subverted by something coming into view from offscreen. Such an event is a literal representation of the psychoanalytic situation where an unwanted insight drifts up from our dreams to disturb our sense of the rational order we depend on. If something completely unexpected were to enter, it would register as surprise, but if a mood is set (primarily through plot and music), where the viewer feels something is threatening to intrude, this is suspense. The burden of the suspense can be made to rest entirely with the viewer, as opposed to the protagonist, in a situation where the viewer knows something the protagonist does not, and where the viewer watches helplessly while the protagonist's need-less apprehension about a harmless situation unwittingly leads him or her into certain danger or death.

This resembles Lacan's description of the subject's inauguration into language, where the word (the symbolic) is gained at the expense of the world (the Real that, henceforth, can only be mediated, incompletely, through the Symbolic

Order).[7] In terms of suspense, the subject's (illusory) mastery is defined as having the ability to look, and through that masterful gaze, to see all there is to see. Helplessness, and an uncomfortable awareness of having been constructed, is configured in a suspense film by a discovery that you are being watched, or (amounting to the same thing) that there is more out there, beyond or behind you, than you are able to see. In the classic Hollywood film, these two positions—mastery versus helplessness—are gendered as masculine and feminine: men look and women watch themselves being looked at. In Hitchcockian suspense, the person who is looking, and who is enjoying a presumed sense of mastery, suddenly discovers someone else has been watching him as he (so he thought) was viewing all there was to see. The sense of panic and fragmentation for a masculine subject is two-fold because the character experiences a loss of control that also feels as if he or she is being feminized into a position of helplessness: subject of the gaze, rather than master of it.

For Hitchcock, gender is a perspective, not a biological fact. Subjects appear feminine because they are subjected to a masculine gaze, but, depending on perspective, a female may be the bearer of the masculine gaze, and a man may be feminized by becoming subject to it. This also means men can feminize other men by tricking them into thinking they possess a masculine, controlling gaze, while all the time keeping them under surveillance. If a man who is watching discovers he is being watched, a crisis of helplessness and panic follows, not least of all because such a discovery is akin to feeling suddenly feminized. In Hitchcock's *Vertigo*, for example, Jimmy Stewart falls in love with a woman, unaware she has been hired by another man to dress, act, and speak in the manner he has grown to love.[8] When Stewart discovers she is acting (with the added

---

[7]Both reading and attending the cinema are activities that have been compared to the dream state. The dream state, in Lacanian theory, organizes what the subject's conscious narration of gender/identity myths elides, and, thus, the language of the unconscious speaks through the gaps of conscious discourse. From yet another point of view, this suggests why there is both panic and pleasure in the experience of suspense. Something our reality excludes is given freeplay (the monster escapes the grave!), and suspense provides the terror of this, but also provides a forum where this monster is hunted down and explained. Slavoj Zizek (1991), discussing the detective story, offered a brilliant description of the tension between symbolic reality and the unrepresented Real—a tension that is fundamental to suspense: "At the beginning there is thus the murder—a traumatic shock, an event that cannot be integrated into symbolic reality becasue it appears to interrupt the 'normal' causal chain. From the moment of this eruption, even the most ordinary events of life seem loaded with threatening possibilities; everyday reality becomes a nightmarish dream as the 'normal' link between cause and effect is suspended ... The detective's role is precisely to demonstrate how 'the impossible is possible' (Ellery Queen), that is, to resymbolize the traumatic shock, to integrate it into symbolic reality" (p. 58).

[8]For a more detailed anlaysis of love and identity in *Vertigo*, see Leonard (1990) entitled, "A Fall from Grace: The Fragmentation of Masculine Subjectivity and the Impossibility of Femininity in Hitchcock's *Vertigo*." Relative to my discussion here, I assert at the close of this research, "[Hitchcock's] belief that cultural myths about 'masculinity' and 'femininity' can shift unexpectedly under one's feet is the cornerstone of suspense in his films" (p. 291). For a thorough examination of Hitchcock from the perspective of feminist theory and gender construction, see Tania Modleski's (1988) *The Women Who Knew Too Much: Hitchcock and Feminist Theory.*

complication that the part of her that is not acting loves him too), his nearly murderous rage focuses on this absent viewer who has been watching him the whole time he thought he was (masterfully) watching her: "He dressed you, didn't he? He taught you how to act? How to speak?" This "other man" who caused Stewart to fall in love with a woman he (the director) constructed, is Hitchcock's metaphor for how a film director manipulates feelings of subjectivity in the audience. But beyond this, the movie *Vertigo* raises, in the uncomfortable manner we experience as suspense, the possibility that all love objects are constructed so as to correspond to, and satisfy, an insatiable lack at the base of the construction of identity.

In *Psycho*, Norman Bates removes a painting from the wall so he can peep at an unsuspecting woman who is undressing in her hotel room. Our point of view is his: we are shown his very view through this jagged hole. But just at the point where Marion is about to remove her brassiere, the perspective shifts to a side-view of Norman Bates watching what we have just been prevented from seeing. This editing reflects back to us our status as voyeurs, but it also makes us uncomfortably aware that we are being watched by the director; in the midst of a quintessentially masculine moment (objectifying a woman's sexuality through the gaze), we are feminized as someone subject to the director's gaze. Such an editing maneuver fractures our illusory sense of voyeuristic mastery. In a similar manner, the Jimmy Stewart character has a nervous breakdown when he realizes the woman he loves "naturally" is, in fact, another man's construct. Such a realization exposes the extent to which his subjectivity, which he also believes in as innate, is a fiction. Suspense, then, is also produced by an oscillating effect, a movement from feeling one possesses the controlling gaze, to the unexpected discovery there is another gaze watching one watch.

In Poe's (1976) "The Tell-Tale Heart," the narrator's final decay into incoherency and madness is triggered by his sudden belief that, far from controlling the gaze of the police (by only showing them what he wants them to see, like a film director), they have been watching him the whole time—fully aware of everything he has done (they have not): " 'Villains!' I shrieked, 'dissemble no more! I admit the deed! Tear up the planks! here, here! It is the beating of his hideous heart!' " (p. 262). In a sense, the ending of the story returns to the beginning, because it is there we learn the narrator's urge to murder the old man was really an urge to murder the gaze he always discovered watching him: "Object there was none. Passion there was none. I loved the old man. He had never wronged me . . . I think it was his eye! Yes it was this! . . . Whenever it fell upon me, my blood ran cold; and so by degrees—very gradually—I made up my mind to take the life of the old man, and thus rid myself of the eye forever" (p. 260). Although the murder of the old man appears to extinguish this intolerable gaze, this eye, the narrator, in fact, experiences only a brief, false reprieve from his sense of being watched, and then the terror builds again; this time signaled by the increasingly loud sound of the dead man's beating heart. Now we see that the gaze the narrator wishes to murder is the gaze by which he imagines himself, and in relation to which he constructs the fiction of his identity; it is an internalized gaze he projected on to the hapless old man. Poe's narrator understood the cause of his own crumbling identity construct to be the fault of the old man's gaze. On the one hand, his instinct is correct that he is dependent on the gaze of the Other, but on the other hand, he is quite wrong in selecting, at random, an individual to stand in as the presumed originator of this gaze. The narrator is like the viewer of a horror film who mistakes the destruction of the monster as the murder of the hostile gaze of the Other, and, in an opposite manner, likewise mistakes the gaze of a coveted love object as a permanent acquisition of a benevolent gaze from the Other (a permanently assured and consistently authenticated sense of self).

Murdering this gaze, then, is a murder of the self. Indeed, in his short story "William Wilson," Poe (1976) has the narrator stab a man who has shadowed him for years, exposing him every time he cheats or lies. After stabbing him, the narrator notes "not a line in all the marked and singular lineaments of his face which was not, even in the most absolute identity, mine own!" (p. 283). The primary suspense of the story—would William Wilson show up yet again to expose him—is revealed to be the result of an internal suspension, as Wilson himself finally explains to the dying narrator: "In me didst thou exist—and, in my death, see by this image, which is thine own, how utterly thou has murdered thyself" (p. 283). To give a similar example from Hitchcock's brand of suspense, Norman Bates kills his mother in *Psycho*; but the absence of her gaze on him is so intolerable, he digs up her corpse, stuffs her (his hobby is taxidermy!), and supplies her with a voice so she can continue to berate him, just as she did when she was alive. We in the audience do not know Mrs. Bates is dead. We assume she is performing the murders, and her son is cleaning up after her. The biggest shock of the movie, then, is to have Marion's sister (searching for her disappeared sister) approach Mrs. Bates from behind. As Mrs. Bates slowly turns to face directly into the audience (a metaphorical equivalent of the airplane in *North by Northwest*), suddenly her skull and empty eye sockets stare straight out at the audience. She has no eyes! Where is the gaze located? Panic! Disorientation! Marion's sister screams and we scream (a common occurrence when the movie was first released), because we suddenly have no idea where we are—who is looking at whom—and yet we are cognizant of tremendous danger, a danger all the more terrifying because, in the moment of having our (illusory) mastery subverted, we feel powerless to locate the source of this disruption.

As we can see from the Poe story, a hostile gaze is blamed for an incipient nervous breakdown, and for a persistent pattern of supposedly inadvertent self-exposure. Equally disturbing to the fiction of the self, however, is the gaze which is suddenly revealed as blind and indifferent. Of course, in the long resolution of *Psycho*, we are told, by an hilariously overconfident psychiatrist, that Norman Bates is now utterly mad, and he has become his mother. But as he drones on about how Norman is nothing like a normal person, the camera appears to wander out the doorway and down the hallway to the padded room where Norman is being kept. A voice-over starts, and we hear the mother's voice, although Norman's lips do not move; Whether this is her actual voice, as remembered by Norman, or his imitation of it, we have no way to determine). In other words, her voice, just like the heartbeat in "The Tell-Tale Heart," is now presented as being audible to us, and to the character in the story or movie, despite the impossibility of this. In both "The Tell-Tale Heart" and *Psycho*, what we are seduced into observing is nothing less than the illusion on which the reality of subjectivity is based: The imagined perspective of something or someone outside of ourselves, authenticating the (illusory) coherency and autonomy of our existence. In Lacanian theory, this recapitulates the situation of the mirror stage where individuals observe their complete reflection in the mirror, then glance at the gaze of another to confirm they are the equivalent of this image (they are not). Henceforth, one's belief in one's identity is dependent on the actual or imagined gaze of an authenticating Other.

In Poe's story "The Tell-Tale Heart" the narrator insists on the reality of a deafening noise caused by the beating of a dead man's heart. He further assures us that the police, who cannot know anything of the crime, can hear the heart too—a heart that could not possibly be beating—and that they are looking at him in a knowing way, and laughing at his rising mania. Insisting on the reality of the absent gaze, swearing that one hears an impossible heartbeat, and other such moments of suspense achieve their effect by making us vaguely aware of the fictions we believe in—the gazes and voices we suspend our sense of self from—in order to authenticate our self. For the audience the suspense is resolved when the story or film reassures us we were tricked into identifying with something now declared mad and criminal, and, therefore, no longer a threat to the presumed natural order. Of course this resolution of the suspense is based on a new denial of the unrepresented Real that always threatens to subvert a given construction of reality. What I describe here, in such sophisticated terms, is better known as the happy ending. In the genre of suspense, the happy ending explains the disruption to the natural order in such a way that it can be discounted as an aberration, and finally dismissed as something utterly foreign to the nature of reality.

In more recent suspense films, however, and quite often for Poe's narrators, madness is figured as an undercurrent of life, rather than something reassuringly separate from it. In the recent remake of *Cape Fear*, the resolutely cheerful happy ending of the original version is replaced with one where the family has survived the onslaught of a madman. But the wary and guarded glances they give one another, coupled with the haunting voice-over of the girl reminiscing how, from that day on, nothing ever was quite the same again, make the point that the apparently seamless fabric of normality can be ripped apart by the eruption of an unexpected and unidentifiable force, a force that poses as coming from the outside but like William Wilson, acts out an internal contradiction. Likewise, David Lynch's film *Blue Velvet* problematizes the convention of the happy ending by having a robin—harbinger of spring—perch on a windowsill. But the camera slowly zooms forward, and then we see, clutched in the beak of the bird, a worm desperately writhing. This appears to be a sort of postmodern happy ending where the threat to the natural order is vanquished, but the restoration of this order still reveals something that cannot be incorporated—even if it is something as harmless and trivial as a worm; these happy endings declare their tenuousness even as they are presented in a tone of complacent finality.

Pascal Bonitzer makes the point, with specific reference to the films of Hitchcock, that any suspenseful encounter must be preceded by an invitation to the reader or viewer to presuppose a natural order. Following on this, suspense slowly builds as this supposedly natural order is exposed as false, constructed by someone or something we don't understand, and therefore not the whole story.[9] In the opening line of Poe's (1976) "The Tell-Tale Heart," the narrator tells us: "True!—nervous—very, very dreadfully nervous I had been and am; but why will you say that I am mad?"(p. 259). The generation of suspense in the reader is instantaneous because a natural order is insisted on ("why will you say I am mad?"), even as the possibility of madness and chaos is hastily admitted ("very dreadfully nervous I had been and am"). In other words, the narrator heightens our sense of his abnormality the more he pleads with us to regard him as normal: "If still you think me mad, you will think so no longer when I describe the wise precautions I took for the concealment of the body. . . . First of all, I dismembered the corpse" (p. 261). Of course, what we think no longer is that this narrator might be sane. The suspense, for the reader, is in determining when to stop taking direction from the narrator as a possible guide through the story, and begin viewing him as an unreliable voice lost in events we suddenly realize he can only pretend to understand.

But even after determining the narrator can be trusted no longer, where are we? We are in the middle of the story, with no way back, and no way forward. The narrator is undoubtedly lost, but he is the only guide we can expect to have. No longer believing what he says, we have no choice but to listen. But we search, now, not for the meaning of what he says—clearly this is useless—but for some clue to help us glimpse all he is not able, or not willing, to tell us. We feel

---

[9]According to Bonitzer (1992), "Hitchcock's films can . . . work only if a natural order is presupposed. Everything is proceeding normally, according to routines that are ordinary, even humdrum and unthinking, until someone notices that an element in the whole, because of its inexplicable behaviour, is a stain. The entire sequence of events unfolds from that point" (p. 20). What Bonitzer calls a stain is comparable to what Lacan calls the Real. It is something that, although impossible to integrate into the fabric of reality, nonetheless cannot be gotten out. Bonitzer (1992) offered an example from *North by Northwest*, specifically the famous airplane scene that I discuss as well, to show how a character confident of his reality can be exposed as the one person who has no idea what is going on: "Cary Grant is looking for someone, he is on the look-out for the slightest sign of recognition, but this recognition, which would restore things to their rightful place, does not occur. Everything remains overhanging, and finally it is he, Cary Grant, who is a stain in the picture, and whom others, as we learn, are trying to 'eliminate' " (p. 21).

suspense, in other words, because we must learn who he thinks he is—there is no question his notions about this are false—in order to understand what it is he is unable to say. In the absence of any other guide, we continue to follow him, but with the heightened apprehension of someone thinking on two levels at once: Meaning is contained, not in anything he says, but in something beyond his discourse that is directing him to say it. He tells us what he sees, and we listen to it in order to decipher who or what it is that is watching him, or that he imagines is watching him. In a spy thriller, for example, it is a common scene for a character to start lying because he wishes to mislead someone he knows is secretly listening to what he says. For the audience in such cases, it is clear that the person listening will need to discover the hidden gaze of this person—whom they think, mistakenly, they are secretly watching—if he or she is to understand the real message.

Effective suspense seduces us into deciding to go a little further, in a direction increasingly hopeless, because to stop reading, or viewing, would be to admit we, too, are capable of being fooled. The reality we have come to believe in is exposed as a symbolic construction rather than a natural essence. On the other hand, if we certify the narrator's point of view as unreal, as an excuse for abandoning it, we cannot forget that we took it to be real at the beginning. Our memory of certitude at the beginning of the story or the film drives us on, in the hopes that we will be able to return to it, somehow. When the reader or viewer reflects on the feelings of certitude with which he or she began the story, and compares it to a growing sense of unease now, the unavoidable conclusion is that reality can be constructed as a fantasy and still elicit a feeling of belief. In suspense, doubt, for the audience, is always doubt about one's own certitude, one's own illusions of mastery, even as we attribute this feeling to the effect of watching the mounting terror of a baffled and bewildered protagonist. We enjoy suspense for the same reason Poe's narrator enjoys planning to murder the old man night after night: the story, or movie, or old man's evil eye, offers an objective corollary to the sense of incertitude that is always operational at the base of human constructions of subjectivity. We, as viewers or readers, can give free rein to this normally dangerous feeling because something other than our selves appears to be its cause.

Suspense, then, is the growing realization that something we rely on as natural, or real, often turns out to be someone else's construction. We thought we could see everything there was to be seen, but, beyond this, someone was seeing us. The cinematic metaphor is most apt: the camera pulls back from an apparent reality, and we see that it is a stage set, and that the people—whose drama we believed in—are acting, and, the landscape we saw as receding out of sight, is in fact painted on a flat canvas. As the ability of the narrator of "The Tell-Tale Heart" to effectively masquerade as sane, or whole, steadily erodes, the reader is forced to experience the extent to which all identity—most pertinently the reader's own—is a fictional construct that depends on highly personalized versions of of reality, versions which, despite their obvious self-serving construction, nonetheless are presented as independent and authentic presentations of all there is to see and know. When we see a character in a suspenseful scene finally recognize the clue that reveals all he or she has been shown and told to be a lie, it is the mythical construction of our own subjectivity we glimpse as we thrill to the presentation of this character's sudden terror.

Again and again in Hitchcock's movies, the protagonist moves through a world that makes sense, a world he or she implicitly believes in, only to notice an anomaly—nothing important, of course, but worth a second look. In *North by Northwest*, Cary Grant is let off a bus somewhere in Kansas to wait for someone he has never met, and anxious to see if the meeting will help him discover who it is other people take him to be. The urgency in understanding this is brought about by the fact these people wish to murder him, but he has no idea who they are, who they have mistaken him for, or why they have done so. "That's strange," says the driver, just before leaving, "there's a plane spraying crops but there's no crops there." Clearly, Grant couldn't care less. He has something else on his mind: What will he be able to learn from this person, presumably already on their way to meet him? The focus of the audience remains on his concern, and therefore is equally indifferent to the speck of an airplane far off on the horizon. But the airplane is a little closer now. Grant glances at it, for no particular reason, passing the time, but it is closer now—it almost appears to be headed for him. How could that be? It makes no sense. He is here to meet someone. Why aren't they here? But, suddenly, it is this meeting with someone he has never met that is subverted as a reality and exposed as a fiction. As with Lacan's Real, the ignored speck of an unacknowledged reality now entirely fills the screen: the man in the airplane is not only headed his way, he has, as his sole mission, a desire to kill him!

The natural order, both for Grant and the audience, is suddenly ripped apart. This is not the scene he thought he was in; this is not the scene we thought we were in: Suspense! Panic! When the apparently innocuous reveals itself as potentially lethal, everything is terrifying, nothing is assured, least of all our survival. As in "The Tell-Tale Heart," the story we were waiting to hear unfold slowly reveals itself as having no basis in reality; in its place, but really there all the time, beyond our awareness, our gaze, our knowledge—which is now revealed as only ours, indeed—is a story we know nothing about, and have no reliable way of finding out about, because we don't understand the vantage point from which it is emanating. Suspense is possible as a subjective effect, even inevitable, because, although none of us, in fact, are capable of knowing the whole story about ourselves, all of us believe we are capable, and this belief is the basis of our (fictional) unity as a (presumably) autonomous subject. Suspense merely calls this belief into question by showing how any view of reality is partial, and therefore vulnerable to subversion by a gaze that sees more than we do, from an alternative perspective we have not even imagined.

The whole time Cary Grant diligently pursues clues supposedly leading to the truth of an illusory reality, what was apparently illusory, or merely strange, reveals itself to have been real, even through the whole period of time he (and the audience) were ignorant of it. Indeed, the discovery has been growing all the time, despite one's indifference to it, and thus creates added panic in the form of a sudden urgency to correct one's course of action, a moment immortalized in the Sherlock Holmes stories by Holmes' trademark exclamation "pray we are not too late, Watson!" The realization that real events have continued to take place, while we pursued our illusion, generates the sense of being too late, which is a hallmark of suspense. In such a moment, what was previously regarded as paramount is suddenly revealed as irrelevant, and the detail we did not think to acknowledge becomes the entry point by which evidence of the unrepresented Real, beyond reality, surges into the character's consciousness in a way that reconfigures everything. No one is on their way to meet Cary Grant, not because they have been waylaid, but because nothing about the meeting was actual except its intent to deceive; Cary Grant, like the audience, was lured there in order that he might be killed (literally for the character, metaphorically for the spectator). For the audience of a suspense film, the danger of the protagonists's death comes to stand in for the unsettling experience of glimpsing the fragmentation and deficiency at the base of their own fictional construction of identity.

As I mentioned earlier, one of the curious features of a suspenseful situation, which distinguishes it from a surprising situation, is that the character is already apprehensive. But this apprehension fails to protect the character—indeed it further blinds him or her—because he or she is apprehensive about the wrong thing; the obvious threat becomes suddenly innocuous even as an overlooked detail reveals itself to be a deadly force. Suspense reminds us that what is denied, far from disappearing, reconfigures itself as something watchful, just on the edge of our awareness. We enjoy suspense because we see someone endure and survive something we experience all the time. The happy ending is important to us because, through it, a new construction of a natural order reasserts itself (the police arrest the narrator of "The Tell-Tale Heart"; a spy ring is exposed and brought to justice in *North by Northwest*; Norman Bates is institutionalized in *Psycho*), and the principle survivors of the story all affirm, completely falsely, that their reality is natural, after all, and it was manifested perversion or insanity, or criminality that called it into question. The disruptive elements, now that they have been ostracized, may be denied anew. One reason suspenseful movies have sequels (there have been three to *Psycho*, and even more than that to *Nightmare on Elm Street*) is that the happy ending is simply dismantled at the beginning of the sequel, and terror and suspense erupt again.

But before any thought of a sequel, the chaos just beneath or beyond the ordinary or the everyday is denied by the happy ending. A good example from a movie not primarily regarded as suspenseful (but very frightening when seen for the first time), is the happy ending of *The Wizard of Oz*. Dorothy rejects the apparent unreality of Oz, for the presumed reality of Kansas. We are left with the premise that Oz does not exist and Kansas is real. In fact, Kansas is the conscious world, and Oz the unconsicous. Oz contains—and depicts through dream imagery—the unrepresented and unmediated Real that always threatens to subvert mediated constructions of reality. The reconfirmed natural order at the end of the film is held sacred by Dorothy once she sees it as holding at bay an intolerable fragmentation and incoherence at the base of human subjectivity. Indeed, the outcome of a suspenseful representation often carries with it this moral: The ordinary may be boring, and you may rail against it, but it keeps you safe from an excess of knowledge about the precarious construction of identity. This is, of course, the moral of *The Wizard of Oz* where Dorothy runs away from home. This action calls forth a tornado from a clear sky that, literally, rips apart her home. When the dust has settled, Dorothy, having barely survived the machinations of bad witches, intones to her self, as though it were a mantra, "there's no place like home." Next time, she will scurry into the cellar with the rest of her family when something ominous—a tornado, an airplane—appears on the horizon. We, along with Dorothy, accept anew the necessity of not exploring too vigorously any reality we need to inhabit a little while longer. The happy ending, in other words, when it serves to resolve suspense, is presented as a resigned acceptance of everyday life—but a grateful one, nonetheless. Dorothy embraces the mundane and the banal because it preserves a fiction of unity manifestly absent from the fragmented and chaotic world of Oz.

We willingly go through the experience of suspense, in viewing a film or reading a text, in order to confirm, yet again, that we, along with the protagonist, can survive the terrifying glimpses of chaos that can be seen when the natural order (on which the structure of our identity depends) somehow gets exposed as not innate or natural. Furthermore, for the viewing subject, there is a curious sense of relief, when viewing something legitimately terrifying in the film or story, brought on by seeing one's nameless fears given a concrete representation. When something evil threatens a group of people, an entire town, or an entire planet, we do not feel so alone, and a course of action difficult to disern in one's own life, becomes a matter of common sense in the face of overwhelming danger. The scene with Cary Grant in *North by Northwest* is a case where something disquieting, but apparently benign, slowly reveals itself as something that has been sent to kill us. Whereas in a general state of anxiety, we are frightened and cannot understand why, Cary Grant begins that scene as already, and for good reason, apprehensive and alert (an attempt has already been made on his life). From there, he becomes, as the airplane approaches, anxious, alarmed, and terrified—but the escalation of suspense and terror is figured in the film as an easily understood reaction to an undeniable danger. The airplane, after all, is getting larger and larger, and, at the last instant, Cary Grant throws himself into a ravine, off the screen, and the airplane—now hideously filling the entire screen—continues to hurtle past him and straight on into the audience, as though, in yet another twist, this had been its intended target all along. Anyone who brings an anxiety or nameless dread to the theater will be given a comfortingly real reason to be scared, and the exposure of this reason will likewise excite the fantasy that the cause of suspense in one's own identity formation can be hunted down and eliminated.

In the case of "The Tell-Tale Heart," we continue to feel more distant from the narrator as he admits, more and more wildly, that he has lost control ("I foamed—I raved—I swore!"). And why? Because he can, he now tells us, hear the beating of the heart of the dismembered dead man under the floorboards. Here, the eventual sense of comfort we take from this story comes from a different direction: We may, in our own lives, feel anxious for reasons difficult to pinpoint, but we are not so unhinged as this! And yet, in exiting from the story, it is we, the readers, who are reduced to saying to ourselves, "true!—nervous—very, very dreadfully nervous I have been and am; but why would anyone say that I am mad?" In the case of Hitchcock, as in all effective suspense, the difference between the character who breaks down and the one who survives, is always a difference in degree, not in kind. Norman Bates asks a woman he will murder in the shower just a little bit later, "We all go a little mad sometimes; haven't you?" "Yes," she replies, "once." One reason suspense may fail to produce its intended effect is there may be too great a polarization implied between good and evil, or mad and sane (why suspense succeeds or fails, though beyond the scope of this chapter, is a question worth pursuing). Hitchcock maintained that a good villain is essential to effective suspense, and by that he meant one that was attractive as well as repulsive and sympathetic as well as unforgivable (the death of a Hitchcock villain is often sad, even as it is a relief).

Often in suspense, the inexplicable detail is confidently approached by the protagonist in order to show mastery of the world, and it is this very mastery that falls apart as the unimportant detail proves impossible to integrate, and slowly becomes more genuine than the identity of the protagonist. This is, for example, the basic movement of the detective in a suspense film or novel. In *The Maltese Falcon*, Humphrey Bogart, in the posture of one who is presumed to know how to find the truth, pursues clues that are intended to clear up an apparent mystery. Accordingly, he confidently pieces together what must have happened. The suspense begins when the person who originally came to him posing as someone bewildered and in need of help, slowly emerges as the one who already knew what they hired the detective to find out. By the end of the film, it is the mystery that is real, and reality that is mysterious. As with "The Tell-Tale Heart," the only way the detctive can recover his self is to have this person arrested by the police; that is to say, because the instigator of suspense represents the intrusion of the Real into a construction of reality, they can never be integrated into society. Instead, they are protectively walled off within it (jailed), or excluded from it (killed) in order to protect the fictional coherency of individual identity within the Symbolic Order.

Let me conclude this chapter with a final comment on the next to last scene in *Psycho*. Norman Bates raises his head, stares straight at the audience, and says "I know they are watching me." It is a moment of communication, one where he speaks what the audience feels. Suspense grows in direct proportion to the feeling that, although we feel it is impossible, somehow we are being watched. For a fraction of a second, his mother's skull is superimposed on his face, and in this moment Norman Bates's split subjectivity—the extent to which he is spoken by something beyond his field of vision—is configured as representative of our own dilemma as human subjects. Just as his subjectivity has been configured by the absent gaze of his mother, the subjectivity of the audience has been directed by the (apparently) absent gaze of Alfred Hitchcock. Indeed, in the scene where we see the eyeless face of Mrs. Bates, Marion's sister raises her hand in fright, knocking into motion, as she does so, a bare lightbulb dangling from the ceiling. The effect of the wildly swinging lightbulb is to make the "eyes" of the dead Mrs. Bates "flicker," not unlike a film projector! Added to this, it is not a coincidence that, on the set of *Psycho*, Hitchcock requested that his name be removed from his director's chair. Having requested that his own identity be erased, what did he have stenciled there instead? The ultimate director, the gaze of the Other, always looking, impossible to kill because long dead or not really there: Mrs. Bates!

REFERENCES

Bonitzer, P. (1992). Hitchcockian suspense. In S. Zizek (Ed.), *Everything you always wanted to know about Lacan . . . but were afraid to ask Hitchcock* (pp. 15–29). London: Verso.

Lacan, J. (1988a). *The Seminar of Jacques Lacan: Freud's papers on technique 1953–54*. New York: Norton.

Lacan, J. (1988b). *The Seminar of Jacques Lacan: Freud's papers on technique 1954–55*. New York: Norton.

Leonard, G. (1993). *Reading "Dubliners" again: A Lacanian perspective*. New York: Syracuse University Press.

Leonard, G. (1990). A fall from grace: The fragmentation of masculine subjectivity and the impossibility of femininity in Hitchcock's *Vertigo. American Imago: A Psychoanalytic Journal for Culture, Science, and The Arts, 47*, 271–292.

Metz, C. (1977). *The imaginary signifier: Psychoanalysis and the cinema*. Bloomington, IN: Indiana University Press.

Modleski, T. (1988). *The women who knew too much: Hitchcock and feminist theory*. London: Methuen.

Poe, E. A. (1976). Fall of the house of usher. In S. Levine & S. Levine (Eds.), *The Short Fiction of Edgar Allan Poe* (pp. 88–98). Indianapolis: The Bobbs-Merrill Company, Inc.

Poe, E. A. (1976). The tell-tale heart. In S. Levine & S. Levine (Eds.), *The Short Fiction of Edgar Allan Poe* (pp. 259–262). Indianapolis: The Bobbs-Merrill Company, Inc.

Poe, E. A. (1976). William Wilson. In S. Levine & S. Levine (Eds.), *The Short Fiction of Edgar Allan Poe* (pp. 271–283). Indianapolis: The Bobbs-Merrill Company, Inc.

Silverman, K. (1983). *The subject of semiotics*. New York: Oxford University Press.

Zizek, S. (1991). *Looking awry: An introduction to Jacques Lacan through popular culture*. Cambridge, MA: MIT Press.

3

The Experience of Suspense: Between Fear and Pleasure

Lothar Mikos
Free University of Berlin

Excitement and suspense are essential patterns of experience in film and television narratives. These specific qualities of experience are sought out by the audience. The expectation of experiencing excitement or suspense motivates the reception of films and television programs, and the promise of such forms of experience is one of their utility values. This chapter focuses mainly on qualities of the experiences of suspense and excitement and the conditions under which they arise.

Up until now, excitement and suspense have been localized as forms of interactive play between the textual characteristics of films and television programs, and a spectator's information processing processes (see, e.g., Bordwell, 1990; Branigan, 1992; Wuss, 1993a). Attempts to differentiate between the fields of suspense, mystery, and surprise often do not elucidate what level of importance the information processing processes assume in understanding the quality of experience. Hitchcock himself pointed out that emotions are "a necessary component of suspense" (Truffaut, 1973, p. 63) and Carroll (1990) identified suspense as "an emotional state" (p. 137); albeit at the intersection of spectators' cognitive activities, because "suspense is a subcategory of anticipation" (p. 137). The experience of suspense goes beyond a pure "play with the deficits of information" (Wuss, 1993a, p. 329). It involves a complex network of the spectator's cognitive and emotional activities that might have been stimulated by various textual characteristics.

Pleasurable flirtation with fear is at the center of the experience of exciting stories. A prerequisite for this pleasurable experience of fear is surety regarding the story's outcome. This corresponds to the meaning of *thrill* as a desire for fear and titillation as described by the psychoanalyst Balint (n.d.). Thrill, as a general type of experience, does not depend on whether subjects are directly involved in the action or whether they merely participate in it as spectators. The degree and form of the thrill is determined in both cases by the structural conditions of the respective narrative situation. The pleasurable experience of fear as a thrill thus represents a special instance within an otherwise everyday narrative situation. So whereas, on the one hand, the structural conditions are constituted in situative contexts during reception, they are constituted within the textual characteristics of film narratives on the other.

First, the phenomenon of desire for fear and titillation is described in more detail. Then, the preconditions of thrill within an audience's specific communicative constellation, within the textual characteristics of the films, and within psychological activity during the generation of thrill as a mode of film experience are presented.

THRILL AS A MODE OF EXPERIENCE

Balint (n.d.) described the phenomenon of the thrill using the example of fairground attractions such as swing-boats, carousels, and roller coasters. Such amusements produce a particular form of fear that according to Balint, is characterized by a loss of balance, stability, and reliable contact with a dependable earth. Three characteristics can be observed here:

1. A certain amount of conscious fear, or the consciousness of a real, external danger.
2. The fact that one exposes oneself consciously and voluntarily to this external danger and to the fear it produces.
3. A more or less confident hope that this fear will be overcome and mastered, and that the danger will pass. It is trusted that one can soon return unharmed to safety. This mixture of fear, delight, and confident hope with regard to an external danger is the basic component of all thrills.

In the following, Balint differentiated, with respect to their reaction to thrills, between two types of people: *ocnophiles* and *philobates*. Both types are based on two different attitudes that stem from object relationships in early childhood. Generally, it can be stated in this context, without delving into the specific implications of Balint's model for developmental psychology, that ocnophiles cling to the beloved object. They do this in order to avoid the danger of being abandoned as they simultaneously strive to build and receive stable object relationships (cf. Klippel, 1990).

The situation is more complex with the philobates. Rather than clinging to the beloved objects, they acknowledge their independence and are able to mourn actively when these objects leave them. This is linked to a learning process: Philobates learn, for example, to avoid dangerous objects and to concentrate on objects that are better for them. At the same time, they develop numerous abilities to influence these objects and to make them useful for themselves. From then on, philobates interact playfully with object relationships and are confident in themselves and the benevolent object world. It is these philobates who enjoy thrills. This is enabled by direct participation in an event as well as through identification and projection as a spectator:

> Ocnophiles live with the illusion that as long as they remain in contact with a safe object, they are safe as well. The philobate's illusion is based on the fact that they don't need any objects outside of their own outfit—and certainly not a single, specific object.... Their optimism is only limited by the compulsive need to observe the world around them; a need which nevertheless yields a large variety of amusements. (Balint, n.d., p. 30)

According to Balint, pleasure for philobates is based above all in a safe distance and a sense of keeping face. The situative contexts and textual characteristics of so-called "thrilling" films contain all the significant elements of thrills: a trusted media relationship, a "viewing contract" (Giles, 1984) between the film and the spectator, and aspects of the film's content and dramaturgy. Let us remind ourselves once again of the main components of a thrill: a certain fear that is characterized by a loss of control; the consciousness of external danger; conscious confrontation of this fear and thereby of the correlated danger; the hope of being able to make a quick return to safety; and the possibility of enjoying the thrill through participation and observation.

The cinema's and film's dispositive structure enables the feeling of safety to be greater than during actual participation in an actual dangerous situation. Even ocnophiles seem able to enjoy the sensation of fear under these conditions. They can bask in familiar security in the absence of any real danger. The thrill becomes a "positive form of experience" (Klippel, 1990, p. 85) given that no danger really threatens their lives, and that it is impossible to access an absence of relationships. Film and television provide a basic prerequisite for thrilling experiences due to their apparative assignation: security for the spectator.

Whatever happens on the movie or television screen, it generally remains of no consequence to the spectator's real life. This, of course, is seen separately from the symbolic aspects of adaptation, for example, the mediation of role patterns in everyday life based on role patterns observed in films. The spectators can only watch and not participate directly in the action. The great majority act in this way willingly and consciously; they are not coerced into doing so.

The unique quality of the communicative relationship in the media, constituted through participation via observation, forms a framework for thrilling experiences that the spectator can turn to consciously and purposefully. Nevertheless, this framework alone does not provide the possibility for losing control, as the prerequisites would then have to be uncertain. Spectators, however, are absolutely sure that the fictional quality of fear will be upheld in the cinema or in front of a television screen. They are certain that fictionalized danger will not become real. This is so even when the subject of the film itself is a screen hero stepping from the screen into everyday life, as in *The Purple Rose Of Cairo* (Woody Allen, 1985) or *Last Action Hero* (John McTiernan, 1993).

Still, a film aims to create a lifelike illusion of danger with the impression of reality that it transmits. This illusion is part of the communicative constellation between the film and the spectator. Films merely convey an impression of reality that spectators recognize as an "as if" reality within the framework of an aesthetic position. The realistic illusion that "a text is a true reproduction of a real and existing world stems from the fact that the contrived quality of the text is suppressed" (Ang, 1986, p. 50). The spectators are so involved in what is going on in the movie or on the television screen that they experience it as quasi-real. The experience of a thrill is possible because, in addition to being part of the reception activities, the situation of "being a spectator of a film" is regarded as such by the spectators.

Balint's (n.d.) typical mixture of "fear, delight and confident hope" (p. 21), which constitute the thrilling experience, appears in several works and, in his examination of excitement, in different contexts. Barthes (1988) described excitement as an exacerbated form of distortion. It not only keeps a narrative sequence open and, thereby, strengthens the contact with the reader (as well as with the spectator), but it also exposes them to an incomplete sequence or disruption of logic that they absorb with anxiety and pleasure: " 'Suspense,' therefore, is a game with structure, designed to endanger and glorify it, constituting a veritable 'thrilling' of intelligibility: by representing order (and no longer series) in its fragility, 'suspense' accomplishes the very idea of language" (p. 133).

Although the thrilling quality of excitement refers to the intelligible, it is absorbed by anxiety and pleasure and is, thereby, accompanied by an emotional state. For Barthes, the Balintian element of loss of control is part of the construction of the fragility of order. Borringo (1980) assumed, in his work on excitement, that "suspense is to be regarded via its basic components of fear and hope as a 'generator of fear' " (p. 50). Nevertheless, he also assumed that spectators can both sympathize with and integrate the hero's fear. Spectators may also experience a thrill without feeling the hero's fear (e.g., when the hero does not suspect that there is any danger, as in the famous sequence with the little boy and the bomb in Hitchcock's *Sabotage*). Wulff (1985, 1994c) considered both excitement and fear to be emotions of expectation. He pointed out that the expectation of fear is an ambivalent one as it is accompanied by the hope that the expectation of fear will not be met (Wulff, 1985). The combination of fear and hope as a moment in experiencing excitement and suspense during film reception appears as a complex interplay of the spectators' cognitive and emotional activities. These emotional activities can accompany the cognitive ones as well as exist on their own.

Fear and hope are linked during the experience of excitement and suspense because on the basis of security, which is transmitted to the spectators by the media constellation, a pleasurable feeling of fear is possible. Thus, the spectators have what they perceive to be control over the fictitious action within the framework of realistic illusion. This fictitious action is, nevertheless, constantly called into question by the characteristics of the text. The framework of the apparative and dispositive structure guarantees the spectators a sense of security and a removed quality from the events on the movie or television screen. It is the ongoing task of the formal and dramaturgical tools to call this security into question by stimulating the spectators' emotional and cognitive activities. This leads to a pleasurable sense of fear and a temporary loss of control. These textual characteristics transform the experience of a thrill into the terror of uncertainty (Grixti, 1989). The incitement of fear constantly calls hope into question. The spectator, thereby, is enfolded in a double sense of security. This is guaranteed by the apparative and dispositive structure (also cf. Baudry, 1975) on the one hand, and by the narrative structures, which are situated in most cases in the realm of genre conventions, on the other.

GENRE CONVENTIONS AND THE VIEWING CONTRACT

Genres are narrative patterns and conventions that have unfolded during the course of cinema history. They may be seen as the media counterparts of film literacy that spectators have developed during their cinematic socialization. According to Berger (1992), they may be seen "as the result of constant reading and viewing of texts in various genres, readers and viewers discern patterns and formulas that define the genres and differentiate them from other genres. These conventions are well-known" (p. 34).

Film literacy is geared toward routinizing cognitive and emotional activity during reception and appropriation. They are thereby partially optimized, as well. Genres standardize and optimize technical production, economic, narrative, and dramaturgical structures (see Schweinitz, 1987). They serve to simplify communication within the framework of the communicative process by creating a sense of behavioral security, simultaneously optimizing the result of comprehension and interpretation. Genres, therefore, structure communication within the context of situative structures of relevance. In this sense, genres are forms of cultural praxis that order the broad field of texts and meanings that circulate in society.

They service, in this manner, both producers and receivers (see Fiske, 1987). Furthermore, they are based on a reciprocal relationship between producers and their audience (Schatz, 1981). That means that the producers will know that their texts will be understood within a framework of a genre's conventions. The viewers can depend on the fact that the texts will fulfill and satisfy the expectations, wishes, and needs that they associate with certain genres. Thus, genres contribute to the routinization and ritualization of film communication and form the basis of the viewing contract between the film and the audience.

In this sense, a genre is neither a characteristic of a text that refers to specific codes nor a mere characteristic of the audience's expectations. "Approached in this way, genres are not to be seen as forms of intertextual codifications, but as systems of orientations, expectations and conventions that circulate between industry, text and subject" (Neale, 1987, p. 19). Nevertheless, genres do not have hermetic structures and undergo dynamic changes. This is because with each new film within a genre, the genre is varied and thereby changes. Still, these changes remain part of the communicative overlap of producers, texts, and recipients.

Numerous genres have developed during the course of cinematic history that make it possible to experience excitement, suspense, and mystery: gangster, detective, and police movies; psycho and spy thrillers; western, action, and science-fiction movies; road movies; horror and splatter films; and so on. All promise an experience of excitement and suspense in the form of thrill. Each sticks, in its own way, to the given conventions of its genre. They thus promise practical value for audiences, which, in turn, motivates them for reception.

Within the framework of the conventions of the genre, the film experience facilitates a *controlled thrilling experience*. To a certain extent, audiences accept that emotions, such as anxiety, fear, shock, disgust, horror, and so on will be played on. They know that the viewing contract will not be violated and that the conventions of the genre will be adhered to. "By the terms of the viewing contract, desire will be engaged, then domesticated by the textual strategies; fear will be aroused, then controlled" (Giles, 1984, p. 39).

The experience of fear becomes even more pleasurable the more the film transports the spectators to the edge of losing control with its textual strategies. In doing so, it appears to dissolve the viewing contract in order to leave the spectators alone with their anxiety and free of the conventions of the genre. This, however, is only part of the game. Whereas fans of certain genres have learned to depend on these conventions, those new to the genre are uncertain as to how to react. Horror fans depend heavily on the conventions that give rise to fear and horror. Furthermore, they have developed individual strategies for avoiding fear that form the basis for their enjoyment of horror films. Viewers who see a horror film for the first time are not sure about the conventions of the genre and have not developed personal strategies for avoiding fear. The reception of the horror film, then, frequently turns into a real horror for first-time viewers. Newcomers cannot yet rely on the viewing contract and its inherent possibilities for experiencing different forms of terror. The conventions of the genre satisfy hopes for a conventional end to the story, whereas the textual strategies induce the experience of fear in part by continually calling these promises into question.

A twofold framework exists for the spectators, in addition to the apparative and dispositive structure, together with the conventions of the genre and its promise of utility. Within this framework the spectators can get caught up in the loss-of-control game in order to enjoy the thrill. The attraction of the thrill genre lies exactly within this interplay of security and insecurity, control and loss of control, which enables the enjoyment of anxiety, fear, horror, and disgust. The genre film's promise of utility not only refers to its textual structure and conventional narrative form, but also to the experience per se insofar as it is bound to the film's reception. A genre film promises the spectators knowledge and an experience, similar to that they have gained watching other films of the same genre.

Cawelti (1969, 1970) designated the conventions of individual genres as *formulas*. These represent in their entirety a conventional system for structuring cultural products. Still, as they are made up of a mixture of convention and the variation and integration of new elements, they are as dynamic in and of themselves as the genres are. These conventional narrative forms are important because they correspond to individual unconscious reference figures, suppressed desires, needs, and fears in each society. Thus, as symbolic objectifications they are simultaneously the expression of these wishes, needs, and fears (Cawelti, 1969).

Collective fears, particularly in the genre films, are staged using specific formulas that observers can experience in a controlled manner. They also refer to the external reality by way of the concretely staged situation. Thus, for example *Terminator 2—Judgement Day* (James Cameron, 1990) stages the fear of all-powerful machines. This fear is experienced, nevertheless, in concrete situations during the film, which lies within the conventional framework of the action film. *Jurassic Park* (Steven Spielberg, 1993) stages the fear of unbridled gene manipulation, and the fear of what is past and has been suppressed. This not only involves collective social fears, but also staged specific fears: fear of the dark, fear of descending into dark cellars, fear of falling from great heights, and others. These fears correspond to everyday situations. The mere fact that the finale of *The Silence of the Lambs* (Jonathan Demme, 1990) takes place in the serial murderer's cellar means that, independently of the film's concrete action in that situation, the locale is interpreted as a place of fear via the classification of the film within a genre.

The Inducement of Fear

The experience of fear during reception is induced in the various genres in different ways. The conventional narrative forms of the individual genres differ in time, place, lead and supporting characters, plots, themes, sequence of events, and set designs (see Berger, 1992). These are joined by different technical and dramaturgic creative tools. Still, there are common patterns in provoking fear. These include (in addition to light and sound effects) all techniques that open up a space external to the frame in which the content is unknown. It can contain a monster that has previously been introduced, or an as yet unknown horror. The staging of the experience of fear is amplified when the camera focuses on people who are obviously scared. This is a favored practice in such films as *Evil Dead II* (Sam Raimi, 1987) or *The Exorcist* (William Friedkin, 1973). Sometimes in these genres, the darkness off screen is even portrayed as something protective. Generally, however, it is shown as something threatening and thereby corresponds to the spectators' real fears of the dark, whether in the pitch black of the woods or in dark cellars.

Whereas in this case the spectator's anxiety is based on something that is not seen on screen, fear can also be staged in a situation that is shown. There is a sequence in *Jurassic Park* in which the characters' experience of fear is staged: when the velociraptors chase both children into the chrome-mirrored kitchen. The spectators know as well as the kids in the film do that velociraptors are dangerous animals, because it was explained earlier on. One can and should be afraid of animals portrayed as dangerous through the frightened childrens' emotional reactions (they are afraid), their gestures and facial expression (they show fear), and their attempts to flee. Whether the spectators are scared in this sequence depends on whether they interpret the situation as a scary one. It is also contingent on their being able to identify with the role of the kids as those being chased within the framework of the situation schema: "being chased by dangerous animals."

Genres, insofar as they are systems of orientations, expectations, and conventions, exhibit special characteristics that justify the communicative overlap between producers, texts, and recipients. Above all, it is the textual characteristics of a film that prestructure an audience's acts of comprehension, interpretation, and the variations of their experiences. Whereas an audience can rely on their film literacy and the viewing contract on the one hand, their expectations are simultaneously being toyed with on the other. This way, the textual characteristics create a space for the spectator's cognitive and emotional activities (see Wulff, 1994c). Specific formulas, narrative conventions, and dramaturgic tools can create room to experience excitement and suspense as thrill within the framework of an individual genre. Excitement and suspense can be defined as a quality of experience that is based on specific constellations of the spectator's emotional and cognitive activities. However, they also may be situated below the level of cognitive activity on the level of direct scenic comprehension.

EXCITEMENT AND SUSPENSE AS MODES OF RECEPTION

Two basic types of emotion can be identified during film reception:

1. So-called feelings of expectation that are closely linked to cognitions.

2. Emotions as situative qualities of experience and sensual experience, which are based on the spectator's previous, biographically significant experiences. It is, thereby, of particular importance that emotions not be seen as isolated, intraindividual steps toward stimulation, but that they always exhibit a relationship to the individual's social reality. They only crop up within the situative framework of social interaction. The communicative relationship of film text and spectator in the reception situation is viewed in the same terms.

According to Bloch (1985), one can differentiate between positive and negative feelings of expectation. He counted anxiety, fear, terror, and despair among the negative ones, hope and confidence among the positive ones. Expectations always refer to the future and are, above all, indeterminate and diffuse. This differentiates them from *filled emotions*, which according to Bloch are bound to ideas of memories. Expectations play a large role in experience, excitement, and suspense. The hope that the security of the apparative and dispositive structure will hold up, as well as the hope that the story will have a happy end, run parallel to the negative expectations of fear, anxiety, and despair that are experienced pleasurably. As the spectators must interpret the situations in the medium as frightening, it is clear that the expectations have a cognitive component (see Wulff, 1985). Thus, fear during the film experience is less grounded in the fact that the spectators empathize with the heroes, who themselves are scared, than constructed within a framework of cinematic conventions and genre patterns that make the spectator expect anxiety, fear, or fright.

Wulff (1994b, 1994c) and Carroll (1990) both referred to the situation dependency of the experience of suspense and excitement. Carroll (1990) stated: "The object of suspense is a situation or an event" (p. 143). The situation is interpreted within the medium, with the help of cognitive pools of information, as one that holds the promise of a threatening plot, or is scary. Only when this succeeds can the audience be taken in emotionally; the thrill sets in. In particular appropriate feelings of expectation are staged for the spectators in psycho thrillers, westerns, action, detective, cop, horror, sci-fi, and gangster films.

During the reception of film and television texts, the hope for a happy ending is always latently present within the framework of a coherent correlation of meaning within the narrative as well as within the conventions of their genres. This is true even when a negative emotion of expectation such as anxiety or fear predominates during reception. This is where the moment of pleasurable fear or the thrill is based. The film's plot and the emotions it provokes take the spectators in because they can expect (as a result of their general film literacy and their special knowledge of the genre) that the film will end in a good and emotionally satisfying way. Still, fright or scare can also produce emotional satisfaction. Those who willfully and purposefully expose themselves to a horror film or a psycho thriller expect to find excitement, suspense, thrill, and horror in the tenor of the reception experience. The spectator is disappointed in the film when these experiences are not present (cf. Wulff, 1994c).

The purpose of staging expectations is to create a space for the spectators within which they can activate previously experienced past feelings based on ideas that spring from their memories. This is joined by the emotional experience of anxiety, pleasure, fear, horror, or disgust, generally by the emotional experience of all forms of curiosity or tense expectation. As these feelings are generally bound to social interaction, memories can trigger them and they can be reanimated and felt anew. In this way, the situations in the medium can be directly felt via a moment of *scenic comprehension.*

Past experiences and the emotional constellations associated with them can be reactivated through visual correspondence between scenic arrangements or situations on television and scenic arrangements in the spectator's imagination and memory (see Mikos, 1994, in press). The staging of fear in narrative situations assumes great importance in the excitement and suspense genre. This is because the emotional experience of fear or horror can be directly scenically induced. On the level of emotional assignment of importance during reception, psychological activities, such as transference, projection, and identification with social roles, are significant. This assignment occurs as a reactivation of personal, past experience through memories of previous scenic experiences. The spectators' primary identification with their own gaze (see Metz, 1990) is overlapped in their film experience by secondary and tertiary identification. This particularly includes identification with social roles.

During reception itself, the reactivation of these scenes causes the emotions associated with the scene to be felt again. The spectators cry, are sad, jealous, envious, disgusted, afraid, repulsed, and so on. They feel this way not because the characters do, but because the scenic arrangements remind them of events from their own biographies. The emotional content of the events in the film experience is also relived through scenic comprehension. The scenes in the film are thereby linked to the spectators' biography via their psychological activities. As in other narrative fictional genres, the plot situations shown are based on patterns of interaction that are also significant within the spectators' lifeworlds.

A *scenic arrangement* (Lorenzer, 1973, 1986) from the film *The Silence of the Lambs* might help to clarify this point. Agent Clarice Starling first visits the cannibalistic serial killer Hannibal Lecter in the high-security ward of an asylum for psychopathic criminals. Spectators are already familiar with Clarice Starling's character and her situation. They only know about Lecter through the stories of other characters. Starling's situation is defined as that of a trainee who has to pass a test: finding a serial killer, Buffalo Bill (alias James Gumb) who is at large, with the help of Lecter, who is in jail. The high-security ward is in the cellar of the asylum. Thus, Starling has to descend into it. The gates and doors close behind her as she enters the hallway leading to Lecter's cell. In this sequence, spectators expect danger and fear that something will happen to her. Furthermore, they wonder whether Lecter will help her, and if not, whether she can carry out her assignment.

On the level of scenic comprehension, past personal emotions are reactivated involving different aspects of this plot situation and their positions within the overall story's framework. Spectators know that Starling is in a trainee situation and that gaining Lecter's help is a sort of test problem. Thus, her entering the high-security ward can be scenically understood in a direct way just as the spectators' personal feelings of fear before an exam may be reactivated. These are joined by fears associated with going into cellars by virtue of the fact that the high-security ward is located in the cellar of the asylum. Furthermore, the situation is defined as one in which Starling must meet someone she has never seen in the flesh before. This situation is also familiar to the spectators from their everyday structure of interaction and they associate it with feelings of tense expectation, curiosity, and anxiety. Therefore although the scene is defined as a concrete plot situation for the protagonist, it also abstracts from this situation. It does so by linking patterns of interaction (the test situation, the cellar, the anxiety of meeting someone new, notorious, and dangerous) from different situations within its textual characteristics that the spectators recognize as frightening from their own life experience. It is thereby possible for spectators to understand the situation in sensual and scenic terms.

This example shows that films deal with structures of experience that relate to spectators' unconscious fears and wishes. Symbolic satisfaction of desires and a symbolic working through of fears occur by means of the reactivation of these structures of experience and the emotions associated with them. These fears can be experienced safely and pleasurably within the framework of a secure apparative and dispositive structure. They can also do so within the bounds of the conventions of a genre. Films and their symbolic representations of scenic arrangements can be seen, in this sense, as a set of instructions for or a challenge to spectators to engage in psychological activity and to pleasurably experience excitement, suspense, disgust, horror, revulsion, and so on, pleasurably.

CONCLUSION

Scenic comprehension, transference, projection, and identification are indissolubly bound to one another. During the film, spectators complete the on-screen narrative using their own biographical experience. These, however, are not purely individualistic but socially structured. The way in which specific spectators experience a certain film depends on the makeup of their identity, structure of experience, and social engagement in the web of their lifeworld. Thus, spectators experience specific films differently. Still, there are certain common patterns. On the one hand, the structures of experience represented in the film are variations of collective structures of experience. On the other, the spectators belong to a common cultural context. It is possible, in this way, to stage structures of experience in films of the so-called suspense genre that refer to the everyday fearful and suspenseful situations of the spectators.

Spectators in films within the suspense genre consciously seek out the thrill's specific mixture of fear, anxiety, and hope (as Balint described it) as a quality of experience. In experiencing this pleasurable anxiety they can both test their limits and work out past experiences and the negative emotions they have learned to associate with them. Pleasure while experiencing fear is possible because the apparative and dispositive structures of the cinema and film provide the assurance that the narrative is fiction and that the illusion is realistic. Furthermore, the spectators can place their faith in the conventions of the genre within the framework of the viewing contract. Thus, play can be created between the security and insecurity, control and loss of control, and certainty and doubt activated within the spectators. Excitement and suspense, as qualities of experience in the reception of films, are determined by a pleasurable experience of anxiety, horror, and other negatively pegged emotions. Therein lies their fascination.

REFERENCES

Ang, I. (1986). *Das Gefühl Dallas. Zur Produktion des Trivialen* [Watching "Dallas": Soap operas and the melodramatic imagination]. Bielefeld, Germany: Daedalus.

Balint, M. (n.d.). *Angstlust und Regression. Beitrag zu einer psycholgischen Typenlehre* [Thrill and regression. Contribution on a psychology theory of character types]. Stuttgart, Germany: Klett.

Barthes, R. (1988). Einführung in die strukturale Analyse von Erzählungen [Introduction to the structural analysis of narration]. In R. Baltes (Ed.), *Das semiologische Abenteuer* (pp. 102–143). Frankfurt: Suhrkamp.

Baudry, J.-L. (1975). Le dispositif. *Communications, 23,* 56–72.

Berger, A. A. (1992). *Popular culture genres. Theories and texts.* Newbury Park, CA: Sage.

Bloch, E. (1985). *Das Prinzip Hoffnung* [The principal of hope]. Frankfurt: Suhrkamp.

Bordwell, D. (1990). *Narration in the fiction film.* London: Routledge.

Borringo, H.-L. (1980). *Spannung in text und film. Spannung und Suspense als Textverarbeitungskategorien* [Excitement in text and film. Excitement and suspense as categories of text-processing]. Düsseldorf, Germany: Schwann.

Branigan, E. (1992). *Narrative comprehension and film.* London: Routledge.

Carroll, N. (1990). *The philosophy of horror or paradoxes of the heart.* New York: Routledge.

Cawelti, J. G. (1969). The concept of formula in the study of popular literature. *Journal of Popular Culture, 3,* 381–390.

Cawelti, J. G. (1970). *The six gun mystique.* Bowling Green, OH: Bowling Green University Press.

Fiske, J. (1987). *Television culture.* London: Methuen.

Giles, D. (1984). Conditions of pleasure in horror cinema. In B. K. Grant (Ed.), *Planks of reason: Essays on the horror film* (pp 38–52). Metuchen, NJ: Scarecrow.

Grixti, J. (1989). *Terrors of uncertainty: The cultural contexts of horror fiction.* London: Routledge.

Klippel, H. (1990). Böse Bilder. Horrorfilm und Angsterleben [Nasty images. Horror film and the experience of fear]. *Frauen und Film, 49,* 78–90.

Lorenzer, A. (1973). *Sprachzerstörung und Rekonstruktion. Vorarbeiten zu einer Metatheorie der Psychoanalyse* [Speech-destruction and reconstruction. Preliminary work to a meta-theory of psychoanalysis]. Frankfurt: Suhskamp.

Lorenzer, A. (1986). Tiefenhermeneutische Kulturanalyse [Depth-hermeneutic analysis of culture]. In H.-D. König (Eds.), *Kultur-Analysen* [Culture analysis] (pp. 11–98). Frankfurt: Fischer.

Metz, C. (1990). *Psychoanalysis and cinema: The imaginary signifier.* London: Macmillan.

Mikos, L. (1994). *Fernsehen im Erleben der Zuschauer. Vom lustvollen Umgang mit einem populären Medium* [Television as experience of the viewer. The pleasurable use of a popular medium]. Berlin: Quintessenz.

Mikos, L. (in press). "Souvenir-écran" and scenic comprehension: Understanding film as a biographical drama of the spectator. *Iris, 19.*

Neale, S. (1987). *Genre* (3rd ed.). London: British Film Institute.

Schatz, T. (1981). *Hollywood genres: Formulas, filmmaking, and the studio system.* New York: McGraw-Hill.

Schweinitz, J. (1987). Stereotyp—Vorschlag und Definition eines filmästhetischen Begriffs [Stereotype. Proposal and definition of a film aesthetical term]. *Beiträge zur Film und Fernsehwissenschafte, 28*(29), 111–127.

Truffaut, F. (1973). *Mr. Hitchcock, wie haben sie das gemacht?* [German translation of Truffaut (1983) Hitchcock]. München: Hanser.

Wulff, H. J. (1985). Die Erzählung der Gewalt [Narration of violence]. Münster: MAkS Publikationen.

Wulff, H. J. (1994a). Aktcharakteristik und stoffliche Bindung [Characteristics of action and material relationship]. *Montage/AV, 3*(1), 142–146.

Wulff, H. J. (1994b). *Spannungserleben und Erfahrungskonstitution: Vorüberlegungen zu einer phänomenologischen Untersuchung* [Excitement and the constitution of experience. Preliminaries to a phenomenological work]. Paper presented at the conference Medien, Erfahrung und Wirklichkeit, Münster, Germany.

Wulff, H. J. (1994c). *Texttheorie der Spannung* [Textual theory of excitement]. Unpublished manuscript, Westerkappeln, Germany.

Wuss, P. (1993a). *Filmanalyse und Psychologie. Strukturen des Films in Wahrnehmungsprozess* [Film analysis and psychology. Cinematic structures in perceptive processes]. Berlin: Edition Sigma.

Wuss, P. (1993b). Grundformen filmischer Spannung [Forms of cinematic excitement]. *Montage/AV, 2*(2), 101–116.

4

▼▼▼▼▼▼▼

Narrative Tension
in Antonioni

Peter Wuss
Academy of Film and Television "Konrad Wolf" Potsdam

TOWARD A COMPREHENSIVE UNDERSTANDING
OF NARRATIVE TENSION

The terms *cinematic tension* and *suspense* have been developed in connection
with the development of popular genres like the detective, crime, and horror film
or thriller, which would probably have lost their right to exist in the cinemas
without the corresponding effects. However, the terms do appear to be rather out
of place when one considers the work of Michelangelo Antonioni. A statement
by the director—that he had aimed for a kind of "inner suspense" (Antonioni,
1964, p. 89) in *L'Avventura*—however, reveals that, even in a dramaturgy that
seems diametrically opposed to the suspense film, tension can play a role—although evidently changing its character a good deal. Theory is challenged not
just to aim solely at finding tension in the narrowly defined understanding of
the suspense genre, but to contemplate how the concept could be extended or
modified so as to be applicable for those phenomena that at first glance, would
appear to be miles apart.

The academic deliberations concerning a comprehensive understanding of
tension that would also allow for distinctions to be made have only just begun.
An important reason for this situation lies in the fact that, on the one hand,
tension is prefabricated within the work structure. On the other hand, however,
it is based on psychologically relevant functional forms, that is, it amounts to a
specifically aesthetic reaction that necessitates an interdisciplinary approach to
examine it that is able to draw on findings from both film studies and psychology.

51

The following thoughts go in this direction. They attempt to make use of cognitive psychological findings to depict film perception so that a general and yet differentiated model, which can mediate between that exterior tension with suspenselike qualities, such as the kind Alfred Hitchcock developed in practice and theory, and the inner tension that Antonioni employs is created for narrative tension. The fact that quite different forms of creating tension are deployed in Antonioni's oeuvre gives us the chance to incorporate transitional forms as well as extremes.

TENSION AND SUSPENSE: ASPECTS OF DEFINITION

It is well known that the deliberations over both cinematic and narrative tension have been stimulated particularly by Hitchcock's concept of suspense. The basic principle of suspense, which I interpret as a particularly special case of tension, was once illustrated very vividly by this master of the genre of suspense through a film situation in which some people were sitting around a table under which there was a bomb that could have exploded at any moment. Unlike the viewers, who are informed of this, the protagonists do not know the danger they are in (cf. Truffaut, 1986). This prototypical situation allows one to identify some general prerequisites for tension and suspense in a film. Thus, tension is conditional on:

1. The probable occurrence of a relevant (often menacing) event in an undefined course of events.
2. The possibility of the protagonists being able to be active in bringing the course of events under control by certain forms of conduct (i.e., preventing the negative outcome of events).

Whereas these two conditions may, in general, apply to narrative tension in film, another characteristic is also applicable to suspense:

3. There is a difference between the information viewers have about the uncertain situation and the kind of information to which the protagonists are privy.

Hitchcock once used the final sequence of *Young and Innocent* to demonstrate in detail how the sequence of events in the film have an influence on tension and suspense. It all comes down to a relevant decision: whether the murderer will be successfully unmasked, thus saving an innocent man from a prison sentence. The efforts of the protagonists here also have an influence on the course of events. In the case of a successful criminal investigation, the situation would have been brought under their active control, that is, changed to the benefit of the innocent man. We are shown a girl, who is on the side of the innocent hero, looking for the murderer who will be recognized by his twitching eye in a first-class hotel during teatime using the services of a tramp. The mass of people in the hotel foyer, however, make it difficult to conduct the search. Thus, the uncertainty of the situation can hardly be resolved by the protagonist, as she needs information about where the wanted man is situated.

Hitchcock now explains that, just at the point when the tramp airs his doubts about whether one can really ever expect to find a man with a small imperfection of his eye in such a throng, the camera is situated below the ballroom's ceiling and gradually travels toward the musicians in the dance band. When it gets so near to the drummer that his eyes fill the screen, one sees the lids twitch: the aforementioned twitchy eye. When talking about the conditioning of viewers considering this suspense scene, Hitchcock said: "The audience is provided with information the characters in the picture don't know about. Because of this knowledge, the tension is heightened as the audience tries to figure out what's going to happen next" (Truffaut, 1986, p. 102). The camera has focused the viewer's field of attention. They now know that the murderer really is in the room, and this enables them to make a better prognosis of the chances of realization for chasing after the criminal. The circumstances, however, always ensure that these chances keep on changing: For example, the drummer sees the girl and the tramp speaking with a policeman and becomes so nervous that he infects the whole band with his bad playing, which results in their stopping and the interruption of the dancing. At the same time, the two "detectives" move to leave the ballroom. This would be the drummer's salvation, but because he is so afraid, he loses consciousness, and the girl, who wants to give him first aid, recognizes him by his twitching eyelids. Until the moment when the clarifying pragmatic information is provided, the elimination of uncertainty for the protagonists occurs in a successive manner—by a slow and often artificially delayed journey to the plot's outcome. At the same time, the tension that arises shortly before the denouement may also be experienced by viewers as a personal feeling of emotion. Indeed, the processes of film experience, which have normally been described here as plot-based and seen from a cognitive aspect, also have a clear emotive dimension.

NEED FOR CONTROL, EMOTIONS, AND TENSION

The examples of suspense cited from Hitchcock dramatize and illustrate a very general trait of human behavioral determination, the "need for control" (Dörner, Reither, & Stäudel, 1983, p. 63). In order to hold their own in their environment, humans must permanently put themselves in situations that allow them to influence the course of things in a practical way. Where this cannot be achieved directly, that is, in the form of active control, they at least try to achieve the possibility of a better prognosis, that is, passive control (cf. Dörner, Reither, & Stäudel, 1983), which, in its own way, reduces the uncertainty of the events.

Control is always connected with cognition, but on closer examination, it can be seen that it also has consequences for the construction of emotions: "Emotions are, in our opinion, reactions to felt or anticipated loss or reclamation of control" (Dörner, Reither, & Stäudel, 1983, p. 66). As a rule, the regaining of a state of control and the repression of uncertainty is accompanied by positive emotions, a loss of control by negative ones. It is connected with the involvement of the viewers in the lives and conflict situations depicted in the film—so that the emotional state of the figures is, to a certain extent, also communicated to them although they cannot actively influence the events because they only have the possibility of passive control in the anticipation of events. Following Fraisse, Leontjew (1979) identified a relationship between two factors responsible for the general materialization of emotions: "The exceptional quality of emotions can be found in the fact that they reflect relationships between motives (needs) and the success or the possibility of the successful realization of the subject's corresponding activity" (p. 189). In the previously mentioned bomb scene, the desire of the protagonists (and the viewers sympathizing with them) is that the bomb will not explode, and the emotions are triggered because the chance of this intention being realized is put into question. In *Young and Innocent*, the heroine and the viewer are interested in the murderer being caught and the innocent man being saved. Emotions arise from the fact that their intentions cannot be achieved straightaway because they lack certain pieces of information. The aforementioned relationship between motivating need and the chance of realization of the subject in a story can also be described within the framework of a comprehensive theoretical concept of information processing as being an information deficit. According to Simonov (1975), certain "pragmatic pieces of information" are necessary to satisfy a need, and, as this writer says, one can "see emotion as a specialized neural mechanism which serves to compensate for the information deficit which the organism needs to organize its process of adaptation" (p. 83). The unsatisfied desire for such pragmatic information is always the source of emotional tension. The degree of tension depends, quantitatively, on both the intensity of the needs and the difference between those amounts of information that are anticipated as being necessary and those that one then actually receives. Thus, in addition to needs or motives, the compensation mechanism is also always receiving prognostic estimations that indicate whether additional information is necessary.

These comments are valid, to start with, for situations in real life; but they are also applicable—although certainly in modified form—to the fictional situations in films. Insofar as a film plot tells a more or less dramatic story, it uses the conflict established therein to construct a problem situation for viewers—and this situation can be resolved by the players. The emotional tension is bound up as much with the content of the pending resolution as with the knowledge of the chances of realization. Instructive in this context is the connection between the events in a film and the resolution of problems: Although one can usually recognize the operation in a feature film of those three components that, from a psychological perspective, characterize a problem-solving situation—an unwelcome (conflict-loaden) initial situation, a desired final situation and a barrier that in a given situation prevents the transformation from initial to final situation (cf. Dörner, 1979)—an analytical approach with this model concept is unusual. There is certain to be connection with the fact that, as a rule, the problem situation and goal within a dialectical film narrative are hard to define and that there is little known about the means of overcoming the barrier. This is quite different with many suspense films, though, and so it really does make sense to speak of a problem-solving situation. In detective films, the reason why the described moments are so comprehensible is because the abstract concept of information, which amounts to the significance of a news item for viewers, comes very close to the trivial concept of information. A simple piece of information is needed that enables a very rational approach to the stores of knowledge touched on. Viewers are then able to appreciate the characters' information deficits with corresponding ease. In the case of *Young and Innocent*, it basically comes down to the heroine having to know where the man with the twitching eye can be found.

The ability to define characters' information deficits seems to be a precondition for suspense. It in fact puts viewers in the position of being able to compare their own level of knowledge with that of the protagonists and to realize the difference. This clearly raises the underlying emotional tension because the prognosis of the necessary increase in information becomes that much easier. In *Young and Innocent*, the direction ensures—through that traveling camera movement that lets the viewers discover the man with the twitching eye in the room without the two "detectives" finding out—that there is a considerable restriction to the uncertainty in the clearly defined problem area, which is given something of a topographic dimension here. Admittedly, this occurs in a game in which, subsequently, the uncertainty in the course of events changes yet again. The emotional tension is clearly not only heightened as a result of the detective story coming to a head, but as a result of metacognitive prerequisitives in viewers who become increasingly aware of their emotions.

The emotions, doubtless, can also have a different character in situations in which the conflicts lead to a less comprehensible problem situation and in which viewers are much less aware of the narrative relationships and their goals; the viewer does not know any more than the characters about the situation. To clarify this interrelationship, it seems important, though, to give a more precise description of the foreknowledge and prognosis that viewers have on events because this has consequences for the narrative strategy and bestows a different kind of coloring on both the expectations and the development of tension.

SCHEMA FRAMEWORK: THREE BASIC STRUCTURES OF NARRATION

Psychology has an apparatus that allows greater differentiation of the knowledge about a situation that Hitchcock noted from character and viewer to the extent that it incorporates the various cognitive schemas underlying this knowledge. It assumes that this formation of schemas operates in processes and runs in phases in equal stages. As I have shown on a previous occasion (Wuss, 1993), film perception can be described within the framework of the concept of information processing as a process that is not just controlled by the depicted events but also by the artistic abstractions deployed at the same time. Events in films are the result of an appropriation of external structures in the memory of authors or directors, together with their cognitive schema formation, and they create the basis for such formation of schema in the viewers. This processing of appropriation or learning during film perception is undertaken in several phases that have already been distinguished from each other by the work's form. Rumelhart (1980), who defined the scheme as a "data structure for representing the generic concepts stored in memory" (p. 34), also pointed out that schemata represent "knowledge at all levels of abstraction" (Rumelhart & Ortony, 1977, p. 40). In an analogy to the cognitive formation of invariants in perception, thought, and subject that have their own respective specification (cf. Klaus, 1966), three structural forms with varying characteristics can be defined in film. The processing of information during the reception of a film occurs quite differently depending on whether (a) an external structure caught on film is to be appropriated in the context of perceptional formation of invariants by the internal model of the viewer, or (b) whether it has already had a sufficient mental representation so that it can already submit itself to thought, or (c) whether its shape has long since been formed into a stereotype by communicative use.

Three types of filmic structure can be distinguished: (a) perception-based structures, (b) conception-based structures, and (c) stereotype-based structures. These structural relations can vary depending on the degree of evidence and awareness, learning behavior in reception, their semantic stability, and their storage in memory. A characteristic, which is bound up with the principle of repetition, makes their distinction from one another particularly reliable on an empirical level: Perception-based structures must be repeated several times within a film to have an effect; a single appearance is sufficient for conception-based ones; and stereotypes only start to develop as a result of repeated use within several films of a cultural repertoire so that they acquire the character of sec-ondhand structures in current experience.

Every cinematic composition can be roughly seen as a network of structural relations with various degrees of schema or processing. One can observe considerable differences between films regarding the expression, correlation, and respective dominance of these structures' components. All three types take an effect, in their own specific way, in the semantic process, and only begin to form the meaning of the whole through their interaction within the cinematic composition.

If a structural relationship is present from beginning to end in a film, or is at least temporarily present, then it will be narratively effective and help create the story. All three types contribute to the establishment of specific basic structures for the narration. Perceptive-based structures lead to topic lines of narration, conception-based ones form the basis for causal chains, and stereotypes lead to real story schemas or narrative stereotypes. Film stories can make equal use of all three basic structures, feature one or two of them, or just let one dominate on its own.

The causal chain is the most well-known and widely researched of the basis structures. Since the time of Aristotle, who deduced the plot of a play from the existence of significant occurrences and their causal linkages, one has preferred to depict narrative structures through concept-based relations that have been termed as a "sequence of causes and effects" (Lessing, 1954, p. 165) or—referring to film—as "plot" or "syuzhet" (Lotman, 1977, p. 101), and also "narrative" (Bordwell & Thompson, 1979, p. 50; Branigan, 1992, p. 3). Many forms of narration considered open or plotless—as one knows from episodic or epically constructed films—are based on the fact that viewers constantly filter reoccuring invariant moments from the loose series of events according to pattern of the perceptive cycle. Through their active and controlled process of perception, they create an inner relation between these moments, which then appears as the link between the presented events. These latter assume the character of concentrated phenomena and form the narrative basic structure of topic lines.

As for dominant stereotype-based narrative structures in the form of permanent motifs, myths, and archetypes, as well as conventional plot patterns of classic or popular genres (which viewers are already aware of from other situations in cultural communication or from such frequent use that they tend to be noticed only in passing and are hardly given any attention), they ensure, in their own way, that cinematic events are each experienced as interconnected information blocks, as larger information units, as chunks. They establish the basic narrative structure of the story schema or narrative stereotype. As has already been said, the basic forms hardly appear on their own in a film's narration, but are linked together mostly in variable interactions that range from semantic cooperation to semantic conflict. What one might prefer to term the narrative structure in film stories is, thus, not homogeneous, but potentially consists of components with varying degrees of awareness and evidence. In addition, it does not have to orientate itself to those conceptualized structural components of the causal chain that are the easiest to analyze. If cinematic narration is based on the perception of events during the course of which uncertainty can be reduced, then the narrative structure always has an effect on the emotional strategy and tension. Various strong anticipations in the form of hypotheses about the occurence of future events take effect in the course of the perception of a film in the dependency on the cognitive schemas, which define each of the narrative basic forms of a film's story. Viewers experience this as anticipation of varying degrees of stability; the spectrum ranges from somewhat latent expectations in the area of perception through specific expectations based on the conceptualization of external structures to normative expectations grounded in stereotype concepts that have been developed in a process of cultural communication and socialization.

BASIC STRUCTURES OF NARRATION
AND TENSION IN THE OPENING SEQUENCE
OF *PROFESSIONE: REPORTER*

A film sequence from Antonioni's *Professione: Reporter* (1975) demonstrates
how the three basic film forms can operate and create the basis for various kinds
of comprehensive basic forms, which, in turn, result in a varying development
of suspense: The film's action begins with an English journalist arriving in an
African village in a jeep. He goes into a workshop where there are several natives,
but, one after another, they leave the room evidently wanting to avoid speaking
with the stranger. One of the Africans still sitting there motions for a cigarette
and is given one but he also leaves as the reporter keeps looking for his lighter.
Outside, the new arrival then goes up to another man who also wants to scrounge
something to smoke. He, however, is no more prepared to talk than the others.
The protagonist speaks in English and French to a boy who has gotten into the
jeep. Vague signs answering his questions as to the right direction only result
in him driving the car into a barren landscape where the boy then leaves him.
While the journalist waits in the desert on his own, he passes the time of day
with a bedouin passing by on a camel. The rider pretends that he has not seen
the stranger and passes by without saying a word. A native comes out of his
nearby dwelling and takes the waiting man into the mountains. The only thing
he says about the destination is that it is a kind of military camp, but he is not
prepared to give any more information. When the two have climbed a rock face
and caught sight of a caravan down in the valley—something the guide had
evidently not expected—they make their way back again without saying a word.
The sequence ends with the hapless reporter, whose jeep is stranded in the desert,
coming back to the hotel. He knocks on the door of the room next to his, but
there is no reaction. When he comes into the room, however, he sees that the
other man is lying motionless on the bed. He turns him over as if wanting to
speak to him, but a conversation is not possible because the other man is dead.
    The remarkable thing about this opening sequence is that it initially consists
of a situation in which viewers find it very difficult to orientate themselves
because they can only divine from the reporter's questions to his companion that
he wants to make contact with the African liberation front. Although the hero's
enterprise has a goal and a respective action program—and thus represents a
"cyclical unity" (Oesterreich, 1981, p. 12) through which viewers can inform
themselves and make note—viewers are nevertheless kept in the dark for a long
time about what the protagonist actually intends to do here. However, a certain
state of anticipation, as well as a form of more internal emotional tension
regarding the course of events, develops. Given the uncertainty of the course of
events, viewers may try to orientate themselves by using the few regularities that
appear in the events (i.e., he undertakes abductions, looks intuitively in the plot
for invariant moments on the perceptual level). This occurs according to the

principle of probability learning or autocorrelation, which "occurs 'inevitably' according to the law of given probabilities or frequencies" (von Cube, 1965, p. 159). In the case of the film sequence, a certain probability distribution of events is effected by having similar things repeating themselves in all of the hero's part actions: An unsuccessful result follows from the attempt at communication.

The pattern of stimuli, with its recurrence of homologous forms that become succinct and developed into a "semantic gestus" (Mukařovský, 1974, p. 49), turns into a topic line that provides the foundation for the story. Eco (1987), writing about the reading of literary texts, claimed that a topic "is what van Dijk has called 'aboutness' " (p. 114). In film, one could see topics in those concentrated constructs that are created as a result of latent expectations about abduction. The resulting cognitive activity also leads to inner tension. Viewers suffer with the protagonist from a deficit in pragmatic information, especially because the uncertainty about the course of events deprives them of the ability to predict and every kind of passive control. This does not lead to suspense, as the level of the viewers' knowledge of the situation is still below that of the protagonist.

Within the described sequence, there are instances in which the conflict of unrealizable communication is so evident that it begins to be conceived as a structural relationship within the film's action (i.e., when the bedouin ignores the European's greeting or when the man in the next room is no longer capable of communication). The structural work then moves onto the level of the formation of invariants of thought, to that of the concept-based forms that enable a much simpler intellectual reflection of events. This level of abstraction is also preserved when the reporter discovers that the other man is dead. He switches on a tape-recorder, on which there is a recorded conversation with his neighbor, and learns that this man had been in close contact with the African underground movement. Unlike the hapless reporter, he had evidently been able to offer them practical aid: as an arms dealer, as we later find out. The verbal pronouncements—which are given to the thought processes and thus also presuppose a corresponding level of invariant and schema formation—help viewers to textually identify and evaluate the previously obscure film events. They also contribute to the formation of dramatic conflict, which confronts viewers with the question of what will happen if the reporter makes the desired contact using false papers that would make him appear to be an arms dealer. According to Aristotelian dramaturgy, this should have given rise to tangible exterior tension in the plot that is steered by a specific anticipation (i.e., the resolution of the conflict). Antonioni decided, though, against the plot in the future.

We are shown how the reporter appropriates the dead man's papers and sticks his own photograph in his passport (i.e., undergoes a change of identity), but the film does not follow this action through in a logical manner. There is no practical involvement by the journalist for the Africans' cause, and so the dramatic conflict hardly deepens any further. The reporter may go to several secret meetings around Europe, which had been arranged with representatives of the African liberation front, but, instead of helping, he gets into their debt by taking money from them as an advance for weapons he does not even possess. Thus, viewers wait in vain for an explanatory event; when the reporter is killed at the end—evidently by opponents of the underground movement who see him as being the real enemy—the uncertainty is hardly reduced, and that famous, endlessly wandering pan during the murder scene at the end of the film does not help either. Specific external tension is deliberately avoided. It is more a case of the viewers' attention remaining involved with the topics of disturbed communication during the action. Their line extends into a subject of disturbed or frustrated engagement.

An interesting aspect in the development of the opening sequence is fact that the level of abstraction constantly changes and the way that the basic form of narration suddenly passes into a narrative stereotype as soon as important character relationships have been resolved on a conceptual level. The forging of the passport brings standardized expectations into play that viewers connect with comparable plots in films of the adventure genre, well known for the motif of the hero who disguises himself, masquerades as somebody else, or changes his identity. Although the opening scenes have actually sensitized viewers to the subtle nuances of his behavior, this will then mean that they will suddenly accept that the hero declares himself to be dead, and will hardly ask any further about the psychological probability of this action. Cultural memory enables them to make this turnaround in thinking. The absorption of information probably experiences a certain channeling in the familiar adventurous basic situation. It follows previously stored stereotypical processes and, by assuming the form of the events, also takes on the respective perspectives and perceptual dispositions to both the events and the corresponding emotional attitudes and value criteria. In the final third of the plot though, the suspense is in fact not dominated by the conflict between the false arms dealer and the duped Africans, but by an additional motif: The protagonist is pursued by a television crew, which includes his wife who is working on a report on the man who supposedly died. This motif intensifies the standardized tension introduced by the narrative stereotypes of the adventure genre. As the narrative state of the film's story moves from the level of the topic line to one of narrative stereotypes and passes quickly over the usual conceptualization, it creates a form of tension that is deliberately heterogeneous by, on the one hand, following a principle of "inner suspense" within the framework of tense behavioral observation, and, on the other, by submitting the artificially dynamized action to the norms and outwardly suspenseful plots of adventure stories. The analytical eye of the observer is transported, to a certain degree, at a faster rate through the events.

Antonioni's personal style can probably be best understood from the perspective of this area of conflict. His stories are hardly ever defined by conceptual causal chains leading to the plot. What makes them so remarkable for the processes of film stories is more their permanent link to the perception-based structures and the topic lines founded on them.

TOPIC LINES AND "INNER SUSPENSE" IN *L'AVVENTURA*

The topic mode of narration had its heyday in the first half of the 1960s when the famous tetralogy *L'Avventura* (1960), *La Notte* (1960), *L'Eclisse* (1962), and *Il Deserto Rosso* (1964) were made.

In an analysis of *L'Avventura*, Eco (1977) suggested that one was dealing here with one of those film works "which broke decisively with the traditional storytelling structures to show a series of events where no dramatic connection existed in the conventional sense, a story where nothing happens or where things happen, which no longer have the appearance of something narrated, but rather of something that happened by coincidence" (p. 202). Indeed, one is missing the syuzhet that would intensify a series of causal-linked events (subsequently appearing as plot points) into conflict situations, thereby conceptualizing them and making us aware of them. This results in the presentation of analog moments in the behavior of the main characters and in their environment that order and topicalize the events (i.e., submit to being regulated). Thus, in the opening sequence of *L'Avventura*, one observes how Anna, the heroine of the film, complains in a number of scenes about her dissatisfaction with life with her partner—although this knowledge will not result in any kind of practical consequence that would change the situation. Viewers have a contradictory situation systematically constructed before them where existing inner conflicts are, indeed, regarded with pain and clearly articulated. However, in the end, they are suppressed once more. Antonioni (1964) coined the term "disease of the emotions" (p. 97) for the psychological state of his heroes and showed that the most comprehensible of symptoms for this illness can be found in eroticism. The topics of *L'Avventura* are bonded, above all, to those relationships to Eros that are out of all proportion.

At the center of the film, the heroine Anna disappears without trace while making a boat trip to a lonely island. She is completely forgotten by her acquaintances and friends after they undertake an extensive yet fruitless search for her. Her fiancé, who had already begun an affair with her best friend during the inquiries on the island, loses sight of her just like the others. Viewers watch the characters' behavior with interest and see how the aforementioned contradictory moments gradually become more apparent and succinct. They then follow this leitmotif created by topics through the story's action in such a manner that the mysterious case of Anna's disappearance similarly passes out of their field of vision.

It is an occurrence that, in terms of narrative strategy, is highly paradoxical, but explainable, because the appropriation of a film story normally means that, in the perception of a film, observers will initially follow the most stable schema the film's action has to offer from the perspective of cognitive psychology (i.e., a causal chain that leads to a plot or even a narrative stereotype such as the canonical story [Bordwell, 1989, p. 27] that they already know before being confronted with it again in the story). If, however, these two semantically stable basic forms of storytelling are not developed, or only insufficiently so, the semantic function of the story will be transformed, according to a substitution principle, to the semantically weaker schema formation of the topic line that provides the only possibility of orientation within the stimulant.

This is obviously the case in *L'Avventura*. A plot is not established because the opening situations do not develop a dramatic conflict that could be steered in the direction of a particular narrative. The fact that Anna disappeared from the island could be explained with the same probability as an accident, suicide, or one of those experiments in which she had previously shocked society by leading them to believe she had been attacked by a shark. So, it is impossible to construct a reliable cause–effect relationship that could explain the events and provide them with meaning. Narrative stereotypes do not present themselves either. In retrospect, the events can be reduced to the conflict schema of the love triangle; but there is absolutely no indication before Anna's disappearance that would lead the viewer to this conclusion. Consequently, the topicalized behavior mode of a disease of the emotions dominates, a mode that is clearly able to carry the film's story by its own efforts. I leave unsaid the fact that the truncated German theatrical version (shorter by 40 minutes) spoiled the opportunity that had been set up for a specific connecting thread, removed observations on behavior, and effected a re-evaluation of what was left that made the fiancé's "betrayal" of Anna into the syuzhet-defining event of a violation of moral norms (i.e., approaching once again the run-of-the-mill kind of plot).

Antonioni (1964) said when speaking about the construction of tension in *L'Avventura*, that he had "removed" all the events "which were, in a certain sense, much more precise and were much more interconnected so as to allow the story to take its inner course; indeed, provided this was possible, so that it could attain an inner 'suspense' since it no longer had any connection with the outside world, except through the characters' actions which were in accordance with their own thoughts and fears" (p. 89). The director coined the formula of the *reverse crime film* for the character of the narrative tension in this film (Leprohon, 1964). The composition deliberately dispenses with incorporating narrative stereotypes or simply making use of natural causal links. It attempts, instead, to consciously disappoint corresponding states of expectation. Eco (1977) noted about one small scene:

> In *L'Avventura*, Antonioni creates a situation of tension at a certain point: under a glowing southern sun a man is seen deliberately pouring an ink bottle over a drawing by a young architect. The tension demands a resolution and, in a western, the whole thing would end with a liberating fight ... In Antonioni's film, on the other hand, nothing of the like occurs: the fight seems to break out, but then doesn't after all. Gestures and passions are then sucked up again in the physical and psychological sensuousness that dominates the whole situation.... The disappointment of all the expectations which, according to all the probability criteria, ought

to be satisfied, is so artificial and deliberate that it must be the result of calculation practised on immediate material: in such a way that is exactly why the events appear to be accidental. (p. 204)

Basically, what happens here, in a very restricted context, is the same as Anna's plot line, which remains without a resolution.

If one wants to talk here of narrative tension, or even inner suspense, then it can only be done in the sense that one no longer deals with the control of uncertainty regarding a specific storyline concerning the discovery of Anna. Rather, it is more about removing uncertainty as far as the periodic appearance of the relevant syndrome of that disease of the emotions is concerned in all further situations. Tension tends to be realized on a perceptual rather than a conceptual level, and thus, viewers are almost unaware of its existence. It follows the aspects of abduction and develops along topic lines. In doing so, though, it invariably loses the emphasis on emotion, becomes more analytical, and thus, not surprisingly, remains hidden for those viewers who are not overly sensitized for cinematic observation. In the cited tetralogy, a similar modification of tension went hand in hand with the complete dismantling of the conceptual-based plot.

UNDERMINING OF THE CENTRAL PLOT
AND PSEUDOTENSION

The process of storytelling and creation of tension as practiced in the tetralogy has its origins in the 1950s. One can see in Antonioni's early feature films like *Cronaca di un Amore* (1950), *I Vinti* (1952), and *Le Amiche* (1955) that a remarkable undermining of the usual syuzhet relations is taking place. In the first film, the initially anticipated crime story loses its way. The second film brings three completely autonomous episodes together, and the third one does not have a central plot. Because there are no causal chains, viewers' attention is increasingly devoted to observations of the protagonists' modes of behavior, and the creation of tension thus assumes a corresponding significance. In the case of *Cronaca di un Amore* (1950), an elaborate pseudotension is created as a result of the dismantling of the classic plot.

At first glance, the film appears to be a report about an act of murder that two lovers want to commit on the husband of the married woman. The criminal plan is prompted by investigations the wealthy husband has had carried out about the life of his wife, Paola, before their marriage; these have then drawn his attention to the fact that she had had a lover—Guido—at that time, whose fiancée was killed in a mysterious accident in a lift. When Guido learns of these enquiries, he travels to Paola to inform her about them—a fact that makes viewers suspicious that the couple could possibly be to blame for that past incident. The woman, who has not seen Guido for a long time, is immediately ready to become involved with him again. Between their embraces, the thought of getting rid of the nuisance of a husband secretly surfaces, something that only goes to strengthen the suspicion about the past crime. The murder is to take place on a motorway bridge that the husband passes each day. In the end, however, it never comes to the act of violence because, shortly beforehand, the husband by chance has a fatal accident. However, because Guido leaves Paola, this is not the beginning of the two lovers legally being together as they had always wanted.

It is instructive that, in both cases, the direction deals with the motif of killing. At the beginning, viewers are keen to know whether a crime happened at that time and what will happen with the rightly (or wrongly) accused couple. In a central scene on the motorway bridge, where the husband is to be murdered, it becomes very clear from a conversation between Guido and Paola that they did not intentionally bring about the lift accident but, rather, had simply not done their utmost to prevent it. It can also be seen that their commitment to the atrocity keeps changing. To begin with, Paola is the driving force and Guido refuses to be involved, but then he makes a corresponding proposal and Paola withdraws. This allows one to draw conclusions about the strength of the motive for the crime in both cases. Their love has never been strong enough to provide the basis for an act of desperation like a crime of passion. It is more case of an act committed under the influence of emotion that comes from inner frustration and shows a high degree of arbitrariness.

The chain of events, thus, does not lead to the usual plot or construct a syuzhet. A traditional suspense dramaturgy would have linked the uncertainty of relevant events to questions like: Had they murdered back then, and is this what is now being discovered? Will they now do it again? Within the framework of genre conventions, the two motifs would have definitely experienced a causal linkage so that the present murder plan would seem like a confirmation of the previous crime and its realization an intensifying continuation, something like the repetition of a crime that was covering over its traces. With the scene on the bridge, however, the suspects are exonerated, and their new intentions are also suddenly presented as being very fragile. Both events suddenly appear as being less goal oriented, and they are separated from one other. Thus, one does not have an original suspense based on goal-oriented or latent expectation resulting in the creation of a mood of uncertainty that wants to be dispelled but gets bigger and bigger. On the contrary, viewers are forced by an expectation, which comes about as a consequence of the stereotypical application of motifs of the criminal action, to approach the subsequent events—automatically, so to speak—with analog assumptions. The criminal action has more the character of a subterfuge followed by viewers when it should really be ensuring that they focus and gather such observations on the figures' behavior that say something about the very fragile ethical principles of this couple balanced so remarkably on the edge of crime.

This leads to a perception-based suspense of the topic line of similar behavior patterns; yet this does not happen in an unqualified manner or under its own steam, but tends to be "emotion supported" in the wake of the genre conventions of the crime film. The overlapping of two different expectations—of which one may be suspended with regard to the contents but still continue to have an emotional effect of this tendency—creates that pseudo-tension. For Antonioni, the use of the murder motif thus functions more as an indicator. Introduced into the action, it helps to identify the seriousness of that disease of the emotions. The tension gravitates toward being more analytical. Moreover, the motif of death keeps occurring in a surprising way in Antonioni's works, which are dogged by the image of uneventfulness. But this never leads to that external narrative tension that normally grows from a plot that demands decisions on this scale. The deaths in Antonioni's films do not happen so that uncertainty within conflict situations can be sorted out by relevant events. Rather, they are the director's dramaturgical vehicles, set pieces that are introduced to heighten expectations and so to provide the events with a significance that they would not otherwise have of their own accord. The death motif either has a marking function, or its stereotype character creates a basis for viewers to verify events through subprograms of psychological behavior that would otherwise usually occur with the experience of death. In several films, a death appears at both the beginning and end of a story so that a strange construct is created, a kind of symmetric framework that creates relevant events that normally increase the potential for suspense. This is how Le Amiche (1955) operates with a girl's suicide attempt. Yet, when the same girl really does kill herself at the end, one can see again that death does not represent an inevitable consequence of the events, but that it is more a marker for the inner conflict and weakness of this figure and of the people around her. In Il Grido (1957), the heroine learns at the beginning that her husband has died overseas (something that, surprisingly, causes her little concern); and at the end, she is a witness as her long-standing lover, whom she no longer wants, falls off a tower in what seems to be half suicide and half accident. Viewers can summon up neither a strong feeling of sympathy for the hero nor a particular feeling of tension as they sense, instead, that the film cannot be about an end result resolving something that would have otherwise stayed in the dark. The film's subject is the inner state, the figure's unproductive fundamental behavior that had already revealed itself previously in many similar situations. The death represents the fact that is needed by the melodramatic genre for its finale.

There are examples for such symmetric deaths that frame the action. At the beginning of La Notte, a married couple experience the approaching death of an ill friend; at the end of the film the friend does indeed die, and the living see themselves confronted all the more by the emptiness of their own existence. Zabriskie Point and Professione: Reporter, similarly, begin and end with a death, although this provides more of a "booster" for the emotionally reserved portrayal of behavior than the construction of a plot that offers an excitedly anticipated turn in events. However, the move to behavioral analyses through repeating the same patterns of comportment does not happen as in the 1950s, against the background of a gradual demontage of handed-down narrative structures and suspense strategies. On the contrary, it occurs through their historical rehabilitation and restoration.

SINCE *BLOW UP*: INTEGRATION
OF EXTERNAL TENSION THROUGH STEREOTYPES
OF NARRATION AND GENRE PATTERNS

After Antonioni had constantly moved away from narrative cinema and its development of suspense through his unremitting suppression of the classical syuzhet in the films of the tetralogy, he then made a step back in that direction with *Blow Up* (1966), *Zabriskie Point* (1969), and *Professione: Reporter* (1975) to the extent that he offered stories that corresponded, at first glance, with the Aristotelian dramaturgy. This impression is illusory. The depicted events aim less for an original plot and, instead, want to adhere to certain stereotype schemata, which originate from syuzhet stories by deploying plot conventions from popular genres (i.e., narrative patterns from the detective and adventure film). Consequently, the observation of the figures' behavior and its establishment through corresponding narrative topics according to the sequence principle was not abandoned. They continued to be of interest to the director, but were integrated with procedural schemata recognized by viewers from popular genres; and this doubtless made it easier to understand the events. In addition, there was the fact that the chosen popular genre was crossed with a construct of the classical genres.

Basically, *Blow Up* combines narrative patterns of the detective film with those of the parable, thus creating a polygenre that enables viewers to discover a much deeper philosophical meaning behind the detective story. At the center of the story is that famous sequence in which the photographer looks at some blow-ups of pictures he has just made of some lovers in a park and thinks that he can see someone aiming at the man from the bushes with a gun. In the end, he is, in fact, killed—so the observer with the camera can thus regard himself as a witness to a crime. The film's story shows how the photographer pursues the pieces of circumstantial evidence in an attempt to clarify what happened (i.e., he tries to reconstruct the criminal course of events via the pictures he has blown up). He is constantly drawn back to the park where he does, indeed, find a corpse. However, he finally gets into a situation where he does not have any proper evidence that could uncover the crime, as someone steals all his photos along with the negatives and removes the dead man. Seen in a purely superficial manner, the course of these sequences follows the schema of the detective film. A crime is discovered, the trail is taken up, and complications—barriers, if you like—arise during further investigation that make solving the case impossible. Antonioni uses this narrative convention by following the schema and strictly obeying the phases of the problem-solving situation specific to the genre. Accordingly, an external tension is created, which viewers are also aware of, because the situation becomes conceptual for him in this phase. Admittedly, this tension does not acquire the real character of suspense because viewers never know any more about the situation than the figures do. It also turns out that the way the action is constructed does not keep wholly to the rules of the detective film. There is a certain point at which the photographer is more interested in letting himself be fascinated by his involvement in a mysterious situation than in solving the murder case. It is exciting for him that the empirically sensuous experience he gets from the photographs appears remarkably fragile and revocable. The detective story then turns into a parable reflecting on the situation of a man searching for truth in an environment that is permanently making him distance himself from his individual perception and disturbing experience of the world. For many people, *Blow Up* is a detective film; but for others, it is more of a cinematic parable about a poorly motivated man, searching for truth, who is only too easily distracted from his path.

The essential aspect for this interpretation of the events is this question: To what degree do viewers grasp the topic line that comes out of the behavioral study of the hero and the beat generation he belongs to? A gesture at the end of the film is characteristic: A singer smashes his guitar during a beat concert, and the audience fights for the pieces. The photographer is vehement in his efforts to get hold of the torso of the guitar, but then he carelessly throws it away as soon as he is back outside in the street. Once again, he shows himself to be actionist but not particularly innerly motivated and, thus, is easy to distract. Even the detective work in the photo lab and the following events are increasingly interrupted by phases of distraction; the fact that women play a role in this seems, however, to be arbitrary. It is a question of the hero's fundamental position, which is contestable through other influences. Thus, Antonioni remained true with *Blow Up* to the cinema of behavior that had characterized his personal style until then—also as far as its specifically analytical tension was concerned. The narrative stereotypes from the genre culture ensured, however, that this tension could be brought together with a criminological perspective as well as with the generalizing top view of life events known as the parable.

In following the story schema of the tale of a dropout, *Zabriskie Point* has a comparable objective in introducing large action and image stereotypes that make the observation of behavior much easier to comprehend. The cliché-like freaking out of the hero, who has flown an airplane into a no-man's land in the desert, is as much part of this as the hippy dream of communal love, or the girl's ideal of the super villa exploding the social establishment going up in smoke at the end of the film.

Neither *Professione: Reporter* nor *Zabriskie Point* are able to maintain the specific tension of a plot or the standardized one of a trivial genre. The latter can be recognized, among other things, by the fact that the heroes differ in their intentions and strategies from those of the syuzhet and genre stories. The reporter loses interest in the African liberation front after the first contacts and faked arms deals. At the end, when he will be killed, he hardly knows anymore why he is going to the meeting. The dropout in *Zabriskie Point* is as honest as he is irrational in the way he comes back in the stolen airplane to the place where, after the murder of the policeman, they have been looking for him, and where he will then be executed. It is instructive to compare the director's attitude toward his protagonists with *Easy Rider*, made at almost the same time, which portrays the hippie generation in a road movie. Right up until the end, the authors have secured the viewers' sympathy for their heroes by keeping up a specific tension oriented toward the conceptualized interests of the figures in a dramatic situation dogged by uncertainty.

PERSONAL STYLE AND VARIANCE IN TENSION STRATEGIES

Antonioni's subsequent works like *Il Mistero di Oberwald* (1980) or *Identificazione di una Donna* (1982), which I do not have room to discuss here, have their own particular narrative tension that is grounded in the coexistence of the narrative basic forms of the topic line and of the narrative stereotype. Whereas a semantic cooperation of these structural levels came about in the last examples discussed— so that the multilayered nature of the narration tended to develop according to the principle of a mutual intensification or integration—the films of the 1980s were based more on a semantic conflict of the basic structures, in a similar way to the description of the example of Fellini's *Otto e Mezzo* (Wuss, 1993). It is not a coincidence that the hero in *Identificazione* is also a film director who is in the middle of a creative process and is reflecting on it.

However varied the creation of tension may be in Antonioni, it is certainly always achieved in a different way from Hitchcock. The Italian director has never declared his unqualified support of the plot, of the dominance of the conception-based causal chain guaranteeing the specific external tension; and if he then does borrow from the narrative stereotypes of popular genres, the events are never simplified by him into the kind enabling the solving of a problem under conditions of a differentiated level of information between viewer and protagonist (i.e., a situation that Hitchcock regarded as a prerequisite for suspense).

Topic lines play an ever more significant role in Antonioni's films of the 1950s, in which the syuzhet is intentionally dismantled and the problem situation is always kept extremely complex and consequently incomprehensible. With the beginning of the 1960s, the topic lines covered the narrative events by their own efforts, and the narrative tension thus created was hardly noticed by viewers as it is steered by perception and topic according to the laws of abduction. From the middle of the 1960s, familiar and already stereotypical narrative structures were also drawn from the repertoire of the popular genres as a way of simplifying the information in narrative relations and of channeling the reception processes.

The development of tension consequently became more multilayered and heterogeneous, especially when the narrative stereotypes of the popular genres joined up with the story schemata of classic parables. Without having to abandon his personal style, developed with purist observations of human behavior, Antonioni has been adept at using the stereotype storylines of the trivial genres, with their more externalized tension, to speed up the action and to lead to a completely new, integrated form of tension.

REFERENCES

Antonioni, M. (1964). Die Krankheit der Gefühle [The disease of the emotions]. In T. Kotulla (Ed.), *Der Film. Manifeste, Gespräche, Dokumente. Vol. 2* (pp. 83–110). München: Piper.

Bordwell, D. (1989). A case for cognitivism. *Iris, 5*(2), 11–40.

Bordwell, D., & Thompson, K. (1979). *Film art. An introduction.* Reading, MA: Addison-Wesley.

Branigan, E. (1992). *Narrative comprehension and film.* London: Routledge.

Dörner, D. (1979). *Problemlösung als Informationsverarbeitung* [Problem solving and information processing]. Stuttgart, Germany: Kohlhammer.

Dörner, D., Reither, F., & Stäudel, T. (1983). Emotion und problemlösendes Denken [Emotion and problem solving]. In H. Mandl & G. L. Huber (Eds.), *Emotion und Kognition* (pp. 61–84). München: Urban & Schwarzenberg.

Eco, U. (1977). *Das offene Kunstwerk* [The open artwork]. Frankfurt: Suhrkamp.

Eco, U. (1987). *Lector in fabula. Die Mitarbeit der Interpretation in erzählenden Texten* [Lector in fabula. The assistance of interpretation in narrative texts]. München: Hanser.

Klaus, G. (1966). *Kybernetik und Erkenntnistheorie* [Cybernetics and epistemology]. Berlin: Deutscher Verlag der Wissenschaften.

Leprohon, P. (Ed.). (1964). *Michelangelo Antonioni: Der Regisseur und seine Filme* [Michelangelo Antonioni: The director and his films]. Frankfurt: Fischer.

Lessing, G. E. (1954). *Gesammelte Werke* [Collected works]. (Vol. 6). Berlin: Aufbau Verlag.

Leontjew, A. (1979). *Tätigkeit, Bewußtsein, Persönlichkeit* [Activity, consciousness, personality]. Berlin: Volk und Welt.

Lotman, J. M. (1977). *Probleme der Kinoästhetik. Einführung in die Semiotik des Films* [Problems of film aesthetics. Introduction to semiotics of cinema]. Frankfurt: Syndikat.

Mukařovský, J. (1974). Beabsichtigtes und Unbeabsichtigtes in der Kunst [The intended and the unintended in art]. In J. Mukařovský, *Studien zur strukturalistischen Ästhetik und Poetik* (pp. 31–65). München: Hanser.

Oesterreich, R. (1981). *Handlungsregulation und Kontrolle* [Regulation of activity and control]. München: Urban & Schwarzenberg.

Rumelhart, D. E. (1980). Schemata: The building blocks of cognition. In R. J. Spiro, B. C. Bruce, & W. F. Brewer (Eds.), *Theoretical issues in reading comprehension: Perspectives from cognitive psychology, linguistics, artificial intelligence, and education* (pp. 33–58). Hillsdale, NJ: Lawrence Erlbaum Associates.

Rumelhart, D., & Ortony, A. (1977). The representation of knowledge in memory. In R. C. Anderson, R. J. Spiro, & W. E. Montague (Eds.), *Schooling and the acquisition of knowledge* (pp. 99–135). Hillsdale, NJ: Lawrence Erlbaum Associates.

Simonov, P. V. (1975). *Widerspiegelungstheorie und Psychologie der Emotionen* [Theory of reflection and psychology of emotions]. Berlin: Volk und Gesundheit.

Truffaut, F. (1986). *Mr. Hitchcock, wie haben Sie das gemacht?* [Hitchcock]. München: Heyne.

von Cube, F. (1965). Kybernetische grundlagen des lehrens und lernens [Cybernetic foundations of learning and teaching]. Stuttgart, Germany: Klett.

Wuss, P. (1993). *Filmanalyse und Psychologie. Strukturen des Films im Wahrnehmungsprozeß* [Analysis of film and psychology. Cinematic structures in the perceptional process]. Berlin: Edition Sigma.

5

▼▼▼▼▼▼▼

The Paradox of Suspense

Noël Carroll
University of Wisconsin

THE PROBLEM

It is an incontrovertible fact that people can consume the same suspense fiction again and again with no loss of affect. Someone may reread Graham Greene's *This Gun for Hire* or re-view the movie *The Guns of Navarone* and, nevertheless, on the second, third, and repeated encounters be caught in the same unrelenting grip of suspense that snared them on their first encounter. I myself have seen *King Kong* at least 50 times, and yet there are still certain moments when I feel the irresistible tug of suspense.

However, although the suspense felt by recidivists like me is an undeniable fact, it appears to be a paradoxical one. For there seems to be agreement that a key component of the emotion *suspense* is a cognitive state of uncertainty.[1] We feel suspense as the heroine heads for the buzzsaw, in part, because we are uncertain as to whether or not she will be cleaved. Uncertainty seems to be a necessary condition for suspense.

However, when we come to cases of recidivism, the relevant readers and viewers know Anne Crowder will stop the onset of world war, that the guns of Navarone will plunge into the sea, and that King Kong will be blown away. After all, we have already read the novel or seen the film; we know how the fiction ends, because we have read it before.

---

[1]Examples of theorists who take uncertainty to be a key element of suspense include Chatman (1978), Vale (1982), Ortony, Clore, and Collins (1988), Walton (1990), Gerrig (1993), and Michaels (1992).

71

How then can it be possible for us to feel suspense the second, the third, or the 50th time around? Or is it possible only because recidivists with respect to suspense fictions are somehow irrational, perhaps psychically blinded by some process of disavowal or denial, of the sort psychoanalysts claim to investigate?

And yet this variety of recidivism with respect to suspense fictions hardly seems to portend any psychological abnormality or pathology. It is well known that successful suspense films like *Raiders of the Lost Ark, Die Hard*, and *The Fugitive* require repeat audiences in order to be the blockbusters that they are, and it is also a fact that there are classic suspense stories, like "The Most Dangerous Game" by Richard Connell, that are often reread without diminution in their capacity to deliver a thrill. Furthermore, there are lots of classic suspense films (like *North by Northwest*), as well as TV and radio shows, that entice re-viewing and relistening.

So there is, in short, too much recidivism for it to be regarded as so pathologically abnormal that it requires psychoanalysis, unless nearly everyone is to be diagnosed. Yet, nevertheless, the phenomenon is still strange enough—indeed, some researchers even call it *anomalous suspense* (Gerrig, 1989a, 1989b, 1993)— that an account is in order of the way in which it can be rational for a reader or a viewer to feel suspense about events concerning whose outcomes the audience is certain.

To state the paradox involved here at greater length, we may begin with the assumption that, conceptually, suspense entails uncertainty. Uncertainty is a necessary condition for suspense. When uncertainty is removed from a situation, suspense evaporates. Putatively, if we come to know that the heroine will not be sawed in half, or that she will be, then we should no longer feel suspense. Moreover, if a situation lacks uncertainty altogether, no sense of suspense can intelligibly arise. It would be irrational for people to feel suspense in such contexts. And yet, apparently rational people are seized by suspense on re-encountering well-remembered films like Alfred Hitchcock's *The Thirty-Nine Steps* or novels like Tom Clancy's *Patriot Games*. Indeed, such consumers often seek out these fictions in order to experience once more that same thrill of suspense that they savored on their first encounter with the fiction. But surely, then, they must be irrational.

Of course, one might try to explain away the recidivism here by saying that with something like *The Thirty-Nine Steps*, filmgoers do not return for the suspense, but for something else—Hitchcock's cinematic artistry, the undeniable humor, the acting, the ambience, and so on. And undoubtedly, these features of the film, among others, certainly warrant reviewing. However, although we need to acknowledge that such features might reasonably motivate recidivism, it is not plausible to suppose that we can rid ourselves of the paradox of suspense by hypothesizing that every case of recidivism can be fully explained away by reference to good-making features of the fiction that have nothing to do with suspense. For recidivism may recur not only with respect to works of substantial literary merit by people like Greene, Elmore Leonard, and Eric Ambler or works of substantial cinematic achievement by people like Hitchcock, Fritz Lang, and Carol Reed; we may also be swept into the thrall of suspense on the occasion of re-viewing a fairly pedestrian exercise like *Straw Dogs*.

In some cases, our propensity to be recaptivated by an already encountered suspense fiction may be explained by the fact that we have forgotten how it ends. This happens often. However, I do not think this can account for every case; I know it does not apply to my 49th reviewing of *King Kong*. Instead, I think that we must face the paradox head on. There are examples—I think quite a lot of examples—where the consumers of fiction find themselves in the enjoyable hold of suspense while responding to stories, read, heard, or seen previously, whose outcomes they remember with perfect clarity; in fact, quite frequently, these audiences have sought out these already familiar fictions with the express expectation that they will re-experience the pleasurable surge of consternation and thrill that they associate with suspense once again.

But how can they rationally expect to re-experience suspense if they know— and know that they know—the outcome of the fictional events that give rise to suspense? For, *ex hypothesi*, suspense requires uncertainty and I certainly know how *The Thirty-Nine Steps, This Gun for Hire*, and *King Kong* end. To put it formulaically, the paradox of suspense—which might be more accurately regarded as an instance of the paradox of recidivism[2]—may be stated in the following way:

1. If a fiction is experienced with suspense by an audience, then the outcome of the events that give rise to the suspense must be uncertain to audiences.
2. It is a fact that audiences experience fictions with suspense in cases where they have already seen, heard, or read the fictions in question.
3. But if audiences have already seen, heard, or read a fiction, then they know (and are certain) of the relevant outcomes.

Although each of the propositions in this triad seems acceptable considered in isolation, when conjoined they issue in a contradiction. In order to solve the paradox of suspense, that contradiction must be confronted. However, before we are in a position to dismantle this contradiction, we need a more fine-grained account of what is involved in suspense.

---

[2]What I am calling the paradox of suspense may be regarded as a subparadox in the family of paradoxes that might be titled *paradoxes of recidivism*—that is, paradoxes that involve audiences returning to fictions whose outcomes they already know—such as mystery stories and jokes as well as suspense tales—but which they enjoy nonetheless for their being twice- (or more) told tales.

A THEORY OF THE NATURE OF SUSPENSE[3]

Before proceeding further, it will be useful to be clear about our topic. First, we are talking about suspense as an emotional response to *narrative fictions*. Inasmuch as we are focusing on fictions, we are not talking about suspense with respect to "real-life" experiences, although some comments about the relation between the two will be made. Furthermore, inasmuch as we are speaking about narratives, we are not talking about so-called musical suspense.

Suspense, as I am using the term, is an emotional response to narrative fictions. Moreover, these responses can occur in reaction to two levels of fictional articulation. They can evolve in reaction to whole narratives, or in response to discrete scenes or sequences within a larger narrative whose overall structure may or may not be suspenseful. For example, the attack on Jack Ryan's home is a suspenseful episode or sequence in Tom Clancy's novel *Patriot Games*, which novel, on the whole, is suspenseful, whereas the ride of the Klan to the rescue in D. W. Griffith's film *The Birth of a Nation* is a suspenseful sequence within a work that is probably not best categorized as a suspense film.

Sometimes fictions are categorized as suspense because they contain suspenseful scenes, especially where those scenes come near the end and appear to "wrap up" the fiction. In other cases, the entire structure of a fiction appears suspenseful—not only are there suspenseful scenes, but these suspenseful episodes segue into larger, overarching suspense structures. For example, in *This Gun for Hire*, scenes in which Anne Crowder averts discovery and death are not only locally suspenseful; they also play a role in sustaining our abiding suspense across the whole fiction about whether she can stop the outbreak of war in virtue of what she knows, a prospect about which we are highly uncertain, because she confronts so many dangers, but which uncertainty is kept alive every time she eludes apprehension or, at least, destruction.

Finally, before proceeding, it needs to be emphasized that the emotion of suspense takes as its object the moments leading up to the outcome about which we are uncertain. As the frenzied horses thunder toward the precipice, pulling a wagonload of children toward death, we feel suspense: Will they be saved or not? As long as that question is vital, and the outcome is uncertain, we are in a state of suspense. Once the outcome is fixed, however, the state is no longer suspense. If the wagon hurtles over the edge, we feel sorrow and anguish; if the children are saved, we feel relief and joy.

However, suspense is not a response to the outcome; it pertains to the moments leading up to the outcome, when the outcome is uncertain. Once the outcome is finalized and we are apprised of it, the emotion of suspense gives way to other emotions. Moreover, the emotion we feel in those moments leading up to the

---

[3]This section represents a refinement and attempted updating of earlier essays by me that advance a theory of suspense, including Carroll (1984), and Carroll (1990).

outcome is suspense whether the outcome, once known, is the one we favored or not.

Suspense is an emotion that besets us when we are confronted with narrative fictions that focus our attention on courses of events about whose outcomes, in the standard case, we are acutely aware that we are uncertain. However, suspense fictions are not the only narrative fictions that traffic in uncertainty. So, in order to refine our conception of suspense, an instructive first step is to differentiate suspense from other forms of narrative uncertainty, of which, undoubtedly, mystery is the most obvious.

The mystery story, which engenders a sense of mystery in us, is a near relative to suspense fiction. Indeed, it seems to me that the two species are so close that some theorists often confuse them.[4] However, although they belong to the same genus—call it fictions of uncertainty—they are clearly distinct. For in mysteries in the classical detection mode, we are characteristically uncertain about what has happened in the past, whereas with suspense fictions we are uncertain about what will happen.[5]

In mysteries in the classical detective mode, our uncertainty about the past usually revolves around how a crime was committed and by whom. This is why this sort of fiction is most frequently referred to as a *whodunit*. The TV programs *Perry Mason* and *Murder, She Wrote* are perfect examples of the whodunit. To become engaged in a whodunit is to be drawn into speculation about who killed the nasty uncle, along with the related questions of how and why it was done. We conjecture about an event whose cause, although fixed, is unknown to us. Of course, the cause will be revealed in the process of the detective's analysis of the case, but of that outcome we remain uncertain until it is pronounced.

However, our uncertainty here does have a structured horizon of anticipation. The outcome about which we are uncertain has as many possible shapes as we have suspects. If the nasty uncle could have been killed by the maid, the cousin, the butler, or the egyptologist, then our uncertainty is distributed across these four possibilities. A mystery of the classical whodunit variety prompts us to ask a question about whose answer we are uncertain and about which we entertain as many possible answers as there are suspects. But suspense is different.

With suspense, the question we are prompted to ask does not have an indefinite number of possible answers, but only two. Will the heroine be sawed in half or not? Moreover, when looking at the distribution of answers available in a mystery fiction, one realizes that one has no principled guarantee that the competing answers are ultimately exclusive. After all, some or even all of the suspects can

---

[4]For example, I would argue that Dove (1989) mistook suspense for mystery throughout his book *Suspense in the Formula Story*, which might have been better titled *Mystery in the Formula Story*.

[5]I do not mean to preclude the possibility of fictions that mix elements of suspense and mystery hierarchically. *This Gun for Hire* is probably an example of such a mixed genre case—because, up to a certain point, there are whodunit questions about who is ultimately behind the assassination—however, in the main it seems to be a suspense novel.

be in cahoots or, as occurs in *Murder on the Orient Express,* a knave can be killed by more than one culprit. So, the classical detective story not only encourages uncertainty about an indefinitely variable number of answers to the question of whodunit, but those answers need not bear any special logical relation to each other.

However, in the case of suspense, the course of events in question can have only two outcomes, and those potential outcomes stand in relation to each other as logical contraries—either the heroine will be torn apart by the buzzsaw or she will not be. Both mystery fictions and suspense fictions confront us with questions, but the way in which those questions structure our uncertainty differentiates the two kinds of fictions. For with mystery, our uncertainty is distributed over as many possible answers as there are suspects, whereas with suspense, we are "suspended" between no more than two answers, which answers stand in binary opposition. The answers we entertain with respect to mystery fictions are, in principle, indeterminate and logically nonexclusive, whereas the answers pertinent to suspense are binary and logically opposed.

However, even if we have established that suspense proper in fictions of uncertainty takes hold only when the course of events that commands our attention is one whose horizon of expectations is structured in terms of two possible but logically incompatible outcomes, we still have not told the whole story about fictional suspense. For clearly, one can imagine fictions in which characters and readers alike confess that they simply do not know whether it will snow or not tomorrow (in the land of the story), but where, nevertheless, at the same time, there is still no question of suspense.

Of course, the reason for this is obvious, once we think in terms of "real life" suspense. For in "real life," suspense only takes charge when we care about those future outcomes about which we are uncertain. We are not inclined toward suspense about whether or not the bus will start unless we have some stake or concern in its starting or not starting. Where we are impervious to outcomes, even though the relevant outcomes are uncertain, there is no suspense, because "real life" suspense requires a certain emotional involvement with the outcome, along with uncertainty about it. Interests, concerns, or at least preferences must come into play. I feel suspense about the results of my blood test not only because I am uncertain about what they will be, but also because I have a vested interest in them.

Similarly, when it comes to fictions, suspense cannot be engendered simply by means of uncertainty; the reader must also be encouraged to form some preferences about the alternative outcomes. As Rodell (1952) put it, speaking from the author's point of view, suspense is "the art of making the reader care about what happens next" (p. 71). Moreover, as an empirical conjecture, let me hypothesize that in suspense fiction, the way in which the author typically provokes audience involvement is through morality.

"Real life" suspense requires not only uncertainty about which outcome will eventuate from a course of events; it also requires that we be concerned about those outcomes. In constructing suspense, authors must find some way of engaging audience concern. Of course, the author has no way of knowing the personal concerns and vested interests of each and every audience member. So in order to enlist our concern, the author must find some very general interest that all or most of the audience is likely to share. One such interest is what is morally right. That is, one way in which the author can invest the audience with concern over a prospective outcome is to assure that one of the logically opposed outcomes in the fiction is morally correct as well as uncertain. In the novel *Airport* by Arthur Hailey, it is morally correct that the jetliner not be destroyed, but whether this outcome will eventuate is uncertain; similarly, in the novel *Seven Days in May* by Fletcher Knebel and Charles Bailey what is presented and perceived to be morally correct—democracy as we know and love it—is at risk.

If the emotion of suspense presupposes not only uncertainty but concern, then presumably a crucial task in constructing a suspense fiction involves finding some way in which to engage the concern of audiences, of whom the author possesses little or no personal knowledge. Nevertheless, the author is typically able to overcome this debit by resorting to morality in order to appeal to the ethical interests of viewers and readers alike. For, all things being equal, the general audience will recognize that sawing the heroine in half is morally wrong, and this will provoke concern about an outcome of the event about which they are uncertain. Likewise, in *This Gun for Hire*, it is presented and perceived that averting war is morally correct, whereas in *The Guns of Navarone* it is given and accepted that the destruction of the Nazi battery is morally right. In suspense fictions, the audience is provided, often aggressively, with a stake in one of the alternatives by having its moral sensibility drawn to prefer one of the uncertain outcomes.

In general in suspense fictions, then, one of the possible outcomes of the relevant course of events is morally correct, but uncertain. In *Patriot Games*, it is righteous that Ryan's family and the Prince and Princess of Wales survive, but when Miller and the terrorists take over Ryan's property, that survival is uncertain. Indeed, it is not merely uncertain; the odds are against it. Moreover, this is the pattern that recurs most frequently in suspense fictions from classic stories like Karl May's *In the Desert* to recent bestsellers like Robert Ludlum's *The Scorpio Illusion*. There are two competing outcomes to the relevant course of events, and one of those outcomes, although morally correct, is improbable or uncertain or unlikely, whereas the logically alternative outcome is evil but likely or probable or nearly certain. Or, to be even more precise, suspense takes control where the course of events that is the object of the emotional state points to two logically opposed outcomes, one of which is evil or immoral but probable or likely, and the other of which is moral, but improbable or unlikely or only as probable as the evil outcome.

Of course, the defeat of the moral outcome cannot be an absolutely foregone conclusion; there must be some possibility that the good can triumph. That is why there can be no suspense about whether the protagonist in the movie

Philadelphia can survive AIDS. For suspense requires that, although what is presented and perceived to be morally right be an improbable option, it must be a live option (i.e., not a completely foregone conclusion) nonetheless. And, for related reasons, in stories, where it is given in the fictional world that the hero cannot be defeated, as it is in many of the scenes in the contemporary film *Crow*, there is no suspense.

Summarizing then, as a response to fiction, generally suspense is

1. an emotional concomitant to the narration of a course of events
2. which course of events points to two logically opposed outcomes
3. whose opposition is made salient (to the point of preoccupying the audience's attention)[6] and
4. where one of the alternative outcomes is morally correct but improbable (although live) or at least no more probable than its alternative, while
5. the other outcome is morally incorrect or evil, but probable.

Surely this formula works for run-of-the-mill cases of suspense—as the heroine is inexorably pulled toward the buzzsaw, it seems hardly likely that she will live. On the other hand, the alternative outcome, her death, is evil but probable.

Perhaps one way to confirm this formulation would be to accept it provisionally as a hypothesis and to see how well it accords with our pretheoretical sorting of the data; another way might be to use it as a recipe for constructing fictions and to assess how viable it is in inducing audiences to experience suspense.

This analysis of suspense in fiction corresponds nicely with the the definition of suspense advanced by the psychologists Ortony, Clore, and Collins (1988), who stated: "We view suspense as involving a Hope emotion and a Fear emotion coupled with the cognitive state of uncertainty" (p. 131). What we hope for is the moral outcome (which is improbable or uncertain), and what we fear is the evil outcome (which is more likely).

The evil that plays such a key role in suspense fictions need not be human evil, but may be natural evil, as it is in the novel *Jaws* or the film *Earthquake*. In these cases, we still regard the destruction of human beings by brute, unthinking nature to be morally offensive. Of course, it is generally the case that suspense fictions involve pitting moral good against human moral evil: the settlers against the rustlers, the Allies against the Nazis, civilization against the barbarians.

Moreover, the reader's or spectator's moral allegiances in response to a suspense fiction do not always precisely correlate with his or her normal repertory of moral

---

[6]Some fictions may contain courses of events that may have rival outcomes that are uncertain but the text may make nothing of them. Thus, they do not generate suspense. The preceding condition acknowledges this possibility and, in consequence, requires that the course of events in question must be one that is made salient, that is, ones where the audience is alerted to the importance of the rivalry between alternative outcomes.

responses, and, indeed, the audience's moral responses are frequently shaped by fiction itself. For example, caper films represent persons involved in perpetrating crimes that we do not customarily consider to be upstanding ethically. However, the characters in such fictions are standardly possessed of certain striking virtues such that, in the absence of emphasis of countervailing virtues in their opposite number, or possibly given the emphasis on the outright vice of their opponents, we are encouraged to ally ourselves morally with the caper. The virtues in question here—such as strength, fortitude, ingenuity, bravery, competence, beauty, generosity, and so on—are more often than not Grecian, rather than Christian. And it is because the characters exhibit these virtues—it is because we perceive (and are led to perceive) these characters as virtuous—that we cast our moral allegiance with them.

Quite frequently in mass fictions, characters are designated as morally good in virtue of their treatment of supporting characters, especially ones who are poor, old, weak, lame, oppressed, unprotected women, children, helpless animals, and so on. Good characters typically treat such people with courtesy and respect, whereas your standard snarling villain, if he notices them at all, usually does so in order to abuse them—to harass the woman sexually, to taunt the child, to kick the dog, or worse. With respect to mass fictions, we may generalize this point by saying that the protagonists typically treat their "inferiors" with courtesy and respect, whereas the villains treat such characters with contempt and disdain, if not violence. I suspect that it is fairly obvious that when it comes to mass entertainments, there is a clear-cut rationale for investing the protagonists with democratic or egalitarian virtue, whereas the villains are painted in the colors of elitist vice.

As these conjectures suggest, it is my view that character—especially at the level of virtue—is a critical lever for guiding the audience's moral perception of the action. This is why one may find oneself morally sympathetic to characters who represent moral causes with which one usually does not align oneself—for example, one may find oneself rooting for the colonialists in *Zulu* even if one is, on the whole, anti-imperialist. Here we are drawn into the film's system of moral evaluations by its portrayal—or lack thereof—of characters with respect to virtues. That is, in many suspense fictions—involving imperialism, war, international espionage, and the like—the protagonists are represented as having some virtues, whereas their opposite number are presented either as having no virtues whatsoever or, more pointedly, only negative personal and interpersonal attributes. And in these cases, the balance of virtue is sufficient to fix our moral assessments of the situation.

If the protagonists are represented as possessed of some virtues and their opponents are less virtuous, altogether bereft of virtue, or downright vicious, suspense can take hold because the efforts of the protagonists and their allies will be recognized as morally correct in the ethical system of the film. Of course, it is probably the case that generally the actions of the protagonists are morally correct in accordance with some prevailing ethical norms that are shared by the majority of the audience. However, in cases in which this consensus does not obtain, the protagonist's possession of saliently underlined virtues will project the moral valuations of the fiction and, indeed, incline the audience toward accepting that perspective as its own. Thus, it turns out that sometimes even an antagonist can serve as an object of suspense, as long as he or she is presented as possessed of some virtues.[7]

The emphasis that I have just placed on the relevance of the characters dovetails significantly with some recent psychological research.[8] There appears to be experimental evidence that suspense is generated in cases in which spectators or readers are said to "like" characters. However, when one looks closely at the factors that contribute to this pro-disposition toward characters on the part of spectators or readers, the most important ones seem to be moral. For example, whether the character is an antisocial recluse, a good man, or a fine individual is relevant to the spectators' or readers' registration of suspense.[9]

Some researchers are prone to discussing this relation between the characters and the spectators in terms of identification (see Brewer & Jose, 1984). But I, like others, think this is ill-advised, insofar as most often characters and spectators are cognitively and emotionally too unalike to warrant any presumption of identity— that is, we know more than Oedipus does for a large part of *Oedipus Rex* and, at the conclusion, when Oedipus is racked by guilt, we are not; we feel pity for him.[10] Thus it makes little sense to talk about identification in cases like this, which are quite frequent, and, if we can do without identification in cases like this one, economy suggests that we can probably do without it in other cases as well.

Of course, I would not say that suspense necessarily requires that we focus on characters who are presented as virtuous. Suspense may take hold when our attention is not riveted on individual characters but on movements that are perceived to be morally correct—as in the case of the socialist mass hero in films like *Potemkin*. Nevertheless, I suspect that we will find empirically that more fictions project the moral assessments relevant for suspense through the virtues of individual characters than through the rightness of social movements perceived as aggregates.

The factors that I have hypothesized that go into appreciating the morality of the outcomes in a suspense framework are broader than what would be considered

---

[7]This happens with the character Raven at points in *This Gun for Hire*.

[8]See, for example, Zillmann and Cantor (1977), Zillmann, Hay, and Bryant (1975), Zillmann (1980), and Comisky and Bryant (1982).

[9]See Comisky and Bryant (1982) for experimental testing along these lines. These experiments were suggested by earlier findings by Zillmann and Cantor (1977) that indicated that subjects responded positively to the euphoria of a boy character when that was subsequent to benevolent or neutral behavior on his part, whereas they responded negatively when the euphoria was subsequent to malevolent behavior by the boy.

[10]For opposition to the identification model, see Zillmann (1980), Carroll (1990), and Harding (1968); Harding's article is a development of an earlier article entitled "The Role of the Onlooker," in *Scrutiny, VI*(3), December, 1937.

matters of morality in certain ethical theories, because in my account, what constitutes the morally correct is not simply a matter of ethical purposes and efforts, but virtues, including pagan virtues, and mere opposition to natural evil. Admittedly, this is a wider conception than what many ethical philosophers would include under the rubric of "morality," but I think that it does converge on the way in which people tend to use the terms "good" and "bad" in ordinary language when they are speaking nonpractically and nonprudentially; and, furthermore, I suspect that one should predict that such an expanded, everyday conception of morality would be the one toward which suspense fictions, which aspire to popularity, would gravitate.

Suspense requires not only that consumers rate certain alternative outcomes to be moral and evil; suspense, with respect to fiction, also requires that the moral outcome be perceived to be a live but improbable outcome, or, at least, no more probable than the evil outcome, whereas the evil outcome is generally far more probable than the moral one. That is, readers, listeners, and viewers of fictions not only rate the alternative outcomes in terms of morality, but also in terms of probability. Of course, the sense of probability that I have in mind here is the probability of the outcomes prior to the moment in the fiction at which one of the alternatives is actualized, because after that moment there is no uncertainty.

Moreover, I am talking here about the probability of the event in the fictional world, or, to state it differently, the probability internal to the fiction, or what falls within the scope of the fictional operator (i.e., "It is fictional that . . ."). It is the audience's access to this internal probability (henceforth usually called just "probability") that is relevant, because from a viewpoint external to the fiction, there is no probability that King Kong will be killed because King Kong does not exist.[11]

Suspense correlates with the course of events prior to, but not including the relevant outcomes. For after one of the rival alternatives eventuates, there can be no suspense. Morever, the sense of internal improbability that possesses the audience for the duration of its experience of suspense is relative to the information provided within the scope of the fiction operator to the audience by the narrative up to and including the moments when we are gripped by suspense. This is meant to preclude the relevance of such "real-world" knowledge, as that

---

[11]This notion of internal probability is crucial to specifying the content of what the audience is to imagine in the course of consuming a suspense fiction. For from a point of view external to the fiction, we do not believe that the events in question have any probability. Likewise by focusing our attention on what is internal to the fiction, we do not imagine that the fiction was, for example, written by Karl May. From the external point of view, we know that *In the Desert* is by Karl May, but we do not imagine that as part of what it is to follow the story. It is not part of the story, nor should it be part of our imaginative response to the story. This is also why our knowledge that heroes almost always triumph in stories does not disturb our internal probability ratings. For it is not information that is inside the fiction operator. It is not part of the story and, hence, not something we are supposed to imagine.

the hero always wins the day, from our estimates of the probabilities of certain fictional events. Instead, we gauge the relevant probabilities relative to the information available in the story preceding and during the interlude of suspense but bracket the information available after and including the moment when one outcome emerges victorious.

The idea of probability that the spectator works with is not technical; it is not a product of deriving probability from a calculus. Rather, when the reader, listener, or spectator entertains the thought that some outcome is either internally probable or improbable, that means that he or she thinks it is likely or unlikely to occur, or that it can reasonably be expected to occur or not, given all the available information provided for the consumer by the relevant parts of the fiction. This hardly requires a consumer deriving specialized probability rankings subvocally; instead, just as I surmise immediately and tacitly that a baseball headed toward a bay window is likely to shatter it, so my estimate that, in a given fiction, it is unlikely that the detailment of the bullet train can be averted, requires no specialized calculations.

It seems to me that much of the suspense sequence in a novel or a film or whatever is preoccupied with establishing and re-emphasizing the audience's sense of the relevant probabilities of alternative lines of action. That is, it appears to be the case that with most suspense sequences we are already apprised of the moral status of the rival parties before the various episodes of suspense take hold. So, what primarily comprises those interludes—at least most frequently—is an emphasis on the relative probabilities of the competing outcomes.

In film and TV, suspense scenes are often elaborated with cross-cutting.[12] As Lois Lane and Jimmy Olsen are apprehended by bandits, we cut to Superman who is struggling to resist the effects of kryptonite. This establishes the probability that evil will befall Lois Lane and Jimmy Olsen and the improbability of their rescue by Superman. By the time that the bandits are mere seconds away from executing Lois and Jimmy, there is a cross-cut to Superman finally aloft, but because he is so far away, the shot re-emphasizes how unlikely it is that he will be able to save them.

Likewise, toward the end of *The Guns of Navarone*, the director, J. Lee Thompson, cuts between shots of the British rescue armada and shots of the ammunition hoist for the Nazi artillery, stopping just before the demolition charges that the Allies hope will take out the cannons. But each cut, insofar as they carry the information that the charges fail to detonate, makes it more probable in the fiction that the guns will have the opportunity to wreak havoc on the fleet once it is in range. A great deal of the work that goes into a suspense sequence—whether it is visual or verbal—depends on keeping the relative probabilities of the alternative outcomes of the relevant course of events vividly before the audience.

Certain sorts of events—including chases, escapes, and rescues, among others—are staples of popular fiction just because they so naturally accommodate suspense, possessing, by definition, logically exclusive, uncertain outcomes that

---

[12]Of course there are comparable narrative structures in literature as well.

can be so readily invested with moral significance. Also, suspense scenes often feature such recurring devices as time bombs. In my view, bombs attached to fizzling fuses or ticking timepieces work so well in generating suspense because, as each moment passes, time is running out on the good, and therefore evil is becoming ever more likely, even as the prospects for righteousness become more and more improbable. I would not want to diminish the importance of time bombs and chase scenes for suspense. I only urge that one be wary of reducing suspense to these devices. Rather, the serviceability of the devices themselves needs to be explained by the kind of general theory of suspense fiction that I have advanced in this section.[13]

---

[13]Because establishing and re-emphasizing the relative probabilities of the competing outcomes to courses of events will undoubtedly take time, the expositional duration of the event will reflect this. Thus, I would not deny that the passage of time figures in the articulation of suspense. However, I have not included it as a central ingredient, in its own right, of suspense. In this I perhaps reveal my suspicions with regard to theorists of suspense who claim that it arises as a consequence of time being "distended" or outcomes being "delayed" in the exposition of suspense scenes.

My problem here is that notions like that of temporal distension entail a contrast with something else—presumably the event represented is supposed to contrast to the duration of the event "in nature." However, with fiction, there seems to be nothing "in nature" to which we can compare the represented event.

Recently, however, there has been some psychological research that maintains that—at least in film—there is an available contrast to the representation of the event, which contrast makes talk about temporal distensions and delayed outcomes intelligible. And that contrast is the time that the audience expects the event to take in order to resolve itself. So, for example, suspense will be accentuated where the outcome of an event occurs after that point in time when the audience expected it. Researchers have not claimed that such a temporal prolongation can carry suspense by itself. Rather, they have only claimed a role for time structures in exacerbating or undercutting suspense.

This research is certainly intriguing. However, I still have some reservations. Because so many representations of events in film differ in duration from the same kind of events "in real life" (e.g., wars and the decisive battles of world history are always shorter in the movies than they are in "real life"), one wonders how audiences form expectations about how long cinematic representations of events should take. Here, it has been suggested that we form our expectations insofar as we develop norms about event lengths on the basis of the other representations in the film. But how, then, do we undergo suspense with respect to the opening scenes in a film?

I would feel more comfortable with this conjecture in general if more could be said about the computational mechanism that putatively enables us to estimate what we feel is the right amount of time, for example, for a suspenseful battle to take in a film about intergalactic revolution. Without a convincing specification of such a mechanism, I am not sure I can make much sense of what people say about their expectations concerning when fictional representations of events should (as a matter of prediction) end.

Also, we experience suspense not only while watching films, but in reading literature. It seems to me that the experience of suspense, whether seen or read, is pretty much the same. However, it is virtually unfathomable to me how people could form expectations about on what page a scene should end. Indeed, on the basis of introspection, I find it difficult to observe such expectations in me. Consequently, if the analysis of suspense in literature and the visual arts should be roughly the same, and if it seems unlikely that readers predict what they take to be the appropriate length of the exposition of events in literature, then why should we suppose that a prediction of the length of the exposition of the event is an essential ingredient in film suspense?

SOLVING THE PARADOX OF SUSPENSE

Suspense, in general, is an emotional state. It is the emotional response that one has to situations in which an outcome that concerns one is uncertain. Uncertainty and concern are necessary conditions or formal criteria for suspense. Where care and uncertainty unite in a single situation, suspense is an appropriate or fitting emotional response. That is, suspense is an intelligible response to such a situation. If I have no concern whatsoever for the outcome in question, a response in terms of suspense is unintelligible. Indeed, if I claim to be in a state of suspense about something about which I genuinely protest that I have not one jot of concern, then I sound as though I am contradicting myself; but if I believe that an outcome that I care about is uncertain, then suspense is in order.

The care and concern required for suspense are engendered in audiences of fictions by means of morality. That is, the audience is given a stake in the outcome of certain events in the fiction when the relevant outcome is presented as morally righteous, at the same time that the rival outcome is represented as evil. When the righteous outcome appears improbable, relative to the information provided in the story up to that point, suspense is a fitting or intelligible reaction.

Improbability, relative to the information available at the relevant point in the fiction, and moral righteousness are typically the standard conditions or formal criteria for suspense when it comes to fiction. Where a morally righteous outcome is imperiled to the point where it is improbable, our concern for the morally right can be transformed into suspense. For consternation at the prospect that the morally correct is in danger or that the good is at risk is an appropriate or fitting response. That is, just as fear is an appropriate response to the prospect of harm, suspense is an appropriate response to a situation in which the morally good is imperiled or at risk.

Of course, when we say that fear is an appropriate response to the prospect of harm, we do not thereby predict that everyone will feel fear when confronting what is harmful. After all, bungee jumpers, lion tamers, and mountain climbers do exist. Nevertheless, it is always intelligible to feel fear in the presence of the harmful, and it is always intelligible to feel suspense when we perceive the good to be imperiled.

When we feel suspense with regard to our own projects and prospects, it is because we believe that some outcome about which we care—say winning at bingo—is not certain. Here, the cognitive component of our mental state is a belief. We believe that it is uncertain or improbable that we shall win at bingo. But when it comes to fictions, we need to modify our conception of the cognitive

---

On the other hand, if these sorts of worries can be allayed, perhaps I shall have to grant that time plays a more integral role in the generation of suspense than I have acknowledged heretofore.

For interesting research on this topic that favors the conclusion that time is an integral element of suspense, see de Wied (1991).

component of our emotional states; since my anger at Leontes in *The Winter's Tale* cannot be based on my belief that he is an unjust person, because I do not believe that there is someone, Leontes, such that he is an unjust person. Leontes is a fictional character, and I know it.

However, it is not the case that the only mental state that can do the requisite cognitive work when it comes to emotion is belief. Emotions may be rooted in thoughts as well as beliefs.[14] What is the difference? If we describe believing *p* as a matter of holding a proposition in the mind as asserted, then thinking *p*, in contrast, is a matter of entertaining a proposition in the mind unasserted, as one does when I say "Suppose I am Charles the Bald."

Furthermore, one can engender emotional states by holding propositions before the mind unasserted. Thus, when I stand near the edge of the roof of a high building and I entertain the thought that I am losing my footing, I can make myself feel a surge of vertigo. I need not believe that I am losing my footing; I merely entertain the thought. And the thought, or the propositional content of the thought (that I am losing my footing), can be sufficient for playing a role in causing the chill of fear in my bloodstream. For emotions may rest on thoughts, and not merely on beliefs.

Fictions, moreover, are readily conceived to be stories that authors intend readers, listeners, and viewers to imagine. Indeed, fictions are the sorts of communication where the author intends the consumer to recognize the authorial intention that the consumer imagine the story. That is, in making fictions, the author is intentionally presenting consumers with situations that they are meant to entertain in thought. The author, in presenting his or her novel as fiction, in effect, says to readers "hold these propositions before your mind unasserted"—that is, "suppose *p*," or "entertain *p* unasserted," or "contemplate *p* as a supposition" (Scruton, 1972).

Furthermore, insofar as thoughts, as distinct from beliefs, can support emotional responses, we may have emotional responses to fictions concerning situations that we believe do not exist. For we can imagine or suppose that they exist, and entertaining the propositional content of the relevant thoughts can figure in the etiology of an emotional state.

Needless to say, in maintaining that the imagination of the consumer of fiction is engaged here I do not mean to suggest that the activity is free or unbounded. The consumer's imaginative activity is, of course, guided by the object—by the fiction in question. That object—the fiction—has certain properties. Specifically, it presents certain situations as having certain properties (in terms of morality and internal probability) which properties, given the psychology of normal consumers, induces certain emotional responses or, as Hume might have it, sentiments in us.

That is, I maintain that the fictions in question can be identified as suspenseful in terms of features of the fiction (such as the logical exclusivity of outcomes,

---

[14]For further arguments on behalf of this contention, see Greenspan (1988).

and their morality and internal probability ratings) that we can specify independently of the responses they induce in a regular fashion in consumers of fiction. These features are naturally suited to raise the affect of suspense in us. The extension of what counts as being suspenseful in fiction is, then, codetermined by the normal (as opposed to the ideal) appreciator's tendency to respond with feelings of suspense and the independently characterizable structural features of suspense fictions adumbrated earlier.[15] In the relevant cases, the appreciator's attention must be focused on those structural features of the the fiction, and his or her imagination is guided or controlled by them. In such cases, the thoughts that he or she is prompted to entertain as unasserted by what is in the fiction (as opposed to whatever passing fancies fleetingly strike her) will raise appropriate feelings of suspense.

Nor should it seem bizarre that thinking various thoughts, in addition to having certain beliefs, should figure in the generation of emotional states. For from an evolutionary perspective, it is certainly a distinctive advantage that humans have the capacity to be moved by thinking p as well as by believing p, because this capacity enables humans to be educated about all kinds of dangers that may come to pass in the future, but that do not exist and do not confront us in the here and now. The imagination is surely an asset from the Darwinian point of view; it provides a way in which not only cognition but the emotions, as well, can be prepared for situations that have not yet arisen. Adolescents vicariously learn about love and parental responsibility by imagining these things, and these acts of imagination serve to educate their feelings.

Certain emotions are cognitively impenetrable, and this impenetrability can be explained in terms of the adaptive advantages it bestows on the organism. Adopting the role of armchair evolutionary biologists, perhaps we can speculate that, in the case of many emotions, they can be induced by mere thoughts and thereby are insulated from exclusive causal dependency on particular beliefs, because of the overall adaptive advantage this delivers to humans in terms of educating the emotions in the response to situations and situation types not already at hand.

However, be that as it may, suspense fictions present audiences with situations that we are to imagine. For example, we entertain (unasserted) the thoughts that the train is about to derail with the much-needed medical supplies and that this outcome is all but unavoidable. Because we entertain this thought as unasserted, we do not call the police to alert them. Nevertheless, this thinking does help generate the affect of suspense in us. And this affect, in the case under discussion, is appropriate, fitting, and intelligible. For it is always intelligible that we feel consternation when we entertain the supposition that the good—something that is morally correct—is threatened or is unlikely to come to pass.

---

[15]I am indebted to Dong-Ryul Choo for pointing out some of the realistic commitments of my theory of suspense. He develops his insights in his *How to be an Aesthetic Realist*, a doctoral dissertation in progress at the University of Wisconsin at Madison.

What does all this have to do with the paradox of suspense? According to the paradox, if a fiction is experienced by readers, listeners, or viewers as suspense, then the outcome of the events that give rise to suspense must be uncertain to said listeners, readers, and viewers. On the other hand, it seems that it is simply a fact that audiences experience suspense in reaction to fictions they have already seen, heard, or read. But how is that possible, since if they've already seen, heard, or read the fiction, then they know how the fiction ends—that is, they know the relevant outcome—and, therefore, they cannot believe, for example, that the righteous alternative is uncertain? This contradicts the earlier presumption that audiences gripped by suspense must be uncertain of the outcome.

However, if what has been claimed about the emotions in general, and the emotion of suspense in particular, is right, perhaps there is a way out of this conundrum. A presupposition of the paradox is that the response of suspense on the part of audiences requires that they be uncertain of the relevant outcomes. I understand this to mean that the audiences must *believe* that the relevant outcomes are uncertain or uncertain to them. For example, they must believe that the relevant moral outcome is improbable. Yet the audience cannot believe this if they actually know the relevant outcomes already, because they have encountered the fiction in question beforehand.

But notice that the problem here resides in the assumption that suspense would only take hold if the audience believes the outcome is uncertain. But why suppose this? The audience may not believe that the relevant outcome is uncertain or improbable but, nevertheless, the audience may entertain the thought that the relevant outcome is uncertain or improbable. That is, even though we know otherwise, we may entertain (as unasserted) the proposition that a certain morally good outcome is uncertain or improbable. If an emotional response can rest on a thought, then there is no reason to remain mystified about the way in which audiences can be seized by suspense even though they know how everything will turn out.

For they are entertaining the thought that the morally correct outcome is improbable relative to the information within the scope of the fiction operator that is available up to the relevant point in the fiction. That is, the paradox of suspense disappears once we recall that emotions may be generated on the basis of thoughts, rather than only on the basis of beliefs. Indeed, emotions may be generated in the course of entertaining thoughts that are at variance with our beliefs.

Nor is the recidivist reader, listener, or viewer of suspense fictions irrational or perverse in any way. For in contemplating the proposition unasserted—that the heroine in all probability is likely to be killed—the recidivist, despite what he or she knows about the last-minute rescue, recognizes a situation in which the good is unlikely, and it is always appropriate or intelligible to undergo consternation in reaction to even the thought of such a prospect.

In terms of the way in which I set forth the paradox of suspense in the opening section of this chapter, the strategy that I have just employed to dissolve the paradox involves denying its first premise, viz., that if a fiction is experienced with suspense by an audience, then the outcome of the events that give rise to suspense must be uncertain to the audience. This seems to me to be the best way to dispose of the contradiction.[16]

Competing proposals might suggest that we reconsider the second proposition in our inconsistent triad, to wit: It is a fact that audiences experience fictions with suspense in cases where they have already seen, heard, or read the fictions in question. The motivation for this seems to be a theoretical conviction that it is just impossible to undergo suspense when one knows how a fiction will end—impossible, that is, for anyone who holds the first and the last propositions in the paradox. But here it seems to me that theory is recasting reality in its own image; for it appears obvious that people do re-experience suspense with certain fictions with which they are already familiar. As I noted earlier, the existence of blockbuster movies like *The Fugitive* and *Jurassic Park* depends on recidivists for their astronomical success; it is the people who go back to see the films from 6 to 16 to 60 times who turn these films into box office legends.

Perhaps a more popular route in negotiating the paradox of suspense is to deny the last proposition in the triad—if audiences have already seen, heard, or

---

[16]As I understand him, Kendall Walton makes a similar move in dissolving the paradox of suspense. He draws a distinction between what one knows to be fictional and what is fictional that one knows. Thus, if I have already seen *The Guns of Navarone*, then I know it to be fictional that the artillery is destroyed; but as I watch the film a second time and play my game of make-believe, I make believe that I am uncertain about whether the guns will be destroyed, or, to put it differently, it is fictional that I am uncertain about whether the guns will be destroyed (in my occurrent game of make-believe).

However, I think that my characterization of the mental state in terms of imagination is superior to Walton's discussion in terms of make-believe, because Walton's games of make-believe seem to require so much more activity than mere imagination. For in some games of make-believe, Lauren is paralyzed by her fear for Jack in the Beanstalk, whereas in others, it is fictional that she is hit by the gravity of the situation of Jack's theft of the goose that lays the golden egg, or, yet again, fictionally she is emotionally exhausted when Jack defeats the giant. Playing games of make-believe in Walton's examples seems to involve readers in playing roles or acting. Playing games of make-believe involves more than merely imagining *p*—merely entertaining the proposition *p* unasserted. Thus, solving the paradox of suspense in terms of imagination seems more economical than talking about make-believe.

Although Walton sometimes speaks of make-believe as imagination, when he gives examples of what he has in mind, it seems far more structurally complex than mere imagining. Consequently, I maintain that my solution to the paradox of suspense is more economical than Walton's, because all I require is a notion of the imagination that we are already willing to endorse outside the context of fiction, whereas Walton employs the more complicated machinery of make-believe or fictional games, which even if called the imagination is really an elaborate version thereof. For a discussion of the relevant examples, see Walton (1990).

Moreover, Walton's overall argument for the efficacy of his concept of make-believe is indirect. He advances his case by showing that his own approach solves more puzzles—such as the paradox of suspense—than do contending approaches. Thus, if the solution offered here by me is superior to Walton's, then one of the major struts supporting Walton's theory is undermined. For pressure on some of the other struts, see Carroll (1990).

read a fiction, then they know (and are certain) of the relevant outcomes. One way to do this is to postulate that when confronting fictions, audiences are induced into a special sort of psychological state that might be described in terms of self-deception, denial, or disavowal. This way of dealing with the paradox accepts the phenomenon of anomalous or recidivist suspense as contradictory and then postulates disavowal as a psychological mechanism that enables us to live with the contradiction—it is a mechanism that suffers mental states during which one both knows and does not know by repressing the former. Thus, the disavowal account resolves the paradox (or contradiction) of recidivist suspense by portraying the audience as irrational.

Psychoanalytic theorists are particularly prone to this mode of explanation, because they believe that people are extremely susceptible to disavowal anyway. For example, male fetishists—of whom (if psychoanalytic film theorist Laura Mulvey, 1989, is correct) there are more than you might expect—are said to be involved pervasively in the disavowal of their knowledge that women lack penises, because that knowlege would stir up male anxieties about castration.

Yet if there is some comparable process of disavowal in operation when audiences consume fictions, then this sort of explanation requires, it seems to me, a parallel motivation for our denial or disavowal of our knowledge of the outcomes of fictions. That is, why would we be compelled to disavow our knowledge of the end of a story? It is hard to imagine generalizable answers to that question.

Recently, a nonpsychoanalytic explanation of anomalous suspense, which also appears to undermine the supposition that recidivist audiences in suspense contexts unequivocably know the relevant outcomes, was advanced by Gerrig (1993). He wrote:

> What I wish to suggest, in fact, is that anomalous suspense arises not because of some special strategic activity but rather as a natural consequence of the structure of cognitive processing. Specifically, I propose that readers experience anomalous suspense because an expectation of uniqueness is incorporated within the cognitive processes that guide the expectations of narratives.... My suggestion is that anomalous suspense arises because our experience of narratives incorporates the strong likelihood that we never repeat a game. Note that this expectation of uniqueness need not be conscious. My claim is that our moment-by-moment processes evolve in response to the brute fact of nonrepetition. (pp. 170–171)

For Gerrig, we are possessed of a uniqueness heuristic, which evolved under the pressure to secure fast, optimal strategies rather than massively time-consuming, rational strategies of information processing; the fact that we can undergo the experience of anomalous suspense is simply a surprising consequence or a kind of peripheral fallout from one of the optimizing heuristics that we have evolved. Gerrig sees this heuristic as an expectation of uniqueness that resides in the cognitive architecture linking inputs to outputs.

In some ways, Gerrig's resolution of the problem of anomalous or recidivist suspense is more palatable than what the disavowal model promises. However, it must be noted that Gerrig's approach still does render recidivists irrational, even if in the long run they are victims of a higher rationality (a.k.a. optimality). And this seems to me to be a problem.

Recidivist readers, listeners, and viewers of suspense fictions very frequently re-encounter fictions with the express expectation of re-experiencing the thrill they experienced on earlier encounters. They remember the thrill, and they remember the story, too. Gerrig seems to argue that their cognitive processing of the story the second or 60th time around is insulated from that knowledge. This seems to me to be highly unlikely.

Think of a relatively simple version of the game show *Concentration* in which there are so few squares that it is very easy to hold all the matching pairs and the image fragments and the saying that solves the rebus in mind after the game is over. Run the game several more times. Quickly, I predict, it will become boring. But how can it become boring if we have this uniqueness heuristic? On the other hand, one can sit through several showings of a suspense film like *The Terminator* and never become bored before one is thrown out of the theater. But if it is a uniqueness heuristic that explains anomalous suspense, shouldn't it also predict equal staying power in the *Concentration* example? But that seems hardly compelling.

Suspense recidivists are perfectly normal, and not for the reason that they, like everyone else with the same cognitive architecture, diverge from the canons of strict rationality for the sake of optimality. Rather, it is because it is perfectly intelligible that people respond to suspenseful situations in fictions with consternation, because not only beliefs, but also thoughts can give rise to emotions. Indeed, thoughts that are at variance with a person's beliefs can give rise to emotions. Thus, effectively asked to imagine—that is, to entertain the thought—that the good is at risk by the author of a fiction, the reader appropriately and intelligibly feels concern and suspense.

In this case, we focus our attention on the relevant, available information in the story up to and for the duration of the interlude in which suspense dominates. That we may not use our knowledge of earlier encounters with the fiction to drive away our feelings of suspense here is no more irrational than the fact that our knowledge of entertainment conventions or regularities, such as that the hero almost always prevails, does not compromise our feelings of suspense on a first encounter with a fiction, because our attention is riveted, within the scope of the fiction operator, to the unfolding of the story on a moment-to-moment basis. And so focused, our mind fills with the thought that the good is in peril, a prospect always in principle rationally worthy of emotional exercise.

ACKNOWLEDGMENTS

I would like to thank Elliott Sober, David Bordwell, Berent Enc, Gregory Currie, and Sally Banes for their assistance in the preparation of this chapter.

REFERENCES

Brewer, W. F., & Jose, P. E. (1984). Development of story liking: Character, identification, suspense and outcome resolution. *Developmental Psychology, 20*(5), 911–924.

Carroll, N. (1984). Toward a theory of film suspense. *Persistence of Vision, 1,* 65–89.

Carroll, N. (1990). *The philosophy of horror or paradoxes of the heart.* New York: Routledge.

Chatman, S. (1978). *Story and discourse: Narrative structure in fiction and film.* Ithaca, NY: Cornell University Press.

Comisky, P., & Bryant, J. (1982). Factors involved in generating suspense. *Human Communication Research, 9*(1), 48–58.

de Wied, M. (1991). *The role of time structures in the experience of film suspense and duration: A study of the effects of anticipation time upon suspense and temporal variations on duration experience and suspense.* Unpublished doctoral dissertation, University of Amsterdam, Department of Theatre Studies.

Dove, G. N. (1989). *Suspense in the formula story.* Bowling Green, OH: Bowling Green State University Popular Press.

Gerrig, R. J. (1989a). Reexperiencing fiction and non-fiction. *The Journal of Aesthetics and Art Criticism, 47,* 277–280.

Gerrig, R. J. (1989b). Suspense in the absence of uncertainty. *Journal of Memory and Language, 28,* 633–648.

Gerrig, R. J. (1993). *Experiencing narrative worlds: On the psychological activities of reading.* New Haven, CT: Yale University Press.

Greenspan, P. S. (1988). *Emotions and reasons: An inquiry into emotional justification.* New York: Routledge.

Harding, D. W. (1968). Psychological processes in the reading of fiction. In H. Osborne (Ed.), *Aesthetics in the modern world* (pp. 300–317). New York: Weybright & Talley.

Michaels, M. (1992). *Structures of fantasy.* Washington, DC: MES Press.

Mulvey, L. (1989). Visual pleasure and narrative cinema. In L. Mulvey (Ed.), *Visual and other pleasures* (pp. 14–28). Bloomington: Indiana University Press.

Ortony, A., Clore, G. L., & Collins, A. (1988). *The cognitive structure of the emotions.* Cambridge, UK: Cambridge University Press.

Rodell, M. (1952). *Mystery fiction: Theory and technique.* New York: Hermitage House.

Scruton, R. (1972). *Art and imagination: A study in the philosophy of mind.* London: Routledge & Kegan Paul.

Vale, E. (1982). *The technique of screen and television writing.* New York: Simon & Schuster.

Walton, K. (1990). *Mimesis as make-believe.* Cambridge, MA: Harvard University Press.

Zillmann, D. (1980). Anatomy of suspense. In P. H. Tannenbaum (Ed.), *The entertainment functions of television* (pp. 133–163). Hillsdale, NJ: Lawrence Erlbaum Associates.

Zillmann, D., & Cantor, J. R. (1977). Affective responses to the emotions of a protagonist. *Journal of Experimental and Social Psychology, 8,* 155–165.

Zillmann, D., Hay, T. A., & Bryant, J. (1975). The effect of suspense and its resolution in the appreciation of dramatic presentation. *Journal of Research in Personality, 9,* 307–323.

6

▼▼▼▼▼▼▼

The Resiliency of Suspense

Richard J. Gerrig
State University of New York, Stony Brook

What does it mean to say that suspense is *resilient*? According to *Webster's New Collegiate Dictionary* (1977), to be resilient is to be "capable of withstanding shock without permanent deformation or rupture" or "tending to recover or adjust easily to misfortune or change" (p. 985). To fit suspense to this schema, we must believe it to be an emotion that survives under conditions in which we might expect it readily to be destroyed. In this chapter, I argue that suspense is exactly such an emotion. To begin, I make some general observations about the narrative circumstances that encourage suspense. In that context, I examine the situations in which suspense endures in the face of adversity.

THE ORIGINS OF SUSPENSE

To understand why suspense is resilient, we must have a theory that specifies the circumstances that give rise to it. Such a theory will no doubt make reference both to readers and to narrative structures: Suspense will arise when readers possessing some particular range of cognitive processes interact with a particular range of narrative features. (For convenience, I use *author*, *reader*, and *narrative* to span all the roles in which individuals create and experience suspense.) In this view, we can best study suspense by examining how narrative structures encourage readers to experience certain types of thoughts.

My research on the origins of suspense has been rooted in two complementary types of expertise. On the one hand, I have examined the sorts of techniques professional suspense makers use to heighten their readers' experiences. Here, we can learn what techniques authors use to nudge their readers' thoughts in a certain direction. On the other hand, I have asked readers themselves to reproduce in brief the types of situations they believe will lead them to experience suspense. Here, we can learn under what narrative circumstances readers are willing to let authors control their thoughts.

WHAT AUTHORS KNOW

For a primer on the sorts of things authors know about suspense, we can turn to a proven expert, Alfred Hitchcock. In conversation with Truffaut (1984), Hitchcock analyzed a number of suspenseful moments in his films. He described, for example, a moment in his early film *Easy Virtue* when a switchboard operator

> is tuned in to the conversation between the young man and the woman who are discussing marriage and who are not shown on the screen. That switchboard operator is in suspense; she is filled with it. Is the woman on the end of the line going to marry the man whom she called? The switchboard operator is very relieved when the woman finally agrees; her own suspense is over.... In the usual form of suspense it is indispensable that the public be made perfectly aware of all of the facts involved. Otherwise there is no suspense. (p. 72)

Thus, in Hitchcock's view, suspense requires that the reader be in possession of enough information to appreciate that there exists a range of outcomes. Suspense occurs when the readers, using only their own resources, cannot determine which of these outcomes will obtain.

What, perhaps, made Hitchcock so successful as a perpetrator of suspense was that he developed explicit models of what readers would count as their own resources at a given moment—and he used that knowledge against them. Consider his analysis of *Psycho* (Truffaut, 1984, p. 269):

> You know the public always likes to be one jump ahead of the story; they like to feel they know what's coming next. So you deliberately play upon this fact to control their thoughts.... You turn the viewer in one direction and then in another; you keep him as far as possible from what's actually going to happen.... *Psycho* has a very interesting construction and that game with the audience was fascinating. I was directing the viewers. You might say I was playing them, like an organ.

The general success of Hitchcock's movies stands as evidence of his success at controlling his public's thoughts.

If we were to boil aspects of Hitchcock's advice down to a testable hypothesis, it might look something like this: To create suspense, make your audience aware that there are unattractive alternatives to the one they desire—and then make that attractive outcome seem increasingly distant. In more cognitive psychological terms, we can suggest that one reliable way to create suspense would be to increase readers' feelings of uncertainty by modeling a course of troubled problem solving (Gerrig, 1993). To see how this might work, consider this passage from Ian Fleming's (1954) novel *Casino Royale* which occurs after James Bond has been captured by his enemy, Le Chiffre:

> He [Bond] felt thoroughly dispirited and weak in resolve as well as in his body. He had had to take too much in the past twenty-four hours and now this last stroke by the enemy seemed almost too final. This time there could be no miracles. No one knew where he was and no one would miss him until well on into the morning. The wreck of his car would be found before very long, but it would take hours to trace ownership to him. (p. 105)

Let us assume the modal reader would like Bond to exact revenge on Le Chiffre. By putting us inside Bond's head, Fleming has allowed us to experience the logical elimination of a number of possible paths to escape. This process of modeling what amounts to unsuccessful problem solving, seems to have the effect of providing heightened feelings of suspense.

Bernardo and I (Gerrig & Bernardo, 1994) sought to test explicitly this putative technique of enhancing suspense by modeling processes of problem solving. Much previous research on suspense has been directed toward identifying the general narrative structures that most readily give rise to experiences of suspense (Brewer & Lichtenstein, 1981, 1982; Brewer & Ohtsuka, 1988a, 1988b). By contrast, my research with Bernardo is intended to take advantage of the analogy with problem solving to predict *relative* levels of suspense among narratives that share the same overall structure.

It should be the case, for example, that readers experience relatively more suspense when they believe some potential escape route to have been eliminated, because a possible solution has been cut off. To test this hypothesis, we wrote alternative versions of a narrative that was based on another scene from *Casino Royale*. We told our readers this:

> The following is an excerpt from Fleming's first James Bond novel, *Casino Royale*. In this book, Bond has been assigned to "ruin" a criminal figure named Le Chiffre by, as it happens, causing Le Chiffre to lose a considerable amount of money gambling. Along the way, Bond has acquired a lady interest named Vesper. Although Bond has, in fact, brought about the gambling losses, Le Chiffre has laid a successful trap for Bond. Bond and Vesper are now the prisoners of Le Chiffre and his two gunmen.

The opening paragraphs of three versions of the excerpt were identical: Bond tries but fails to escape from Le Chiffre. At that point, the versions diverged in subtle ways. Consider the neutral version of the excerpt:

Like lightning the Corsican [i.e., the second gunman] slammed himself back against the wall of the passage and, as Bond's foot whistled past his hip, he very quickly, but somehow delicately, shot out his left hand, caught Bond's shoe at the top of its arc and twisted it sharply. As he crashed to the ground, Bond rolled agilely and, with a motion in which he took great pride, he righted himself with minimal damage.

"Search him," barked Le Chiffre.

The two gunmen dragged Bond to his feet. While the thin man kept his gun trained on Bond's unquiet chest, the Corsican roughly stripped Bond's revolver out of its shoulder holster. He twisted Bond around brusquely in search of other weaponry.

Le Chiffre observed his assistant's work attentively. Then, as if reading Bond's thoughts, he crossed the room and said, "Come, my dear friend. Let's not waste time."

A second version of the excerpt was identical except that it made it clear that Bond wished to retain his fountain pen:

As he crashed to the ground, Bond rolled agilely and, with a motion that he hoped went unnoticed, moved his fountain pen deeper into his breast pocket.

A third version included both this mention of the pen and also a second revision in which the pen is taken away:

Le Chiffre observed his assistant's work attentively. Then, as if reading Bond's thoughts, he crossed the room and snatched away Bond's fountain pen. "Come, my dear friend," said Le Chiffre. "Let's not waste time."

Our goal, again, was to make predictions about how much suspense about Bond's fate readers would experience in each version of the story. The analogy to problem solving suggests that the mention of the pen should, on balance, not appreciably change feelings of suspense: Some readers will experience more suspense because they wonder how Bond will use the pen; others will experience less suspense because they believe whatever powers the pen gives Bond will enable him to escape with ease. By contrast, the version of the excerpt in which the pen is removed should unambiguously lead to more suspense: A possible solution has been eliminated, so readers should feel Bond's situation to be just a bit more desperate.

Roughly 50 students at the University of the Philippines read each version of the excerpt and provided suspense ratings on a scale that ranged from 1 (*not very suspenseful*) to 9 (*extremely suspenseful*). Mean ratings on the version that did not mention the pen ($M = 3.43$) were virtually identical to ratings for the version that mentioned, but did not remove the pen ($M = 3.47$). However, ratings for the version in which the pen was removed ($M = 4.06$) differed reliably from the other two. This pattern suggests that even though readers almost certainly had no specific idea of exactly how the fountain pen would have functioned, they were sensitive to the removal of a potential solution.

In a second experiment, Bernardo and I demonstrated that the object removed loses its meaning if it has been shown to have its ordinary function. Our analogy, in this case, was to the classic problem-solving phenomenon of *functional fixedness*, in which individuals fail to find a solution because they are unable to overcome a tendency to associate an object with only one function (Duncker, 1945). For this experiment, we wrote two versions of a Bond excerpt that focused on a comb rather than a pen. In one version, Bond put the comb to its ordinary use:

> Bond looked in the mirror of his hotel room to make certain that his black tie was centered in his collar. He noticed that his hair was just the least bit mussed, so he extracted his comb from his pocket and smoothed his wandering locks back into place.

In a second version, the comb was not mentioned:

> Bond looked in the mirror of his hotel room to make certain that his black tie was centered in his collar. He noticed that he had a white thread on his lapel, and removed it. Bond smiled at the elegant figure he presented.

In both versions, Le Chiffre removed Bond's comb. However, those individuals who had read the version in which the comb had been seen to function as an ordinary comb reported reliably less suspense ($M = 3.41$) than those who had not ($M = 3.96$). We see again that readers' relative ratings of suspense can be predicted by analogy to processes of problem solving. Bernardo and I (Gerrig & Bernardo, 1994) carried out other variations on this theme to bolster this theoretical link. In general, our incorporation of the techniques of expert suspense makers has yielded successful predictions of relative levels of suspense.

Note how these experiments serve the general theme that suspense results from an interaction of the characteristics of reader processes and narrative structures. There is nothing deterministic about our narratives, in the sense that some readers may not succumb to the problem-solving effects: In real problem-solving situations, individuals may or may not overcome something like functional fixedness. We could make our predictions only because research has shown that cognitive processes create a general tendency to experience problems in a certain way. That is why we feel most comfortable concluding that features of the narrative *encourage* a certain type of thought. With the right type of encouragement, many readers will experience suspense.

WHAT READERS KNOW

A second approach to understanding the origins of suspense is to ask readers what kinds of situations they believe are likely to foster this experience. The premise of this approach is that readers' most readily available suggestions should accurately reflect the types of situations that have regularly promoted feelings of uncertainty (see Slovic, Fischhoff, & Lichtenstein, 1982, for a similar analysis of perceived risk). From this analysis, we can learn, therefore, something about the distribution of suspense situations that readers encounter. We can learn, that is, about readers' habits of suspense.

With this goal of letting the readers themselves reveal their knowledge, 40 Yale undergraduates were given the following instructions:

> Suppose that you are reading a novel. We want you to try to imagine three different sentences (i.e., three different situations) you might arrive at that would immediately make you feel suspense. Try to make the sentences as brief as possible.

The students were encouraged to make the sentences brief so that they would be forced to lay out what they believed to be the minimal prompt for suspense. Also, so that it was most likely they would really write down the first situations that came to mind, the students were allowed only about 5 minutes.

Overall the students provided 103 sentences. Five of those responses suggested that the students had not understood the instructions (e.g., they provided scenarios, rather than sentences). The majority, however, appeared to have some merit for inspiring suspense. Table 6.1 presents an informal taxonomy for the responses. These categories are not intended to be definitive, but rather to capture the general flavor of the students' strategies. Note, also, that some of the students' responses could fit into more than one category (e.g., the example I have given for "doors" also mentions "darkness").

The majority of the responses made some explicit reference to what I have termed *classic suspense schemas*. For example, 15 of the 98 sentences mentioned doors, 11 mentioned darkness, and 12 mentioned potential physical harm. Each of these references, I believe, evokes prototypical scenes in which readers are likely to have experienced suspense in the past. Their popularity suggests that individuals have reasonably consistent notions of the identity of those prototypical scenes.

TABLE 6.1
A Taxonomy of Suspense Responses

I. Classic Suspense Schemas
    A. Doors: "As she entered the dark room, the door slammed behind her."
    B. Darkness or lurking danger: "He awoke to find a pair of yellow eyes staring at him through the darkness."
    C. Footsteps or danger from behind: "The footsteps behind her quickened."
    D. Potential physical harm: "He felt the cold hands wrap themselves around his neck."
    E. Despair: "He was trapped and there was no escape."
    F. Fear: "As she rounded the dark corner, Nancy drew a quick breath."
II. Modeling a Lack of Knowledge
    A. In the narration:
       "She answered the phone [and] uttered softly, 'Oh my God.' "
       "And what she saw before her cannot easily be described."
    B. Alongside the character:
       " 'I'm watching you,' said the voice."
       "Her eyes opened wide as she stared at the scene before her."

The other major category I have called *modeling a lack of knowledge*. These sorts of sentences seemed to me, in one way or another, to include within them some direct marker for uncertainty. In some cases, the uncertainty was expressed within the narration: The character already knows something, but the reader has yet to be informed or the reader knows something of which the character is not yet aware. Other times, the character's lack of knowledge was mentioned as a direct model for the reader. These sentences echo the earlier characterization of suspense as problem solving in the sense that they attempt to elicit suspense partially by virtue of engaging a particular type of processing.

The students' original task was to produce sentences that would "immediately" make readers feel suspense. To see how successful they had been, I asked a second group of 24 undergraduates to attach suspense ratings to a randomly selected group of 20 of the original responses. They were given the following instructions:

> We would like you to read each of the following sentences, and answer the question: How successfully do you think this sentence evokes a scene that would make you feel suspense? If you read a sentence, and it calls to mind a scene that is very suspenseful, you should give it a high rating. If it calls to mind a scene that isn't very suspenseful, you should give it a low rating.

The students gave ratings on a 7-point scale from 1 (*not very suspenseful*) to 7 (*very suspenseful*). Table 6.2 presents the results for the 20 sentences. To the

TABLE 6.2
Mean Ratings for Suspense Sentences

How this unfortunate situation came to be is a long, sad story.	1.54
Jack opened the big brown box.	1.79
But he didn't arrive at the appointed time.	2.00
He opened the door and descended the basement stairs.	2.08
And then what happened?	2.46
A shot was heard, but no one knew from where it had come.	3.00
He got the results back, but did he really want to know the results?	3.04
As Bertha was watching T.V. she heard some footsteps downstairs.	3.79
Just as she exhaled her pent-up breath with relief, the house shuddered and creaked.	3.83
All of a sudden the door swung open and there he stood. Even though it was dark he thought he saw movement but was it just his eyes playing tricks on him?	3.96
He saw a man staring at him eerily.	4.00
She heard something behind her.	4.21
She struggled against the current, wondering if she would reach dry land in time.	4.33
As she entered the dark room, the door slammed behind her.	4.42
"I have something important to tell you," he said, at the moment a bullet whistled through his chest.	4.50
A drop of blood landed on his head.	4.92
She didn't notice that the window behind her was slowly opening.	5.21
The agent fled down the hallway hearing the relentless steps of his pursuers closing on him.	5.25
She raised her hand containing the knife as her husband looked on in horror.	5.42

extent that there is a pattern in these data, they seem to suggest that the classics of suspense prevail. Even so, the mere mention of certain motifs is not enough. The sentence "He opened the door and descended the basement stairs" is not sufficient to inspire suspense. What improves the image immensely, at least in these students' judgments, is to include darkness and a mysterious agent: "As she entered the dark room, the door slammed behind her." We might, therefore, look to configurations of elements to best explain how readers undergo suspense.

What have we learned from this exercise? It is perhaps not surprising to see that readers have consistent ideas about the sorts of situations that are likely to inspire suspense. These data remind us, however, that we should expect some sorts of narrative situations to bring about strong suspense responses in large part because they have a prior history of doing so. We cannot, that is, have a theory of suspense that ignores the patterns of experiences that accumulate over readers' lifetimes. The resiliency of suspense may be abetted by the existence of categories of outcomes that are reflexively registered for uncertainty.

ANOMALOUS SUSPENSE

Let us return for a moment to Alfred Hitchcock. Why is it that people who repeatedly view Hitchcock's films still can experience suspense? Hitchcock's fans may continue to feel uncertainty about the figure in the rocking chair in *Psycho* or the seeming resurrection of Madeleine Elster in *Vertigo* even after many viewings. When Hitchcock recommended that "the public be made perfectly aware of all of the facts involved" it seems he might even have added that they could be made aware of the very outcome that will obtain. I call this type of suspense that survives in the face of perfect knowledge of the outcome *anomalous suspense* (Gerrig, 1989a, 1989b, 1993). Anomalous suspense puts us squarely back at the definition of resiliency. Here, suspense is clearly "capable of withstanding" . . . "rupture" and "misfortune."

The paradigm case of anomalous suspense was laid out by Walton (1978):

> [S]uspense may remain a crucial element in our response to a work almost no matter how familiar we are with it. One may "worry" just as intensely about Tom and Becky while rereading *The Adventures of Tom Sawyer*, despite one's knowledge of the outcome, as would a person reading it for the first time. A child listening to *Jack and the Beanstalk* for the umpteenth time, long after she has memorized it word for word, may feel much the same excitement when the giant discovers Jack and goes after him, the same gripping suspense, that she felt when she first heard the story. (p. 26)

What is "anomalous" here is that suspense perseveres in the face of perfect knowledge of an outcome. Because we most often gloss suspense as uncertainty, and suspense arises particularly in response to unknown outcomes, we should let ourselves be very puzzled by anomalous suspense. For it to exist—for suspense to be resilient in this way—suggests that inherent properties of cognitive architecture conspire to make suspense a prominent emotion. What might those properties be?

To approach a theory of anomalous suspense, I sought to recreate it in an experimental setting (Gerrig, 1989b). A first goal of these experiments was to demonstrate the generality of the phenomenon. Walton's theoretical treatment of anomalous suspense, similar to others in the philosophical literature, relies on special aspects of readers' experience of fiction (for a review, see Gerrig, 1989a). None of these explanations can be adequate, however, if anomalous suspense extends to instances of nonfiction (or, at least, normal considerations of parsimony argue against alternative theories for fiction and nonfiction). My research began, therefore, with nonfictional outcomes toward which college undergraduates experience no uncertainty:

- The Eiffel Tower is in the city of Paris, France.
- The United States dropped an atomic bomb on Japan.
- The Beatles recorded the song "I Wanna Hold Your Hand."

The next step was to write brief stories that created suspense, in a gentle fashion, with respect to these outcomes. Consider the fate of the Eiffel Tower:

> The Eiffel Tower came about because of one man's dream. Alexandre Eiffel wished to build a tower in his home city, Lyons. The city fathers were delighted at this idea. They hoped that Eiffel's planned tower would attract many visitors. The citizens of Lyons were dazzled by Eiffel's models.

Imagine, after reading this brief story, that you were asked to verify the statement "The Eiffel Tower is in the city of Paris, France." If the cognitive processes that give rise to anomalous suspense are sufficiently robust—and, in particular, if they do not rely on properties of fiction—we would expect readers to find it just a bit more difficult to verify this assertion than they ordinarily would. That, after all, is the evident phenomenology of anomalous suspense. A child does know that Jack escapes the giant. We would only expect him or her to find it a bit more difficult to access that knowledge while re-experiencing Jack's story.

To make an appropriate comparison—to operationalize "a bit more difficult"—some experimental participants read a version of the Eiffel Tower story that excluded suspense:

> The Eiffel Tower came about because of one man's dream. Alexandre Eiffel wished to build a tower taller than all others. The city fathers of Paris were delighted at this idea. They hoped that Eiffel's planned tower would attract many visitors. The citizens of Paris were dazzled by Eiffel's models.

We can now make a comparison between situations with and without suspense. Even this, however, is not quite enough to afford a rigorous demonstration of anomalous suspense. We want to rule out the possibility that we are doing nothing more than using the suspense stories to confuse readers. There are many things that we could do, to make readers less capable of demonstrating their knowledge, but very few of them would be relevant to theories of discourse comprehension. To rule out the possibility that delayed verification could reflect nothing more interesting than confusion, another pair of stories (one each with and without suspense) began with what I call a *prior warning*: The story began with the exact sentence that served as the target for verification. Consider:

> The Eiffel Tower is in the city of Paris, France. Alexandre Eiffel wished to build a tower in his home city, Lyons. The city fathers were delighted at this idea. They hoped that Eiffel's planned tower would attract many visitors. The citizens of Lyons were dazzled by Eiffel's models.

In this case, there can be no doubt that readers had recently considered the fact toward which the story was intended to create suspense.

Participants in the experiment read 32 stories that were evenly divided among stories with and without prior warning and with and without suspense. Half of the stories were followed by a true statement (e.g., "The Eiffel Tower is in the city of Paris, France") and half were followed by a false statement (e.g., "The Beatles did not record the song 'I Wanna Hold Your Hand' "). The readers' task was to judge each statement as true or false as swiftly and accurately as possible.

The readers were much aided in their judgments by the inclusion of prior warning. When a story began with an exact statement of the target assertion, the average response time was 2.260 seconds. Without a prior warning, the average was 2.643. This difference suggests that the prior warning did function to make the right memories accessible. The introduction of suspense also had an appreciable effect on response times. Readers were able to verify statements like "The Eiffel Tower is in the city of Paris, France" in 2.326 seconds without suspense, but in 2.586 seconds with suspense. Critically, however, there was no interaction between prior warning and suspense. Thus, the introduction of suspense had roughly the same effect on response times with prior warning (2.131 vs. 2.391 seconds) or without (2.526 vs. 2.764). Even, that is, when readers had been recently reminded of the appropriate real-world outcome—a reminder that benefited performance—suspense still wielded an influence. Further experiments showed that the effect of the suspense stories endured at least for 10 minutes after the stories had been read. Readers were much more than momentarily confused. This is strong evidence that suspense can be resilient for both fictional and nonfictional outcomes.

To explain anomalous suspense, I have suggested that cognition is structured so that it incorporates an *expectation of uniqueness* (Gerrig, 1989b): Because life is made up of unique experiences—we undergo repeated types, but not repeated tokens—readers do not ordinarily have reason to search memory for *literal* repetitions of events. This principle is intended to capture the sense that individuals who experience anomalous suspense do not forcibly remove themselves from an unfolding narrative to determine whether they have prior knowledge of the outcome. An important implication of this principle, for current purposes, is that our cognitive architecture almost requires experiences of suspense. If our natural stance—as we are immersed in the ongoing stream of life—is always to act as if we cannot know what is going to happen next, we are likely to find our moment-by-moment existence routinely punctuated by minor and major bouts of suspense.

What the expectation of uniqueness presupposes, even so, is that a narrative, as it unfolds, must be sufficiently compelling to draw the reader into its narrative world. We need this to be true because there are quite clearly circumstances in which readers do *not* experience anomalous suspense—circumstances in which suspense is *not* resilient. Carroll (chap. 5, this volume) provides a compelling example of just such circumstances. He suggests that someone watching the same moments of the game show *Concentration* many times over would become increasingly bored. I share Carroll's intuition. I am not as certain, however, that the example stands against the operation of an expectation of uniqueness. What strikes me as most salient about anomalous suspense as a cognitive psychologist is not so much what happens—the enduring feelings of suspense—as much as what does not happen—a rush of pertinent information from memory that would spoil the suspense. When I began to study anomalous suspense, I did not know of any cognitive psychological mechanism that could explain the failure of this information to become available. The expectation of uniqueness was intended to fill this gap with a principle that I believed to be consistent with the types of uses to which readers would ordinarily put their memory.

How then does this analysis apply to *Concentration*? The expectation of uniqueness is only in trouble if we can demonstrate that what makes the show increasingly boring is automatic access to memories for past experiences of the game. If viewers are effortfully calling the outcome to mind, the expectation of uniqueness is not especially relevant. If I forced the subjects in my experiment to stop reading and remind themselves of the true location of the Eiffel Tower, I have few doubts that evidence of anomalous suspense would virtually disappear. In that sense, Carroll is correct to assert that the phenomenon relies in part on the readers' attention being riveted to the unfolding of the story on a moment-to-moment basis. To the extent that a narrative is engrossing, readers will not expend the extra effort to remove themselves from the narrative world to engage in purposeful uses of memory. The crowding of attention cannot, however, explain why it would be impossible for readers to obtain automatic access to the information that would spoil anomalous suspense. We carry out many reasonably complex cognitive tasks in an unconscious, automatic fashion (Logan, 1988,

1992). For example, we are never so engrossed while we read that we lose our automatic ability to recover word meanings and piece together syntactic structures. What we need to explain, thus, is why the type of memory access that would reveal known outcomes to narrative dilemmas is not similarly automatic. We can accept Carroll's account of the swirl of thoughts that surrounds anomalous suspense without eliminating the need for an explanatory principle like the expectation of uniqueness.

These considerations suggest that we should have two different criteria for a successful theory of suspense. We must, in the first place, explain what narrative structures initially give rise to suspense, and why and how they do so. We must explain why, for example, the introduction of a ticking bomb could keep even *Concentration* viewers on the edges of their seats. We must then explain why some, but not all, narrative structures engage readers in a way that gives rise to anomalous suspense. Will that ticking bomb create a situation sufficiently engrossing to allow repeat viewings? By differentiating these two classes of narratives, we should acquire important insights into how narrative structures are situated with respect to cognitive structures.

CONCLUSIONS

The main evidence for the resiliency of suspense comes from situations in which uncertainty prevails against the force of perfect knowledge of an outcome. This phenomenon of anomalous suspense led me to suggest that theories of suspense must ultimately specify which types of narratives permit the experience, but not the re-experience of suspense, and which permit both. My own research into the origins of suspense has taken its inspiration from the insights of both authors and readers. From both of these sources, we can learn what kinds of narrative structures habitually foster suspense.

REFERENCES

Brewer, W. F., & Lichtenstein, E. H. (1981). Event schemas, story schemas, and story grammars. In J. Long & A. Baddeley (Eds.), *Attention and performance IX* (pp. 363–379). Hillsdale, NJ: Lawrence Erlbaum Associates.

Brewer, W. F., & Lichtenstein, E. H. (1982). Stories are to entertain: A structural-affect theory of stories. *Journal of Pragmatics, 6,* 473–486.

Brewer, W. F., & Ohtsuka, K. (1988a). Story structure, characterization, just world organization, and reader affect in American and Hungarian short stories. *Poetics, 17,* 395–415.

Brewer, W. F., & Ohtsuka, K. (1988b). Story structure and reader affect in American and Hungarian short stories. In C. Martindale (Ed.), *Psychological approaches to the study of literary narratives* (pp. 133–158). Hamburg, Germany: Buske.

Duncker, K. (1945). On problem solving. *Psychological Monographs, 58* (5, Whole No. 270).

Fleming, I. (1954). *Casino royale.* New York: Macmillan.

Gerrig, R. J. (1989a). Reexperiencing fiction and non-fiction. *Journal of Aesthetics and Art Criticism*, *47*, 277–280.
Gerrig, R. J. (1989b). Suspense in the absence of uncertainty. *Journal of Memory and Language*, *28*, 633–648.
Gerrig, R. J. (1993). *Experiencing narrative worlds*. New Haven, CT: Yale University Press.
Gerrig, R. J., & Bernardo, A. B. I. (1994). Readers as problem-solvers in the experience of suspense. *Poetics*, *22*, 459–472.
Logan, G. D. (1988). Toward an instance theory of automatization. *Psychological Review*, *95*, 492–527.
Logan, G. D. (1992). Shapes of reaction-time distributions and shapes of learning curves: A test of the instance theory of automaticity. *Journal of Experimental Psychology: Learning, Memory, and Cognition*, *18*, 883–914.
Slovic, P., Fischhoff, B., & Lichtenstein, S. (1982). Facts versus fears: Understanding perceived risk. In D. Kahneman, P. Slovic, & A. Tversky (Eds.), *Judgement under uncertainty: Heuristics and biases* (pp. 463–489). New York: Cambridge University Press.
Truffaut, F. (1984). *Hitchcock* (Rev. ed.). New York: Simon & Schuster.
Walton, K. L. (1978). Fearing fictions. *The Journal of Philosophy*, *75*, 5–27.
Webster's New Collegiate Dictionary. (1977). Springfield, MA: G. & C. Merriam.

7

vvvvvvv

The Nature of Narrative Suspense
and the Problem of Rereading

William F. Brewer
University of Illinois at Urbana–Champaign

This chapter attempts to give an account of the nature of narrative suspense and to explain why people read and enjoy suspense stories. It outlines an elaborated version of our structural-affect theory and shows how this theory deals with narrative suspense. The empirical literature on narrative suspense is reviewed, and I examine the degree to which this literature supports the elaborated structural-affect approach to suspense. The next sections of the chapter examine how various theories of story enjoyment deal with the problem of rereading narrative texts. Finally, I report the results of an experiment that examines the ability of the structural-affect theory to deal with the rereading of artificially constructed entertainment texts.

ENJOYMENT OF NARRATIVE SUSPENSE

Positive or Negative Affect?

The Random House Dictionary (1987) defines *suspense* as "a state or condition of mental uncertainty or excitement, as in awaiting a decision or outcome, usually accompanied by a degree of apprehension or anxiety" (p. 1917). This description of suspense leads to a serious paradox: Why would anyone read suspense stories for entertainment? Clearly, most people do not want to subject themselves to situations that lead to negative affective states such as apprehension or anxiety.

It must be the case that in some situations suspense can have a positive affective valence. This position is supported by other descriptions of suspense.

For example, *Webster's Third New International Dictionary* (1986) gives a meaning for suspense that has positive valence: "pleasant excitement as to a decision or outcome" (p. 2303). Literary discussions of suspense have made the point more vividly. Barnet, Berman, and Burto (1971) described suspense as a "curious mixture of pain and pleasure" (p. 107). Bartholomew (1977) referred to the "delicious agony" of narrative suspense (p. 23) and Esenwein (1924) referred to the "sweet pain of anxiety" (p. 202). Thus, one important part of understanding the nature of narrative suspense is to give an account of the affectively positive aspects of suspense in fiction.

Positive Affective Valence in Nonnarrative Suspense

Psychologists interested in emotion, motivation, and affect have noted the "anomalous" positive valence of some forms of suspense. The problem is to account for the fact that children find the experience of falling very aversive, yet children frequently enjoy being thrown in the air and caught. Similarly, most adults would find the experience of losing their brakes while driving down a steep mountain road to be very aversive, yet the same individuals will pay to ride on a roller coaster. Researchers in this area have proposed two basic accounts for these phenomena.

Arousal Jag. One approach is to argue that a mild state of excitation followed by relief gives rise to a positive affect. Thus, Woodworth (1921) stated that for situations such as those already described, "The joy of escape more than pays for the momentary unpleasantness of fear" (p. 489). Berlyne (1960) stated that a positive valence is produced when "the drive is aroused to a moderate extent, and . . . the arousal is promptly followed by relief" (p. 198).

Arousal Boost. A second approach is to argue that mild forms of arousal can have an intrinsically positive valence. Hebb (1955) stated that "up to a certain point, threat and puzzle have positive motivating value, beyond that point negative value" (p. 250). Berlyne (1971) stated that one can have a "situation in which a moderate arousal increment is pursued because it is satisfying in itself, regardless of whether it is promptly reversed or not" (p. 136).

This review of theories of nonnarrative suspense gives us two accounts of situations in which suspense can have positive valence. In the next sections I examine the application of these accounts to the case of narrative suspense.

Why Feel Suspense for Fictional Characters?

In attempting to transfer the construct of suspense from the real world to the fictional world we immediately run into another paradox that was nicely stated in the title of an article by Radford and Weston (1975)—"How can we be moved by the fate of Anna Karenina?" The problem is clear. In the nonfictional world, you feel emotions when you see other human beings placed in certain situations. Thus, most human beings would feel suspense if, during a flood, they watched the flood water rise toward a person stranded on a rooftop waiting for rescue. The difficulty is why one should feel suspense when reading about the same scene in a narrative in which one knows the character at risk is purely fictional.

Reader Involvement. It seems to me that to solve the puzzle of concern for fictional characters one must invoke some basic notion of involvement. It appears that when human beings read about a fictional world they can engage in a "willing suspension of disbelief" (Coleridge, 1817/1975, p. 169) and become absorbed in the events of the fictional world. A necessary condition for involvement in a fictional world is some degree of detail in the description of the events and characters of the fictional world. Thus, an abstract plot summary of a suspenseful novel can give the basic event sequence, yet it does not elicit an emotional response in the reader. A commonplace example of involvement with fictional worlds occurs in watching films. Almost everyone has had the experience of becoming deeply absorbed in a film and then having someone in the audience make a sound or movement that causes a momentary disengagement from the fictional world of the film and a shift to awareness of the actual world of the movie theater. The constructs of willing suspense of disbelief and reader involvement seem to me to provide an account of how the actions of fictional characters can give rise to actual emotions in the reader. However, one needs additional theoretical development in order to give an adequate account of the particular emotions a reader will feel.

Identification Theories. One very common approach to solving this problem is to postulate that the reader of fiction *identifies* with the character and thereby comes to feel the emotions that are being felt by the fictional character (cf. Zillmann, 1994, for a good review of this position).

Even though the identification theory is probably the most frequent solution to this problem, it suffers from severe difficulties. Both Carroll (1984) and Zillmann (1994) provided powerful critiques of the identification theory. In particular, they both note that the reader's affective state is frequently quite different from that of the character. For example, if the reader knows that the character's drink has poison in it, but the character is not aware of this fact, the reader feels suspense, but the character does not. Yet, under these circumstances, the identification theory would have to predict that the reader (who is identifying with the character) would feel no suspense.

Sympathy Theories. The other approach to the problem of predicting which emotions the reader will feel is to postulate that the reader feels emotions for fictional characters that are like those the reader would feel for nonfictional individuals in similar circumstances. This view has the advantage that it does not necessarily predict that the reader and the character will be feeling the same emotions. If both the reader and the character are aware that the character is in danger then both should be feeling the same emotions. However, if the reader knows the character is in danger, but the character does not, the reader can feel suspense whereas the character is perfectly calm. Zillmann (1991, 1994) gives a careful discussion of these issues.

STRUCTURAL-AFFECT THEORY OF NARRATIVE SUSPENSE

Over a period of years at the University of Illinois we have been developing a structural-affect theory of story appreciation. In essence we have taken some of the constructs about the nature of affect from the work of Berlyne (1960, 1971), Hebb (1949), and Woodworth (1921) and applied them to the domain of narrative, using constructs taken from structuralist literary theorists such as Chatman (1978), Culler (1975), and Sternberg (1978).

We have examined our theoretical ideas with artificially constructed texts (Brewer, in press-a; Brewer & Lichtenstein, 1981), with short stories (Brewer, in press-b; Brewer & Ohtsuka, 1988a, 1988b), with fables (Dorfman & Brewer, 1994), with children's responses to texts (Jose & Brewer, 1984, 1990), and with cross-cultural data (Brewer, 1985).

In essence, the structural-affect theory relates particular structural features of narratives to particular affective responses in the reader and then relates the postulated structural/affective patterns to story liking.

Discourse and Event Structure

A core assumption in the structural-affect theory is that there is a distinction between the events that underlie a narrative and the linguistic presentation of these events in the narrative. This distinction was made explicit in the work of the Russian formalists (Erlich, 1980) and has continued to play an important role in structuralist accounts of narrative (e.g., Chatman, 1978; Sternberg, 1978). We refer to the organization of the events in the underlying event world as the *event structure*, and we refer to the temporal arrangement of these events in the narrative text as the *discourse structure*.

Common Entertainment Discourse Structures

We have hypothesized that three of the most important discourse structures used in entertainment stories are surprise structures, curiosity structures, and suspense structures. We assume that each of these structures is based on a different arrangement of the discourse structure with respect to the underlying event structure and that each leads to a unique affective response in the reader. Figure 7.1 shows the basic event–discourse relationships and the postulated affective curves.

Surprise. We hypothesize that surprise is produced by including critical expository or event information early in the event structure, but omitting it from the discourse structure. By critical information we mean information that is required for the correct interpretation of the event sequence. Thus, in a surprise discourse structure, the author withholds the critical information from the initial

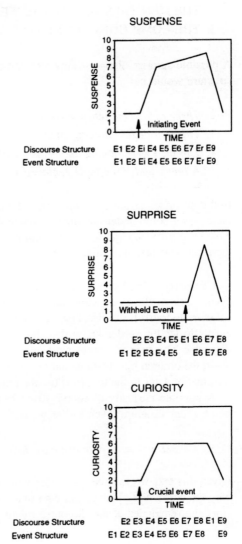

FIG. 7.1. The event–discourse relationships and postulated affect curves for three fundamental modes of discourse organization.

portions of the text and does not let the reader know that the information has been withheld. Then, later in the text, the author discloses the unexpected critical information, producing surprise in the reader and forcing the reader to provide a new interpretation of the events in the text.

For example, consider the following event structure:

1. ALFRED H. PUTS A BOMB UNDER A TABLE.
2. THREE MEN COME INTO THE ROOM.
3. THE MEN BEGIN PLAYING CARDS ON THE TABLE.
4. THE MEN TALK ABOUT THE WEATHER.
5. THE BOMB GOES OFF KILLING THE MEN.

A possible surprise discourse structure that could be constructed from this event structure would be:

2. *Three men came into the room.*
3. *The men began playing cards.*
4. *The men were talking about the weather.*
5. *A bomb under the table exploded killing the men.*

In this surprise narrative the author has deliberately not informed the reader that there was a bomb under the table, so when the bomb went off the reader should have been surprised and forced to rethink his or her assumption that the table in the room was just an ordinary table.

Curiosity. We hypothesize that curiosity is produced by including a crucial event early in the event structure. In a text with curiosity structure (unlike a surprise discourse) the discourse contains enough information about the earlier events to let the reader know that the information has been omitted from the discourse. This type of discourse organization causes the reader to become curious about the omitted information, and the curiosity is resolved by providing enough information later in the text to allow the reader to reconstruct the missing event.

A possible curiosity discourse structure that could be constructed from the bomb event structure given earlier would be:

5. *A bomb under a table exploded killing three men.*

Given this text we assume the reader will be curious about who the men were, why the bomb was planted, and who planted the bomb. In a traditional mystery story the remainder of the discourse might consist of having a detective try to solve the mystery of who and why the bomb was planted (cf. Bennett, 1979, for a more detailed account of the structure of this genre).

Suspense.   We hypothesize that suspense is produced by including an initiating event or situation in the underlying event structure. An *initiating event* is an event that has the potential to lead to a significant outcome (good or bad) for one of the main characters in the narrative. In addition, we hypothesize that the event structure must contain the outcome of the initiating event. In general, suspense discourse is organized with the initiating event early in the text and with considerable intervening material before the outcome is presented. The initiating event causes the reader to become concerned about the potential consequences for the character, the intervening material prolongs the suspense, and the eventual occurrence of the outcome resolves the suspense.

A possible suspense discourse structure that could be constructed from the bomb event structure would be:

1. *Alfred H. put a bomb under the table.*
2. *Three men came into the room.*
3. *The men began playing cards.*
4. *The men were talking about the weather.*
5. *The bomb under the table exploded killing the men.*

The initiating event was the placement of the bomb by Alfred H. This event had the potential to lead to a very significant outcome for the characters in the text. The initiating event comes early in the text, and so the reader should be in suspense about the outcome for the characters. The eventual explosion of the bomb brings to a close the events set in motion by the planting of the bomb and so should resolve the reader's suspense.

Suspense discourse structure differs from that of surprise and curiosity in one important respect. In order to produce the affects of surprise and curiosity, the discourse structure must diverge from the underlying event structure in the ways outlined. However, for suspense it is possible for the discourse structure to run completely parallel with the underlying event structure, as long as the text has an initiating event and a character for the reader to become concerned about. In actual suspense texts, authors frequently do not keep the discourse structure and event structure parallel. For example, authors of suspense texts often use flash-forwards to give hints of events yet to come in order to increase reader suspense (cf. Smiley, 1971; Sternberg, 1978). Brewer (1980), Sternberg (1978), and Oht-suka and Brewer (1992) have provided additional discussions of techniques for arranging the discourse with respect to the underlying event structure.

One important technique available to authors is to decide whether to give the reader knowledge that the character does not have (cf. Friedman, 1955). Authors of suspense texts often chose to give the reader knowledge of potential difficulties that the character does not know about in order to increase reader suspense.

Story Liking.   In structural-affect theory the various discourse organizations are related to reader enjoyment. In particular we have hypothesized that readers will enjoy narratives with discourse structures that produce surprise and resolution, suspense and resolution, or curiosity and resolution.

Just World Organization.   A crucial aspect of story content that must be considered in an overall theory of story liking is the interaction of character valence (good or bad character) and outcome resolution (positive or negative outcome for the character). Both Zillmann (1980) and Jose and Brewer (1984) proposed that adult readers will like texts in which good characters receive good outcomes and bad characters receive bad outcomes, but they will not like texts in which good characters receive bad outcomes and bad characters receive good outcomes. Jose and Brewer (1984) argued that this pattern of story preferences reflects a belief in a "just world" that derives from a more general sense of moral justice.

Hitchcock on Surprise and Suspense.   One possible source of confirmation of theoretical accounts of the structure of entertainment genres is through the discussions of these issues by those who produce texts and films for a living. It is encouraging to discover that the theoretical accounts just given are completely consistent with those of one of the world's most skillful crafters of suspense— Alfred Hitchcock. In a famous interview with Truffaut (1967) Hitchcock discussed these issues and continued:

> We are now having a very innocent little chat. Let us suppose that there is a bomb underneath this table between us. Nothing happens, and then all of a sudden, "Boom!" There is an explosion. The public is surprised, but prior to this surprise, it has seen an absolutely ordinary scene of no special consequence. Now, let us take a suspense situation. The bomb is underneath the table and the public knows it. . . . In these conditions this same innocuous conversation becomes fascinating because the public is participating in the scene. The audience is longing to warn the characters on the screen: "You shouldn't be talking about such trivial matters. There's a bomb beneath you and it's about to explode!" In the first case we have given the public fifteen seconds of surprise at the moment of the explosion. In the second case we have provided them with fifteen minutes of suspense. (p. 52)

ELABORATED STRUCTURAL-AFFECT MODEL FOR SUSPENSE

For the purposes of the present chapter, I elaborate on some aspects of the structural-affect model as it applies to suspense.

Significant Outcome.   We have asserted that the initiating event has to lead to a significant outcome. We made this assumption because we felt that events that led to insignificant outcomes did not tend to produce suspense. Thus, if a reader read a text in which the initiating event was that the main character's shoelace was weak, it seems unlikely that the reader would feel much suspense when they read that the character tied his shoe.

Positive or Negative Potential Outcomes.   We have asserted that the potential outcome can be of either positive or negative valence. Bartholomew (1977) concluded that suspense results from potential negative outcomes and Zillmann (1980) made similar suggestions, although he was more ambivalent. It seems to us that an event sequence in which a character has the potential for winning a lottery is clearly capable of producing suspense, and so we retain the assumption that the potential outcome can be either positive or negative for the character. However, we agree with Zillmann (1980) that, in practice, the vast majority of suspense texts involve a potential negative outcome for the character.

Good Versus Bad Characters.   Zillmann (1980) hypothesized that readers will not feel suspense for bad characters, whereas Klavan (1994) argued that one can build suspense for bad characters just as well as for good characters. I tend to agree with Alfred Hitchcock, who stated that one could build suspense for negative characters, but that the suspense would not be as strong as for a positive character in the same circumstances (Truffaut, 1967).

Outcome Likelihood.   A number of writers have speculated about the relation of suspense to the reader's subjective estimate of the likelihood of a particular outcome. Bartholomew (1977), Vale (1973), and Vanderbilt (1991) all argued that suspense is maximum when the forces of good and evil are balanced so that the odds of a particular outcome are 50–50. Carroll (1984) suggested that maximum suspense will occur when the odds are either very high or very low for a good outcome. This is another issue on which I do not have strong opinions; however, if forced to take a position, I would disagree with these theorists and suggest that maximum suspense will occur when the odds of a good outcome are very low. This is clearly a topic that needs some empirical investigation.

There is a peculiar property for all of the odds given in the previous discussion. In most formulaic suspense genres it is required that good characters have good outcomes. Thus, in practice, the odds are always extremely high that a good character will come to a good outcome. Therefore, it would appear that all of the odds given are calculated under some form of willing suspension of disbelief, in which the reader (and the theorists) ignore this genre-based information and calculate the odds strictly within the world of the story. Zillmann's (1991) view is one exception to this general assumption. He hypothesized that suspense is maximum when the character is placed in a situation with a low probability of a good outcome. However, he included the genre-based expectations in his calculations, so he stated that for standard formulaic texts the odds for a good outcome are very high. Therefore, he was forced to make the quite counterintuitive prediction that readers do not feel suspense while reading formulaic texts.

Character Sympathy. We have stated that when there is the potential for a significant outcome for a character, the reader must be concerned about the character in order for the reader to feel suspense for the character. On this issue we have clearly chosen to adopt a character sympathy approach and not a character identification approach. There are a number of good reasons to prefer the character sympathy approach. The one that has seemed decisive to us is that, in a suspense text in which the reader has been given information that the character has not, the reader's affect is frequently not the same as the character's affect (cf. Brewer, 1985; Brewer & Lichtenstein, 1982). Thus, the reader's affect is not identical to that of the character, as predicted by the identification theory, but tends to be similar to what a sympathetic individual would feel for a nonfictional person that the individual observed in those same circumstances.

Outcome Resolution. We have postulated that a successful suspense text must include the outcome of the initiating event. We made this assumption for two reasons. We thought that it was necessary for the suspense to be resolved in the discourse structure if the positive valence of suspense texts was going to be accounted for by Berlyne's arousal jag theory. In addition, many practical books on how to write suspense stories made strong arguments that successful suspense texts need a resolution. For example, Esenwein (1924) stated that "Readers still mentally threaten to pummel the author if the suspense is not satisfactorily relieved" (p. 202).

Mini Suspense and Resolution Episodes. In preparing this chapter it has become clear that there is one important aspect of our previous accounts of suspense that needs to be extended. We have always focused on the overall suspense and resolution curve for suspense (cf. Fig. 7.1). However, many of the authors of practical books on writing suspense stories have emphasized that to keep up reader suspense one needs a number of "mini" suspense and resolution episodes along the way, in addition to the macro suspense and resolution structure (cf. Bartholomew, 1977; Boulton, 1975, p. 53; Vanderbilt, 1991). Zillmann, Hay, and Bryant (1975) made a very similar argument to account for their empirical finding that children's liking of an unresolved suspense text increased with increasing degrees of suspense. Zillmann et al. noted that "Apparently, the suspense-resolution format applies not only, as a master plot, to the whole presentation but also to the smaller episodes of which the presentation is composed" (p. 322). Given these arguments it seems clear that the structural-affect account of suspense ought to be extended so that it includes mini suspense and resolution episodes (i.e., for longer texts the suspense curve in Fig. 7.1 ought to be "sawtoothed").

EXPERIMENTAL STUDIES OF SUSPENSE

As the preceding sections show, there has been much theoretical discussion of suspense and of suspense texts. Even though most of the hypotheses that have been proposed in this literature are open to experimental investigation, in practice, there have only been a modest number of empirical studies of these issues.

Significant Events. Brewer and Lichtenstein (1981) used experimentally constructed texts to examine the issue of whether significant events lead to suspense. In that study we had subjects read two texts (e.g., about a man driving home from work) that were identical except that one text also included an initiating event (a bomb with a timer had been planted in the man's car). As subjects read the texts, they were stopped at fixed points and asked to make a series of affect judgments. The data showed that the inclusion of significant events led to a strong rise in rated suspense.

Positive Outcomes. Brewer and Lichtenstein (1981) also provided data that make it possible to examine the issue of whether suspense can be produced when the potential significant event has a positive valence. Two of the texts used in the Brewer and Lichtenstein study used potential negative outcomes for the character (bomb in car, approaching tidal wave), and one used a potential positive outcome (finding a sweepstakes ticket worth $100,000). Examination of the rated suspense data show that all three texts (including the one with a potential positive outcome) produced high levels of rated suspense.

Good Versus Bad Characters. Jose and Brewer (1984) studied children's responses to suspense stories. We experimentally manipulated character valence (good vs. bad) in the texts used in this study and found that the children rated both forms of the stories as producing suspense, but that the suspense texts with good characters showed reliably higher amounts of suspense.

Character Sympathy. All of the suspense texts used in Brewer and Lichtenstein (1981) were designed so that information about the significant event was provided to the readers early in the text, but the character did not become aware of the significant event until the resolution at the very end of the text. Therefore, the fact that the readers provided high suspense ratings for the portions of these texts before the character was aware of the significant event shows that reader affect can be quite different from character affect in suspense texts.

Outcome Resolution. Zillmann, Hay, and Bryant (1975) studied children's responses to a television presentation of a suspense discourse structure (attack by a wild lion). They used various measures of physiological arousal (e.g., skin temperature, heart rate) and found that these physiological measures of arousal showed a drop right after the segment of the program that provided a resolution of the initiating event (shooting of the lion). Brewer and Lichtenstein (1981) measured reader suspense before and after the presentation of the outcome of the significant event in suspense texts. In the segment of text right after the outcome there was a dramatic drop in rated suspense that reduced suspense almost to the original base level.

Story Liking: Arousal Boost.   Zillmann, Hay, and Bryant (1975) found that television programs without clear resolution that were constructed to produce higher suspense also produced higher liking ratings. Brewer and Lichtenstein (1981) examined story liking for texts with an initiating event but no resolution and for texts without an initiating event (i.e., control texts). The texts with unresolved suspense were given higher liking ratings than were the control texts. Brewer and Ohtsuka (1988a) had readers (from the United States) read a set of American and Hungarian short stories and rate them at fixed points. We carried out correlational studies and found that overall suspense rating had the highest correlation with overall story liking. Thus the data seem to support Berlyne's (1971) arousal boost hypothesis as applied to narrative suspense.

Story Liking: Arousal Jag.   Zillmann, Hay, and Bryant (1975) found that experimentally produced television programs with clearly resolved outcomes were liked better than programs with less clearly resolved outcomes. Brewer and Lichtenstein (1981) examined story liking for texts with an initiating event and resolution (i.e., suspense discourse structures) and for texts without an initiating event (i.e., control texts). The texts with a resolved suspense discourse structure were given considerably higher liking ratings than were the control texts. Brewer and Ohtsuka's (1988a) study of American and Hungarian short stories showed that story liking was reliably correlated with story completeness (i.e., story resolution). These studies provide support for Berlyne's (1960) arousal jag theory as applied to narrative suspense.

Mini Suspense and Resolution Episodes.   As discussed earlier, Zillmann, Hay, and Bryant (1975) found that unresolved suspense television programs with higher suspense showed higher liking ratings. They were not expecting this finding and suggested that it might have occurred because their television programs had smaller elements of suspense and resolution imposed on the macro suspense and resolution structure. Gerrig and Bernardo (1994) carried out an experiment using modified texts from a James Bond novel. In Experiment 1 they compared one version in which Bond tries to hide his fountain pen, but is unsuccessful, with a version in which this episode is omitted. The version in which Bond tried and failed to hide his pen showed reliably higher ratings of suspense than did the other version. Gerrig and Bernardo interpreted these results as supporting their hypothesis that suspense is produced when the reader believes "that the quantity or quality of paths through the hero's problem space has become diminished" (p. 460). It seems to me that this finding might be better interpreted as showing that mini suspense and resolution episodes can increase overall narrative suspense.

Conclusion. Although there has only been a limited amount of empirical work in this area, the research that has been done tends to provide considerable support for the major components of the structural-affect model of suspense. The data support the hypothesis that suspense is produced by having an initiating event in the discourse that has the potential to lead to significant outcome for one of the characters. The data support the view that suspense can be produced by events that have the potential for either good or bad outcomes and that suspense can be produced when either good or bad characters are at risk, although higher suspense is produced when there is the potential for a bad outcome for a good character. The data show that when the outcome of the initiating event is given in the discourse suspense drops. Finally, the data show that both the simple occurrence of suspense and the occurrence of resolved suspense lead to higher story liking.

THE PROBLEM OF REREADING FOR THEORIES OF SUSPENSE

The issue of rereading is a significant problem for theories of story enjoyment. The data are simple. Many readers will reread a book for a second time (cf. Smith, 1985). Yet, this simple fact provides serious constraints on theories of suspense. In this section of the chapter, I review a number of theories of rereading and work out the implications of these theories for the topic of narrative suspense.

Uncertainty Theories. Many theories of suspense assume that suspense derives from psychological uncertainty. For example, one important recent discussion of psychological theories of emotions (Ortony, Clore, & Collins, 1988) states that suspense involves a "Hope emotion and Fear emotion coupled with the cognitive state of uncertainty" (p. 131). Kintsch's (1980) theory of what makes a text interesting is an example of this approach applied to stories. Kintsch stated that "Interest in a story derives mainly from the unpredictable but well motivated turn of events; conflicting expectations are aroused in the reader about where it is all going and what will happen next" (p. 89).

Uncertainty theories make a clear prediction about rereading. On a second reading, the reader will know what is going to happen next; therefore there will be little uncertainty. If there is little uncertainty there will be little affect, and so rereading should not occur. Thus, these theories are descriptively inadequate to account for rereading.

Willing Suspension of Memory (Voluntary Amnesia).   Another approach to the problem of rereading is to adopt the uncertainty approach to story affect, but then invoke a special form of suspension of disbelief in which it is hypothesized that the reader ignores information gained during the first reading during subsequent readings. For example, Walton (1978) described the case of a child hearing a text for a second time and argued that "She is engaged in her own game of make-believe during the reading, a game in which make-believedly she learns for the first time about Jack and the giant as she hears about them" (p. 26).

De Beaugrande and Colby (1979) also appear to hold a form of this theory. They stated that during subsequent readings the reader "must at every narration, compute the consequences of actions and reactions all over again. At turning points, audiences keep reconstructing the alternative disastrous states that the tracks inherently tend to lead toward, even though those states will not be attained" (p. 50).

Gerrig (1989) also appears to adopt a variation on the amnesia theory. He stated that "we have incorporated an *expectation of uniqueness* into the cognitive processes that guide our experience of the world" (p. 279). He noted that rereading a text violates this expectation, but that the reader ignores the information obtained from the previous reading and maintains "an unfailing expectation of uniqueness" (p. 279).

The theories that postulate some form of amnesia about the earlier readings make just the opposite prediction about the consequences of rereading from that made by the uncertainty theories. The theories based on the willing suspension of memory about the earlier readings predict that readers should enjoy rereading just as much as the original reading because there should be no change in the reader's affect produced by the later readings. (Publishers may not like this theory much because it also implies that one could be quite content with owning just one very suspenseful book!)

Shift of Motivation Theories.   The next type of theory is frequently held by theorists who have strong opinions about the differences between entertainment fiction and true literature. These theorists often accept an uncertainty view for first readings, but account for the rereadings of *literary* texts by postulating that other motivations come into play with later readings. For example, Allen (1986) stated, "It is characteristic of literary interest, interest in the work itself rather than in vicarious emotional involvement, that one wishes to read again and that works written with literary merit bear second and third readings, whereas those written only to produce vicarious feelings (thrillers, popular romances) do not" (pp. 64–65). Perrine (1959) proposed a similar view. He assumed some form of uncertainty theory for popular entertainment fiction. For example, he stated "If we know ahead of time exactly what is going to happen in a story, and why, there can be no suspense" (p. 64). However, he stated that a good interpretive story "should be as good or better on a second or third encounter—

when we already know what is going to happen—as on the first" (p. 64). He stated that on the later readings the reader obtains satisfaction from the fact that the characters are interesting or that the story is "morally penetrating."

Lever (n.d.) gave a very clear version of this type of theory. She stated, "A good novel needs and deserves re-reading; a bad novel cannot be re-read. Re-reading of a novel is thus a sound test of quality. . . . If the novel is good, we do not miss the suspense of not knowing what is to happen next" (p. 50). She concluded that during a rereading, "We are not hurried along by curiosity and thus have more inclination to observe details. These details now carry a significance we could not note at the time" (p. 51).

The shift of motivation theories make the clear prediction that people will reread literary fiction but not popular entertainment fiction. Because many people do reread popular fiction, this class of theories is descriptively inadequate.

Modes of Reading.   C. S. Lewis (1947) proposed a theory similar to the shift of motivation theory except that he applied it to different types of readers instead of different types of genres. He noted that some readers read primarily for excitement, which he defined as "the alternate tension and appeasement of imagined anxiety" (p. 93). He stated that "excitement . . . is just what must disappear from a second reading" (p. 102). He proposed that "We do not enjoy a story fully at the first reading. Not till the curiosity, the sheer narrative lust, has been given its sop and laid asleep, are we at leisure to savour the real beauties" (p. 103). He noted that other readers read the same texts for the atmosphere and the imagination and that the way to distinguish the two types of readers is that those who read for excitement will not reread texts, whereas those who read for atmosphere and imagination will engage in multiple readings.

This theory makes a strong individual difference prediction, hypothesizing that some readers will reread and some will not, and that the two types of readers will show different affective states during both first and second readings.

Character Identification.   Another common approach to story enjoyment is to postulate that the reader's affective states are derived by his or her identification with one or more of the characters in the fictional world (see Zillmann, 1994, for a review of these theories). In general, character identification theories will predict no change in reader affect and enjoyment during rereading, because the characters' circumstances and emotions will remain constant on a second reading. Thus, these theories, like the willing suspense of memory theories, predict that there should be no change in the reader's affect with repeated readings.

Vicarious Doubt.   Lipsky (1956) developed a somewhat more sophisticated version of identification theory. He stated that "emotional identification is the basic thing on which storytelling depends" (p. 108). He made a distinction between real doubt (i.e., uncertainty) and vicarious doubt. He asserted that suspense is based on the reader experiencing vicarious doubt, which he defined as "doubt shared by the reader with the fictional actor as to the outcome of the fictional intention. This sharing of doubt arises through emotional identification of the reader with the fictional actor" (pp. 107–108).

Lipsky made the explicit prediction (p. 107) that with rereading, actual doubt is eliminated but vicarious doubt remains and so some suspense is retained during rereading. Thus, this theory gives an account of why readers might engage in rereading.

Memory–Forgetting. Most of the theories of rereading already discussed assume that the reader has retained all the information gathered from the first readings. However, in real life I suspect that most rereading occurs after a period of time, so considerable forgetting should occur. Under these circumstances, all of these theories would predict that after a period of time rereading could occur, based on the particular mechanisms postulated to account for suspense on a first reading.

Memory–Capacity Limitations. Another aspect of human memory could also play a role in rereading. It seems obvious that readers simply cannot retain all the information in a book after a first reading. Therefore any information that was not retained could play its expected role in producing suspense on a second reading. Boulton (1975) made this point. She asked, "Does even an experienced reader ever take in a novel as a whole?" (p. 47) and concluded that, "This imperfection in our response is of course one reason why it is worth while to read a book, hear a symphony, or gaze at a painting more than once; but we may never exhaust it" (p. 47). The memory capacity theory would predict the occurrence of rereading, but with reduced suspense on a second reading.

Memory–How. Another variation on the memory capacity hypothesis is to argue that after a single reading one may recall basic elements of the plot such as the outcome, but not the details of *how* the outcome was achieved. Thus, one could postulate that rereadings lose some affect due to the recall of the outcome, but that rereading information about the details of how the outcome was achieved will still produce enough suspense to produce enjoyment on a second reading.

Armstrong (1977) seems to hold this position. She stated, "A good suspense story operates, even though you've read the book before. So curious is the suspension in which he is held, the reader can know exactly how it all comes about and still be caught up in the razzle-dazzle of the proceedings" (p. 13).

De Beaugrande and Colby (1979) also appear to have adopted this approach as one way to account for rereading. They stated that:

> Interest is upheld during repetitions of the same narrative because the audience predicts only global data, and rediscovers local data each time. It would follow

that enduring narratives—and perhaps art objects of all kinds—manifest inherent structural complexities whose processing demands, even after repeated exposure, remain above a certain threshold of cognitive storage abilities. (p. 49)

STRUCTURAL-AFFECT THEORY AND REREADING

This section of the chapter works out the implications of rereading for the structural-affect theory. Our theory is more complex than most of the theories of suspense discussed earlier. As noted earlier, the structural-affect theory assumes a discourse–event distinction and postulates three different discourse organizations associated with three different affective states. Therefore the phenomena of rereading provide a severe test for our theory.

Event–Discourse Relation Unchanged. One possible approach is to apply the suspension of disbelief hypothesis to the structural-affect theory. This approach would assert that the information about the discourse structure and the event structure gained in the first reading has no impact on subsequent readings. Thus, this hypothesis predicts no change in the levels or types of affect on a second reading.

Events Only. Another possible approach is to assume that on a second reading the reader responds to the text with the full knowledge of the underlying events that were obtained from the first reading. This hypothesis makes some rather interesting predictions. It predicts that curiosity should be essentially eliminated during second readings because the reader knows the true state of affairs and should no longer be curious about the outcome (e.g., the reader now knows how and why Alfred H. hid the bomb under the table).

The prediction for suspense texts is more subtle. If suspense is assumed to be based on reader uncertainty then it should be eliminated on a second reading because the reader will no longer be uncertain about the underlying event sequence. However, if suspense is based on the reader's concern for the plight of the character, then it should show little or no reduction during a rereading.

The events-only hypothesis predicts that surprise will be eliminated on a second reading because the reader knows the actual state of affairs in the event structure. However, it also makes the prediction that in many cases there will be a *qualitative shift* in the type of affect felt during the rereading of a surprise story. Consider Hitchcock's bomb example. There is a bomb underneath the table (a fact unknown to both the reader and the characters) and it goes off during the innocent card game. According to the structural-affect theory, on a first reading, this should lead to surprise. However, on a second reading, the events-only hypothesis predicts that the readers will not be surprised because they now know the bomb is under the table. However, during this second reading they should feel suspense as the characters carry on their everyday conversation about the weather because the readers now know that there is potential danger for the characters.

REREADING EXPERIMENT

This section of the chapter gives a preliminary report on data from a study of rereading carried out by Edward Lichtenstein and myself.

Method

The texts used in this experiment were similar to those used in Brewer and Lichtenstein (1981). There were three texts, all using the same set of underlying events. One text was arranged in suspense form, one arranged in surprise form, and one was a base form that did not include an initiating event. The initiating event early in the suspense texts let the reader know that the character was at risk, but the character was not aware of the risk until the outcome at the end of the text. Subjects were asked to read a text and then at fixed points were asked to make a series of affect judgments. Subjects carried out a brief filler task and then were given back their original booklet and asked to reread the text and make new affect judgments.

Results

On first reading the suspense texts showed an initial high level of suspense with a strong drop in the text segment containing the outcome (replicating the findings of Brewer & Lichtenstein, 1981). On second reading there was a strong overall reduction in the suspense ratings, but not quite down to the level of the base narrative.

On first reading the surprise texts showed an initial low level of surprise with a sharp rise in the text segment in which the crucial information was given (replicating the findings of Brewer & Lichtenstein, 1981). On second reading the surprise was reduced to the level of the base narrative. However, on the suspense scale the surprise narrative showed an initial small rise above the base level, with a drop below the base narrative on the text segment that contained the crucial information.

IMPLICATION OF REREADING DATA
FOR THEORIES OF NARRATIVE SUSPENSE

Story theories based on suspension of disbelief predict no change in affect with rereading. The data showing strong reduction in suspense and surprise with rereading provide severe problems for this class of theories.

Story theories based on identification of the reader with the character's emotion also predict no change in affect with rereading. The data showing strong reduction in suspense and surprise with rereading thus also provide severe problems for this class of theories. In addition, the identification theories cannot account for the initial rise in suspense for the suspense texts on first reading. In the initial segments of the suspense text, the character is not in suspense, yet the readers who know that the character is in peril report high levels of suspense.

Overall, the structural-affect theory fares considerably better. The theory provides a good account of the shape of the surprise ratings on first reading and their severe drop on second reading. The theory gives a good account of the shape of the suspense ratings on first reading. The finding that the suspense ratings on second reading show a strong, but not complete drop can be accounted for by adopting the memory limitations theory and assuming that our subjects were not able to recall every detail of our texts on a second reading. It could also be accounted for by a variation on Lipsky's (1956) hypothesis, in which reader suspense is postulated to be a combination of uncertainty about outcome (which drops with rereading) plus concern about outcome (which does not drop with rereading).

Our experiment was deliberately designed to be a very extreme form of rereading. By giving the subjects back their original booklet we set up the situation so that the subjects had to know that all of the information in the discourse was going to be repeated exactly as they had seen it before, so there was no possible uncertainty. In addition we used short simple texts so the memory load was minimal.

With more complex texts (e.g., those containing rich characterization and descriptions) it seems likely that the memory capacity hypothesis might come to play a stronger role in rereading. Similarly, with longer time intervals one might expect that the memory forgetting hypothesis might come to play a more important role in producing reader suspense during rereading. The structural-affect theory can be used to make a number of predictions about the rereading of natural texts (e.g., readers will be more likely to reread suspense stories than surprise stories). All of these issues remain to be tested.

ACKNOWLEDGMENTS

Much of the theoretical and empirical work reported in this chapter was carried out in close collaboration with Edward H. Lichtenstein. I would like to thank Gregory Murphy for discussions about some of the issues in this chapter and I would also like to thank Ellen Brewer (a serious rereader) for reading and commenting on an earlier draft of this chapter.

REFERENCES

Allen, R. T. (1986). The reality of responses to fiction. *British Journal of Aesthetics, 26,* 64–68.
Armstrong, C. (1977). The three basics of suspense. In A. S. Burack (Ed.), *Writing suspense and mystery fiction* (pp. 9–13). Boston: The Writer.
Barnet, S., Berman, M., & Burto, W. (1971). *A dictionary of literary, dramatic, and cinematic terms.* Boston: Little, Brown.

Bartholomew, C. (1977). The man in the closet. In A. S. Burack (Ed.), *Writing suspense and mystery fiction* (pp. 21–26). Boston: The Writer.

Bennett, D. (1979). The detective story. *PTL, 4,* 233–266.

Berlyne, D. E. (1960). *Conflict, arousal, and curiosity.* New York: McGraw-Hill.

Berlyne, D. E. (1971). *Aesthetics and psychobiology.* New York: Appleton-Century-Crofts.

Boulton, M. (1975). *The anatomy of the novel.* London: Routledge & Kegan Paul.

Brewer, W. F. (1980). Literary theory, rhetoric, and stylistics: Implications for psychology. In R. J. Spiro, B. C. Bruce, & W. F. Brewer (Eds.), *Theoretical issues in reading comprehension* (pp. 221–239). Hillsdale, NJ: Lawrence Erlbaum Associates.

Brewer, W. F. (1985). The story schema: Universal and culture-specific properties. In D. R. Olson, N. Torrance, & A. Hildyard (Eds.), *Literacy, language, and learning* (pp. 167–194). Cambridge, UK: Cambridge University Press.

Brewer, W. F. (in press-a). Good and bad story endings and story completeness. In R. J. Kreuz & M. S. MacNealy (Eds.), *Empirical approaches to literature and aesthetics.* Norwood, NJ: Ablex.

Brewer, W. F. (in press-b). Short story structure and affect: Evidence from cognitive psychology. In B. Lounsberry (Ed.), *Proceedings of the Second International Conference on the Short Story.* Westport, CT: Greenwood.

Brewer, W. F., & Lichtenstein, E. H. (1981). Event schemas, story schemas, and story grammars. In J. Long & A. Baddeley (Eds.), *Attention and performance, IX* (pp. 363–379). Hillsdale, NJ: Lawrence Erlbaum Associates.

Brewer, W. F., & Lichtenstein, E. H. (1982). Stories are to entertain: A structural-affect theory of stories. *Journal of Pragmatics, 6,* 473–486.

Brewer, W. F., & Ohtsuka, K. (1988a). Story structure, characterization, just world organization, and reader affect in American and Hungarian short stories. *Poetics, 17,* 395–415.

Brewer, W. F., & Ohtsuka, K. (1988b). Story structure and reader affect in American and Hungarian short stories. In C. Martindale (Ed.), *Psychological approaches to the study of literary narratives* (pp. 133–158). Hamburg, Germany: Helmut Buske Verlag.

Carroll, N. (1984). Toward a theory of film suspense. *Persistence of Vision, 1,* 65–89.

Chatman, S. (1978). *Story and discourse.* Ithaca, NY: Cornell University Press.

Coleridge, S. T. (1975). *Biographia literaria.* London: J. M. Dent. (Original work published 1817).

Culler, J. (1975). *Structuralist poetics.* Ithaca, NY: Cornell University Press.

de Beaugrande, R., & Colby, B. N. (1979). Narrative models of action and interaction. *Cognitive Science, 3,* 43–66.

Dorfman, M. H., & Brewer, W. F. (1994). Understanding the points of fables. *Discourse Processes, 17,* 105–129.

Erlich, V. (1980). *Russian formalism.* The Hague: Mouton.

Esenwein, J. B. (1924). *Writing the short-story* (rev. ed.). Springfield, MA: The Home Correspondence School.

Friedman, N. (1955). Point of view in fiction: The development of a critical concept. *PMLA, 70,* 1160–1184.

Gerrig, R. J. (1989). Reexperiencing fiction and non-fiction. *Journal of Aesthetics and Art Criticism, 47,* 277–280.

Gerrig, R. J., & Bernardo, A. B. I. (1994). Readers as problem-solvers in the experience of suspense. *Poetics, 22,* 459–472.

Hebb, D. O. (1949). *The organization of behavior.* New York: Wiley.

Hebb, D. O. (1955). Drives and the C.N.S. (Conceptual Nervous System). *Psychological Review, 62,* 243–254.

Jose, P. E., & Brewer, W. F. (1984). Development of story liking: Character identification, suspense, and outcome resolution. *Developmental Psychology, 20,* 911–924.

Jose, P. E., & Brewer, W. F. (1990). Early grade school children's liking of script and suspense story structures. *Journal of Reading Behavior, 22,* 355–372.

Kintsch, W. (1980). Learning from text, levels of comprehension, or: why anyone would read a story anyway. *Poetics, 9,* 87–98.

Klavan, A. (1994, May). The uses of suspense. *The Writer, 107*(5), 13–15, 22.

Lever, K. (n.d.). *The novel and the reader.* New York: Appleton-Century-Crofts.

Lewis, C. S. (1947). On stories. In D. Sayers, J. R. R. Tolkien, C. S. Lewis, A. O. Barfield, G. Mathew, & W. H. Lewis (Eds.), *Essays presented to Charles Williams* (pp. 90–105). London: Oxford University Press.

Lipsky, E. (1956). Suspense. In H. Brean (Ed.), *The mystery writer's handbook* (pp. 103–112). New York: Harper.

Ohtsuka, K., & Brewer, W. F. (1992). Discourse organization in the comprehension of temporal order in narrative texts. *Discourse Processes, 15,* 317–336.

Ortony, A., Clore, G. L., & Collins, A. (1988). *The cognitive structure of emotions.* Cambridge, UK: Cambridge University Press.

Perrine, L. (1959). *Story and structure.* New York: Harcourt, Brace.

Radford, C., & Weston, M. (1975). How can we be moved by the fate of Anna Karenina? *Proceedings of the Aristotelian Society* (Supplementary Volume), *49,* 67–80.

Random House Dictionary of the English Language (Unabridged, 2nd ed.). (1987). New York: Random House.

Smiley, S. (1971). *Playwriting: The structure of action.* Englewood Cliffs, NJ: Prentice-Hall.

Smith, L. A. (1985). Rereading: A response to literature. *Dissertation Abstracts International, 45,* 2382-A.

Sternberg, M. (1978). *Expositional modes and temporal ordering in fiction.* Baltimore: Johns Hopkins University Press.

Truffaut, F. (1967). *Hitchcock.* New York: Simon & Schuster.

Vale, E. (1973). *The technique of screenplay writing* (rev. & enlarged ed.). New York: Grossett & Dunlap.

Vanderbilt, H. (1991, January). How to put suspense in your story. *The Writer, 104*(1), 19–21, 47.

Walton, K. L. (1978). Fearing fictions. *Journal of Philosophy, 75,* 5–27.

Webster's Third New International Dictionary (Unabridged). (1986). Springfield, MA: Merriam-Webster.

Woodworth, R. S. (1921). *Psychology: A study of mental life.* New York: Henry Holt.

Zillmann, D. (1980). Anatomy of suspense. In P. H. Tannenbaum (Ed.), *The entertainment functions of television* (pp. 133–163). Hillsdale, NJ: Lawrence Erlbaum Associates.

Zillmann, D. (1991). The logic of suspense and mystery. In J. Bryant & D. Zillmann (Eds.), *Responding to the screen: Reception and reaction processes* (pp. 281–303). Hillsdale, NJ: Lawrence Erlbaum Associates.

Zillmann, D. (1994). Mechanisms of emotional involvement with drama. *Poetics, 23,* 33–51.

Zillmann, D., Hay, T. A., & Bryant, J. (1975). The effect of suspense and its resolution on the appreciation of dramatic presentations. *Journal of Research in Personality, 9,* 307–323.

8

▼▼▼▼▼▼▼

Cognitive Modeling of Suspense-Inducing Structures in Narrative Films

Peter Ohler
University of Passau

Gerhild Nieding
Technical University of Berlin

THE COGNITIVE PERSPECTIVE

Cognitive psychology is concerned with the study of cognitive structures and the processes underlying human information processing. This approach generally assumes that information about all aspects of the environment that are important for a natural cognitive system, is mentally represented. Cognitive operations are carried out on these representations to produce an integrative representation of the environment that allows adequate behavioral responses.

The cognitive information processing that takes place during the process of reception of a film story is dominated by the organization and content of the mental model the viewer forms of the story. So-called situation models (a specific type of mental models, cf. van Dijk & Kintsch, 1983) describe the representation of the central actors in a story and their motives, the development of the plot, the central themes, and so on (cf. Ohler, 1994). Whereas mental models of more complex film stories may vary from viewer to viewer (both during the reception process and after reception of the whole story), the set of cognitive operations, which is responsible for the construction and modification of mental models, remains quite constant.

Cognitive psychology assumes that cognition—which, alongside motivation and emotion, is one of the basic human psychological functions—plays the dominant role in predicting the experience of suspense during the viewing of a film.[1]

---

[1]Emotional processes evoked by the viewing of audiovisual texts are seen as subordinate to the cognitive processing of the film. Before the viewer can experience the emotional impact of a film,

The cognitive processes underlying the experience of suspense are seen as being largely of an automatic rather than conscious nature.

COGNITIVE MODELING OF THE RECEPTION
OF SUSPENSE-INDUCING STRUCTURES

Cognitive analyses of suspense phenomena may be carried out by either focusing on the text as a calculated structured proposal for the information processing of the viewer (cf. Wulff, 1994; Wuss, 1993a) or by focusing on the reception process (considered here as information processing). When emphasis is laid on the reception process, it is necessary to extend Wulff's assumption, developed from Bordwell (1985) for text analysis based on cognitive theory. Wulff (1993) assumed that text may be modeled as a "program for its own reading" (p. 327). Although his assumption may well lead to a fruitful heuristic for a research program, it would lead to a limiting standardization of viewers if applied to the analysis of reception processes. The "text may produce a model of the addressees" (p. 327) but it may not determine their method of reception.

A possible description of the suspense-inducing structural components, which may be realized during the different phases of the film production process from script conception to final cutting, can be used to generate implicit working hypotheses about the effects of the suspense viewers' experience. Such hypotheses may stand or fall on empirical testing of actual reception processes. Viewers would be free to develop their own mental representation of the text. (*Free* here is not used in the sense of having a completely free choice, but rather in the sense of viewers being free to choose their own idiosyncratic sequence of schema activation.) This modeling of the viewers' information processing would take a greater variety of individually generated internal mental models of the text into account than a text-oriented analysis (at least a variety of textual models that correspond to the dominant ways of reading of different viewers). It is just this variety of ways of reading texts, in which it is revealed which dimensions of the text are represented relatively consistently and which vary strongly from viewer to viewer, that throws light on the processes at work during reception.[2]

---

the text must be mentally represented—at least in a rudimentary form. Motivational processes are seen as the energy-related components of cognitive processing mechanisms.

[2]Researchers working in the field of reception aesthetics (Iser, 1990; Warning, 1975) have pointed out the imprecision of a literary text whose meaning only becomes clear through the act of its reading. It is doubtless that a similar criticism may be made for the process of film viewing. Nevertheless, in text-oriented approaches to reception aesthetic research, the "empty slots in the text" (*Leerstellen*), which allow for the different ways of reading, are overemphasized and unambiguous parts of the text are ignored. In contrast, in our reception-oriented approach, we believe that more emphasis should be placed on the interdependence of precision and imprecision in a text. Despite interindividual differences in the mental models readers form of a text generally, each model is commonly coherent in itself. Whereas empty slots allow for differences in interpretation, more precise text elements and structures are used to establish internal coherence within each mental model.

A text with a conventional form has a well-formed and closed cognitive sequential gestalt for the makers that, when looked at in retrospect, ideally organizes a configuration of schemata into an unbroken thread running through the text (Glowalla, 1981). Despite all dramatically motivated twists and turns, the text is coherently represented by a single abstract and congruent superschema. Nevertheless, such a superschema contains only the coherence structures inherent to the story, which are, in turn, settled at different hierarchical levels. The specific connections to the knowledge structures different viewers allocate to these coherence structures and the cognitive functions that control the reception process are not part of the textual superschema. Were such a complete description of the text structure available to the viewers during their online information processing, then they must not "switch" between different cognitive schemata. The viewers must, however, repeatedly modify their current cognitive schemata or group of schemata in order to follow the flow of information and to build up an organized model of the situation underlying the story.

Synopses of suspense texts may be written corresponding to manifest texts (cf. Wulff, in press), but not about the online processing during reception. The openness of the reception processes and the story development schemata created during these processes is no less than a prerequisite for the generation of suspense.

In the viewer-oriented approach, the different levels of expertise viewers have in dealing with suspense-inducing texts are a deciding factor in determining the viewing experience. From the information-processing standpoint, the complexity of different levels of knowledge—general knowledge about the world, narrative knowledge, knowledge of film presentation forms, knowledge about genre, and so on (cf. Ohler, 1994)—is responsible for different ways of viewing. During the formation of a situation model of a film story, experienced viewers construct an expectations horizon (*Erwartungshorizont*) that contains more hypotheses for the continuation of the story than that of inexperienced viewers. However, for strongly stereotypical films, rich in genre-typical structures, experienced viewers often construct a more precise expectations horizon with fewer hypotheses than their inexperienced colleagues. Because experienced viewers make more accurate interpretations of the text, they do not need to switch between [super-]schemata as they have pre-established expectations that will not be broken during the course of the story.

A further difference between the text- and viewer-oriented approaches to the experience of tension can be derived from the work of Bordwell (1985). His program for a cognitive film theory, developed from the point of view of the production process, emphasizes that the reception process may be understood from a constructivist standpoint. This means that particular elements of a text have the character of cues for constructive activities of the viewer, such as the loading of schemata. In the perceptive process, in this case in the perception of audiovisual text, only a part of the information necessary for the complete understanding of the text is available and viewers' knowledge, in, for example, the form of schemata, is required to form the whole or gestalt. Bordwell, however, assumed a rational viewer whose information processing is always bound up in goal-oriented processes, an assumption which, in our opinion, brings a restriction for the modeling of the experience of tension. It appears doubtful to us that this assumption of rationality can be valid for the specific question of the experience of suspense in the reception process. Modeling of the ongoing suspense-inducing process, which takes place in the context of the viewers' forming of hypotheses (e.g., about the development of the plot), cannot restrict itself solely to revealing the rules viewers follow. Furthermore, for a more complete understanding of a cognitive-induced experience of suspense, it is necessary to take account of factors such as specific variable assignment in schemata, associative moments in thinking and memory processes, implicit learning during the process of film reception, and intuitions about the rhythmical timing of a text. The disappointment of an expectation is a moment in information processing that clearly reveals a momentary deficit in adequate rules. Rules that normally would help the viewer schematically form a coherent internal model of the story are set out of use.

Two important information-processing mechanisms, which in conventional films evoke tension phenomena in everyday viewers (but not necessarily in theoreticians or critics), are characterized in the following. Note that all suspense-inducing mechanisms mentioned here are described with an average Hollywood production in mind as the standard film type.

1. The strategy adopted in the text succeeds in creating expectations horizons for viewers in which the probability of each possible outcome for the protagonist in a particular scene is similar; the outcome is "held in balance."

2. The strategy adopted in the text succeeds in systematically transcending the expectations horizon of viewers. A particular example of this strategy is when:

2a. The strategy adopted in the text succeeds in interrupting viewers' cognitive preference for building an internal model using a global coherence strategy. Through the use of suitable text structures, such as the strategic positioning of temporal ellipses in the audiovisual text, viewers are forced temporarily to fall back on primary local coherence building.

Expert and everyday viewers are able to see through the intended suspense construction (in which case the film will not be experienced as exciting) when the text does not succeed in irritating, questioning, or attacking the structure of expectations and hypotheses that the viewers form in the course of watching the film. This would be the case, for example, when suitable macrostructures, which allow global coherence building, are always available and the coherence-building process is not disturbed. Furthermore, an increase in suspense cannot occur when possible outcomes for the protagonists have already been reduced to certainties in the reception process. Here, Wulff (1994, in press) correctly pointed out that text-oriented analyses must also include a historical dimension. That which has been found to be exciting must not always remain so. When the strategy by which a plot unfolds becomes so conventionalized that the intended unpredictability is no longer guaranteed for the viewers, when the strategic game with their knowledge structures no longer succeeds, then the suspense-inducing construction degenerates into a transparent shell without excitement.

MODELING OF UNCERTAIN OUTCOMES FOR THE PROTAGONIST USING SCHEMA THEORY

In the majority of the more conventional thriller, detective, adventure/action, and horror films, which do not rely mainly on shock effects, the viewer's experience of suspense is based on the establishment and maintenance of a simple double-option decision situation (binary decision) of possible outcomes for the protagonist. The simplest example is the so-called trivial case (Kessler, 1994; cf. also Carroll, 1984): Does the hero manage to catch the bus or not? Such double-option decisions, however, are generally interwoven in a more complicated form within the plot as a whole and are most effective at "turning points in the plot" (*plot points*; cf. Wuss, 1993a, 1993b). Here, the potential for suspense is based on dichotomies of the sort: Is the protagonist dreaming everything or is he proceeding in the reality of the world of the story?

An example of a more recent Hollywood production with a dichotomy anchored on a central plot point may be found in a scene from the film *Total Recall* (1990; Paul Verhoeven). The outline of this science fiction film is as follows: A secret agent from the Martian government is implanted with a new identity in order to uncover the leader of a revolt of the Martian inhabitants against their governor. The protagonist (played by Arnold Schwarzenegger) is not aware of his role in this plan and believes that he is acting from his own motives, which, in itself, is a part of the implantation. To get behind his apparently lost identity, he visits the Recall Institute to experience an imaginary episode on Mars. After this is aborted, and a following "mad chase," he eventually travels to Mars himself. In researching into his identity, he unwittingly almost helps realize the plans of the Martian governor and his alter ego (the secret agent who allows himself to be implanted with another identity). But as his new identity has started to achieve a more stable psychic state, he succeeds in opposing the reintegration of his former self. At the last minute, therefore, he manages to help the morally justifiable cause of the Martian inhabitants to victory.

The scene we should use to describe the connection between a plot point and the dichotomy of outcomes for the protagonist takes place in the Mars Hilton. The theme of the conversation between the main protagonist (Schwarzenegger), a female agent who is said to be his wife (played by Sharon Stone), and a supposed doctor from the Recall Institute, is the question: Is the protagonist really on Mars or is he still in the virtual reality of his adventure in the Recall Institute? If he is still captured in an electronically simulated adventure on Mars, as the doctor and his "wife" suggest to him, then the female agent is really his wife and the doctor truly wants to help him out of a "schizophrenic embolism." On the other hand, if he should find himself in the reality of the science fiction world, then both his "wife" and the "doctor" are instruments of a giant conspiracy, and the main protagonist (at that point in time) is fighting against the dealings of the Martian authorities. Both possibilities are held open until the end of the scene, at which point the protagonist realizes that he must be based in reality because the doctor, in his function as a virtual projection, is not really in danger and has no reason to sweat in fear. Development of the rest of the plot is dependent on the outcome of this scene. According to the outcome here, the film will either develop into a modern variation of the psychiatry thriller or into a spy thriller. The function of the "wife" is similar to the function of the leading women in many of the "Innocent on the Run" stories from Hitchcock (cf. Möller-Naß, 1986) for example, in which, as here, suspense is often nourished (bearing in mind the connection between the romance plot and the action plot) from the simple basic dichotomy: Does she really love him or is she only a refined tool in the service of the real perpetrator?

The experience of suspense comes mainly from the tacit expectation of the viewers that they will find in the current scene the decisive piece of evidence necessary to make a decision between the dichotic alternatives that are of utmost importance to the protagonist. The construction of suspense comes from the game that the director, scriptwriter, and others involved in filmmaking play with the control of information. The viewer knows more than the protagonist, but not as much as the maker (cf. Wuss, 1993a, 1993b, on the difference in available information between protagonist and viewer). When this narrative strategy is used to sustain a general atmosphere of suspense for the viewer throughout a complete film, it is important that a particular number of such dichotomous alternatives remain open in the plot, or that they are opened or reopened as others are closed.

It is possible to model such information processing during the viewing of this type of film using schema theory and to characterize exclusively the suspense-inducing mechanism in terms of information processing without recourse to additional empathy processes. Before this is specified more exactly, however, it is necessary to provide a short introduction to the fundamentals of schema theory.

Human beings mentally represent objects, situations, and events in their memories that are relevant to their actions in the environment. These objects, situations, and events are organized into schemata that can be retrieved from memory according to need; for example, the presence of relevant stimuli in the environment. Schemata can generally be thought of as permanently stored structures and processes that actively provide the best "interpretation" of the information perceived from the environment. They consist of (generic) data structures that represent many layered configurations of stimuli from the environment as abstract information in a unified form. Schemata connect concepts and sets of concepts in mental representations to coherent structures according to principles of their causal, spatial, and temporal relationships. Moreover, they represent the typical properties and attributes of objects, spaces, scenes, events, and actions.

The concepts contained in schemata and their possible attributes are modeled as *fillers* that fit in so-called *slots* of schemata. The slots can be thought of as variables and the fillers as the different values each variable can take. So, for example, the age-range slot of guests at a birthday party can be thought of as a variable dependent on different subschemata (children's birthday, teenager's, and so on), that can then take on quite different values according to the subschema. The variables convey information about possible assignments during the encoding and assimilation of incoming information from the environment. Schemata are automatically activated during information processing and they organize the incoming information. The instantiation of a schema, that is, the successive assignment of (constant) values according to the best fit of incoming information to the variable slots, is the basis of this organization process in schema theory. The variable slots of a schema (cf. Minsky, 1985) can also be described as a statistical distribution of possible values the variable can take (cf. Rumelhart, 1980). Incoming information fits better into the variable slot of the schema the smaller the distance on the x-axis of the distribution between the value of the information and the modal value of the statistical distribution. When incoming information does not allow the instantiation of a specific variable slot, then the variable is assigned the pre-existing modal value (the default value; Minsky, 1985). The existence of a party place with candles would be assumed, for example, although these are not mentioned in a story about a children's birthday party. It is further assumed in schema theory that the variable slots are dependent on one another. Should a variable slot be assigned a value, then all other value ranges and statistical distributions (and modal values) of not instantiated variable slots in the activated schema will also be newly defined.

The information presented in audiovisual texts, however, cannot, even with conventional stories, be represented generally by a single schema, and it is usually necessary to use a configuration of schemata to represent coherently complex information or situations. The most suitable schema relevant to each specific aspect of the information is then activated and instantiated according to the encoded incoming information. Furthermore, all relevant and already activated schemata conceptually control the processing of new information.

The schema theory just presented can now be used to describe the information processing that takes place during the suspense-inducing double-option decisions situation in film reception described earlier. The schema or the configuration of schemata for the "outcome for the protagonist" variable slot (Minsky, 1985) does not have a single default value, but rather two, each with a similar probability of occurrence. Therefore, when a variable slot is seen as a statistical distribution of possible values (Rumelhart, 1980), there is not a single modal value (one default value) but a bimodal distribution (two peaks in the distribution, or two default values). While encoding the story, viewers attempt, in an automatic process, to reach a decision regarding the value allocation; they attempt to assign a fixed value to the variable slot of the activated schema or configuration of schemata concerned with the outcome for the protagonist. To do this, significant cues in the audiovisual text are sought. In the case of a variable slot with one default value or unimodal distribution of possible values, a delay in the value assignment because of a lack of significant cues that have been held back in the audiovisual text does not lead to any particular cognitive state in the viewer. The variable slot is temporarily assigned with the default value and this situation remains as long as no further textual cues provide information to the contrary. In contrast, in the case of a variable slot with two default values or a bimodal distribution of possible value allocations, viewers are not able to carry out an unambiguous preassignment. Their cognitive systems vacillate between two default values and they energetically seek the necessary significant cues they require to allocate a value to the variable slot (i.e., the elements and structures in the viewers' mental models of the story that correspond to the outcome for the protagonist are activated very much more than average).

When significant cues necessary for solving such a double-option decision are held back over a whole scene, particularly one in which aspects of the outcome for the protagonist in the viewer's mental model of the story are very important, then the demands on the cognitive system's allocation of variable slots are particularly high. These high demands form the cognitive basis of the experience of suspense and thereby the resulting emotional reaction to double-option decisions about alternatives for the protagonists.

The experience of suspense is heightened when significant cues for a value allocation that are required to clarify already activated schemata that are crucial to the further development of the whole plot are sought in the audiovisual text. In this situation, in the configuration of schemata, which are activated because of their relevance to the further development of the plot, many variable slots must be held open (i.e., they cannot be assigned with default values[3]). Until a variable slot with a binding function for the assignment of many other variable slots, which themselves are important for the further development of the plot, is assigned a fixed value, no default values for the unfolding of the plot can be instantiated. Therefore double-option decisions about the outcome for the protagonist at plot points (cf. Wuss, 1993a, 1993b) are potentially very suspense inducing.

The viewer-oriented description of the occurrence of suspense described here can be found in production-oriented publications and theory building as well as in film dramaturgically oriented work (e.g., Carroll, 1984) and is thereby nothing

---

[3]This aspect of the dynamic linking of a number of schemata is modeled in schema theory using, among others, a specific type of variable slot that contains procedural references to other schemata as possible values. In this way, splits in the plot development can be modeled.

substantially new. The value of the description based on schema theory presented here, however, lies in that the simplest form of suspense (but nevertheless one frequently occurring in conventional films) is modeled in a form that makes experimental testing of reception processes possible in the laboratory.

Despite similarities in their descriptions, there are substantial differences between the model presented here and the approach of Carroll (1984). Carroll assumed that viewers of narrative films with suspense elements unconsciously ("automatically" in our terminology) form expectations about the development of the plot, expectations that may be conceived of as implicit questions (and therefore Carroll named his approach a *tacit question model*), which they expect to be answered in following answer scenes. He described a type of question with binary alternative answers that can be seen as being analogous to the representation, in our approach, of double-option decisions about outcomes for the protagonist. Carroll (1984) also differentiated between *micro* and *macro questions*, which approximate, respectively, our minimalistic binary outcomes (of the type: catch the bus? yes / no) and our outcomes after pivotal points in the plot. On the basis of his model, Carroll introduced suspense as follows: "Suspense arises when a well-structured question—with neatly opposed alternatives—emerges from the narrative and calls forth an answering scene. Suspense is a state that accompanies such a scene up to the point when one of the competing, alternative outcomes is finalized" (p. 71). Alongside this question–answer structure, Carroll introduced the uncertainty of the outcome of the alternatives, which occurs in the question phase in the form of an either–or dichotomy, as a second factor in his description of suspense. As in our approach, narrative suspense depends on the effect of the relative probability of each of two possible outcomes of a situation: "Specifically, suspense in film generally results when the possible outcomes of the situation set down by the film are such that the outcome which is morally correct in terms of the values inherent in the film is the less likely outcome (or, at least, only as likely as the evil outcome)" (Carroll, 1984, p. 72).

Carroll specified the outcomes of situations in terms of two factors: their probability, and their desirability for the protagonist.[4] Carroll emphasized the viewpoint that suggests that a specific combination of mutually exclusive logical outcomes is responsible for suspense in answer scenes: The outcome desirable for the protagonist has a lower probability, and the negative or damaging outcome for the protagonist has a higher probability of occurrence.

On this basis, differences between our model and Carroll's concept may be seen clearly. We assume that suspense is induced when there is an approximately similar probability for each outcome and not when there is a bias in favor of the undesirable outcome. Carroll, too, presupposed uncertain outcomes in his model that would not

---

[4]Desirability for the protagonist himself but also for the viewer, because the protagonist represents morally desirable values such as excellence, efficiency, courage, commitment, and so on, for the viewer.

make sense for outcomes with a highly asymmetrical probability. It appears that Carroll would not accept the occurrence of an asymmetry of probabilities that would be strong enough to render an outcome no longer uncertain. Furthermore, Carroll (1984) used the term *probability* in a nontechnical sense and excluded the fact that viewers themselves, in one way or another, execute operations with these probabilities: "The idea of probability that I have in mind in this formula is a non-technical one. For a spectator to believe that x is probable is not for the spectator to assign x some ranking or value in terms of the probability calculus. . . . Nor does this imply that the audience is in its seat actively calculating probabilities of either the technical or non-technical sort" (p. 77).

This is the essential difference between the two concepts: We use the term *probability* in a much more technical sense than Carroll. Probabilities may be technically interpreted under the premise that suitable information for the unambiguous allocation of an internally preset value is not present (Minsky's assignment of default values cannot be executed in a simple way), whereas an internally preset value must nevertheless be allocated. Technically seen, probabilities can be interpreted as the values of the probability distribution of the possible variable values for the outcome for the protagonist variable slot. The probability density function for uncertain double-option outcomes for the protagonists would be expected to show a bimodal distribution for scenes with this type of suspense construction. Our model can be tested by gathering empirical data on viewers and computing the frequency of assignments at different points in suspense scenes.

Like Carroll, we do not assume that viewers "actively calculate" (Carroll, 1984, p. 77) in the sense of a consciously carried out operation. The allocation of a variable in a schema occurs automatically, but the operations thereby carried out may be simulated (e.g., as numeric operations on a computer). In so doing, it is possible to simulate with a computer program the hypothetical variable allocation in mental models of viewers. It is thereby assumed that the viewers function in a way that may be represented using operations with probabilities.

In our model, text processing mechanisms form the basis for the experience of suspense. In contrast to Carroll (1984), the occurrence in every scene of a specific value in a morally good–bad dimension is not a prerequisite for the experience of suspense. In the course of the reception of a film story, action elements and motives are brought together with a protagonist or group of protagonists in the viewer's mental model.[5] This foregrounding serves to establish a specific narrative structure in the mental model of the viewer where the protagonist is an organizing node for a specific perspective toward the entire story. Thereby, among other things, perspectives are established from which the desirability of possible outcomes is evaluated. Carroll's allocation of moral values, as described in the previous paragraph, is, from our point of view, nothing

---

[5]This can also—but does not have to—contain the allocation of prototypical attributes in moral dimensions.

other than an ongoing scene-specific adoption of protagonist-specific perspectives. This allows the retention of a pure cognitive description with only minimal recourse to evaluative processes. We do agree, however, with Carroll's assertion that it is not necessary to take account of ongoing empathic identification processes in the modeling of this type of experience of suspense.

MODELING OF TRANSCENDENCE OF VIEWERS' EXPECTATIONS HORIZONS USING SCHEMA THEORY

As already implied, a second suspense-inducing phenomenon is the possibility of transcending the viewers' expectations horizons. We have explained how elements of an audiovisual text provide cues for the viewers' hypotheses and schema updating. By transcending the viewers' expectations horizons, we mean that the presentation of cues in a text is manipulated so that the cues cannot be integrated into the viewers' mental models of the story. The viewers under those conditions are forced to fundamentally revise their systems of assumptions and expectations.

In the dramaturgy of suspense, as Wulff (1993) outlined, "a manipulation of anticipated future events" (p. 331) is attempted. This statement can be used as a heuristic for the description of the manifest narrative text and the production process of suspense films. It is a structural description of at least the dominant, planned, but not resolved potential expectations of the viewers. On the other hand, neither a description of the text nor of its ideal unfolding in the course of the reception can fully capture the online information processing of the viewers. The reception process itself may be described as a succession of repudiations (falsifications in the world of the story, so to speak) of schemata, thought, up to that point in the reception process, to be valid, and the following search for new schemata. The basis on which suspense is induced here lies in the systematic unpredictability of the plot development and in turns in the story, which in the idiosyncratic knowledge of the viewers about the genre and their particular memory traces for a particular type of stereotypical story, are either not known or forgotten.[6]

A master of the art of playing with the expectations of the viewer was Alfred Hitchcock. His dramaturgical film conception explicitly included the viewers and their most probable expectations so that the expectations of viewers could, on this basis, be transcended in a systematic way. In interviews with Truffaut (1989) Hitchcock commented: "That is right. They go to the cinema, sit down and then

---

[6]Suspense can only be induced with this mechanism when viewers, either during or before the reception process, build up a tacit expectation that their expectations will be manipulated. Besides that, an infringement of the viewers' expectations may not transcend the boundaries of a very abstract mentally represented frame for stories of that type. Should one of these conditions not be satisfied, transcending the expectations of the viewer becomes a means of creating "surprise" rather than suspense and, in extreme cases, it can lead to disorientation.

say: 'Show us something.' And they always think they know everything in advance: 'I know what's going to happen.' And I am forced to react: 'You know it, do you? Let's see, shall we?' In *The Birds* my aim was always not to let the public know in advance what the next scene would bring" (p. 279).

When the audiovisual text transcends the expectations horizons of the viewers, they search for similar experiences in a more local processing mechanism in their long-term memories. Something about the unexpected turn of events in the film they are currently viewing reminds them of something similar in another film, or in another context in life. Through this process, other schemata are activated and are used, in collaboration with schemata previously activated, to construct a coherent mental model of the film currently being processed.

A model of this phenomenon of schema elaboration assumes that pointers from previously activated schemata are placed on other knowledge bases according to primarily associative mechanisms so that informational cues may be matched with previously existing knowledge (cf. Schank, 1982). This matching process usually takes place automatically and is not the result of a conscious cognitive adherence to rules.

During the memory search and the associated reorganization of their mental models, viewers are in a cognitively unbalanced (because it is unorganized) state. Their cognitive system strives to return as quickly as possible to macrostructures that allow the development of the plot of the story to be organized in a global way. Furthermore, extensive updating of the variables allocated to date may need to be undertaken in particular situations, when, for example, the function of characters in the narrative framework is completely different to that which has been assumed so far.

A second key scene in the film *Total Recall* may serve to illustrate the process of transcending the expectations horizon and the necessity of extensively updating a mental model. On Mars, the protagonist is taken prisoner after he has assisted, seemingly unintentionally, in the identification of the ringleader of the revolutionary Martian colonists. Should viewers not anticipate the possibility that the implantation of a different identity was part of an overall plan to identify the leader of the revolt, they will be surprised to realize in the discovery scene, which takes place in the office of the governor of Mars, that the protagonist has been acting, probably against his will, as a double agent from the start of the story. This changes the protagonist's function for the whole of the story. A revision, which requires a reassignment of many of the variables in the mental model that has been developed up to this point, of the viewer's narrative perspective takes place: Is the protagonist in reality a villain? Does his new identity up to this point disintegrate? Can his female collaborator continue to trust him?

It is only in the next scene that this state of imbalance is resolved and it is revealed that the new identity of the hero does, after all, triumph over the old. Viewers, who had not anticipated the possibility that the implantation was part of an overall plan, may once again follow the development of the text on the basis of an updated mental model and with the aid of old but modified macro-strategies. Transcending the expectations horizons of viewers creates uncertainty corresponding with a dominance of local mechanisms of information processing in the anticipation of the further development of the action and the underlying motives. To put it metaphorically, the viewer's cognitive system is in a state of increased suspense.

Suspense constructions based on transcending viewers' expectations horizons run the risk of failing to trigger suspense as a result of excessive conventionalization. If viewers of *Total Recall* have anticipated the unexpected turn of events, they will no longer have an immediate sensation of suspense and will merely be able to identify it as an element of the dramaturgical structure. We believe, therefore, that this type of suspense construction would not play a significant role when a film is seen several times. This requires empirical investigation, however.

In terms of schema theory, the process of conventionalization can be described with recourse to the model proposed by Schank (1982). Information, especially if it runs contrary to the expectations of the viewer, is represented additionally in an episodic form. According to Schank's model, every time the viewers' expectations horizons are transcended, an episodic memory trace is opened. These experiences, which run counter to expectations, lead to the formation of indices for possible reasons for deviations from schemata. On the basis of these indices, these unexpected experiences are linked to the inappropriate schemata that were active in the situation of schema transcending. Furthermore, these indices are linked to viewers' memory traces whose context sensitivity was better suited to the interpretation of the information than the original schemata. If, at a later point in time, one of these previously indexed schemata is activated in a reception situation, then the indices for possible reasons for deviations from the schema will also be activated. These indices, in turn, activate information that refers to inadequacies of the schema for the organization of information in the current situation; they also activate index-related memory traces that may permit a better and more consistent information integration with a higher expectation conformity than the one in the reception situation first activated schema. Should viewers frequently encounter a particular type of information contrary to their expectations, they will, step by step, generate new abstract schemata from the combination of schemata, episodic memory traces, and indices involved in their attempts to interpret the situation. The new schemata guarantee a better interpretation of the particular type of information. Because they are systematically caught up by the viewer's learning processes, suspense constructions of the "transcending the expectations horizon" type must be innovative in order to work.

There is a comparable situation in the area of comedy. When Charlie Chaplin was asked if slapstick comedy would some day exhaust itself because everyone would know immediately how to interpret a banana skin on the road, he replied that the actor would then need to step over the banana skin and fall down an open drain. When that was sufficiently conventionalized, the observer would anticipate the open drain. Hence, the observer would, in the course of a learning process, infer from the examples of banana skins and drains an abstract formula such as "FUNCTION (Object 1 for possible mishap: unproblematic) (Object 2 for possible mishap: problematical)." In this context, therefore, slapstick must not only generate new causes and objects for mishaps, but also new scenic forms in order to achieve the intended effect.

A further local form of the irritation of the viewers' expectations horizons frequently used to induce suspense in films is the strategic placement of a temporal hiatus in the film text. Temporal ellipses are omissions of time with relevant action sequences in the audiovisual text that the viewer must bridge by inference processes. If the omitted information can only be reconstructed from the subsequent development of the plot or action sequence, the viewer is forced to generate hypotheses for the development of further plot or action sequences by means of anticipation processes that help preserve the textual coherence when ellipses occur. If they are to be effective in generating suspense, temporal ellipses must not be such that they can be bridged easily by generation of obvious inferences from the viewer's general knowledge about the world. Under these circumstances, suspense motivated entirely by the textual structures is evoked.

The information-processing mechanisms used to bridge temporal ellipses automatically can be described as follows. In the formation of a mental model of a story, cognitive systems prefer processing strategies directed to the creation of global text coherence (cf. van Dijk & Kintsch, 1983). If, for example, viewers can use a story schema (cf. Mandler, 1984) to globally organize current text information, local links between information units received from the audiovisual text only play a subordinate role. Representation of the text takes place via the instantiation of the story schema. This is cognitively more economical than the successive assembly of a text base as a result of the possibility to organize the information currently available. Local coherence merely serves to check the instantiation of activated schemata for consistency but is itself not integrated into the mental model.

At the time of the occurrence of a temporal ellipsis in the text, viewers have constructed a mental model of the story that should permit current information to be connected by the use of macrostructures. The temporal discontinuity in the action sequence, however, temporarily prevents the normal process of updating this mental model. The global schemata that were applied up to the point of the ellipsis remain stored in memory and new macrostructures are automatically generated that permit the organization, on a global level of coherence, of the text received after the ellipsis. These macrostructures, however, contain a high degree of uncertainty, as they do not yet contain enough information to bridge the gap. In this situation, the viewers' information-processing systems must take recourse to local coherence-building mechanisms in order to close the temporal hiatus and to find new bearings in relation to the plot (i.e., place, situation, character configuration).

The cognitive system attempts to integrate information elements of the locally constructed text base into the mental model as quickly as possible and to create a continued instantiation of the stored schemata relevant to the development of the plot. Any delay in these operations leads to an imbalance of the system and thereby forms the basis for the development of suspense experience.

A further scene from *Total Recall* can serve as an example. While still on earth, the protagonist repeatedly manages to shake off his pursuers from the Martian government. After a last successful escape attempt, viewers know that his new destination is Mars. Here, the film has a temporal ellipsis. Viewers see a spaceship landing. The color coding gives viewers the cue that this spaceship is landing on the "red planet" (Mars). The macroschema established in the situation model generates the expectation that the protagonist is landing on Mars. However, viewers cannot know this with certainty because they have not been present with the protagonist during the leap in time (and they cannot even be sure that it is a leap in time as the scene could also be showing a parallel scene taking place on Mars concurrently with the last scene). In the following scene, the protagonist is apparently not present in the immigration zone of the Mars colony. Largely resulting from knowledge of the genre, viewers have the expectation that the protagonist will only be able to arrive in the Mars colony if he is suitably disguised. This expectation, however, is not enough to enable them to completely organize the information they receive in a top-down mode. Here, the information-processing system is forced to switch to a more local mode. The elements of the actions present in the current scene are assimilated. Dominated by bottom-up processes, a schema of the scene and its spatial and functional conditions in the immigration zone is established. An abstract schema remains activated that the protagonist aims to penetrate this Mars colony, which is, as a result of the bottom-up-oriented information depiction, now mentally represented as well secured. Viewers search for significant cues in the film that will help them to anticipate how the protagonist will manage to enter the hermetically sealed Martian colony. Finally, it becomes clear that the strange fat woman will play a role in the scene. This assumption is linked with the search for the protagonist and the assumption is made that, in spite of the dissimilarity of the characters, the fat woman must be the protagonist in disguise. From this point on, the viewers leave the primarily local mode of the integration of information. Event-specifying macroschemata again guide the establishment of a coherent mental model of the story.

Temporal ellipses as a text strategy evoke an element of retardation in the processing of the information that induces suspense. It is not only the necessity of anticipating the development of the plot and the use of the text "to temporarily suspend the viewer's answering of questions" (Möller-Naß, 1986, p. 277) that are constitutive to these elements of suspense in the processing of information. The temporary invalidation of the schemata that would be able to perform this task most efficiently in the normal mechanism of information processing is also constitutive. Temporal ellipses, which can be bridged too easily by general knowledge about the world, are not able to induce this form of suspense. In such cases, inference is drawn directly and the macrostructures are able to unfold their organizing function in text processing without any interruptions.

THE FUNCTION OF PROBLEM-SOLVING PROCESSES IN SUSPENSE PHENOMENA

This brings us to our last point. It considers whether, and to what extent, the conscious adherence to rules, a domain that plays an especially important role in problem-solving psychology, has any significance in cognitive processes underlying the experience of suspense by the viewer. We include this point here because the German scientific literature on suspense in film often has recourse to psychological problem-solving processes. Wuss (1993a, 1993b) suggested, specifically for films with a continuous narrative structure and a causal chain between events, that the presentation structure of the film, that is its narrative strategy, could be regarded as the construction of a problem-solving space. As an innovative approach for a textual/production-oriented description, this model seems to us to be very fruitful. Thought processes, such as those described in the psychology of complex problem solving (cf. Funke, 1986), are also seen to play a major role in the reception of art films, which are mainly directed by the portrayal of ideas. The reception of such films demands a high degree of conscious, reflective information processing from the viewer who is striving to understand them. It can also be noted that in "suspense" genres such as detective films, viewers generally create a mental representation of problem spaces in the form in which they appear from the perspective of a protagonist. Wuss (1993b) suggested in this context that "Each feature film composition constructs . . . with the conflict it establishes a problem situation before the viewer, and this problem situation requires a solution; it is the film composition which controls the supply of pragmatic information which is suitable for the solution of this *problem solving situation*" (p. 103, italics in original).

Here, too, in our estimation, the viewers construct a representation of a portrayed problem situation or a problem-solving situation. In conventional films, that is, "nonart" and, in particular, suspense films, however, the heart of the mechanism of information processing, and the associated experience of suspense, seems, in our estimation, not to be, in itself, problem-solving processes of the viewers. The fact that viewers create representations of a portrayed problem situation does not mean that they act cognitively in the same way as a problem solver confronted with the sort of tasks commonly used in problem-solving psychology. In our opinion, Wuss aimed to provide a description of the calculated structured proposals of films that is as complete as possible and includes manifest perception and processing possibilities contained in the text itself. We believe that his approach should not be misunderstood as a reception theory in which the information processing in conventional films is modeled as a problem-solving process. Viewers of suspense films always have the option of mental relaxation, a state in which they can simply allow the problems inherent in the film to be solved by the film itself. Commonly, everyday viewers proceed in this manner and in their relaxed mental attitude, they still find suspense in the film. This attitude indicates that a fundamentally different form of information processing takes place in film reception than in situations in which test subjects are confronted with the tasks of problem-solving research.

In our opinion, the expectations viewers develop should not be modeled as problem-solving attempts. Even with simple interpolation problems (cf. Dörner, 1974; Dörner, Kreuzig, Reither, & Stäudel, 1983), problem spaces and the solving of problems are characterized by a consciously processed sequence of steps that is designed and able to lead to a specific goal. Even here then, we are faced with a rational, conscious adherence to certain rules that apply even more to the solution of complex problems. On the other hand, cognitive processes that evoke suspense experiences are usually the result of automatic mechanisms of information processing (e.g., in the example of the value assignments of a schema in double-option decisions). In cases in which viewers' expectations horizons are transcended, a significant role is played by associative processes of reminding (something reminds one of something else) that, at least to some extent, are neither conscious nor guided by adherence to rules.

The psychology of problem solving, then, does not, at this point, provide a suitable model for the processes of information processing in the viewer. Both in simple interpolation problems and in so-called synthesis problems (known original state, known final state, unknown operators for the transformation of states; cf. Hussy, 1993) normally achieving an intermediate goal brings the problem solver closer to the final goal. In both these forms of problem solving, in contrast to the reception of films with suspense constructions, the achievement of an intermediate goal cannot delay the overall goal. In film stories, however, this can happen to the protagonist. Achieving an intermediate goal in his or her goal hierarchy may make the protagonist conscious of the fact that his or her overall goal is far more difficult to achieve than originally assumed. The goal may even change dynamically. In the reception of films, it is quite normal for completely new spheres of action to arise from the resolution of a dichotomy and, with that, for the previous expectations of the viewer to transpire to be a dead end. This is something fundamentally different from a failed problem-solving attempt in interpolation and synthesis problems, which leads to new attempts at solving a problem.

A further difference between problem-solving processes and the deception of expectations in films with suspense constructions lies in the fact that, although in problem-solving processes it is possible to make mistakes as a result of false assumptions about the problem space, the problem solver is not led by the information provided to systematically make mistakes (as in some films that transcend the expectations horizon of the viewer).

Problem-solving processes for so-called dialectical problems (unknown original state, unknown final state, unknown operators for the transformation of states; cf. Dörner et al., 1983) are generally more similar to the process of transcending the expectations horizon. The difference is that dialectical problems are completely devoid of a clear specification of goals, which the problem solver has to reach, whereas the processing of conventional films by the viewer can also be organized mentally in terms of an anticipated goal (causa finalis; cf. Wuss, 1993a).

The concepts of problem-solving psychology are, therefore, suitable for the modeling of widely defined structures in the film text itself, which are enriched by latent reception mechanisms, and also for the modeling of the reception of very open, conceptually based works of film art, but not as a model for the processing of conventional films with a suspense structure as considered here.

ACKNOWLEDGMENTS

We would like to thank Dr. Hans Jürgen Wulff for his many helpful comments and Alan Amos for translating the text into English.

REFERENCES

Bordwell, D. (1985). *Narration in the fiction film.* London: Methuen.

Carroll, N. (1984). Toward a theory of film suspense. *Persistence of Vision, 1,* 65–89.

Dörner, D. (1974). *Die kognitive Organisation beim Problemlösen* [Cognitive organization in problem-solving processes]. Bern: Huber.

Dörner, D., Kreuzig, H. W., Reither, F., & Stäudel, T. (Eds.). (1983). *Lohhausen. Vom Umgang mit Unbestimmtheit und Komplexität* [The impact of uncertainty and complexity in problem-solving]. Bern: Huber.

Funke, J. (1986). *Komplexes Problemlösen. Bestandsaufnahme und Perspektiven* [Complex problem-solving: Overview and perspectives]. Berlin: Springer.

Glowalla, U. (1981). *Der rote Faden—ein handlungstheoretisches Modell zur Textverarbeitung* [The unbroken thread—an action-theoretical model of text processing]. Unpublished doctoral dissertation, Technical University of Braunschweig.

Hussy, W. (1993). *Denken und Problemlösen* [Thinking and problem-solving]. Stuttgart, Germany: Kohlhammer.

Iser, W. (1990). *Der Akt des Lesens. Theorie ästhetischer Wirkung* [The act of reading: The theory of aesthetic impact]. München: Fink.

Kessler, F. (1994). Attraktion, Spannung, Filmform [Attraction, suspense, filmstructure]. *Montage/AV, 2*(2), 117–126.

Mandler, J. M. (1984). *Stories, scripts, and scenes: Aspects of schema theory.* Hillsdale, NJ: Lawrence Erlbaum Associates.

Minsky, M. A. (1985). A framework for representing knowledge. In R. J. Brachmann & H. J. Levesque (Eds.), *Readings in knowledge representation* (pp. 245–262). Los Altos, CA: Morgan Kaufmann.

Möller-Naß, K.-D. (1986). *Filmsprache. Eine kritische Theoriegeschichte* [The language of film: A critical history of film theory]. Münster: MAkS-Publikationen.

Ohler, P. (1994). *Kognitive Filmpsychologie. Verarbeitung und mentale Repräsentation narrativer Filme* [Cognitive film psychology: Information processing and mental representation of narrative films]. Münster: MAkS-Publikationen.

Rumelhart, D. E. (1980). Notes on a schema for stories. In D. G. Bobrow & A. Collins (Eds.), *Representation and understanding: Studies in cognitive science* (pp. 211–236). New York: Academic Press.

Schank, R. C. (1982). *Dynamic memory: A theory of learning in computers and people.* Cambridge, UK: Cambridge University Press.

Truffaut, F. (1989). *Mr. Hitchcock, wie haben Sie das gemacht?* [Mr. Hitchcock, how did you do that?]. München: Heyne.

van Dijk, T. A., & Kintsch, W. (1983). *Strategies of discourse comprehension.* New York: Academic Press.

Warning, R. (Ed.). (1975). *Rezeptionsästhetik* [Reception aesthetics]. München: Fink.

Wulff, H. J. (1993). Testsemiotik der Spannung [Text-semiotics of suspense]. *Kodikas/Code, 16,* 325–352.

Wulff, H. J. (1994). Spannungsanalyse. Thesen zu einem Forschungsfeld [Analysis of suspense: Theses in a field of research]. *Montage/AV, 2*(2), 97–100.

Wuss, P. (1993a). *Filmanalyse und Psychologie. Strukturen des Films im Wahrnehmungsprozeß* [Film analysis and psychology: Film as a calculated structured proposal for the perception process]. Berlin: Edition Sigma.

Wuss, P. (1993b). Grundformen filmischer Spannung [Basic principles of suspense in film]. *Montage/AV, 2*(2), 101–116.

9

▼▼▼▼▼▼▼

Suspense, Predictive Inference, and Emotion in Film Viewing

Ed Tan
University of Amsterdam*

Gijsbert Diteweg
Leyden University

AIMS AND SCOPE OF THIS STUDY

Studying predictive inference in suspense films is necessary because the psychological status of viewer expectation is subject to current controversy. On the one hand, the notion of suspense is inextricably bound up with the concept of expectation; suspense is the very situation in which film viewers have to hang on (the literal meaning of suspense) to see whether or not any event outcomes will meet their expectations. Because suspense is very common as a device used in films, it would seem that the film viewer is very often projecting expectations. On the other hand, the research literature on narrative comprehension gives the researcher good reason to believe that predictive inferences are hardly ever made online, that is, immediately on decoding information that affords prediction. At the same time, research of the process of predictive inference generation is particularly scarce. This study is meant to fill this gap; more specifically, an attempt is made to predict predictions, that is, to specify in advance exactly what predictive inferences a particular example film allows its viewers to generate. The position is defended that suspense is a textual procedure that allows for specific predictive inferences, and that predictive inferences as part of an emotional response tend to be generated by necessity. The emphasis of this study is on identifying predictive inferences afforded by suspense film sequences in methodical fashion. Showing that they are actually generated online will be a secondary concern. The extensive analysis of

---

*The author is now at Free University Amsterdam.

the film's inference potential will also bring to light sources of entertainment other than suspense, and their relations with suspense.

SUSPENSE AS A NARRATIVE PROCEDURE

Writers and dramatists use suspense to evoke entertaining tension in the readership or audience. It is a member of a larger class of tension-provoking procedures. The concept of *dramatic tension* has figured in drama theory for a long time (e.g., Freytag, 1911; Pfister, 1977). Suspense has also been treated as the result of any retardation in closing the structure, in a wide sense, of a narrative text. Bordwell (1985) described various forms of suspense in narrative film distinguished by the source of uncertainty. For instance, action outcomes may dangle for some time, but the unfolding of some pattern of film style, say a series of frames of increasing size, or the development of a single long take, may also take some time, during which the viewer has to deal with uncertainty. Finally, suspense is often mentioned as one of three rhetorical devices in fiction, the other two being surprise and mystery (see Cupchik, chap. 10, this volume). Probably the best documented discussion of these three devices is in Sternberg (1978). Brewer and Lichtenstein (1982) demonstrated that the presence of each of them contributes to the readers' appreciation of a discourse as a story and their liking of it. According to Brewer and Lichtenstein, in all three procedures, there is an *Initiating Event* (IE) that creates anticipatory worry in the subject about the fate of a protagonist, and an *Outcome Event* (OE), an event of major importance to the protagonist's fate. The ordering of the plot determines temporal relations between the IE and OE. In suspense, ordering is chronological, and tension builds up during the interval between the two events (see also Brewer, chap. 7, this volume). In mystery, the IE is left out conspicuously, and the plot presents us with the gradual unfolding of the IE, creating curiosity. In surprise, the IE is left out as well, but inconspicuously, and the subject is unexpectedly confronted with both the OE and the IE. In suspense, events during the interval between the IE and OE act as retardation and thus strengthen tension in the subject (see de Wied, 1991). Alternatively they may heighten worry about the protagonist's fate (see, e.g., Tan, 1986), that is, increase hopes and fears, the responses seen as typical for the procedure's effects.

THE EMOTIONAL RESPONSE TO SUSPENSE

The response to suspense in film has hardly been investigated, but the experience of viewers of suspenseful television drama, closely related to that of film viewers, has been the subject of quite some research, notably by Zillmann and his coworkers (e.g., Zillmann, 1980, 1991; see also Zillmann, chap. 11, this volume).

Zillmann (1980) offered a review of experimental studies, some of which are referred to later, and Zillmann (1991) surveyed existing conceptualizations of suspense. His own definition can be regarded as common sense among researchers, and at the same time it reflects the typical narrative structure of the most popular suspenseful media drama. The latter concerns especially the sympathetic disposition viewers need to have in order to experience suspense. According to Zillmann (1991):

> The *experience of suspense* . . . is brought on by exposure to dramatic presentations as an affective reaction that characteristically derives from the respondents' acute, fearful apprehension about deplorable events that threaten the liked protagonist, this apprehension being mediated by high but not complete subjective certainty about the occurrence of the anticipated deplorable events. (p. 287)

The experience of suspense involves an emotional response, a state of fearful apprehension. Fearful apprehension may be seen as a prospect-based emotion, a class of emotions including hope, fear, and others, characterized by prospects in the stimulus of events that seriously harm or benefit the subject (Ortony, Clore, & Collins, 1988). In terms of a general theory of emotion (Frijda, 1986), suspense as a procedure causes the viewer to create a specific appraisal of the situation, in which another's fate is at stake, the other has relevance and a positive value to the viewer, the other's well-being is under threat, urgency is high, and the viewer cannot act on the situation. De Wied (1991) defined the response to suspense as an anticipatory stress reaction, prompted by an initiating event in the discourse structure, and terminated by the actual presentation of the harmful outcome event.

Suspense adds to the viewers' fun because the response to it always involves a sense of promise. Even if suspense involves a negative emotion, such as intense fear, there is always some prospect of relief, a promise of improvement, or at least an ending to the suffering. In Tan (1991, 1995) *interest* is proposed as the emotion that is sensitive to promise. It is the dominant emotion in film viewing, regardless of genre and phase of the plot. Every narrative film creates a twofold difficulty for the viewer, consisting of: (a) a felt lack of knowledge of the complete series of events and the ultimate situation in the fictional world, and (b) a problem faced by a sympathetic protagonist. Events subsequently shown contribute in some way to a final representation of the complete story that is rewarding as a solution to both difficulties. Interest is a response to promise of improvement rather than to the immediate effect of input events on the actual situation. More specifically, interest is a function of proximity and value of the final representation. The closer an outcome that is important for the final representation and the higher the value of the envisioned final state of affairs in the fictional world, the higher interest intensity is. Interest's action tendency consists of an inclination to allocate attention from a limited capacity to the stimulus, more specifically to: (a) actively elaborate input events, (b) anticipate future developments, and (c) invest sympathy in the protagonist and belief in a particular view of the fictional world. Interest is low when the final representation has low value, or is too remote, or both. Now in suspense, some important progress on the way to a valued final situation is sensed to be near. This is typically due to an acute threat to the protagonist's well-being. The promise is that an outcome is felt to be near, and this outcome is anticipated to bring certainty about a major part of the final situation in the fictional world, typically life or death for the protagonist. As a consequence, interest is high. A sympathetic attitude toward the protagonists, mentioned in Zillmann's definition, heightens promise and interest, as their fate is valued more strongly.

A WORKING DEFINITION OF SUSPENSE

By integrating the various conceptions of suspense as a narrative procedure and the viewer's emotional response to it, suspense scenes in traditional narrative films can be characterized as follows:

1. An IE occasions expectations regarding the nature of an OE.
2. The IE has relevance for the fate of a protagonist; it is appraised as a threat.
3. The OE is perceived to be imminent and to eliminate threat by materializing an unfavorable result; it is appraised as uncertain.
4. The fate of the protagonist is relevant to viewers; they sympathize with the protagonist.
5. Viewers feel that they are unable to act.
6. In observing the events as witnesses, viewers respond emotionally with fear, that is, the anticipation of the unfavorable OE, and the desire for the protagonist to escape from it.
7. Another emotional response in viewers is increased interest and tension, a readiness to witness the OE.

SUSPENSE AND EXPECTATIONS

Expectations generated by viewers of traditional films have been the subject of theorizing in cognitive film studies (Bordwell, 1985; Branigan, 1992; Carroll, 1988, 1990). Carroll's theory is the most general. He proposes that films have an *erotetic structure*, that is, events and sequences of events call up questions that are answered by events and sequences of events occurring later in the narrative (Carroll, 1988, 1990). Macroquestions ("Will good conquer, or will evil?") are posed and answered by clusters of events distributed across larger portions of the plot, whereas microquestions are posed by parts of separate actions, and made salient by stylistic means such as framing. Questions control the viewers' expectations. Bordwell's extensive account of viewers' activity in watching a film includes an extensive discussion of the kinds of *hypotheses* that viewers frame and test (Bordwell, 1985). He distinguished these from assumptions, on the one hand, and inferences on the other. Inferences, according to Bordwell, are conclusions drawn from implicit, schematic knowledge. Hypotheses are expectations about upcoming story information. Following Sternberg (1978), he distinguished curiosity and suspense hypotheses. A curiosity hypothesis pertains to past action that the text has not yet specified; a suspense hypothesis sets up anticipations about forthcoming events. Note that at any given moment of presentation time, both kinds of hypotheses involve an expectation of what is to be presented, be it events localized in fictional time earlier or later than the moment of fictional time represented at a given moment. In other words, in the construction of the complete sequence of story events, viewers have expectations of forthcoming events, some of which fill gaps in the provisional sequence as presented so far, whereas others extend the front of the sequence. Kintsch (1980) dubbed this twofold framing of hypotheses *bidirectional processing*, a combination of forward and backward inferencing, and deemed it a favorable condition for cognitive interest. Branigan's (1992) position deserves mention here, because he does not use the term *expectation*, or any direct equivalent of it, such as hypothesis. Instead, he studies film narrative as a way of perceiving by the viewer (a) fictional events, under the illusion that they occur, and (b) the ways the events are perceived and shown. Although Branigan described construction processes making use of schematic knowledge that goes beyond what is given, his account of narrative comprehension remains close to what is, step-by-step, immediately given on screen.

Bordwell (Bordwell, Staiger, & Thompson, 1985) described in some detail how the narrative within the classical scene regulates expectation:

> Limited kinds of resolution occur *early* in the scene, as old lines of action get closed off. And the dangling cause often leaves the scene unresolved, open, and leading to the next. The classical scene progresses steadily toward a climax and then switches the resolution of that line of action to another, later scene. From the standpoint of reception, this pattern enhances the viewer's confidence in understanding the story action . . . short-term resolutions also promise a final resolution as well. (p. 65)

Every scene, then, sustains curiosity hypotheses, by way of a dangling cause, and generates suspense hypotheses that anticipate short-term resolutions. These hypotheses may be tentative and crude. It may be that suspense scenes, in a narrower sense, afford generation of expectation that is particularly well articulated.

The functioning of suspense-driven expectation in film viewing and story processing has been demonstrated more or less directly. Cantor, Ziemke, and

Sparks (1984) reported a higher emotional response in conditions under which viewers receive a warning preceding a fear-provoking scene. This may increase the salience of the initiating event, thus favoring generation of specific expectations concerning the outcome. The results of a number of well-known experiments carried out by Lazarus and his group during the 1960s may be interpreted in a similar vein (Lazarus, Averill, & Opton, 1970; see also references in de Wied, 1991). They showed films that signaled threat. Anticipatory fear was measured and fearful expectations appeared sensitive to experimentally induced coping. Albritton and Gerrig (1991) made plausible that readers generate *preference responses*, that is, hopes and preferences in terms of outcomes relevant for the protagonist's goal. They demonstrated effects of outcome preference manipulation on verification of sentences stating an outcome. Outcomes that were not hoped for had longer verification times than ones that were preferred throughout reading. Gerrig (1989, chap. 6, this volume) showed that in stories about historical and well-known events, readers temporarily forget, neglect, or disbelieve facts that they normally know immediately after suspense has been created. Resolving suspense eliminated the effect. Although the mechanism underlying it is far from clear, it seems like subjects' expectations of outcomes outweigh firm knowledge acquired earlier. The experiments just discussed, and those by Albritton and Gerrig (1991) and Gerrig (1989) in particular, render it plausible that outcomes are represented in memory in some form before they have actually occurred in the text. In other words, they support the notion of expectations.

THE STATUS OF EXPECTATION AND PREDICTIVE INFERENCE

Despite support for the existence of expectation, there is a lot of debate about the status of predictive inferences in research of cognitive processes in discourse comprehension. Expectation as referred to earlier, is—like Bordwell's hypotheses—future oriented, that is, a set of predictive inferences. To be more precise, they specify a causal consequence that is as yet to be presented. There is a logical argument to be made against predictive inferences made during film viewing. In film, as in other narrative forms, the action unfolds by itself, and closure of the plot is guaranteed if one just sits and waits. Causal consequences may not be anticipated, but generated post hoc, as explanations of events that occurred earlier in the discourse, and possibly only formed when the subject is prompted to give an account. In their recent and encompassing overview of the research literature on inferences made during narrative comprehension, Graesser, Singer, and Trabasso (1994) pointed out that, "Researchers have frequently proposed that causal consequences are not made on-line because there are too many alternative hypothetical plots that could possibly be forecasted, because most of these alternatives would end up being erroneous when the full story is known or because it takes a large amount of cognitive resources to forecast a single hypothetical plot" (p. 382).

In reviewing existing studies, Graesser et al. made it plausible that online comprehension involves mostly explanation of new input in terms of what is already known. (It can be shown that this strategy is computationally more efficient than the alternative, i.e., expectation-based understanding, in which each input is compared to expectations generated by earlier inputs; see Dyer, 1983.) Graesser et al. discussed six theoretical positions concerning the status of online inferences, only two of which explicitly allow for predictive inferences. The *minimalist position* on online generation of inferences (McKoon & Ratcliff, 1992) deserves special mention here. According to this extreme position, readers hardly make any inferences at all. They only form a more detailed image of the situation described to the extent that the necessary information is directly available. Readers barely look beyond the boundaries of the present situation. McKoon and Ratcliff (1992) gave an example of a situation that seems very similar to many suspense fragments: The sentence, "The actress fell from the fourteenth story" does not automatically generate the inference that she will die, in their view, unless local coherence requires that it is generated.

The minimalist position is in strong contrast with prevailing views on film suspense. It is hard to believe that a film sequence portraying a character falling out of the window would not evoke an expectation that the character will die. In cognitive film theory, a minimalist position on the issue of viewer expectations may be ascribed to Branigan (1992), as we have seen. Some caution is in order, as he did not deal explicitly with expectation. So-called priming experiments by McKoon and Ratcliff provide no proof that inferences based on causality are developed with respect to the outcomes of the narrative at a later stage. In their view, previous research, which ran counter to these findings, is not convincing.

The minimalist position has not remained unchallenged. For instance, it has been shown that readers routinely construct a representation of the protagonist's emotional state (Gernsbacher, Goldsmith, & Robertson, 1992) and the protagonist's mental view of objects and locations (Morrow, Bower, & Greenspan, 1989; Wilson, Rinck, McNamara, Bower, & Morrow, 1993). Also, and more importantly for the present discussion of expectations, readers have been shown to make inferences about causally related events that are globally, rather than locally, connected with presented events (Huitema, Dopkins, Klin, & Myers, 1993; Suh & Trabasso, 1993). For further discussions of experimental evidence that counters the minimalist position we refer again to Graesser et al. (1994). McKoon and Ratcliff (1992), however, themselves left open the possibility that inferences that go beyond strictly local coherence are only partially encoded. Graesser et al. similarly did not completely exclude the possibility that predictive inferences may be made during reading, although they stated that, in general, inferences predicting causal consequences tend not to be made: "However, a causal consequence inference is likely to be generated on-line if it is highly constrained by the text and there are a few if any alternative consequences that would be likely to occur" (Graesser et al., 1994, p. 382).

It would seem that suspense passages in film conform to these conditions. Classical cliffhanger scenes are highly limited as to their outcomes, the protagonist falls to death or does not, and it is very hard to come up with any specified alternatives. It would seem, then, that during suspense sequences of a film, after presentation of an IE, predictive inferences are made as to the nature of the OE.

IDENTIFYING PREDICTIVE CAUSAL CONSEQUENCE INFERENCES

In our study, we proceeded as follows. First, a film was analyzed and predictions were made of all important inferences, including causal consequence ones, that could possibly be made from one input action to the next. This procedure resulted in a *model protocol*, representing the course of comprehension of the film by an ideal viewer. Second, suspense sequences were identified in the model protocol on the basis of the working definition of suspense. Third, test subjects viewed the film and were asked about their expectations during suspense sequences and control sequences.

Film Analysis

The Film **Alaska.** *Alaska*[1] (Mike van Diem, 1989) is a short film (45 minutes) about a married couple, Mr. and Mrs. Koole. Mrs. Koole has a secret affair with Mario, an employee of the slaughterhouse owned by her husband. She helps him steal money from a safe in the slaughterhouse, but Mr. Koole catches him accidentally. He finds out that the lovers were about to leave the country together, to start a new life in Buenos Aires. Mr. Koole locks Mario into a freezing chamber, and Mario dies. Mrs. Koole also accidentally finds out what has happened and takes revenge by killing her husband the same way as he had killed her lover. A fuller synopsis of the plot is found in Table 9.1.

Description of the Plot. A detailed and timed shot list was made, which represented the action, including dialogues, and gave a description of cinematography. The consecutively listed actions from the shot list made up jointly the *event list* that was used for identifying suspense sequences and the prediction of suspense projections. The synopsis in Table 9.1, in the usual form of a summary, is an abstract of the event list. An abbreviated form of the complete event list is given in the Appendix.

The film is characterized by a thriller theme involving two murders. It is, however, somewhat less typical in that the temporal structure of the plot is complex. This cannot be seen from the synopsis, which has been made to obey chronology.

---

[1]The authors are indebted to Mike van Diem and the Netherlands Film & TV Academy.

TABLE 9.1
Synopsis of *Alaska* (van Diem, 1989)

1. Mr. Koole is the manager of a slaughterhouse.
2. One Saturday morning, he sets his wife down in town on his way to the slaughterhouse.
3. Mrs. Koole enters a drugstore.
4. Only a moment later, Koole, who is caught in a traffic jam, discovers that his wife left her shawl in the car and he gets out to run after her.
5. To his surprise, he sees that she has gone into a travel agency, where she receives airplane tickets.
6. He does not see that she writes the code of the slaughterhouse safe on one of the tickets.
7. Koole goes his way without signaling his presence.
8. In the late afternoon, when he has returned home, Mrs. Koole steals a key to the slaughterhouse from Mr. Koole's bunch of keys.
9. Accidentally, she drops his glasses, causing them to break.
10. Mario, one of the workers at the slaughterhouse, is having a secret affair with Mrs. Koole.
11. That evening, they meet at a subway station and Mrs. Koole gives him an envelope with a ticket, the safe's code, and the key.
12. Mario visits his little son, Miguel, in a gym and tells him that he, Mario, will be going on a journey.
13. Then Mario goes to the slaughterhouse, climbs over the wall, and enters the office.
14. He opens the safe, takes the money, and sets himself behind the manager's desk.
15. The telephone rings.
16. Mario waits until it has rung twice, he takes off the receiver and lays it down again.
17. He writes a farewell note to his friend at the slaughterhouse: "Disculpame! Mario," and attaches it to a bottle of bourbon.
18. Then, he walks to the freezing chamber to leave a bottle for his friend Carlos, who is also a worker at the slaughterhouse.
19. The same evening, Mrs. Koole leaves her husband.
20. She acts as if she is going to her drawing lessons, as usual.
21. Instead, she goes to the airport where she picks up her luggage.
22. She phones the slaughterhouse.
23. Then she sits and waits for Mario, who does not show up.
24. The airplane leaves for Buenos Aires without them.
25. After taking a look at the slaughterhouse, Mrs. Koole returns home.
26. After Mrs. Koole has left, Mr. Koole wants to assemble a construction kit.
27. He discovers that his glasses are broken and goes to the slaughterhouse to retrieve another pair.
28. In the slaughterhouse, he hears a sound of something hitting the floor but ignores it.
29. Then he hears the alarm of the freezing chamber. He sees Mario in the freezing chamber.
30. He locks the door of the freezing chamber and starts to call the police.
31. While ringing, he notices Mario's bag and the ticket with the safe's code on it.
32. He understands the plot of his wife and Mario.
33. The police answer and Koole puts down the phone.
34. He lowers the temperature of the freezing chamber and observes Mario through the TV camera for some time before turning the monitor off.
35. Mario has managed to hang a medallion Mrs. Koole has given to him on the camera.
36. The next day (it must be the weekend) Mr. and Mrs. Koole act as usual.
37. Mr. Koole goes to the slaughterhouse where he processes Mario's body into food for his husky dogs.
38. He discovers the bottle in the freezing chamber.
39. It has a note on it, saying: "Disculpame! Mario" ("Forgive me! Mario").
40. He mails this note to "Senora Koole."

(Continued)

TABLE 9.1
(Continued)

---

41. Mrs. Koole suspects that Mario has left her alone, and Miguel confirms that he is on a journey. But she is not convinced, and even "Mario's" note fails to put an end to her uncertainty.
42. She packs her things and leaves her husband.
43. She sets out in search of Mario.
44. One or two days later Mr. Koole watches his wife arrive at the slaughterhouse.
45. She talks to Mario's friend, Carlos, and is shown into the freezing chamber.
46. They look into the camera.
47. Koole goes into the freezing chamber and climbs to the camera.
48. He watches the medallion.
49. Then he perceives his wife in the doorway.
50. She locks him in and he hears her start the freezing engine.

In fact, the whole series of events is represented in three consecutive episodes, each limited to the perspective of one of the three main characters. Events belonging to each of the episodes overlap in time, so that some events are shown more than once, but from a different point of view. The episodes are the following:

1. One follows Mario during the first day (Synopsis events 10–18, see Table 9.1). Late in the afternoon, Mrs. Koole gives him a key, the code to the safe, and a ticket. In the evening he burglarizes the slaughterhouse.

2. After this, one goes back to the beginning of the story to follow Mrs. Koole (2–9, 11, 19–25, 41–43). Early in the morning she is shown buying a ticket, stealing Koole's key after he has come home from work, handing it to Mario, and, in the evening, waiting at the airport in vain. Then she returns home. After the weekend, she receives a note and starts to search for Mario, leaving her husband alone.

3. Again, one goes back to the beginning of the story to follow Mr. Koole through the day and to the end (1–7, 26–33, 36–40, 44–50). He is shown watching his wife as she furtively buys the ticket, coincidentally going to the slaughterhouse, and stumbling on Mario, whom he kills. The next day, he deals with the body and the viewer sees him finding and preparing a note. Back home, he sees that his wife has left him. On the Monday, or perhaps 1 or 2 days later, he watches Mrs. Koole's arrival at the slaughterhouse and her conversation with Mario's friend Carlos. Koole goes to the freezing chamber and his wife locks him in.

A complete understanding of the plot requires, above all, the grasping of the two relapses in time, the temporal overlap of the three episodes, the fact that in each episode knowledge is restricted to the character that is followed, and that the last one, the one that focuses on Mr. Koole, extends beyond the end of the former two episodes, ultimately rendering the time of the narration equal to the time in the fictional world. Each episode fills gaps in the representation of events constructed so far. For instance, the viewer does not know how and when Mrs. Koole bought the tickets handed over to Mario in the first episode until the beginning of the second one. Also, only at the beginning of the third episode do we learn that Koole has seen her entering the ticket shop and buying the tickets. Furthermore, repetition of many of the events functions as a cue to the temporal structure of the plot. They include the following actions: Mrs. Koole buys a ticket (Eps. 2 & 3), Mrs. Koole hands it over to Mario (1 & 2), Mrs. Koole rings Mario from the airport (his perspective in 1 and hers in 2), Mario accidentally drops a slaughter knife (shown in 2 and shown to be heard by Koole in 3), and more.

In spite of its relative complexity, the plot has an overall suspense structure in Bordwell's sense: Closure of the causal sequence is suspended until the end and retarded by the narration's repeated receding in time. These relapses, and thus retardations, are considerable. Each episode consists of scenes varying in time and place. Before the point at which the narration assumes the present tense (i.e., Koole witnessing his wife discover what has happened to Mario), curiosity builds up, as the viewer is only gradually informed of the past. It allows Kintsch's bidirectional processing by the viewers, as they are led to reconstruct a past in each new episode. Here then, viewers are led to generate explanation-driven, causal antecedent inferences (Graesser et al., 1994). At the same time, they may frame expectations about the future of the plot, that is, generate predictive, causal consequence inferences. Within each of the three episodes, the film contains a number of suspense sequences in a stricter sense that correspond to the working definition of suspense, as we see shortly.

The Model Protocol

Plot Unit Representation of the Film's Story.   In order to obtain predictions of viewers' expectations, the plot unit summarization model, developed by Lehnert (1981, 1982; Lehnert & Vine, 1987), was applied to the film's event list. The model gives a bottom-up account of narrative comprehension starting from elementary conceptual units and arriving at a complex thematic representation. The model has been shown to explain summarization behavior. It is based on two assumptions: (a) that elementary events are understood as a function of their value in terms of the protagonist's concerns, and (b) that viewers comprehend a story by representing characters' goals and plans. These assumptions are generally accepted and serve as an explanation of the comprehension of fictional narrative and ensuing reader emotion at large (see Oatley, 1992, for a thorough treatment of reader experience along these lines).

The first step in obtaining a narrative's plot unit configuration consists of the identification of the simplest thematic units, known as *simple plot units*, followed by the composition of more complex themes, known as *complex plot units*, consisting of combinations of the simple units. Examples of a simple plot unit are a Success and a Loss. More complex units include Retaliation, Hidden Blessing, and Fortuitous Resolution (uppercase is used to distinguish them from simple units). Situational ironies and other striking forms of regularity or contrast between elements of the action are clearly expressed in Lehnert's model. *In statu nascendi*, the plot unit structure enables the framing of expectations concerning complications and the ensuing solutions and failures. More precisely, in terms of the classification given by Graesser et al. (1994), these are superordinate goal and thematic inferences. According to Graesser et al., evidence as to online generation of thematic inferences is lacking at present.

In terms of the characters' goals and values, the model's primitive states, or *affect states* may be pleasant or positive (+), unpleasant or negative (–), or neutral (M). Those designated as + or – are events or, to be more precise, event outcomes, whereas M reflects a neutral mental state or mental act, such as (having in mind) a goal, a plan, or a preferred state that has yet to be realized. One affect state may relate causally to another in various ways. A mental state is motivated (m-link) by another mental state or an event, or it is the equivalent (e-link) of another mental state, or it is terminated (t-link) by another mental state or an event. An event is an actualization (a-link) of a mental state, or an equivalent of another event, or it is terminated by another event. Any event or mental state may have more than one relation with one or more other events or mental states. Affect state patterns can combine to form *primitive plot units*, such as a Problem (– –m→ M), a Success (M –a→ +), or a Hidden Blessing (– –e→ +). Primitive plot units, in turn, form *complex plot units*. An example is Retaliation (see Fig. 9.1a), consisting of a Mixed Event (+ — –), a Problem (– –m→ M), a Success Born of Adversity (– –m→ M –a→ +), and another Mixed Event (+ — –). In order to account for a thematic structure that is usually left out of summaries, but that is indispensable in comprehension, we have added a Setting category to the model. The Setting generates the main characters' goals and desires in which mental acts and positive and negative affect states originate (see Tan, 1986, for a demonstration of the necessity of this addition).

Alaska's story at the highest level of abstraction consists of two related complex plot units, one pertaining to Mr. Koole, and the other to Mrs. Koole, which together make up a dual Retaliation (Fig. 9.1a). At a more fine-grained level of analysis, Mario's share in the story is represented, as well as details of the two complex units, mostly consisting of nested subgoal plot units. For the sake of clarity, relations among clusters belonging to each of the three characters have been omitted.

The complete plot unit representation in Fig. 9.1b is considered to be the final cognitive representation of the film's story after the whole film has been presented. The events presented during the film can be seen as consecutive inputs that contribute to the piecemeal construction of the final representation. The inputs trigger thematic knowledge structures, that is, larger plot units. Any addition at time t to what is immediately given in input event $E(t)$ and its precursors is considered

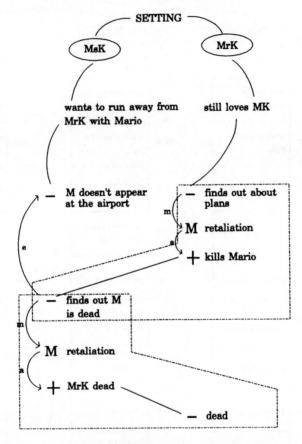

FIG. 9.1a. Complex plot unit Dual Retaliation. Each retaliation includes, from top to bottom, a Mixed Event, a Problem, a Success Born of Adversity, and a second Mixed Event. MsK = Mrs. Koole, MrK = Mr. Koole, + and − are valences of affect states belonging to character in same column.

to be an *inference*. Furthermore, any inference that specifies future input events is considered a *predictive inference*. Not all possible inferences are equally relevant. Those that have an immediate bearing on the plot unit structure as it is, including anticipated parts of it, are by hypothesis considered more relevant than others. Furthermore, some elements of the plot unit structure are more relevant than others. Lehnert (1982) proposed a number of definitions of connectivity within a plot unit representation. These definitions enable one to determine the structural relevance of plot units in terms of the number of relations to other plot units. For instance, a plot unit is pivotal in a cluster if it is not entailed by other plot units in the same cluster and if it has more immediate links with other units than any other plot unit in the cluster (see Lehnert, 1982, for a more complete definition). It is natural to suppose that, given the nature of conventional stories, including that of traditional

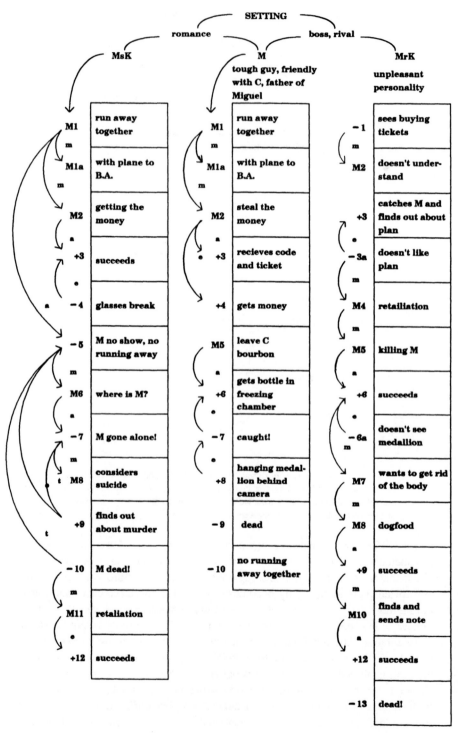

FIG. 9.1b. Detailed representation showing primitive plot units. M = Mario.

films, structural relevance of events is correlated with a more intrinsic relevance. Certain themes, such as death, danger, and love, have been attributed high interest values in other models of narrative discourse processing (see especially Schank, 1979), and, of course, in the historical studies of dramatic situations.[2] Because it is not easy to catch intrinsic relevance of events and themes in any absolute number, we prefer to define relevance of events (and of plot units entailing them) in a relative fashion, that is, in relation to other units of the final representation. In other words, *relevance* means no more than structural relevance within *Alaska*'s plot unit representation.

In view of our working definition of suspense, suspense-driven predictive inferences specifying a (future) negative state are especially relevant. Furthermore, the major negative affect states in the plot unit representation can be ranked according to their structural relevance, that is, their value for the final representation as follows:

1. MrK −13 dead
2. MsK −10 M dead
3. M−9 dead
4. M−7 Mario caught
5. MrK −3A dislikes plans

MrK −13 dead is a pivotal unit in the Dual Retaliation unit, that is, in the largest cluster; MsK −10 M dead is pivotal in the Retaliation (MrK) cluster; and M−9 dead links the two Retaliation clusters. The fourth and fifth negative affect states have more direct links with other affect states than all remaining negative states, and M−7 Mario caught outnumbers MrK−3A dislikes plans in this respect.

Predictive Inferences. The model protocol (see Appendix) specifies for each input event of the event list the new inferences that an ideal viewer can make. On the one hand, inferences are constrained by the requirement of online processing without hindsight, that is, the viewer does not have more information available at any moment than has been presented and possibly inferred so far with the help of standard knowledge of the world. In particular, before the last of the 68 events has been processed, viewers do not have an overview of the story as a whole as it is reflected in the complete plot unit representation. On the other hand, ideal viewers are supposed to make optimal use of the available information. They notice all relevant events as described in the event list. If an inference can be made, they make it.

Inferences have the shape of propositions from the plot unit representation. They consist of an affect state (+, −, or M) from the representation, a certainty index of the plot unit structure involved, and an index for the degree to which the content

---

[2]See Tan (1995) for references.

of the plot unit element is specified. For example, when Mario burgles the slaughterhouse (Event 9), the inference can be made—and is made by ideal viewers—that he may be caught in the act. In the model protocol, this expectation has the notation: (M–7) $ [ ], in which (M–7) is Mario's negative affect state when he is caught, the $ stands for the subjective likelihood that the expected affect state is definitely part of the final representation, and the blank between the square brackets indicates that there is no articulation of the exact nature of the event leading to the affect state. This expectation can be paraphrased as follows: "Mario may be caught, but I don't know the particulars of when, how, or by whom." Expectation aroused by Events 51 and 52 can be contrasted with the former one. These events make the ideal viewer expect with more certainty that Mr. Koole is just about to catch Mario in the freezing chamber. Both the structural certainty index and the content index range from ? (possible/vague guess) through $ (likely/some idea) to $$ (certain/detailed content). It is assumed that ideal viewers make model inferences after the entire input event has been processed.

The model protocol in the Appendix lists the number of the events (Column 1), a description of events (Column 2), new and altered expectations (Column 3), and expectations that are kept in the background (Column 4). Expectations can only acquire complete certainty and complete specification of contents when the last element of the event contributing to certainty and content has been processed, that is, shown in the film. Such expectations are set in bold characters. For example, after Event 10, the inference is made with complete certainty and specification of content that Mario wanted to steal the money: (M M1a) $$ [$$]. Until that moment, there are no grounds in the film for having that expectation with full certainty and content. Certainty and content indexes can be negative. In that case ideal viewers expect a structure and/or content that is opposite to what happens, in actuality, later. Inferences starting with an S refer to the setting. They have a character or a relationship between two characters as their predicate, whereas the argument refers to inferred properties of characters and relationships.

Model inferences are not exclusively predictive, as can be verified readily in the Appendix. They include, for instance, state inferences (i.e., pertaining to setting; e.g., Events 1–6), and superordinate goal inferences (e.g., M M2, Event 9: Mario burgles the slaughterhouse in order to steal money), to use the terminology of Graesser et al. (1994). The latter examples are backward inferences, that is, they serve explanation rather than prediction. Most generally speaking, the model protocol rests on a prediction-substantiation model of online inference generation. According to Graesser et al., in this model, narrative comprehension is largely top-down and expectation driven: Expectations derive from higher order knowledge structures, such as scripts, or, in our case, conventional complex plot unit structures. It is not surprising, then, that most inferences in the model protocol are predictive. Most of them, to follow Graesser et al. (1994), are causal consequence or subordinate goal inferences. As we are interested in the response to suspense, we will limit our discussion to predictive inferences involving a negative consequence for a character.

Dual indexing of expected affect states makes it possible to hypothesize two kinds of important tentative inferences, namely: (a) predictive inferences of specific events that are highly uncertain, and (b) predictive inferences of events of an unspecified nature that have a high certainty. In this way, the kind of expectation figuring in film theory, as well as the possibility of partial encoding of inferences, suggested by McKoon and Ratcliff (1992), have been incorporated in the model protocol. Dual indexing of causal consequence inferences allows for a more flexible elaboration of constraints imposed by the text and the number of alternative consequences proposed by Graesser et al. (1994).

There is another attribute of the model protocol that results in variability of the degree of activation. Predictive inferences can have a foreground or a background status due to their very nature. Predictive inferences serve online comprehension and are generated in the search for specification or (dis-)confirmation. Predictive inferences are attributed a background status when the present event cannot be expected to contribute to their structural certainty or content values. This is the case, for instance, when a scene changes. Predictive inferences that were active in the previous scene do not disappear altogether, but lead a hidden life of sleeping demons until they are again activated by other events. The shifting of inferences back and forth between a foreground and a background memory is also in line with the dynamics of viewer emotion. Interest is sensitive to immediate promise, as we have seen. Predictive inferences that cannot be answered give way to ones that can, due to emotional control. (For an extensive discussion of the activation shift just referred to, see Tan, in press.)

It is reasonable to suppose that deactivated inferences are not kept in a background store forever. For instance, Mario's visit to his son Miguel (Event 8) results in the ideal viewer's (weak) predictive inference that we will learn more about Miguel and Mario's relation to him (Who is his mother? Is Mario divorced?); in other words, more about Miguel's position in the wider Setting of the story: S (Mig) $ [ ]. After Event 10, a scene break occurs, and the inference is deactivated. A long time afterwards, it may be reactivated by Mrs. Koole's questioning of the boy (Event 38). Alternatively, its deactivated state may have lasted too long for it to survive. The shots representing the two events are separated by an interval of almost 15 minutes. Moreover, the interval contains a number of relevant events, and the inference in question is only weak and hardly specified at all. Generally, after some time, predictive inferences will be forgotten. At present, however, we do not have an algorithm available that switches off deactivated inferences altogether.

Suspense Inferences. We can now identify the smaller class of suspense inferences afforded by the film. A *suspense inference* is an emotionally charged inference of a causal consequence of an IE that is accompanied by the emotions interest, hope, and fear. The intensity of the total of emotions corresponds to the activation strength of the inference. Suspense inferences are identified in the model protocol as follows:

A suspense inference is a predictive inference that meets two conditions: (a) it contains a negative affect state, and (b) it has a certainty and content specification that are all but maximal. For the model protocol, this means that the sum of the certainty and content indices equals 3.

The degree of activation of a suspense inference is heightened by the relevance of the expected negative event for the protagonist, in other words, the seriousness of the threat.

The first condition is sufficient for the appraisal of threat to a protagonist's well-being, a feared outcome (Requirement 2 of the working definition of suspense). The second condition is sufficient for the felt immediacy of the feared outcome and precludes absolute certainty as a condition for suspense. The suspense intensifier, seriousness of threat, corresponds to Requirement 3 of the working definition. If there is suspense, its intensity is determined by the relevance of the anticipated negative outcome event. The intensifier corresponds to determinants of fear that are mentioned in various theories of emotion. Frijda (1986) argued that relevance to the subject's concerns is a core component of emotional meaning structure, that is, it is indispensable for any emotion to arise at all. Ortony, Clore, and Collins (1988) viewed desirability as one of the intensifiers of fear as a prospect-based emotion. For seriousness of threat to assume the character of suspense intensifier, it must be assumed that viewers make the protagonist's concerns their own. *Suspense sequences* in the model protocol then, together with their suspense inferences are the following:

1. e16: Mario accidentally pushes a slaughter knife from a table; it hits the floor with an awkward echoing sound. The event is the IE, and it takes place between Actions 18 and 19 in the synopsis (Table 9.1). Suspense inferences: He will be caught: (M−7) $$ [$]. The OE does not occur. Instead the scene ends, to be taken up as part of Koole's episode.

2. ee49−57: The sequence in Koole's episode in which he catches and kills Mario. For the events, see also Table 9.1, 28−34. The IE is, again, the falling slaughter knife; the OE is that Mario is killed. (In all probability, only when Koole is shown with the body is the inference of Mario's death completely certain, e58.) Suspense inferences: Mario will be caught by Koole (M−7) $$ [$], which becomes completely certain in e53. After 53 there is still the suspense inference that Mario will be killed by Koole: (M−9) $$ [$].

3. ee66−69: The final sequence of the film, corresponding to synopsis Events 49 and 50 (Table 9.1). Mrs. Koole entering the freezing chamber where Koole is watching the medallion is the IE. The OE is Koole's sitting down in apathy on hearing the freezing engine start. The suspense inference is that Mr. Koole is going to be killed by his wife in the freezing chamber: (MrK −13) $ [$$].

Because of differences in the seriousness of the expected threat, the strength of the suspense inferences is not equally high in all three sequences. Given the ranking of structural relevance of the expected negative states, it should be highest in the third sequence, followed by the second and the first.

Threat Inferences and Sequences. According to the working definition, suspense is characterized by acute threat. The temporal proximity and certainty of the feared event are high, and the content of the threat, or the nature of the feared event, is clear. In film, there is often a less acute and articulated threat. It can be a foreshadowing of future, more concrete danger by way of music, sudden inserts, or ambiguity of the represented view on the scene ("Whose look is this?"). A location can be sinister, in actuality or due to learning effects related to conventional film signs. The portrayed fictional events themselves can also signal a diffuse threat that is not immediately linked to salient features of the scene. An example is the beginning of the burglary scene in Mario's episode. After his conversation with Miguel, we see Mario climb over the wall of the dimly lit slaughterhouse, without any introduction. It can be assumed that ideal viewers infer a threat to his well-being: He may be caught, or worse. The inference, however, may not be certain and specific enough to fulfill the two conditions of suspense. The situation is appraised as less urgent as well as less focused than in suspense. (The two elements of appraisal are derived from Frijda's, 1986, discussion of components of situational meaning in emotion.) Therefore we define *threat inferences* as follows:

1. It contains a negative affect state.
2. Its certainty and content specification indices are nonzero, but not all but maximal. In terms of the model protocol, they are higher than ?, but their sum is less than three $.

The relevance of the expected outcome event resulting in a negative affect state, or in other words its seriousness, is an intensifier of threat. Threat may or may not precede suspense. In addition, it should be noted that suspense inferences entail threat inferences. *Threat sequences*, then, are:

1. 30–34: Mrs. Koole waits in vain for Mario at the airport (Table 9.1, 23–25). Threat inferences are: Mario may have been caught somehow: (M–7) $ [$]; maybe Mario is dead: (MK–10) $ [$]; or Mario may have left Mrs. Koole alone and has somehow disappeared: MsK (–7) $ [$].
2. 62–63: Mrs. Koole talks to Mario's friend Carlos and is about to discover how Mario has been killed. Threat inference: (MsK–10) $ [$].

Neutral Sequences. For purposes of comparison, sequences can be selected from the model protocol that qualify neither as suspense nor as threat sequences. These will be called *neutral sequences*. Their main feature is that in inferences accompanying viewing of these sequences, negative affect states are absent. Two neutral sequences were chosen for purposes of comparison, namely Events 17 to 21 and Events 22 to 25. In the first sequence, Mrs. Koole receives the tickets at the travel agency and writes the code on one of them. As these events are part of Mrs. Koole's episode, the viewer is not yet aware that Mr. Koole is watching her. In the second one, Mrs. Koole steals a key from Mr. Koole and accidentally breaks his glasses.

It may be expected, then, that in response to suspense sequences, more suspense inferences are framed than in response to threat and neutral sequences. In addition, more threat inferences should be framed in threat sequences than in neutral ones. Level of interest, or excitement, should be highest in suspense sequences followed by threat and then by neutral sequences.

EMPIRICAL SUPPORT FOR THE GENERATION OF PREDICTIVE INFERENCES

Subjects and Procedure

In order to obtain empirical support for the hypothesized suspense and threat inferences in ideal viewers, 15 subjects were presented with the film and asked to verbalize any inferences immediately after the sequence, while the film was (Group I) or was not (Group II) halted. Subjects, all students of social sciences, were tested individually. Group I was asked to watch the film attentively. They were told in advance that the film was going to be halted a few times and that they were to answer some questions. They were asked for their first reaction, and it was emphasized that there were no correct or incorrect answers. In this group, the answers were audiotaped. There were 12 stops, all immediately after the target sequences, except for Stop 10, which occurred during Event 63, just before Carlos wants to climb to the camera. Seven were used for the analysis as they followed directly after a suspense, a threat, or a neutral sequence. The order of the seven target sequences was as follows: Suspense 1, Neutral 1, Neutral 2, Threat 1, Suspense 2, Threat 2, and Suspense 3. During the stops, four questions were asked, in this order:

1. How *exciting* do you find the film at this moment, on a scale from 1 to 14 (1 = absolutely not exciting; 14 = extremely exciting)?
2. What can you tell about the main characters?
3. What do you think they are after?
4. What do you think the outcome will be?

Question 1 is a measurement of the emotional interest response. Reported excitement has been found to be a fairly good index of interest in earlier studies (e.g., Tan & van den Boom, 1992). It may capture empathetic fear as well because significant correlations have been found between excitement ratings and concern for a film's protagonist and fear during suspenseful films (Tan, in preparation). Questions 2 through 4 are meant to catch the inferences predicted in the model protocol. They reflect an increasing degree of specification of inferences, from global and diffuse to local and precise. Also, they were intended to catch inferences about the following plot unit structures: Setting (2, 3), Mental Acts (3, 2), and Positive/ Negative Affect States (4).

Group II, five subjects, was formed as a control for the effect of halting the film. They were asked to watch attentively and, meanwhile, to think aloud and to utter inferences. At regular times they were asked to indicate how exciting they found the film to be on a scale from 1 to 14. The film was not halted. Subjects were told before the showing that, if they had a lot to say, the film could be stopped at their request. No use was made of this possibility. During suspense and threat sequences, and if the subjects' silence had lasted for a longer time, they were prompted by questions: "How exciting do you find the film right now?" and "What do you expect to happen?" In this group, the complete sessions were audiotaped. All subjects were asked to write a 10- to 20-line summary of the story afterwards. In the course of analysis it was decided that subjects who really did not understand the film should be excluded from the analysis. The decision was based on the summary and the responses that were audiotaped. The only grounds for exclusion was the misunderstanding of the film's temporal structure, which leads to the misunderstanding of the whole film. This way, the data from 13 subjects remained in analysis.

Results

As the two groups did not differ markedly in their responses, they were taken together for the analysis. Responses to the seven sequences were scored as follows. If the verbalization did not meet a condition absolutely, a 0 was given. If there was a partial match, a 1 was given. When the condition was verbalized entirely, a 2 was given. The intensifier was scored whenever the state concerned was explicitly mentioned, according to the weights discussed earlier. The state (HK–13) scored a 4, the state (MK–10) scored a 3, the state (M–9) scored a 2, and the states (M–7) and (HK–3a) scored a 1. As an example, consider verbalizations after Suspense Sequence 1. The suspense inference here is (M–7), Mario will be caught. The verbalization, "Something nasty is sure going to happen to Mario," scored 2 on the certainty index and a blank on the content index. The response, "Maybe Mario will be trapped by Koole, but I really don't know for sure," scored a 0 on the certainty index and $$ on the content index. A response like "I'm very sure Mario will not be trapped" did not contribute to any score.

Suspense and threat inferences were also scored for the neutral sequences. The results are shown in Table 9.2. The proportion of subjects that uttered suspense inferences increased over the subsequent suspense sequences, as can

TABLE 9.2
Percentages of Subject Verbalizations Meeting Conditions 1 and 2 Per Sequence

	Sequence								
	Sus1	Sus2	Sus3	Thr1	Thr2	Nt1s	Nt1t	Nt2s	Nt2t
Cond 1	46.2	92.3	100	76.9	69.2	7.7	7.7	46.2	61.6
Cond 2	53.9	92.3	100	76.9	69.2	7.7	7.7	61.6	53.9

Note. N = 13.

be expected, because the seriousness of inferred harm to characters increased over the plot. Support for suspense inferences after Suspense Sequence 3 was maximal. There was substantive evidence for threat inferences being made in response to threat sequences, and few threat inferences were observed in response to the first neutral sequence. The second one elicited considerable predictive inferences, both of the threat and suspense type.

The intensifier affect states were mentioned by a substantial proportion of subjects, as Table 9.3 shows, both for suspense and threat, and the proportion of subjects who mentioned any can be neglected in the neutral sequences. It can be seen that the frequency of explicit mention of an appropriate intensifier increased over suspense sequences, as can be expected. In order to arrive at a measure of activation strength of suspense and threat inferences, an index figure was formed following the rule: index $= (C1 + C2)*$ Intensifier $+ (C1 + C2)$. In this formula, C1 is the score on Condition 1 (ranging from 0 to 2), C2 is the score on Condition 2 (ranging from 0 to 2), and Intensifier is the score for the intensifier (ranging from 0 to 4). Thus the index ranges from 0 to 20. It is again emphasized that weights were added to scores by the experimenters on the basis of the plot unit analysis. In the strength of activation index, the most important contribution is due to the intensifier. The index reflects the degree to which subjects generate suspense and threat inferences. Table 9.4 lists index means per sequence. Differences between sequences were tested using paired t tests, except when stated otherwise. Two subjects who found the film completely uninteresting were removed from the analyses. There were a greater number and stronger suspense inferences in the suspense sequences than in the neutral sequences, as predicted. Suspense 1,

TABLE 9.3
Percentages of Subjects Who Mentioned an Intensifier Per Sequence

Intensifier	Sequence						
	Sus1	Sus2	Sus3	Thr1	Thr2	Nt1	Nt2
1	15.4	15.4	0	30.8	0	7.7	7.7
2	0	76.9	0	15.4	0	0	0
3	0	0	15.4	0	23.1	0	0
4	0	0	84.6	0	46.2	0	0

TABLE 9.4
Means of Suspense and Threat Strength Index Per Sequence

Sequence	Index	SD
Sus1	2.09	2.56
Sus2	10.45	2.52
Sus3	19.18	1.83
Thr1	4.36	4.06
Thr2	12.73	8.91
Ntr1	.36/.73	1.21/2.41
Ntr2	6.45/7.83	7.00/2.46

Note. The indices for Neutral Sequences 1 and 2 represent values for suspense and threat, respectively. $N = 11$.

however, was significantly lower than Neutral 2, when strength index was concerned, although not significantly (two-tailed $p = .09$). The ranking of the suspense sequences in terms of the suspense inference index conformed to prediction, and all differences were significant at the .01 level. Threat 2 was higher than the neutral sequences, but only the difference with Neutral 1 reached significance ($p = .00$). Threat 1 yielded significantly more threat inferences than Neutral 1 ($p = .01$), although less than Neutral 2. The difference was not significant. It would seem once again that the sequences earlier in the film (Suspense 1, Threat 1, and Neutral 1) did not result in as many suspense and threat inferences, or as (emotionally) relevant ones, being made as later sequences.

The excitement marks give an impression of the degree of interest and excitement in the various sequences (see Table 9.5). The level of excitement was rather high throughout. The three suspense sequences were significantly more exciting than both neutral sequences ($p < .02$), except for Suspense 1, which was not more exciting than Neutral 1 ($p = .08$). The differences between Suspense 3 and the two threat sequences in terms of excitement was significant ($p < .01$); Suspense 3, then, was significantly more exciting than any of the other sequences. The other two suspense sequences did not differ significantly from the two threat

TABLE 9.5
Means of Excitement Per Sequence

Sequence	Excitement	SD
Sus1	10.60	1.51
Sus2	11.31	1.95
Sus3	12.22	1.79
Thr1	9.80	2.57
Thr2	9.67	3.08
Ntr1	9.63	1.92
Ntr2	9.00	2.45

Note. $N = 8{-}11$.

sequences. Threat sequences could not be distinguished from neutral ones on the basis of excitement scores, although the direction of differences was in the predicted direction.

The correlation between the (S and T) index and excitement was low, PMC = .20, and .30 with the exclusion of two subjects who experienced the film as totally unexciting. Coefficients were based on all observations from the seven sequences. In both cases the correlation was significant ($p < .03$, $p < .01$, respectively). PMCs calculated per sequence were extremely variable, ranging from −.39 to .46. Due to the small number of observations ($N = 9$–13), they could hardly be interpreted.

Discussion of the Results

The results lend considerable support to the hypothesis that predictive inferences are generated during suspense sequences, because a satisfactory proportion of subjects verbalized inferences predicted by the model protocol, and that suspense sequences result in more, and both emotionally and structurally more important predictive inferences. This result supports the claim that predictive inferences are made whenever they can be made, the assumption on which the model protocol was based. Also, it would seem that causal consequence inferences, rather than any other type of inference, are made in response to suspense. It would seem that both the certainty and specification of the consequence is higher in response to suspense, as compared to threat and neutral sequences, as is witnessed by the appropriate fit between the nature of predicted inferences and obtained verbalizations.

Obviously, the results support the hypothesis of online generation of predictive inferences only so far as the verbalizations reflect immediate and spontaneous encoding of inferences. The questions posed to subjects have undoubtedly acted as prompts, and it is unknown to what degree this has been the case. The exploratory method used in this study does not allow more than tentative conclusions. In particular, a response format is needed that allows a more exact matching of model expectations and subject response. Further research using more accurate online measures and procedures, for instance a priming experiment, will have to decide this issue. It is also important that the weighing of affect state relevance by the experimenters, based on a theoretical thematic analysis, should be verified by way of some sort of subject ratings.

The low correlations between strength of activation of inferences and excitement raises interesting questions. It was observed that excitement had a high level throughout. Also, this level remained stable over subsequent sequences, and a marked increase in excitement was observed only between the sixth and the seventh sequence, that is, from Threat 2 to Suspense 3. These two findings give rise to the surmise that more global expectations may be at work that are difficult to verbalize, even in response to the experimenters' fairly open prompt. It sounds silly to report that "things are going to happen," a verbalization made by some subjects nonetheless. It may be that such an extremely vague expectation remains in the background due to lack of articulation. We come back to this vague expectation later. Suspense sequences afford viewers the opportunity to sharpen a part of their global expectation that is shifted to the foreground store, where inferences are amenable to verbalization. The same goes for threat sequences, to a lesser degree. It may be that threat expectations remain vague for the greater part.

CONCLUDING REMARKS: SUSPENSE AND OTHER PROCEDURES

This study has yielded support for the current conception of suspense as a procedure that affords emotionally charged predictive inferences about the protagonist's fate. It was shown that such predictive inferences can be identified when it is assumed that thematic knowledge is used in comprehension, approximately in the way asserted by the prediction-substantiation model, as it is termed by Graesser et al. (1994). In particular, we obtained some support for the idea that suspense induces causal consequence inferences, a result that is ruled out by a strictly minimalist position concerning online inferencing (McKoon & Ratcliff, 1992). It may be that suspense texts are an exception to the general rule that states that causal consequence inferences are not made in the processing of narrative text, due to the large number of alternative outcomes. As the working definition makes explicit, in suspense, the number of alternatives is limited, and/or a future state of the protagonist has such high relevance that it is encoded in spite of the possibility of poor articulation.

On the other hand, the study throws some light on the limitations of the current notion of suspense. Many prototypical action films, such as *Speed* (de Bont, 1994) or *The Terminator* (Cameron, 1984), create undiluted suspense, whereas others clearly do not. These are not part of a minority in terms of number and are not less interesting. *Alaska* is one of these. First, although our subjects (and other viewers who watched it in Dutch cinemas and on Dutch television) clearly enjoyed the film, suspense was probably only one of the various factors that contributed to this enjoyment. *Alaska* does not elicit strong sympathy for either one of the protagonists, for instance as compared to prototypical film alternatives. There is no portrayal of strong romance hampered by obstacles that would result in sympathy for the secret lovers. Mr. Koole is not presented as a sympathetic victim of betrayal, but, quite the opposite, as a rather sadistic person, whose love for his wife is only shown in passing, and very implicitly. (There is only one sign that he loves his wife: We watch him touching the shawl in a kind of loving way.) Our sympathy, then, is with Mrs. Koole and Mario, but the couple is not made attractive, or morally right, or even interesting. Hence, inferred future negative states may not matter as much to the viewer as they do in the typical case of the suspense movie, which would dampen the effects of suspense. Furthermore, it seems that the plot inhibits suspense. The relevance of negative affect states increases over the plot, but its episodic structure breaks continuity in comprehension. Predictive inferences are pushed to the background status as the next episode starts the story anew, and the fact that new starts are made several times forces the viewer to explanation-driven backward inferencing. The cognitive labor involved in constructing the complete chronological sequence may result in aesthetic enjoyment that is incompatible with sympathy-driven hopes and fears, already relatively weak in themselves. We believe that the construction of the chronology of the plot and concomitant inferences in more complex films deserves separate investigation.

Other narrative procedures mentioned in the introductory section on suspense are a second source of enjoyment that runs counter to or interacts with the emotional effects of suspense. Curiosity and mystery are realized by retarded exposition. It takes considerable time before the viewer knows who Mario is, who Mr. Koole and Mrs. Koole are, and how they relate to each other. Retardation of setting information also results in a lack of comprehension of motives and major plans, from which the complete plot unit structure is dependent. For instance, viewers only get an idea of who Mr. Koole is (S MrK) in the last episode, especially through Events 57 and later, when they witness his sadistic perfectionism. This discovery may provoke anxiety, disgust or anger. An unspecified predictive inference may have been generated as early as Event 1. Curiosity is maintained throughout the two earlier episodes, due to the background activity of this inference. As another example, consider curiosity about the relationship between Mario and Mr. Koole. Viewers may expect to learn more about it after Event 1, which generates a weak predictive inference S (M–MrK). Only in Event 46, where Mario watches Koole and kisses the medallion, do viewers learn that Mario is a rival of his boss, and that Koole was unaware of this. Apart from retarded exposition, interruption of suspense may alter the narrative procedure and promote curiosity. Consider the first suspense inference (M–7) made according to the model protocol after Event 16. The causal consequence inference that Mario will somehow be caught in the slaughterhouse is answered in a sequence other than the one in which it was generated. Event 17 introduces a change of scene, the inference moves to the background, adding to curiosity, and becomes an active expectation again when Mrs. Koole waits for Mario in vain at the airport (Event 29) and starts to search for him (Events 32, 37, and 38).

Surprise can also be identified in the model protocol. It is a surprise that the suspense inference generated by the falling knife just referred to does not get answered. A hot suspense inference is moved to the background. Event 49, where Koole hears the sound of the knife hitting the floor, triggers it again as a suspense inference through surprise. Koole ignores the sound (Event 50), a surprise, which enables the inference that Mario will not be caught, an inference that is falsified, again by surprise, in Event 51, where Koole hears the alarm. Here the old suspense inference is reactivated for the third time. Generally, and in terms of the model protocol, a change in the certainty or content indices of a given plot unit string of some size, say one totaling to two $, may count as a surprise, and predicts surprise in the viewer. When this is accepted, it can be seen from the model protocol that the film is loaded with surprise. New inferences that immediately have a structural and content value summing to two $ represent a surprise. They stand for sudden insights or possibilities. A decrease of certainty or specification of an existing inference has the same effect of surprise assuming the shape of sudden confusion or wonder.

Surprise may be as important for viewer interest as suspense is. As indicated, it may relate to suspense. Suspense inferences can be transformed into background expectation that adds to a more diffuse curiosity, and their appearance or deactivation may constitute a surprise. Finally, there is a last source of enjoyment, the numerous instances of irony that the film narrative of *Alaska*, or any other film, offers. The lack of potential for empathy may be thought to be compensated for by the distant mode of observation that the film imposes on the viewer. Instead of deepening insight into the striving of characters, the film offers viewers amusement in a view of the futility of striving and human frailty. Lucariello (1994) recently showed that people have extensive knowledge of situational irony, a special kind of knowledge of how scripted events can go and do go awry despite human striving and the illusion of control. He showed that people can recognize, with remarkable ease, ironic courses of events, produce examples from real life, and have available rich and complex schemata for ironic events. It would seem that Lehnert's complex plot units capture part of this knowledge, as can be seen from the names given to typical complex plot units like Fortuitous Resolution, Starting Over, and simpler ones that have an ironic flavor, such as Mixed Blessing. These structures seem to contain more than conventional event, goal, plan, and action scripts. The Double Retaliation theme in *Alaska* may be appreciated as fitting a typical ironical script in which not only the retaliation of one is followed by that of the other, but in which there is also an identity of punishments. Mr. Koole dies in the same way as he killed Mario. Accordingly, the diagrams of the plot unit structure exhibit a symmetry at first glance (Fig. 9.1). Furthermore, the causal sequence hinges on a number of silly details that are nonetheless decisive. A few props, in themselves insignificant, are involved in fatal mistakes. If Mrs. Koole had not accidentally dropped Koole's glasses, he would not have returned to the slaughterhouse, he would not have caught Mario, and the whole causal sequence would have been different. If Mario had not put the bottle in the freezer for Carlos—out of friendliness—Koole would not have heard the alarm, and Mario would not have been caught. That Koole first ignores the sound of the knife hitting the floor makes the role of silly details even more salient. (Here we have an interesting combination of suspense, surprise, and situational irony, all contributing to the viewer's enjoyment of the film.)

Koole fails to notice that Mario hangs the medallion by the camera—right under his eyes—and this error proves to be fatal. Many of these ironic courses of events can only be understood in retrospect. They contribute to the viewers' emotions by making them realize what could have happened, and thus they deepen various feelings, such as regret or *schadenfreude*. Some ironic events, however, may be foreseen, and contribute to the specification of suspense inferences, or in some other way facilitate predictive inference of causal consequence. Some of our subjects predicted that Mr. Koole would die in the same way as Mario as this course of events matches a common ironic script. A most general expectation, again, may be that whatever the protagonists are attempting to get at is doomed to fail in an amusing way, and this expectation may take its cue from global indications, such as the atmosphere of the film, that are radically different from the highly specific constraints triggering suspense inferences, such as an IE that leaves open only one or two outcomes. This general expectation may even counteract the generation of specific predictive inferences, because viewers may sense that they are just as helpless in the face of the whims of fate as the protagonists are, and, in this way, they may suppress any effects of suspense. Interest is then fed by the promise of postdictable surprise, an unexpected outcome that makes ironic sense only in retrospect. Our analysis of this film, then, has interesting parallels with the distinction Cupchik makes between prediction and comprehension (Cupchik, chap. 10, this volume). Suspense elicits predictive inference, accompanied by acute excitement, and various other devices, including irony and thematic associations have been identified to operate in parallel. These contribute to curiosity, and to a deeper understanding of the narrative, which results in another set of feelings complementing, or perhaps counteracting, excitement. It seems likely that these procedures provoke generation of inferences as well, but these are less likely to be predictive. Further research will have to show to what degree the inferences involved are made online. Given the fact that grasping the full richness of the meaning of some films requires careful analysis, it seems probable, that deeper understanding of, for example, theme and irony may require watching a film more than once.

In sum, a more general moral may be drawn from studying this film: namely that suspense does not operate in a vacuum, but is mostly one element in an affect structure within which several procedures govern a variety of viewer emotions and their regulation.

REFERENCES

Albritton, D. W., & Gerrig, R. J. (1991). Participatory responses in text understanding. *Journal of Memory and Language, 30*, 603–626.

Bordwell, D. (1985). *Narration in the fiction film.* Madison: University of Wisconsin Press.

Bordwell, D., Staiger, J., & Thompson, K. (1985). *The classical Hollywood cinema: Film style and mode of production.* New York: Columbia University Press.

Branigan, E. (1992). *Narrative comprehension and film.* London & New York: Routledge.

Brewer, W. F., & Lichtenstein, E. H. (1982). Stories are to entertain: A structural affect theory of stories. *Journal of Pragmatics, 6,* 473–486.

Cantor, J., Ziemke, D., & Sparks, G. G. (1984). Effect of forewarning on emotional response to a horror film. *Journal of Broadcasting, 28,* 21–31.

Carroll, N. (1988). *Mystifying movies: Fads and fallacies in contemporary film theory.* New York: Columbia University Press.

Carroll, N. (1990). *The philosophy of horror or Paradoxes of the heart.* New York: Routledge.

de Wied, M. (1991). *The role of time structures in the experience of film suspense and duration.* Unpublished doctoral dissertation, University of Amsterdam, The Netherlands.

Dyer, M. G. (1983). *In-depth understanding. A computer model of integrated processing for narrative comprehension.* Cambridge, MA: MIT Press.

Freytag, G. (1911). *Die Technik des Dramas* [Technique of the drama]. Leipzig: Hirzel.

Frijda, N. H. (1986). *The emotions.* Cambridge, UK: Cambridge University Press.

Gernsbacher, M. A., Goldsmith, H. H., & Robertson, R. R. W. (1992). Do readers mentally represent characters' emotional states? *Cognition and Emotion, 6,* 89–111.

Gerrig, R. J. (1989). Suspense in the absence of uncertainty. *Journal of Memory and Language, 28,* 633–648.

Graesser, A. C., Singer, M., & Trabasso, T. (1994). Constructing inferences during narrative text comprehension. *Psychological Review, 101,* 371–395.

Huitema, J. S., Dopkins, S., Klin, C. M., & Myers, J. L. (1993). Connecting goals and actions during reading. *Journal of Experimental Psychology: Learning Memory and Cognition, 19,* 1053–1060.

Kintsch, W. (1980). Learning from text, levels of comprehension, or: Why anyone would read a story anyway. *Poetics, 9,* 877–898.

Lazarus, R. S., Averill, J. R., & Opton, E. M., Jr. (1970). Toward a cognitive theory of emotions. In M. Arnold (Ed.), *Feelings and emotions* (pp. 207–232). New York: Academic Press.

Lehnert, W. G. (1981). Plot units and narrative summarization. *Cognitive Science, 4,* 293–331.

Lehnert, W. G. (1982). Plot units: A narrative summarization strategy. In W. G. Lehnert & M. H. Ringle (Eds.), *Strategies for natural language processsing* (pp. 375–414). Hillsdale, NJ: Lawrence Erlbaum Associates.

Lehnert, W. G., & Vine, E. W. (1987). The role of affect in narrative structure. *Cognition and Emotion, 1,* 299–322.

Lucariello, J. (1994). Situational irony: A concept of events gone awry. *Journal of Experimental Psychology: General, 124,* 129–145.

McKoon, G., & Ratcliff, R. (1992). Inference during reading. *Psychological Review, 99,* 440–466.

Morrow, D. G., Bower, G. H., & Greenspan, S. L. (1989). Updating situation models during narrative comprehension. *Journal of Memory and Language, 28,* 292–312.

Oatley, K. (1992). *Best laid schemes. The psychology of emotions.* Cambridge, MA: Cambridge University Press.

Ortony, A., Clore, G. L., & Collins, A. (1988). *The cognitive structure of emotions.* Cambridge, MA: Cambridge University Press.

Pfister, M. (1977). *Das Drama* [The drama]. München, Germany: Fink Verlag.

Schank, R. C. (1979). Interestingness: Controlling inferences. *Artificial Intelligence, 12,* 273–297.

Sternberg, M. (1978). *Expositional modes and temporal ordering in fiction.* Baltimore: Johns Hopkins University Press.

Suh, S., & Trabasso, T. (1993). Inferences during reading: Converging evidence from discourse analysis, talk-aloud protocols, and recognition priming. *Journal of Memory and Language, 32,* 279–300.

Tan, E. (1986). Interest when nothing happens. A note on narrative retardation. *Proceedings of the Eighth Annual Conference of the Cognitive Science Society* (pp. 832–842). Hillsdale, NJ: Lawrence Erlbaum Associates.

Tan, E. (1991). *Film als emotiemachine* [Film as an emotion machine]. Unpublished doctoral dissertation, Universiteit van Amsterdam, The Netherlands.

Tan, E. (1995). *Emotion and the structure of narrative film. Film as an emotion machine.* Mahwah, NJ: Lawrence Erlbaum Associates.

Tan, E. (in preparation). *Exposing the affect structure of narrative film: Some empirical studies.*

Tan, E., & van den Boom, I. (1992). Explorations in the psychological affect structure of narrative film. In E. Nardocchio (Ed.), *Reader response to literature. The empirical dimension* (pp. 57–94). Berlin: De Gruyter-Mouton.

Wilson, S. G., Rinck, M., McNamara, T. P., Bower, G. H., & Morrow, D. G. (1993). Mental models and narrative comprehension. *Journal of Memory and Language, 32,* 141–154.

Zillmann, D. (1980). Anatomy of suspense. In P. H. Tannenbaum (Ed.), *The entertainment functions of television* (pp. 133–163). Hillsdale, NJ: Lawrence Erlbaum Associates.

Zillmann, D. (1991). The logic of suspense and mystery. In J. Bryant & D. Zillmann (Eds.), *Responding to the screen. Reception and reaction processes* (pp. 281–304). Hillsdale, NJ: Lawrence Erlbaum Associates.

APPENDIX: MODEL PROTOCOL OF COMPREHENSION PROCESS OF *ALASKA*

Key:
    MsK = Mrs. Koole
    MrK = Mr. Koole
    M = Mario
    t = threat sequence
    s = suspense sequence
    n = neutral sequence
    A double line between two events indicates a change of scene

Event No.	Description of Event	New and Altered Inferences	Background Inferences	Kind of Sequence
1	Mario sees Mr. Koole arriving at the slaughterhouse.	S (M) ? [ ] S (MrK) ? [ ] S (M–MrK) ? [$]		
2	Mario kisses his medallion.	S (M) ? [ ] S (MrK) ? [ ] S (M–MrK) ? [$] (M +8) ? [ ] S (M–MsK) ? [ ]		
3	Mario is boxing with a piece of meat in the freezing chamber.	S (MrK) ? [ ] S (M–MrK) ? [$] (M +8) ? [ ] S (M–MsK) ? [ ] S (M) $ [$]		
4	Mario and his friend Carlos have a drink.	S (MrK) ? [ ] S (M–MrK) ? [$] (M +8) ? [ ] S (M–MsK) ? [ ] S (M) $ [$] S (M–C) $ [ ]		

Event No.	Description of Event	New and Altered Inferences	Background Inferences	Kind of Sequence
5	Mario sees Mr. Koole at the gate after working hours.	S (M–MrK) $ [$] (MrK M4)? [ ]	S (MrK) ? [ ] S (M–MrK) ? [$] (M +8) ? [ ] S (M–MsK) ? [ ] S (M) $ [$] S (M–C) $ [ ]	
6	Mario and Mrs. Koole meet at a station.	S (M–MsK) $ [$] (MsK M1) ? [ ] (M M1) ? [ ]	idem + S (M–C) $ [ ] S (M–MrK) $ [$] (MrK M4)? [ ]	
7	Mario receives an envelope, Mrs. Koole plays with the medallion.	S (M–MsK) $ [$] (MsK M1) $ [ ] (MsK M1a) $ [ ] (MsK M2) ? [ ] (M M1) $ [ ] (M M1a) $ [ ] (M M2) ? [ ] (M +3) $ [ ]	idem	
8	Mario sees Miguel and tells him he will be going abroad (in Spanish).	S (Mig) $ [ ]	idem+ S (M–MsK) $ [$] (MsK M1) $ [ ] (MsK M1a) $ [ ] (MsK M2) ? [ ] (M M1) $ [ ] (M M1a) $ [ ] (M M2) ? [ ] (M +3) $ [ ]	
9	Mario burgles the slaughterhouse.	(M M2) $$ [$] (M +4) $ [ ] (M –7) $ [ ] (M –9) ? [ ]	idem+ S (Mig) $ [ ]	t
10	Mario opens the envelope that contains a ticket with the code and the key of the safe on it. He opens the safe and gets the money out.	(M M2) $$ [$] (M –7) $ [ ] (M –9) ? [ ] (M M1) $$ [$] (M M1a) $$ [$$] (M +3) $$ [$$] (M +4) $$ [$$]	idem	t
11	Mario sits behind the desk.	(M M2) $$ [$] (M –7) $ [ ] (M –9) ? [ ] (M M1) $$ [$] (M M1a) $$ [$$] (M +3) $$ [$$] (M +4) $$ [$$] (M M..) $ [ ]	idem	t

Event No.	Description of Event	New and Altered Inferences	Background Inferences	Kind of Sequence
12	The telephone rings.	(M M2) $$ [$] (M −7) $ [ ] (M −9) ? [ ] (M M1) $$ [$] (M M1a) $$ [$$] (M +3) $$ [$$] (M +4) $$ [$$] (M M..) $ [$] (X M) $ [ ]	idem	t
13	Mario lets the telephone ring twice, takes off the receiver, and lays it down again.	(M M2) $$ [$] (M −7) $ [ ] (M −9) ? [ ] (M M1) $$ [$] (M M1a) $$ [$$] (M +3) $$ [$$] (M +4) $$ [$$] (M M..) $ [$] (X M) $ [ ] (MsK M1) $ [$] (MsK M2) $ [ ] (MsK +3) $ [ ]	idem	t
14	Mario writes the note to Carlos.	(M M2) $$ [$] (M −7) $ [ ] (M −9) ? [ ] (M M1) $$ [$] (M M1a) $$ [$$] (M +3) $$ [$$] (M +4) $$ [$$] (M M..) $ [$] (X M) $ [ ] (MsK M1) $ [$] (MsK M2) $ [ ] (MsK +3) $ [ ] (M M5) $$ [−$] (MsK −7) $ [$]	idem	t
15	Mario goes to the freezing chamber in order to put the note and a bottle there.	(M M2) $$ [$] (M −7) $ [ ] (M M1) $$ [$] (M M1a) $$ [$$] (M +3) $$ [$$] (M +4) $$ [$$] (M M..) $ [$] (X M) $ [ ] (MsK M1) $ [$] (MsK M2) $ [ ] (MsK +3) $ [ ] (M M5) $$ [−$] (MsK −7) $ [$]	idem	t

Event No.	Description of Event	New and Altered Inferences	Background Inferences	Kind of Sequence
16	Mario hits a butcher's axe, which falls from a table.	(M M5) $ [ ] (M −9) $ [ ] (M M2) $$ [$] (M M1) $$ [$] (M M1a) $$ [$$] (M +3) $$ [$$] (M +4) $$ [$$] (M M..) $ [$] (X M) $ [ ] (MsK M1) $ [$] (MsK M2) $ [ ] (MsK +3) $ [ ] (M M5) $$ [−$] (MsK −7) $ [$] (M M5) $ [ ] (M −7) $$ [$] (M −9) $$ [ ]	idem	s
17	Mr. Koole sets his wife down in town on his way to the slaughterhouse.	S (MsK−MrK) $$ [$]	idem + (M M2) $$ [$] (M M1) $$ [$] (M M1a) $$ [$$] (M +3) $$ [$$] (M +4) $$ [$$] (M M..) $ [$] (X M) $ [ ] (MsK M1) $ [$] (MsK M2) $ [ ] (MsK +3) $ [ ] (M M5) $$ [−$] (MsK −7) $ [$] (M M5) $ [ ] (M −7) $$ [$] (M −9) $$ [ ]	
18	Mrs. Koole enters a drugstore.	S (MsK−MrK) $$ [$] (MsK M..) ? [ ]	idem	
19	Mr. Koole drives away.		idem	
20	Mrs. Koole enters a travel bureau and receives airplane tickets.	(MsK M..) ? [ ] (MsK M1) $$ [$] S(MsK−MrK) $$ [$$] (MsK M1a) $$ [$$] (MsK M1)-e- (M M1) $ [$]	idem	n
21	Mrs. Koole writes down the code of the safe on the ticket.	(MsK M..) ? [ ] (MsK M1) $$ [$] S(MsK−MrK) $$ [$$] (MsK M1a) $$ [$$] (MsK M2) $$ [$] (MsK +3) $$ [$]	idem	n

Event No.	Description of Event	New and Altered Inferences	Background Inferences	Kind of Sequence
		(MsK M1)		
		(M M1) $$ [$]		
22	Mrs. Koole steals a key from Mr. Koole's bunch of keys.	(MsK M2) $$ [$$] (MsK +3) $ [$$] (MsK −..)? [ ] (MrK +3) ? [ ]	idem + (MsK M..) ? [ ] (MsK M1) $$ [$] S(MsK−MrK) $$ [$$] (MsK M1a) $$ [$$] (MsK M2) $$ [$] (MsK +3) $$ [$] (MsK M1) (M M1) $$ [$]	n
23	Mr. Koole's glasses break.	(MsK M2) $$ [$$] (MsK +3) $ [$$] (MsK −..)? [ ] (MsK −4) $$ [$$] (MrK +3) $ [ ]	idem	n
24	Mr. Koole makes a remark about making a little trip together.	(MsK M2) $$ [$$] (MsK +3) $ [$$] (MsK −..)? [ ] (MsK −4) $$ [$$] (MrK +3) $ [ ] S (MrK−MsK $$ [ ] (MrK −1) ? [ ] (MrK M2) ? [ ] (MrK −3a) ? [ ]	idem	n
25	(Beginning of the evening) Mrs. Koole acts as if she is going to her drawing lessons.	(MsK M2) $$ [$$] (MsK +3) $ [$$] (MsK −..)? [ ] (MsK −4) $$ [$$] (MrK +3) $ [ ] S (MrK−MsK $$ [ ] (MrK −1) ? [ ] (MrK M2) ? [ ] (MrK −3a) ? [ ] S (MsK−MrK) $ [$] (MsK M1)$$ [$]	idem	n
26	Mrs. Koole meets Mario at the station.	(MsK M1) $$ [$$] (..)? [$$] (MsK M2) $$ [$$] (MsK +3) $$ [$$] S (MsK−MrK)$$ [$$] S (MsK −M) $$ [$$] (M M1) $$ [$$] (..)? [ ] (M M2) $$ [$$] (M +3) $$ [$$]	idem + (MsK M2) $$ [$$] (MsK +3) $ [$$] (MsK −..)? [ ] (MsK −4) $$ [$$] (MrK +3) $ [ ] S (MrK−MsK $$ [ ] (MrK −1) ? [ ] (MrK M2) ? [ ] (MrK −3a) ? [ ]	

Event No.	Description of Event	New and Altered Inferences	Background Inferences	Kind of Sequence
			S (MsK-MrK) $ [$]	
			(MsK M1)$$ [$]	
27	Mrs. Koole goes to airport.	(MsK −5) $ [−$]	idem +	
			(MsK M1) $$ [$$]	
			(..)? [$$]	
			(MsK M2) $$ [$$]	
			(MsK +3) $$ [$$]	
			S (MsK–MrK)$$ [$$]	
			S (MsK −M) $$ [$$]	
			(M M1) $$ [$$]	
			(..)? [ ]	
			(M M2) $$ [$$]	
			(M +3) $$ [$$]	
28	Mrs. Koole phones, the receiver is taken up and put down again.	(MsK −5) $$ [−$$]	idem	
29	Mrs. Koole is waiting (for Mario).	(MsK −5) ? [ ] (M −7) ? [ ] (M −9) ? [ ]	idem	
30	Mrs. Koole enters the plane after last call.	(MsK −5) $ [$] (M −7) $ [$] (M −9) ? [ ] (MsK −7) ? [ ]	idem	
31	Mrs. Koole gets out of the plane.	(M −7) $ [$] (MsK −5) $$ [$$] (MsK −10) ? [ ] (MsK M6) $ [$$] (MsK −7)? [$$]	idem	
32	Mrs. Koole takes a look at the slaughterhouse.	(MsK M6) $$ [$$]	idem + (M −7) $ [$] (M −9) ? [ ] (MsK −5) $$ [$$] (MsK M6) $ [$$] (MsK −7)? [$$]	
33	Mrs. Koole goes home.	(MsK M6) $$ [$$] (M −9) $ [$] (MsK −7) $ [$$]	idem	t
34	Mrs. Koole tries to telephone somebody but no one answers.	(MsK −7) $$ [$$] (M −9) $$ [ ] (M −7) $$ [ ]	idem · (MsK M6) $$ [$$] (M −9) $ [$] (MsK −7) $ [$$]	t
35	Mrs. Koole goes to sleep in her hobby room.	as 34	idem	

Event No.	Description of Event	New and Altered Inferences	Background Inferences	Kind of Sequence
36	Mr. Koole brings his wife breakfast, they act as if nothing has happened.	S (MrK–MsK) $$ [$] (MrK M2) $ [$] (MrK +3) ? [ ] (MrK –3a) $ [$]	idem + (MsK –7) $$ [$$] (M –9) $$ [ ] (M –7) $$ [ ]	
37	Mrs. Koole asks for Mario at a bar.		idem + S (MrK–MsK) $$ [$] (MrK M2) $ [$] (MrK +3) ? [ ] (MrK –3a) $ [$]	
38	Mrs. Koole sees Miguel, who tells her that his father is on a journey.	(MsK –7) $$ [$$] (M –9) ? [$] (M –7) $$ [$$]	idem	
39	Mr. Koole is putting boxes with meat in the freezer.	S(MrK–MsK) $$ [$$] (MrK M2) $ [$] (MrK +3) ? [ ] (MrK –3a) $ [$]	idem + (MsK –7) $$ [$$] (M –9) ? [$] (M –7) $$ [$$]	
40	Mrs. Koole receives Mario's note.	(MsK –7) –$$ [$$] (MsK M8) $ [$$] (M –7) –$$ [$$] (M –9) –$$ [$]	idem + S(MrK–MsK) $$ [$$] (MrK M2) $ [$] (MrK +3) ? [ ] (MrK –3a) $ [$]	
41	The telephone is ringing.	(MsK M8) $ [$$] (MsK –7) ? [$$] (MsK +9) ? [ ] (M –7) ? [$$] (M –9) ? [$]	idem	
42	Mr. Koole sets his wife down in town on his way to the slaughterhouse.	(MrK –1) $ [$]	idem + (MsK M8) $ [$$] (MsK –7) ? [$$] (MsK +9) ? [ ] (M –7) ? [$$] (M –9) ? [$]	
43	Mrs. Koole enters a drugstore, Mr. Koole drives away.	(HK –1) $ [$]	idem	
44	Mr. Koole notices his wife's shawl in the car and returns to give it to her.	(MrK –1) $ [$$]	idem	

Event No.	Description of Event	New and Altered Inferences	Background Inferences	Kind of Sequence
45	Mr. Koole sees his wife entering a travel bureau and receiving tickets. Koole doesn't signal his presence.	(MrK −1) $$ [$$] (MrK M2) $$ [$$] (MrK +3) $ [$] (MrK −3a) $ [$]	idem	
46	Mario sees Mr. Koole arriving at the slaughterhouse and kisses his medallion. After working hours Mario watches Mr. Koole at the slaughterhouse gate.	S (M−MrK) $$ [$$]	idem + (MrK −1) $$ [$$] (MrK M2) $$ [$$] (MrK +3) $ [$] (MrK −3a) $ [$]	
47	Mr. Koole makes a remark about a trip.	(MrK M2) $$ [$$] (MrK +3) $ [ ] (MrK −3a) $$ [$]	idem + S (M−MrK) $$ [$$]	
48	Mr. Koole wants to assemble a construction kit. He discovers that his glasses are broken and goes to the slaughterhouse to retrieve another pair.	(MrK M2) $$ [$$] (MrK −3a) $$ [$] (MrK +3) $ [$] (M −7) $ [$] (M −9) $ [$]	idem	
49	Mr. Koole hears the noise of the falling axe.	(MrK +3) $$ [$] (M −7) $ [$$]	idem + (MrK M2) $$ [$$] (MrK −3a) $$ [$] (MrK +3) $ [$] (M −7) $ [$] (M −9) $ [$]	s
50	Mr. Koole ignores the noise.	(MrK +3) $$ [$] (M −7) −$$ [$$]	idem	s
51	Mr. Koole hears the alarm of the open door of the freezing chamber.	(MrK +3) $$ [$] (MrK M4) $ [ ] (M −7) $ [$$] (M −9) $ [ ]	idem	s
52	Mr. Koole sees Mario in the freezing chamber.	(MrK +3) $$ [$] (MrK M4) $ [ ] (M −7) $$ [$$] (M −9) $$ [$]	idem	s
53	Mr. Koole locks Mario into the freezing chamber.	(MrK +3) $$ [$] (MrK M4) $ [$] (MrK M5) $ [$] (M −7) $$ [$$] (M −9) $$ [$]	idem	s

Event No.	Description of Event	New and Altered Inferences	Background Inferences	Kind of Sequence
54	While ringing the police, Mr. Koole finds the ticket with the safe's code in Mario's bag. Koole looks at a photo- graph of his wife and understands his wife's and Mario's plans.	(M −7) $$ [$$] (M −9) $$ [$] (MrK +3) $$ [$$] (MrK −3a) $$ [$$] (MrK M4) $$ [$] (MrK M5) $$ [$] (MrK +6) $ [$]	idem	s
55	When the police answer, Mr. Koole puts down the phone.	(M −7) $$ [$$] (M −9) $$ [$] (MrK +3) $$ [$$] (MrK −3a) $$ [$$] (MrK M5) $$ [$] (MrK M4) $$ [$$] (MrK +6) $ [$$]	idem	s
56	Mr. Koole lowers the temperature in the freezing chamber.	(M −7) $$ [$$] (M −9) $$ [$] (MrK +3) $$ [$$] (MrK −3a) $$ [$$] (MrK M4) $$ [$$] (MrK +6) $ [$$] (MrK M5) $$ [$$]	idem	
57	Mr. Koole observes Mario in the freezing chamber through the TV camera for a while before turning the monitor off.	(M −7) $$ [$$] (M −9) $$ [$] (MrK +3) $$ [$$] (MrK −3a) $$ [$$] (MrK M4) $$ [$$] (MrK +6) $ [$$] (MrK M5) $$ [$$] S (MrK) $$ [$$]	idem	
58	Mr. Koole goes to the slaughterhouse.	(MrK −7) $$ [$$] (MrK M8) $ [ ] (MrK +9) $ [$]	idem + (M −7) $$ [$$] (M −9) $$ [$] (MrK +3) $$ [$$] (MrK −3a) $$ [$$] (MrK M4) $$ [$$] (MrK +6) $ [$$] (MrK M5) $$ [$$] S (MrK) $$ [$$]	
59	Mr. Koole processes Mario's body into food for his husky dogs.	(MrK −7) $$ [$$] (MrK M8) $$ [$$] (MrK +9) $$ [$$] (M −9) $$ [$$]	idem	

Event No.	Description of Event	New and Altered Inferences	Background Inferences	Kind of Sequence
60	Mr. Koole finds the note and mails it as a farewell letter to Mrs. Koole.	(MrK −7) $$ [$$] (MrK M8) $$ [$$] (MrK +9) $$ [$$] (M −9) $$ [$$] (MrK M10) $$ [$$] (MrK +12) $$ [$$]	idem	
61	Mr. Koole brings his wife breakfast, they act as if nothing has happened. Later he puts the boxes with the meat in the freezer.	(MsK +9) ? [ ]	idem + (MrK −7) $$ [$$] (MrK M8) $$ [$$] (MrK +9) $$ [$$] (M −9) $$ [$$] (MrK M10) $$ [$$] (MrK +12) $$ [$$]	
62	Mrs. Koole goes to take a look at the slaughterhouse.	(MsK +9) $ [ ] (MsK −10) $ [ ] (MsK M11) ? [ ]	idem	t
63	Mrs. Koole talks to Carlos and they look at the camera in the freezing chamber. Mrs. Koole keeps Carlos from climbing to the camera.	(MsK +9) $$ [$] (MsK −10) $ [$] (MsK M11) $ [ ] (M +8) $ [ ] (MrK −6a) $ [ ]	idem	t
64	Mr. Koole watches this on his monitor.	idem	idem	t
65	Mr. Koole goes into the freezing chamber and sees the medallion. He grasps it and watches it pensively.	(MsK +9) $$ [$] (MsK −10) $$ [$] (M +8) $$ [$$] (MrK −6a) $$ [$$] (MsK M11) $ [$] (MrK −13) $ [$$]	idem	s
66	Mrs. Koole appears in the opening of the door.	(MsK +9) $$ [$] (MsK −10) $$ [$] (M +8) $$ [$$] (MrK −6a) $$ [$$] (MsK M11) $$ [$] (MrK −13) $ [$$]	idem	s
67	Mrs. Koole and her husband look at each other silently.	idem	idem	s
68	Mrs. Koole closes the door of the freezing chamber.	(MsK +9) $$ [$] (MsK −10) $$ [$] (M +8) $$ [$$] (MrK −6a) $$ [$$] (MrK −13) $ [$$]	idem	

Event No.	Description of Event	New and Altered Inferences	Background Inferences	Kind of Sequence
		(MsK M11) $$ [$$]		
		(MsK +12) $$ [$$]		
69	Mr. Koole hears the noise of the engines of the freezing chamber.	idem	idem	

10

Suspense and Disorientation: Two Poles of Emotionally Charged Literary Uncertainty

Gerald C. Cupchik
University of Toronto

PREDICTION AND UNDERSTANDING

We bring to aesthetic episodes knowledge from everyday life without which the thoughts, feelings, and actions of protagonists would not be meaningful. Of course, literary and film materials challenge us by restructuring events in original ways and concealing information from us. These transformations induce states of uncertainty that might be divided into two types. One kind of uncertainty concerns *predictions* regarding future events, be they the experiences of characters or the outcomes of their actions. A second kind of uncertainty concerns the *understanding* of ongoing events, which may require the discovery of facts and conditions concealed from us by the author. The contrast between prediction and understanding and the emotions that accompany these states of uncertainty are central to this chapter.

Typically, problems surrounding prediction have been associated with suspense. Scholars are in agreement that suspense involves a concern "about the outcome of the events set into motion by the initiating event" (Brewer & Lichtenstein, 1981, p. 366). According to Sternberg (1978), "Suspense derives from a lack of desired information concerning the outcomes of a conflict that is to take place in the narrative future, a lack that involves a clash of hope and fear" (p. 65). Kreitler and Kreitler (1972) listed a variety of devices that have been used to create suspense, including foreshadowing and unchronological presentation of a story, unexpected resolutions, and a gradual build-up toward a climax across a series of crises. Tan and Diteweg (chap. 9, this volume) define suspense as an expectation of a relevant negative outcome and show what predictions of such outcomes can actually be made in response to a particular film. It has also been suggested (Vorderer, 1993) that personal involvement is essential if the series of unfolding events is to be taken seriously. Film directors such as Hitchcock (see Truffaut, 1967) manipulated their audiences by informing them in excruciating detail about dangers facing the unknowing protagonists with whom they identify.

If suspense is concerned with uncertainty about future outcomes, then what state is associated with understanding the meaning of present circumstances? Some authors have juxtaposed uncertainty against curiosity. Sternberg (1978), for example, stated that "Curiosity is produced by a lack of information that relates to the narrative past, a time when struggles have already been resolved, and as such it often involves an interest in the information for its own sake. Suspense thus essentially relates to the dynamics of the ongoing action; curiosity, to the dynamics of temporal deformation" (p. 65). From the viewpoint of Brewer and Lichtenstein (1978), in "order to produce curiosity in the reader, the author leaves some significant event out of the discourse, but lets the reader know that the information is missing, thus causing the reader to become curious about the omitted events" (p. 366).

Note how *The Oxford English Dictionary* (1989) treats these two terms. Suspense is described as "A state of mental uncertainty, with expectation of or desire for decision, and usually some apprehension or anxiety as well as doubt" (p. 320). With reference to popular literature, a work can be "characterized by the capacity to arouse suspense, excitement, or apprehension" (p. 321). Curiosity, on the other hand, involves "The desire to know or learn about anything, especially what is novel or strange" (p. 143). These definitions suggest that the kinds of uncertainty which motivate suspense and curiosity are different, but the underlying processes are not clearly differentiated.

Indeed, some authors have used these terms in different ways. Kreitler and Kreitler (1972), for example, associated curiosity with plot-related suspense, which is diminished by information provided in the unfolding story. They contrasted uncertainty about event outcome with a problem in understanding the meaning of what is happening in a bewildering and ambiguous moment. This search for situational meaning focuses on "conflicts within a person, among people, between a human being and nature, reality, society, time, death" (Kreitler & Kreitler, 1972, p. 252). Theatre of the Absurd is presented as an example of the kind of literature that stimulates such intellectual uncertainty. Perhaps this is the best way to go, contrasting underlying processes associated with predicting outcomes and understanding meanings, rather than focusing on the words *suspense* and *curiosity*, which are not diametrically opposed.

THE ROLE OF LITERARY STRUCTURE

Collectively, these authors point to a contrast between intellectual uncertainty about plot-related future outcomes and present situational meanings. Both are a product of temporal deformation, the quality that makes narrative discourse structure different from everyday activity. Iser's (1978) concept of *blanks* provides a helpful framework within which to understand these deformations. Blanks "mark the suspension of connectability between textual segments" (p. 195). In other words, blanks occur if the flow of discourse is broken for some reason. When connectability is suspended between textual segments, the reader must enter to provide structure, thereby transforming the unfolding text.

Iser's (1978) analysis shows how breaks in continuity apply to structural processes involved with suspense, as in the case of the 19th-century technique of presenting novels in installment format. Even stories that border on the trivial might hold a reader's attention in this format. The secret lies in the *cutting technique* of the serial story, which "breaks off just at a point in suspense when one would like to know the outcome of a meeting, a situation, etc. The interruption and consequent prolongation of tension is the basic function of the cut. The result is that we try to imagine how the story will unfold, and in this way we heighten our participation in the course of events" (Iser, 1978, p. 191).

By implication the blank has an equally important role to play in evoking and reducing the experience of uncertainty regarding situational or momentary meaning. As the reader's viewpoint wanders through a text it encounters moments in which connectability between textual elements is suspended. The sudden introduction of a new character or a radical shift in venue or activity represents the introduction of a new theme. However, understanding the meaning of this theme requires the adduction of an appropriate horizon against which it is to be understood. This engages the reader who must unravel the reading process, returning to earlier themes in the context of which the current event takes on meaning. This process enhances the reflective activity of the reader and facilitates the attainment of a new level of understanding.

The direction of a reader's wandering viewpoint, either forward (in the case of suspense) or backward (in the search for meaning), can have experiential effects such as modulating the reader's experience of temporal duration. Stutterheim (1966) stated that, "At a formal level we generate suspense when the distance—that is, the duration experienced together with other moments of consciousness—between two elements is greater than normal, which means greater than expected" (p. 177). Cupchik and Laszlo (1994) found that subjects read action-oriented texts more quickly, especially toward the end, whereas they slowed down when reading texts that were rich in the description of experience. De Wied (1991, 1995) showed that the experienced duration of events is longer in suspense scenes, because outcome events are systematically presented later than they are expected. Readers wait with anticipation for all their emotion-filled expectations to be resolved. The end cannot come fast enough, and as a consequence appears to arrive all too slowly.

By extension, one can speculate that uncertainty about meaning is associated with the experience of "frozen" time. Faced with an event the meaning of which is obscure, the wandering viewpoint stops its natural flow forward and is fraught with anxious uncertainty. The reader must reach back in time, selecting possible contexts that bring the immediate moment into relief and render it meaningful. Of course, this frozen moment may seem to never end because the natural flow forward has been arrested and the duration becomes a heavy burden for the reader.

BERLYNE'S BEHAVIORAL CONTRIBUTION: SUSPENSE AND SURPRISE

There is another contrast with suspense that is of potential interest and it involves the emotion of surprise. Berlyne (1971) provided a very helpful discussion of the dynamics underlying suspense and surprise. His analysis links informational structures in everyday and aesthetic stimuli with the experience of arousal. People approach unfolding episodes in terms of prior knowledge and expectations. Accordingly, they form schemas within which an event is understood and then assimilate incoming information to them. This comparative or collative process is responsible for the experience of qualities such as complexity, orderliness, surprisingness, and clarity.

Berlyne (1960) treated the "scheme of progress" in literature in terms of mounting arousal followed by relief. Uncertainty about future outcomes stimulates reading activity and associated arousal reinforces the reading process in two ways. First, the heightening of arousal that occurs as the reader approaches the story climax is stimulating (providing an *arousal boost*). Second, the diminution of arousal that occurs once the outcome is known is also reinforcing (providing an *arousal moderation*). Thus, the close conjunction between states of cognitive uncertainty and states of arousal underlies the dynamics of suspense.

In the Gothic novel or mystery story, extremely unlikely circumstances are posed and then the author provides some explanation that is uncritically accepted. Berlyne (1960) argued that detective novels create suspense, "agonies of belief–disbelief conflict" (p. 253), by offering both a crime, potential suspects, and reasons to discount each of them as responsible for the crime. In subtler fiction or drama, a main character is endowed "with equally strong but opposed motives or personality traits" thereby creating uncertainty surrounding his or her future actions, or opposing characters are given "seemingly equal advantages" with differing aims "so that the outcome is in the balance" (p. 253). In the end comes the denouement that may be happy or tragic but serves nevertheless to "release arousal because it is inevitable or somehow appropriate, or simply because it is too late to do anything about it now and, in any case, it is *only a story*" (p. 253).

The behavioral roots of this analysis of suspense are evident. In an application of the goal-gradient hypothesis (see Miller, 1971), it can be argued that suspense will increase the closer a reader gets to the climax of a scene. As an interesting paradox, this hypothesis holds that the tendency to avoid an aversive goal increases more quickly than the tendency to approach a positive one. In spite of the increasing tension, a reader continues on as if trapped by the need to resolve uncertainty in spite of the aversive emotion. But after all, "it is only a story" and suspense is not quite fear! This dynamic is present in Cohen's (1966) account of the literary process: "Our orientation to the subjective future appears to have the character of a 'gradient of tension': we become more and more vigilant as an expected event draws near in time ... our hearts beat faster" (p. 263).

Berlyne's (1960) analysis of surprise fits extremely well with what has thus far been described as an attempt to understand the meaning of events occurring in the present. A surprising stimulus pattern is one that "fails to agree with an expectation that was aroused by what preceded it" (p. 145). A reader will experience surprise when an event is incongruous with expectations about what will happen in the story. The arousal in this case reflects disorientation and can be resolved when information is brought forward that resolves the uncertainty. Thus, rather than increasing over time, surprise reaches an immediate peak and diminishes over time as relevant information is adduced.

This juxtaposition between suspense and surprise is quite useful. Whereas suspense focuses on the future, surprise pertains to the present. Suspense builds gradually over time in accordance with the author's manipulation of information and, hence, of uncertainty. Surprise is immediate and reflects a disorientation produced by the contrast between facts and expectations. Uncertainty and disorientation would appear to be the operative constructs for suspense and surprise, respectively.

THE KREITLERS' PSYCHODYNAMIC CONTRIBUTION

There are also psychodynamic rather than behavioral accounts of the evocative power that suspenseful narratives have over readers (Kreitler & Kreitler, 1972). Like Berlyne, the Kreitlers adopted a homeostatic model of motivation according to which "psychologically and physiologically the evocation of pleasure in nearly all its varied forms is concomitant with a rise in tension followed by a reduction in tension" (p. 13). However, they add that "the art experience is motivated by tensions which exist prior to its onset, but are triggered through the production of new tensions by the work of art" (p. 16). Why would people expose themselves to stimulating works of art if indeed the homeostatic principle suggests that people seek to reduce tension. Further, "why does a work of art generate new tensions instead of reducing the existing tensions" (p. 27)?

Their answer is that prior tensions in the spectator play an important motivating role. "The work of art mediates the relief of these tensions by generating new tensions which are specific" (p. 19). According to their approach, unresolved personal tension exists as "diffuse tension, whose cause or origin has been forgotten or never clearly identified" (p. 19). In an innovative variation on a traditional behavioral model of emotion, an additional source of stimulation can be specific enough to "serve as a cue for channelizing the tension in a specific direction" (p. 20). This new cue is a further source of arousal. In sum, the work of art produces "variegated and multidimensional tensions" (p. 22) which combine with the prior diffuse tensions in the spectator and "the resolutions of these tensions is attended by pleasure" (p. 22).

The Kreitlers also offered a different way of conceptualizing the evocative stimulus that is particularly relevant to understanding the meaning of an ongoing event. In a traditional behavioral approach, the stimulus is formally defined. It can be a concrete stimulus, such as a threat, or a structural property, for example, uncertainty about the probability of escaping the threat. However, aesthetic stimuli have the potential to be multilayered in the form of metaphor, irony, and so on.

> Multileveledness is the capacity of a work of art to be grasped, elaborated, and experienced in several systems of connected meanings, each of which allows a meaningful, clear, comprehensive, and sometimes even autonomous organization of all the major constituents of the work of art (p. 295). . . . Each level affords a view of the whole, without impairing the wholeness quality of the work of art, produced by many or all of the levels together. (p. 297)

The concept of *multileveledness* applies in particular to that kind of uncertainty regarding the meaning of an episode or event (not of a passage or other technical unit). According to the Kreitlers, it is possible to generate "several equally valid organizations of the same set of stimuli" (p. 298). Schmidt (1982) applied the term *polyvalence* to describe this diversity of literary interpretations and suggested that it is a basis for aesthetic pleasure. Thus, the potential for generating multiple interpretations regarding the meaning of an event is essential for the resolution of uncertainty about meaning. To the extent that an appropriate context is chosen, the event can be understood in a coherent manner and aesthetic tension can be reduced.

The Kreitlers also proposed a possible integration of the processes underlying the search for meaning and suspense. Certain motifs, such as a chase after a perpetrator of evil, can take on a symbolic search for truth, thereby going beyond the social or personal. Thus, the merely suspenseful can take on a more profound level of meaning if approached in the right way. Consequently, suspense can go beyond the release of tension, stimulating a reader to achieve a more profound level of personal and social understanding.

EMOTIONAL PROCESSES UNDERLYING SUSPENSE AND DISORIENTATION

What are the emotions associated with each of the two kinds of aesthetic reception and how are they elicited? Suspense has been related to the general affects of excitement and apprehension, and the specific emotions of hope and fear. The search for contextualized meaning might be initiated by a surprising or puzzling event that gives rise to a sense of disorientation or discomfort, but it may eventually transform into subtle combinations of emotions. It is ultimately an empirical question as to how general feelings related to uncertainty transform into specific emotions in the two kinds of literary events (see Fig. 10.1).

Let us consider a general framework that encompasses both suspense and the search for meaning. Encounters with the world, whether pragmatic or aesthetic, involve both appraisal and reaction (Cupchik, 1995; Cupchik & Winston, 1992). According to Piaget, appraisal can emphasize either the *assimilation* of an event to the recipient's specific knowledge base or an *accommodation* to its unique qualities (Flavell, 1963). Reactions can involve either independent dimensions of response with a bodily flavor, such as excitement or apprehension, or patterns of distinct primary emotions, including happiness, sadness, anger, and so on (Izard, 1971). The essential points of my dual-processing model are that: (a) assimilation is linked to dimensional bodily responses, and (b) accommodation is linked to patterns of primary emotions.

Suspense is an assimilation-type process whereby specific stimulus configurations elicit bodily feelings (i.e., pleasure and excitement).

Generally speaking, if a recipient wants to experience an affective response, such as pleasure or excitement, a specific kind of stimulus is sought. Thus, naive viewers of art generally prefer sentimental themes (e.g., country life or family life) that evoke a sense of warmth through the vehicle of soft edges and nostalgic imagery (Winston, 1992). In the case of suspense, the experience of apprehension (a form of excitement) is all important; excitement produced by something quite specific—such as uncertainty about an aversive outcome in the life of a sympathetic character. However, this excitement is moderated by the fact that it is only a story after all!

However, to the extent that the recipient is vicariously involved in a character's experience, there indeed may be hope that everything works out in the end and fear that it will not. It is unclear, though, whether this is real fear and real hope in the everyday sense. Perhaps experiences of emotions are progressively more "real" (i.e., like everyday emotions) as the boundary between art and reality is eliminated by an engrossing plot (e.g., the movie *Jaws*).

RECEPTION STATE:	Disorientation	Suspense
LITERARY GENRE:	Theatre of the Absurd	Police Thriller
INTERPRETIVE MODEL:	Understanding	Prediction
COGNITIVE/AFFECTIVE PROCESS:	Reflective	Reactive
	↓	↓
	Meaning ←→ Primary Affect Blends (e.g., sadness and anger)	Configurations ←→ Bodily Feeling States (e.g., pleasure and arousal)

FIG. 10.1.   Emotional responses to literature, theater, and film.

There is one important corollary to this principle: The link between stimulus configurations and dimensionalized bodily feelings is constrained by bodily mechanisms such as conditioning, habituation, and stimulus generalization.

According to stimulus generalization, events that are in any way potentially related to the suspenseful outcome (e.g., a new gangsterlike figure appears on the scene) evoke the feeling of anxious excitement. The gradient of tension is an excellent example of a mechanism whereby approaching the climax directly increases the intensity of a feeling. In terms of habituation, the repeated viewing of a suspenseful film should reduce the intensity of its impact.

Disorientation is an accommodation-type process whereby the meanings of novel and surprising events are resolved with the assistance of patterned primary emotions (e.g., happiness, sadness, anger).

A very different kind of process results when a reader or filmgoer encounters an event that appears multileveled, incongruous, or surprising given what preceded it. This leads to the experience of disorientation and evokes a need to find meaning in the episode, usually by reaching back in time and uncovering a relevant fact that serves to explain the event. Thus, a reader is challenged to find a relevant context that makes the event meaningful (Iser, 1978). The reader can bring unity and meaning to a complex scene by integrating earlier events in the text or film with conjectures about possible emotional meanings derived from personal experiences. If the event is approached as multileveled, then a unique meaning can be found that unifies its different aspects.

In sum, the psychological processes associated with suspense and the search for meaning are very different. A suspenseful narrative engrosses the readers' attention and rushes them into the future riding waves of bodily tension. The process terminates when the fictive resolution becomes known. In contrast, a complex, surprising, or disquieting text arrests the readers' attention, prompting an exhaustive search for meanings and emotions that can encompass and explain the event. Suspense and disorientation are symmetrical with reference to the importance of future and past, respectively, in relation to the present. However, they are radically different when it comes to the kinds of interpretive and emotional processes that underlie them.

REFERENCES

Berlyne, D. E. (1960). *Conflict, arousal, and curiosity.* New York: McGraw-Hill.
Berlyne, D. E. (1971). *Aesthetics and psychobiology.* New York: Appleton-Century-Crofts.
Brewer, W. F., & Lichtenstein, E. H. (1981). Event schemas, story schemas, and story grammars. In C. R. Cooper (Ed.), *Attention and performance IX* (pp. 363–379). Hillsdale, NJ: Lawrence Erlbaum Associates.
Cohen, J. (1966). Subjective time. In J. T. Fraser (Ed.), *The voices of time* (pp. 257–275). New York: George Braziller.
Cupchik, G. C. (1995). Emotion in aesthetics: Reactive and reflective models. *Poetics, 23,* 177–188.

Cupchik, G. C., & Laszlo, J. (1994). The landscape of time in literary reception: Character experience and narrative action. *Cognition and Emotion, 8*, 297–312.

Cupchik, G. C., & Winston, A. S. (1992). Reflection and reaction: A dual-process analysis of emotional responses to art. In L. Y. Dorfman, D. A. Leontiev, V. M. Petrov, & V. A. Sozinov (Eds.), *Art and emotions* (Vol. 2, pp. 65–72). Perm, CIS: The Perm State Institute of Culture.

de Wied, M. (1991). *The role of time structures in the experience of film suspense and duration.* Unpublished doctoral dissertation, University of Amsterdam.

de Wied, M. (1995). The role of temporal expectancies in the production of film suspense. *Poetics, 23*, 107–123.

Flavell, J. H. (1963). *The developmental psychology of Jean Piaget.* New York: Van Nostrand.

Iser, W. (1978). *The act of reading.* Baltimore: Johns Hopkins University.

Izard, C. E. (1971). *The face of emotion.* New York: Appleton-Century-Crofts.

Kreitler, H., & Kreitler, S. (1972). *The psychology of the arts.* Durham, NC: Duke University Press.

Miller, N. E. (1971). *Collected papers.* New York: Aldine Atherton.

Schmidt, S. J. (1982). *Foundations for the empirical science of literature.* Hamburg, Germany: Buske.

Sternberg, M. (1978). *Expositional modes and temporal ordering in fiction.* Baltimore: Johns Hopkins University Press.

Stutterheim, C. F. P. (1966). Time in language and literature. In J. T. Fraser (Ed.), *The voices of time* (pp. 163–179). New York: George Braziller.

The Oxford English Dictionary (2nd ed.). (1989). London: Clarendon.

Truffaut, F. (1967). *Hitchcock.* New York: Simon & Schuster.

Vorderer, P. (1993). Audience involvement and program loyalty. *Poetics, 22*, 89–98.

Winston, A. S. (1992). Sweetness and light: Psychological aesthetics and sentimental art. In G. C. Cupchik & J. Laszlo (Eds.), *Emerging visions: Contemporary approaches to the aesthetic process* (pp. 118–136). New York: Cambridge University Press.

The Psychology of Suspense in Dramatic Exposition

Dolf Zillmann
University of Alabama

In this chapter, I focus on cinematic suspense as a phenomenon that defines a most popular genre of contemporary media entertainment and that permeates numerous other entertaining endeavors. I explore the informational structure of suspenseful drama and examine the cognitive and affective reactions to the information flow in such drama. I investigate affective dispositions toward entities in drama as a result of unfolding events, but also as a consequence of traits that respondents bring to the screen. I also probe the consequences for euphoric and dysphoric reactions of these dispositional factors.

After analyzing suspense in conceptual terms, I specify its unique evocative and experiential characteristics. I concentrate on different strategies of informational layout, as well as on cerebral and emotional aspects of elicited experience and, in particular, its appraisal as joyful. In all of this, I proceed from an intuitive analysis to formal psychological and psychophysiological theory. I consider various theoretical approaches and then pursue those best supported by pertinent research findings.

CONCEPTUALIZATION OF SUSPENSE IN DRAMA

According to dictionary definitions, the suspense concept has at least three shades of meaning. Common usage of the term is said to reflect (a) a state of uncertainty in the sense of doubtfulness and indecision, (b) a state of anxietylike uncertainty, and (c) a state of pleasant excitement about an expected event. In other words, suspense is seen as an experience of uncertainty whose hedonic properties can vary from noxious to pleasant. The experience of uncertainty, moreover, is thought to apply to all anticipated social events and environmental happenings considered likely to upset or gratify. Who instigates these events or happenings, the uncertain persons themselves or others, appears to be immaterial in this conceptualization.

The usefulness of such broad definitions for the consideration of suspense in drama specifically, particularly of the enjoyment that the experience of suspense can foster in its wake, is very limited. To obtain a workable definition, it would seem desirable to exclude, first of all, decisional conflict about outcomes that persons are able to influence by their own action, and to restrict the concept to anticipations of events that are merely witnessed. In suspenseful drama, outcomes lie, after all, outside the respondents' control, and the notion of indecision simply does not meaningfully apply to the consumption of fixed narrative.

More importantly, however, the view that uncertainty can assume any conceivable hedonic valence is troublesome. Uncertainty about a future event is obviously the more pronounced the closer the subjective probability of the event's occurrence is to that of its nonoccurrence. Uncertainty is thus at a maximum when the odds for a desired or a feared outcome are 50–50. In the face of such even odds, the experience of uncertainty about a desired outcome should prove noxious because of the relatively high perceived likelihood that the outcome will not materialize. By the same token, the experience of such uncertainty about a feared outcome should prove noxious because of the relatively high perceived likelihood that the feared event will occur. In short, uncertainty at high levels is unlikely to be hedonically neutral or positive. It tends to produce decidedly noxious states (Berlyne, 1960; Zillmann & Zillmann, in press).

The fact that the experience of suspense, in and of itself, has been considered a pleasant one indicates that, in conceptualizing suspense, the experiential properties of uncertainty have been poorly understood. There is no impetus for euphoria in uncertainty per se. Pleasant excitement, it would seem, can result only from the anticipation of desired outcomes when this anticipation is not tempered by a substantial likelihood of alternative, undesirable outcomes. In other words, uncertainty about favorable happenings is likely to be pleasantly experienced only when this uncertainty is negligible. Uncertainty, then, especially at high levels, is unlikely to evoke joyful reactions. Its removal might. However, as it turns out, the concept of uncertainty is altogether less critical to the experience of suspense than its popular definition suggests and many writers pondering suspense have presumed. We return to this issue as I examine the suspense concept for drama specifically.

If general definitions of suspense fail us, so do most that have been provided by scholars struggling with suspenseful narrative as such. Rabkin (1973), for instance, equated suspense with curiosity in proposing that anything that motivates continued interest in a story constitutes a suspenseful element. Barthes (1977) furnished the following opaque elaboration: "Suspense . . . is a game with structure, designed to endanger and glorify it, constituting a veritable 'thrilling' of intelligibility: by representing order . . . in its fragility, 'suspense' accomplishes the very idea of language" (p. 119). Uncounted similar and equally esoteric assessments seem to mystify the suspense phenomenon rather than elucidate it.

Fortunately, there also exist definitions that highlight aspects of drama that seem critically involved in the creation of suspense. A most useful definition of this kind was offered by Carroll (1990): "Suspense in popular fiction is (a) an affective or emotional concomitant of a narrative answering scene or event which (b) has two logically opposed outcomes such that (c) one is morally correct but unlikely and the other is evil and likely" (p. 138). Although this definition does not specify how and why entities (b) and (c) have an emotional concomitant, we accept it as a guide. I clarify the various definitional elements in terms of our conceptualization of suspense, and I explain how and why particular conditions of information flow generate affect and bring about the experience of suspense.

Expositional Properties of Suspense in Drama

I should reiterate that, in suspenseful drama, respondents are witnesses to events involving others, and that the respondents are neither directly threatened nor directly benefited by the witnessed events. Whatever mechanism is presumed to mediate the respondents' affective reactions, suspense can manifest itself only through the anticipation of outcomes that either endanger or benefit others (i.e., protagonists or other members of the cast). It may prove useful, in addition, to be cognizant of further unique and seemingly universal restrictions that apply to the experience of suspense in drama:

1. Drama must preoccupy itself with negative outcomes.
2. Liked protagonists who are deserving of good fortunes must be selected as targets for negative outcomes in order to make these outcomes feared and dreaded by the respondents.
3. High degrees of subjective certainty (rather than uncertainty) about the occurrence of outcomes that threaten liked protagonists must be created in the respondents.

Apprehensions About Harm and Doom. It is generally accepted that *conflict*, especially human conflict, constitutes the very essence of drama (Marx, 1940; Smiley, 1971). The clash of two or more antagonistic forces is viewed as a basic, necessary condition for drama. Any and every dramatic situation is said to arise from such conflict, and it is explicated or implied that drama cannot exist without the display of conflicts and crises in one form or another. Suspense in drama, in turn, has been viewed as the experience of apprehension about the resolution of conflicts and crises (Carroll, 1984, 1990).

This experience of apprehension can derive, in principle, from (a) the fear that a favored outcome may not be forthcoming, (b) the fear that a deplorable outcome may be forthcoming, (c) the hope that a favored outcome will be forthcoming, (d) the hope that a deplorable outcome will not be forthcoming, and (e) any possible combination of these hopes and fears. It has been shown that the fears and hopes in question are largely a function of respondents' affective dispositions toward the antagonistic parties (Zillmann, 1983a; Zillmann & Bryant, 1994; Zillmann, Bryant, & Sapolsky, 1989; Zillmann & Cantor, 1976).

The indicated disposition-theoretical considerations lead to the expectations that: (a) respondents will hope for outcomes that are favorable for liked and deserving protagonists and deplorable for disliked and undeserving ones; and that (b) respondents will fear outcomes that are deplorable for liked and deserving protagonists and favorable for disliked and undeserving ones. With hopes and fears thus confounded, the question arises as to whether suspenseful drama thrives on hopes or on fears.

The issue can be construed in two ways. First, favorable and deplorable outcomes can be thought of as entirely interdependent. A sympathetic protagonist may be up against a hostile environment, for example, and respondents are placed in suspense by watching him face a thousand dangers as he struggles through savage swamps toward safety. The respondents' affective reactions to these events could be regarded as mediated by the fear that the protagonist will be injured or killed. However, they could equally well be considered to result from the hope for the protagonist's welfare. It could be argued that if respondents had no such hopes, they would not have the fear that things might go wrong—that is, the very fear that presumably produces the gripping experience of suspense. This reasoning suggests that hopes and fears are inseparably intertwined in the apprehensions that produce suspense. In fact, the conceptual separation of hopes and fears would seem to be pointless because the two concepts appear to constitute two alternative ways of describing the same phenomenon of apprehension about an outcome.

Second, and in contrast, outcomes can be thought of as events that cause experiences that are hedonically classifiable as either negative or positive. Outcomes can be noxious or pleasant to protagonists, and they can assume the one or the other hedonic valence to different degrees. Death, mutilation, torture, injury, and social debasement can be categorized as negative outcomes, whereas gain of money, glory, and privileges can be classified as positive ones. Essentially, the distinction is between outcomes that constitute annoyances and outcomes that constitute incentives.

If outcomes are conceptualized in these terms, it becomes clear that suspense in drama is predominantly created through the suggestion of negative outcomes. As in the man vs. swamps example, protagonists often fight for dear life. Although some glory may be attached to sheer survival and the avoidance of injury, the provision of incentives is obviously not a necessary condition for the experience of suspense. Generally speaking, the attainment of incentives in suspenseful drama is secondary to the creation of apprehensions about deplorable, dreaded outcomes. Suspenseful drama consequently features events such as bombs about to explode, dams about to burst, ceilings about to cave in, ocean liners about to sink, and fires about to rage. It features people about to be jumped and stabbed, about to walk into an ambush and get shot, and about to be bitten by snakes, tarantulas, and mad dogs. The common denominator in all of this is the likely suffering of the protagonists. It is impending disaster manifest in anticipated agony, pain, injury, and death. Suspenseful drama, then, appears to thrive on uneasiness and distress about anticipated negative outcomes. Put more directly, it thrives on fear—on empathic fear, to be precise.

Apprehensions About Losing Out on Good Fortunes.   This is not to say that suspense cannot be built on the anticipation of good fortunes. As the popularity of television game shows attest, people can be thrilled with uncertainty about grand prizes hidden behind curtains and in chests. This treasure-hunt type of suspense appears to derive in large measure from the expectation of great rewards. The contestants in such games are obviously not placed at risk. The only misfortune that can befall them is the lack of good fortune. Oddly, it is conceivable that the very possibility of losing (i.e., the fear of not winning) is what produces the experience of suspense in these respondents. At any rate, even a cursory inspection of suspenseful drama should suffice in convincing anyone that suspense is characteristically generated through the creation of apprehensions about bad fortunes rather than good ones. In order to be truly suspenseful, drama must show more than the respondents' likely failure to gain incentives. Something more than not winning must be at stake. A car race, for example, devoid of threats and dangers, without risks to the liked protagonist, and with prizes and glory for all, not only would be uncharacteristic of suspenseful drama, it also would fail to induce suspense reactions of appreciable magnitude. The successful creation of the gripping experience of suspense apparently depends on the display of *credible endangerments.* The audience must think it likely, for example, that the protagonist's car will skid on the oil slick, that a wheel will come off, that the motor will catch on fire, or that the driver will fly out of the curve and tumble down the mountain.

In summary, suspenseful drama relies heavily on the exhibition of threats and dangers to protagonists. The information flow is designed, primarily, to evoke apprehensions about decidedly noxious experiences the protagonists are about to undergo. Although suspense can be generated through the anticipation of favorable, pleasing outcomes, this technique of suspense induction is uncharacteristic, even alien, to suspenseful drama as such. It should be recognized, however, that in suspenseful drama the primary technique of suspense induction, namely the creation of apprehensions about deplorable outcomes, is often confounded with the creation of the anticipation of favorable outcomes as a secondary technique (Zillmann, Johnson, & Hanrahan, 1973).

Dispositions Toward Protagonists and Antagonists. It has been stated already that the respondents' hopes and fears regarding likely events that would affect the welfare of protagonists are dispositionally mediated. Research evidence (Zillmann & Cantor, 1977) indicates that (a) a positive outcome is enjoyed when the protagonist whom it benefits is liked or, at least, not disliked. In sharp contrast, (b) a positive outcome that benefits a disliked protagonist is deplored. The inverse applies to negative outcomes: (c) a negative outcome is deplored when the protagonist whom it victimizes is liked or, at least, not disliked; and (d) a negative outcome that victimizes a disliked protagonist, again in sharp contrast, is enjoyed. Note that what I refer to as disliked protagonist is commonly defined as antagonist.

If it is assumed that these affective reactions are precipitated by hopes for and fears about certain outcomes, it follows that the hopes and fears regarding the same events will be totally different for liked and disliked protagonists. Whereas liked protagonists are considered deserving of positive outcomes, the very possibility of disliked protagonists' benefaction becomes deplorable and distressing. Even more important for suspenseful drama, whereas liked protagonists are regarded as undeserving of negative outcomes, the impending victimization of disliked protagonists is usually not only not deplored, but very much enjoyed. After all, disliked protagonists—typically mean, obnoxious, and evil antagonists who demean and torment others—are merely getting their just deserts (Zillmann & Bryant, 1975).

Obvious as the dispositional mediation of suspense may seem, it is not generally recognized. Smiley (1971), for instance, insisted that "suspense *automatically* occurs during all crises" (p. 68, italics added). Expressed in dramaturgical nomenclature, he proposed that any "hint" that (a) two identified, opposing forces will fight, and that (b) the one or the other party will win, produces the experience of suspense in the "wait" (i.e., the period of time in which the fighting is about to erupt or is in progress) for the "climax" that comes with the resolution of the conflict.

Smiley's automatic suspense reaction is not only at variance with what is known about the dispositional mediation of affective reactions, but is noncompelling intuitively. In the case where two intensely disliked parties fight to the finish, for example, onlookers are likely to be utterly indifferent about, rather than fearful of, any particular outcome. In the case where a resented agent is about to walk into an ambush set by liked protagonists, the only source of suspense appears to be the possibility that something could go wrong with the hoped-for destruction of the villain. Not surprisingly, then, suspense in drama favors the projection of negative, feared outcomes for beloved protagonists—not the projection of such outcomes for just any member of the cast.

Moral Considerations. Our treatment of disposition, it should be noticed, entails elements of justice and morality. The assumption that liked characters are judged to be undeserving of bad fortunes, whereas disliked characters are judged to be deserving of them, accords with moral considerations. So does the complementary assumption that liked characters are judged to be deserving of good fortunes, whereas disliked characters are judged to be undeserving of them. It seems that liked characters are always moral and good and disliked characters are always immoral and evil. It would be premature, however, to conclude that moral judgment follows disposition. The opposite is more likely: As characters do things that respondents deem moral, a favorable affective disposition toward them is formed; and as characters do things that respondents deem immoral, an unfavorable affective disposition toward them is formed. The disposition then mediates the moral judgment of subsequent actions and events (Jose & Brewer, 1984; Zillmann & Cantor, 1977).

Carroll (1984, 1990) emphasized the role of moral considerations in the creation of suspense. He argued, essentially, that respondents hope for morally correct outcomes and fear evil ones. To the extent that morally correct outcomes translate to benefaction of protagonists and evil outcomes to their calamity, this accords with our dispositional conceptualization. However, Carroll granted fiction sole responsibility for the moral judgment of events in drama. Morality is seen "in terms of the values inherent in the fiction" (Carroll, 1990, p. 138). Here our conceptualization differs. We recognize that the moral judgment of respondents is highly personal and varies considerably (Kohlberg, 1964), and that respondents bring their own, unique moral considerations to fiction—considerations capable of overwhelming the morality built into narratives.

It might be argued that, for all practical purposes, fictional morality and the respondents' moral judgment coincide, and that consideration of personal morality is an unnecessary complication. This may well hold true for drama that paints characters morally in black and white. Not all drama takes this form, however, and complex characterizations are bound to foster divergent reactions in respondents who see things different morally. Consider a film that features a woman who has been repeatedly stalked by her estranged abusive husband, and who fears for her life as he confronts her again. Women who have suffered similar abuse might find it morally correct to see the abuser shot dead. Men who have abused their spouses are unlikely to see it that way. They might show little sympathy for the woman's plight, experience little if any suspense when seeing her in a state of panic, and consider her defensive action a heinous crime—suggesting that the outcome was "morally incorrect" for them.

This is to make the point that in suspenseful drama, the morality of an outcome is a function of the respondents' potentially idiosyncratic moral judgment. It is not inherent in fiction. At best, fiction can anticipate the pertinent moral considerations of the large majority of respondents and express itself in terms of these presumed considerations.

The conceptualization of subjective affective dispositions toward characters, in part the result of subjective moral considerations, thus appears to be more useful in explaining suspense. On the other hand, it might be considered limiting because of its focus on people, and because it seems to require the anthropo-morphization of nonhuman entities in drama. Both impressions are erroneous, however. Affective dispositions are not limited to persons. We obviously hold them toward spiders, snakes, dogs, and racehorses. Nothing needs to be anthro-pomorphized as we witness, for instance, a lion chase an impala. Those who detest seeing a brutal kill, for moral or other reasons, may find themselves in suspense, fearing the worst, and rejoicing when the impala gets away. Those with the mentality of a hunter may experience suspense only because the impala might escape unscathed. This example illustrates that liking and disliking need not be based on moral judgment. Respondents may morally accept predation for what it is, but still shiver as the disliked lion gains ground on the liked impala.

Affective dispositions, then, are by no means limited to human targets. They can be held toward any agent or event capable of inducing emotions. However, in suspenseful drama such agents or events tend to assume significant roles only to the extent that they can function as protagonists or antagonistic forces. A lightning-sparked inferno, for instance, can be antagonistic to a group of pro-tagonists. Although events of this kind may be interpreted in moral terms, post facto, it appears that suspense can manifest itself on the basis of entities in conflict toward whom or toward which affective dispositions exist that are not the result of moral reasoning.

Subjective Certainty of Apprehensions. It has been suggested already that maximal uncertainty associated with feared outcomes does not necessarily constitute the point of maximal suspense. In fact, it seems quite unlikely that the degree of uncertainty about outcomes and the intensity of the experience of suspense vary proportionally. One would expect, for instance, that witnessing the endangerment of an intensely liked protagonist produces less fearful appre-hensions, and thus less suspense, when the odds for her safety are perceived to be 50–50 rather than, say, 25–75. It would appear that suspense will be more intensely experienced the greater the respondents' *subjective certainty* that the liked protagonist will succumb, this time, to the destructive forces against which she is struggling.[1] Carroll's (1990) earlier cited definition echoes this proposal: Suspense is seen to be pronounced when an evil outcome is deemed likely—and its good fortune alternative unlikely.

However, although even odds (i.e., maximal uncertainty) may indeed constitute a condition of rather moderate endangerment, total subjective certainty about the liked protagonist's forthcoming victimization does not, in all probability, produce maximal suspense. It may be argued that as soon as respondents are confident that

---

[1]The implications of subjective uncertainty, as projected here, are specific to the experience of suspense and the enjoyment of suspenseful drama. Subjective uncertainty about outcomes has entirely different consequences for the enjoyment of mystery. The genre differences between suspense and mystery have been detailed by Zillmann (1990, 1991b). A similar but somewhat sketchy account was provided by Carroll (1990).

a feared outcome is indeed forthcoming, they are no longer in suspense. The respondents may, at this point, start to experience disappointment and sadness. There is reason to believe that certainty about a forthcoming deplorable event will serve a preparatory appraisal function, which protects against overly intense noxious arousal in response to the depiction of the event once it materializes (Leventhal, 1979). Subjective certainty about a deplorable outcome not only seems to terminate the experience of suspense, it also may be expected to minimize the emotional impact of tragic happenings. According to these considerations, then, uncertainty is a necessary condition for suspense, but the experience of suspense will be more intense the greater the onlookers' subjective certainty that a deplorable outcome will indeed befall a liked protagonist. However, as extreme levels of certainty are reached and the outcome is no longer in doubt, the experience of suspense vanishes and gives way to more definite dysphoric reactions.

This proposal concerning the relationship between subjective uncertainty and the experience of suspense has been validated experimentally. The intensity of suspense increased with ascending levels of certainty, as proposed, up to a maximum just prior to total certainty (Comisky, 1978; Comisky & Bryant, 1982).

Episodic Suspense. It might be argued that most popular dramatic fare is incapable of producing intense experiences of suspense because liked protagonists are hardly ever credibly endangered. In television drama series, with recurrent characters and formats, it is clear from the outset that the main protagonists will survive all conflicts in which they are engaged. The situation is not all that different for the movies. Usually there are cues that permit respondents to infer, with considerable certainty, which parties will be victorious in the end. Fearful apprehensions about deplorable outcomes may seem groundless under these circumstances.

The *macrostructure* of drama, the overall plot or theme (Marx, 1940) that terminates with the ultimate resolution of a dramatic presentation, may indeed contribute little, if anything, to suspense. However, in the course of a single play, the experience of suspense can be produced many times over in pertinent episodes. In the *microstructure* of drama, specific plots can show the liked protagonists credibly endangered. Scores of secondary protagonists can suffer fatal blows. Similar loss of life may not be a viable threat to primary protagonists, but loss of limb may have considerable credibility for these characters. Moreover, the possibility that heroes and heroines are beaten, tortured, stabbed, shot, or otherwise subjected to painful, agonizing, and humiliating treatment certainly can have great credibility. Respondents thus need not fear for the primary protagonists' life, but there can be ample cause for worrying about their being hit, raped, strangled, or severely injured.

Suspense thus tends to be created in chains of potentially independent episodes in which endangerments are indicated, dwelled on, and resolved. The overall plot is unlikely to meet these conditions because of the necessary frequent interpolation of information that connects the elements of a story.

Grand Resolution. It would appear that novel, unpredictable dramatic themes lend themselves more than predictable themes to the creation of high levels of suspense. Because the fate of primary protagonists is unknown and their ultimate survival not guaranteed, respondents can more readily reach the point of subjective certainty about these protagonists' victimization, including their death. The likely contribution of unpredictable overall plots to the enjoyment of drama through the facilitation of suspense seems less important, however, than the theme's contribution in moral terms (Carroll, 1984, 1990). The theme's unique contribution to enjoyment, however, has to await the resolution of the narrative and thus is virtually defined by the play's ultimate outcome. This outcome is undoubtedly morally appraised. More specifically, during the course of a play, respondents will have formed notions, however vague, of what fortunes particular protagonists (as well as antagonists) deserve or do not deserve; resolutions that meet these moral dispositions to sanction then are applauded and foster great enjoyment, whereas resolutions that fail to meet them are deplored and cannot be enjoyed as much, if at all (Jose & Brewer, 1984; Zillmann & Bryant, 1975; Zillmann, Hay, & Bryant, 1975). To the extent that the grand resolution is to serve the enjoyment of drama, the principal function of the ultimate outcome is to ensure euphoric reactions to the final events. This objective, it seems, is best accomplished by the provision of a morally acceptable, applaudable final outcome—usually one that yields glory and other incentives to good and liked characters, mostly because they triumphed over and destroyed all evil agents, at the very least the primary antagonist.

Enjoyment of suspenseful drama is, of course, not entirely dependent on morally appropriate final happenings. The reasoning that has been applied to the grand resolution applies equally to all resolutions of dramatic episodes throughout the narrative. The more satisfying the resolutions of suspenseful plots, the more enjoyment can be attained. The experience of such enjoyment can be repeated in plot chains, unlike the necessarily singular euphoric reaction to the grand resolution. Drama that features suspenseful episodes frequently and that accomplishes joyful reactions to the resolution of most of them should be deemed enjoyable overall, irrespective of the grand resolution's contribution to enjoyment.

The Experience of Suspense

I now can define the experience of drama-evoked suspense, in agreement with the various rationales that have been presented, as a noxious affective reaction that characteristically derives from the respondents' acute, fearful apprehension about deplorable events that threaten liked protagonists, this apprehension being mediated by high but not complete subjective certainty about the occurrence of the anticipated deplorable events.

According to this definition, the experience is compromised when protagonists are insufficiently liked or disliked and/or when the subjective certainty about the anticipated deplorable outcome is either at very low levels or total. We can, more-over, define *suspenseful drama* as dramatic exposition that features sympathetic, liked protagonists in apparent peril, frequently so and in a major way, thus having the capacity to instigate sustained experiences of suspense.

Essentials of Information Flow

The preceding definitions entail a prescription for effective suspenseful drama. They emphasize, first and foremost, the importance of character development. Characters toward whom respondents feel indifferent are unlikely to engage the respondents' concerns about their bad or good fortunes (Hoffner & Cantor, 1991; Zillmann & Cantor, 1977). It is imperative, therefore, that narratives create pro-nounced favorable dispositions toward the chief protagonists by displaying their admirable attributes and their virtuous behavior. The analogous creation of un-favorable dispositions toward antagonists or antagonistic conditions is equally essential. In order to be credibly evil, antagonists must initially succeed in doing evil things. Their eventually faltering deviousness must be reserved for particu-larly satisfying resolutions, usually the grand resolution.

Once liked protagonists and disliked antagonists are in place, the information flow must concentrate on the creation of conditions that credibly endanger the protagonists for appreciably long periods of time. The suspense-mediating nox-ious apprehensions would seem to be more intensive the stronger the positive affective disposition toward the endangered protagonists and the greater the risk to their welfare.

Recipes for the creation of acute experiences of suspense tell us little, however, about the enjoyment of suspense. On the premise that the experience of suspense, per se, is noxious, the basis for enjoyment must lie outside the suspense experience proper. Seemingly paradoxically, it is on the termination of the suspense expe-rience, not during its acute manifestation, that enjoyment is determined: Satisfying resolutions will liberate joyful reactions and dissatisfying resolutions will prevent them, fostering disappointment instead (Carroll, 1990; Zillmann, 1980, 1991b). The outcome of the struggle between good and evil characters or forces is the most obvious condition for the hedonic transition from negative to positive. I have already emphasized the involvement of moral considerations in this transi-tion. The temporary or ultimate triumph of the protagonists over the antagonists appears to define the winning formula for resolutions. I return to this crucial issue in explaining the enjoyment that noxious suspense can instigate.

INVOLVEMENT AND EMOTIONS IN RESPONSE TO SUSPENSEFUL DRAMA

Suspenseful drama has, no doubt, the capacity to engage our emotions. Respond-ents subjected to "torturous" suspense scenes have been observed to break out in sweat, bite their fingernails, become exceedingly restless altogether, and cover their eyes, should the experience become too disturbing. Moreover, they are known to cheer and applaud approvingly when their heroes and heroines eventually humiliate and destroy the evil opposition, seemingly irrespective of the degree of brutality and cruelty involved in the accomplishment. Such noxious or joyous affective reactions exhibit an intensity that rivals that of emotions fostered by actual interpersonal conflict or by gratification obtained in direct social exchange.

The great intensity of emotional reactions that drama can elicit, suspenseful drama in particular, has baffled uncounted scholars. Why is it that people exposed to drama lose or, at any rate, abandon their cognizance of the artificiality of the situation? Why do they fail to recognize the contrived, make-believe nature of the setting and respond to it as an interesting retelling or enactment of an actual, liberally modified, or totally imagined occurrence? How can so-called rational beings fall prey to the actors' personas and respond to them as if they were real persons in their immediate environment—either friend or foe?

The Identification Doctrine of Involvement

The seemingly nonrational emotional involvement in fiction, whatever its particular narrative form, has spawned numerous somewhat mystical conjectures that have been accepted as patent explanations. First and foremost in this is the concept of *identification*. The notion that people identify with fictional heroes (Gabbard, 1987; Metz, 1982; Rimmon-Kenan, 1976; Skura, 1981), even with the cruelest of fictional villains (King, 1981), in order to attain "vicariously" the gratifications that these personas experience, has become commonplace psychology (Mendelsohn, 1966). It is the gospel, still, in much of narrative and cinematic analysis (Altenbernd & Lewis, 1969; Kaplan, 1990). Notwithstanding the popularity of the identification concept in considering drama and drama appreciation, the concept's usefulness in this context has been called into question (Zillmann, 1994).

Identification is a Freudian concept (Freud, 1923/1964a, 1921/1964b) whose meaning has been lost to a large degree. Hall (1954), in a popular primer of Freudian psychology, defined it as "the incorporation of the qualities of an external object, usually those of another person, into one's personality" (p. 74). He went on to suggest that "we always tend to identify with people who have the same characteristics that we have" (p. 74). Such an interpretation may have intuitive appeal. However, it seems to reverse the sequence of events specified by Freud. His sequence projects trait likeness to result from identification, rather than to be the cause of it.

Freud developed the concept of identification in connection with the Oedipus complex. To him, identification characterizes the earliest emotional bond between a child and another person. He focused on the male child, who develops an ideal conception of his father, and then seeks to attain this ideal by adopting all aspects of the father's behavior (Freud, 1921/1964b). It is the adoption of mother-directed libido, of course, that eventually creates the Oedipal dilemma.

Irrespective of these complications, Freud apparently believed that identification serves to attain valued, wanted traits, and that it fosters behavioral emulation and the adoption of traits. He insisted, however, that identification is more than overt imitation (Freud, 1900/1968), and that the desire "to be like" an external agent results in the assimilation of this agent. The fact that the specifics of the proposed more-than-imitation assimilation have never been adequately articulated opened the door to interpretations ranging from pretended or actual emulation to transitory or permanent ego confusion.

The concept, as commonly used now, was succinctly articulated by Friedberg (1990): "Identification is a process which commands the subject to be displaced by an *other*; it is a procedure which refuses and recuperates the separation between self and other" (p. 36). If only for a fleeting moment, then, self and other become one (in some unspecified fashion), and eventually separate again to normalcy. Contempt for such magic is rebuffed by the argument that identification is subcognitive and "draws upon a repertoire of unconscious processes" (p. 36). It is implied, of course, that the processes in question are empirically inaccessible, which makes all contentions nonfalsifiable.

Metz (1982) was most specific in his conception of *cinematic identification*. Primary identification, he suggested, is with the vision- and sound-reproducing systems. These systems substitute for eyes and ears in the structured path of camera and microphone. The camera, in particular, forces the respondent's head into a scripted walk during which such primary identification is thought to occur. In Metz's scheme, identification of the Freudian variety—with actors, their personas, or the stars in their extracinematic existence—is secondary identification.

Surely, there have always been a few who thought to be someone else, pathologically so if they had difficulty to return to self. Equally certain is that a great many people, dissatisfied with themselves and their lot, envy others and wish to be in their place. They may well try, as best as they can, to imagine themselves in these others' place and thereby seek access to the gratifications denied them in their own lives. Whether such efforts bear fruit or result in further despair remains to be seen. Particularly unclear is whether the unimaginatives' or the imaginatively passives' imagination is mechanically engaged by merely witnessing persons or their personas who display desired traits and fortunes.

Freud's (1905–1906/1987) answer is unmistakably positive. He pointed to the powers of the playwright and actor. These agents are seen as providers of a *Scheinwelt* that enables the spectator, characterized as "a poor soul to whom nothing of importance seems to happen, who some time ago had to moderate or abandon his ambition to take center stage in matters of significance, and who longs to feel and to act and to arrange things according to his desires" (pp. 656–657), to attain the fulfillment of his thwarted wishes. The spectator, said Freud, "wants to be a hero, if only for a limited time, and playwrights and actors make it possible for him through *identification* with a hero" (p. 657, author's translation). Accordingly, the cinema and all other narrative formats may be seen as forums that offer a cast of heroes and heroines or others with desirable characteristics among whom respondents, depending on their desires, can choose a party for identification. In fact, they are free to enter into and abandon identifications. However, it is generally held that there be identification with only one party at a time. Lastly, identification with fictional characters is presumed to be rather effortless, not requiring particular imagination skills or deliberate cognitive maneuvers.

The question is whether these proposed mechanics can explain the affective behavior of respondents to cinematic presentations and alternative narrative art forms. Do respondents place themselves, however tentatively, into essentially envied personas and then "share" the emotions displayed by these personas? Can respondents vicariously (i.e., in place of others) experience the personas' emotions and thereby gain access to the gratifications experienced by them?

A *Gedankenexperiment* should help to clarify the issue. I call on early childhood experiences that most of us are likely to have had: experiences with the puppet theater, like the Punch-and-Judy show or the German *Kasperletheater*. In order to avoid the sexism of Punch and Judy, I focus on Kasperle, a paragon of goodness who fights all evil with a club he usually holds over his shoulder.

Anybody who has ever watched the behavior of children in response to Kasperle's antics will be able to confirm that this character, although thoroughly liked, does not evoke parallel, congruent, or concordant affect through identification. This is most apparent in the characteristic suspenseful tease of the children, when Kasperle enjoys, say, a present he has received while a crocodile or the devil himself is sneaking up behind him, ready to inflict harm. The onlooking children will simply *not* share and display the euphoria of their hero—which they should, had they put themselves in his stead. Rather, they surely will scream in distress, trying to avert harm to Kasperle. Shouts like "Watch out!," "Look behind you!," or "There's a crocodile coming!" signal a desire to intervene and thereby reveal that the children respond as observers, as third parties, who did succumb to the theatrical illusion that social reality unfolded before them. They respond to Kasperle and his foes in much the same way they respond to friends and foes in their actual, immediate social environment. When their theatrical hero finally manages to bring justice to the situation, the children can enjoy this restoration of justice. The assumption that they enjoyed a just resolution because they thought to have been Kasperle and acted on his behalf is simply not necessary, violates parsimony of explanation, and most importantly, is empirically unfounded.

This assessment is not changed by the likely emulation of Kasperle. Children are encouraged to emulate positive models and are generally rewarded for doing so. Thus, even if some children were to adopt Kasperle's mannerisms, it would be premature to infer that they seek to enter into the totality of his existence—or that they must have identified with their hero during his theatrical existence.

Adolescent and adult audiences have learned to inhibit intervention attempts. Theatrical convention condemns attempts of this kind as inappropriate. They disclose, after all, the succumbing to a somewhat embarrassing illusion. Oddly, the expression of approval of action is allowed, and audiences are free to applaud, literally, the protagonists' triumph over evil, even the often brutal restoration of justice. Such behavior gives further evidence to the respondent-as-observer interpretation of affect mediation.

Independent of intervention attempts and action approval, any suspense cliché provides evidence against identification. The wild west hero, for instance, who calmly and collectedly rides into an ambush, with shotguns aimed at him from all rooftops, is unlikely to project his sense of security on the audience. The audience, instead, is likely to be taken in by the impression of impending harm. This reaction reveals once again the audience's concern for the welfare of heroes, responding to them as if they were personal friends.

Hitchcock's (1959) suspense prototype of a couple on a sidewalk, approaching an open manhole while engaged in lively conversation, makes the same point. As witnesses, respondents to the cinematic event experience emotions that are based on the fear that the couple, although only a reflection of light off a screen, might stumble, fall, and knock their teeth out.

All these examples show that respondents treat theatrical personas as friends or foes similar to friends and foes in their immediate social environment, that they experience emotions accordingly, but that they eventually learn to hold back any actions to intervene in the activities before them.

Metz's (1982) cinematic concept of primary identification,[2] an identification that is supposedly forced on respondents by the subjective vision of the camera, also is far from compelling and can readily be accommodated by the witness conceptualization. The iconic trace produced by camera and microphone simply can be considered a first-witness record that is rewitnessed by respondents. Even if we were to grant the camera the status of a first experiencer, there is no reason to assume that presentation of such first experience compels anyone to abandon consciousness of self and to place himself or herself existentially in the camera's stead—or in place of a person whose perceptual experience the camera record is thought to represent. The latter pertains to the simulation of another person's vision by a roaming camera. The makers of horror, for instance, insist that having the camera chase a victim through the bushes, having it look down on the fallen, pleading person, and having it show how the far end of a dagger moving away from the camera right through the victim's abdomen ensures identification with the murderer and thus provides the thrill of forbidden experiences to anybody who cares to watch (King, 1981). However, identification is not ensured. Respondents simply rewitness what the murderer must have witnessed during primary experience. This, at least, is what must be concluded from the scarce research on this topic (Sapolsky, cited in Zillmann, 1994).

Notwithstanding the lingering popularity of the identification concept in discussions of involvement with fiction, then, the concept is without empirical foundation

---

[2]A detailed discussion of Metz's conceptualization and its problems was presented by Zillmann (1994).

and amounts to an act of faith. It would appear that the time has come to abandon the notion and replace it with a conceptualization whose components and interdependencies can be demonstrated empirically.[3]

Empathic Mediation of Involvement

Empathy is a concept that, in contrast to identification, has generated a considerable amount of research and now can be considered firmly established empirically. Moreover, the empathy concept is entirely compatible with the respondent-as-witness approach that we have advocated. It is, in this context, capable of explaining much of the respondents' affective reactivity that is instigated by fictional as well as nonfictional events.

The empathy concept is comparatively new. It is said to derive from German aesthetics at the turn of the century (Brentano, 1874/1924; Lipps, 1903, 1906, 1907; Prandtl, 1910; Worringer, 1908/1959). The term *Einfühlung*, translatable as "feeling into" another entity, gained acceptance during this period and eventually entered into general psychology (Wispe, 1987). Titchener (1915) appears to have popularized the concept in U.S. psychology.

It would be misleading, however, to credit German aesthetics with the invention of the concept. Under the heading of *sympathy*, empathic processes have received much attention and have been scrutinized by numerous scholars (Baldwin, 1897; Ribot, 1897; Scheler, 1913; Spencer, 1870; Spinoza, 1677/1985). The British philosopher Smith (1759/1971) might be considered the authority on the subject, having dealt with it more sensitively than others. Smith recognized the automatic features of many empathic responses, as well as the cognitive instigation and mediation of complex feeling states. He also identified the anticipatory nature of numerous empathic reactions, stating that, "When we see a stroke aimed and just ready to fall upon the leg or arm of another person, we naturally shrink and draw back our own leg or our own arm" (p. 3). Perhaps most importantly, he recognized the empathy mediation of the pleasures that may be derived from any kind of storytelling: "How selfish soever man may be supposed, there are evidently some principles in his nature, which interest him in the fortune of others, and render their happiness necessary to him, though he derives nothing from it except the pleasure of seeing it" (p. 1).

The various conceptualizations of empathy have been reviewed by Zillmann (1991a) and integrated as follows: *Empathy* is defined as any experience that is

---

[3]It should be noted that the discussed problems with the concept of identification concern identification with a singular unique entity, such as a particular human being. The concept of *social identification*, as used in theories of social identity (Abrams & Hogg, 1990; Tajfel, 1982) and social categorization (Turner, 1985), is devoid of these problems. The simple reason for this is that persons who believe themselves to be members of a group, however tentatively defined this social aggregate may be (e.g., fans of a rock group or a sports team; cf. Zillmann & Bhatia, 1989; Zillmann & Paulus, 1993), fully retain cognizance of the separation of self and others.

a response (a) to information about circumstances presumed to cause acute emotions in another individual and/or (b) to the bodily, facial, paralinguistic, and linguistic expression of emotional experiences by another individual and/or (c) to another individual's actions that are presumed to be precipitated by acute emotional experiences, this response being (d) associated with an appreciable increase in excitation and (e) construed by respondents as feeling with or feeling for another individual.

This definition allows one to consider empathic, first and foremost, any concordant reflexive or reflective emotional reaction to witnessing others express emotional reactions. The condition of concordance (Berger, 1962) must be met, at least in terms of hedonic compatibility, to ensure that respondents can construe their reactions as feeling with or feeling for these others. However, the definition extends to causal circumstances that eventually may foster emotional expression in affected others, as well as to others' emotionally nonexpressive actions that imply their emotions.

Such extended conceptualization of empathy allows us to consider the experience of suspense and the accompanying excitatory activity as an anticipatory emotion that is primarily elicited by the comprehension of causal circumstances that threaten harm to an entity of concern (Frijda, 1986). Returning to Hitchcock's (1959) manhole illustration of suspense, suspense cannot be considered elicited by affect expressed on the part of the potential victims. The protagonists are oblivious to the impending disaster and express, if anything, positive emotions. Empathy thus cannot be in response to the protagonists' facial or bodily expression of their recognition of danger. It must come, and according to Hitchcock it does, from the respondents' appraisal of the situation. This appraisal, in turn, must activate the anticipatory emotion of suspense.

Hitchcock's illustration should not be misconstrued as a claim that protagonists need to be oblivious to their potential victimization. They may eventually, if not from the outset, comprehend their dilemma and express their concern verbally, paralinguistically, facially, or bodily in the appropriate emotions: anxiety, acute fear, or panic. Such expression provides ample opportunity for empathy, for feeling for or with, by respondents. In the creation of suspense, then, both the respondents' appraisal of conditions threatening protagonists and the immediate empathic reaction to their plight are essential contributors.

It should be noticed that we limited the list of emotional expressions capable of eliciting or intensifying the experience of suspense to withdrawal-linked emotions, such as fear. The protagonists' expression of approach-linked affect, such as anger and rage, is considered to signal their ability to cope successfully with the endangering conditions, thereby diminishing apprehensions. The expression of positive emotions, such as belittling amusement, should have the same consequence. An investigation by Bergman (cited in Zillmann, 1980) shows, in fact, that a protagonist's apparent ability to ward off and punish an assailant compromises the respondents' concern and thereby the experience of suspense.

Theories addressing empathic phenomena are usually grouped into three categories: (a) those that posit that empathy is due to innate, reflexive processes, (b) those that posit that empathy is acquired through processes that entail neither awareness nor deliberate cognitive operations, and (c) those that focus on deliberate cognitive maneuvers.[4] The proposed mechanisms actually correspond rather closely with a commonly employed taxonomy of empathic processes. Innate, reflexive empathy models (Lipps, 1907; McDougall, 1908) concentrate on motor mimicry. Models suggesting deliberate cognitive efforts at putting oneself into another's place (not in the sense of identifying with that other, but as an attempt at understanding as much as possible of this other's experiential state) address perspective or role taking (Rogers, 1967; Stotland, 1969). The learning-theoretical approaches (Aronfreed, 1970; Berger, 1962; Hoffman, 1973; Humphrey, 1922) focus on affective reactivity and, especially, empathic reactivity. The latter is a part of the former, the part that subsumes emotional reactions that are concordant with explicit, implicit, or impending similar reactions witnessed in others.

The empirical research pertaining to these mechanisms of empathy and emotional involvement has been presented and discussed elsewhere (Zillmann, 1994). Suffice it here to say that all of them attracted considerable research support. In response to suspenseful expositions, we thus may expect relatively primitive mimicry reactions to expressed emotions and actions (such as respondents' jerking their heads backward on seeing a protagonist receive a blow to the face that jolts his head backward) and largely acquired concordant affect (such as crying on seeing a protagonist cry or becoming tense as a protagonist is witnessed becoming tense), as well as perspective taking (such as a better comprehension of a protagonist's dilemma by imagining oneself in a similar situation). Reflexive and acquired response dispositions, because they do not require cognitive elaboration, are most directly responsible for immediate empathy. Perspective taking can be considered a modifier, primarily, of empathy induced by other mechanics. However, its frequent application may result in greater empathic sensitivity as a trait (de Wied, Zillmann, & Ordman, 1994). High empathic sensitivity, formed in this fashion, may then be expected to foster particularly strong suspense reactions to expositions that thrive on the expression of apprehensions and fear.

Empathic reactivity, however, it should be recalled, does not depend on emotional displays by protagonists and other cast members. It can be instigated by the comprehension of threatening circumstances and the anticipation of harm to entities of concern, usually persons, in the absence of anybody's expression of emotion.

Consideration of the role of empathic reactivity to drama, of the enjoyment of drama in particular, would be patently incomplete, however, without recognition of conditions under which concordant affect does not materialize—in fact, of

---

[4]The interested reader is referred to a review by Zillmann (1991a) that features a comparative and integrative analysis of the pertinent empathy theories.

conditions under which discordant affect comes about. Suspenseful drama is obviously laden with situations in which some individuals' humiliation and destruction prompts euphoria. This situation is essential to satisfying resolutions, especially to grand resolutions. However, this very situation is one that calls for the suspension of all empathic inclinations. There must be conditions, then, under which respondents can readily abandon empathic concerns and behave in ways that are utterly inconsistent with empathy. We now turn to such counterempathic emotional behavior.

Dispositional Override of Empathic Involvement

Theories of empathy naturally concern themselves with concordance of affect in model and observer. Situations of nonconcordance and outcomes opposite to concordance, usually referred to as *counterempathy*, are acknowledged, but their prediction has not been systematically integrated in the theories.

McDougall's (1908, 1922) theorizing constitutes an exception to the rule. He held that empathy is an innate response disposition that continually compels observers to experience the emotions of witnessed others. McDougall feared, in fact, that individuals could get so caught up in empathizing with the miseries and joys of others, especially with the former, that this innate disposition would prove pathogenic. His apprehensions forced him to develop theoretical amendments capable of saving those who would come to grief over the grief of others—or as in suspenseful drama, over the anticipated grief of others. Focusing on persons who are resentful toward those they witness undergo misfortunes, he proposed a theory of amusement that essentially projects gaiety as a response that relieves morally inappropriate empathic grief. The conversion of empathic grief to amusement was, of course, to secure the welfare of all innately motivated, universal empathizers.

Zillmann (1980, 1991b) similarly focused on affective dispositions toward witnessed agents, but proposed very different consequences of these dispositions. Based on the three-factor theory of empathy that integrates reflexive, acquired, and deliberate empathic reactivity (Zillmann, 1991a), it is suggested that, with the likely exception of reflexive reactions, affective dispositions toward persons or their personas virtually control empathy. Specifically, it is posited that positive affective dispositions toward models foster empathic reactions, whereas negative affective dispositions impair, prevent, or hedonically reverse them. The intensity of these empathic or counterempathic reactions is in turn projected to be a function of the magnitude of positive or negative initial affect toward the observed entity: The stronger the positive affect, the more intense the empathic reactions; the stronger the negative sentiment, the more intense the counterempathic reactions.

These expectations are associated with the assumption that positive affective dispositions motivate the approval of good fortunes and the disapproval of misfortunes that are experienced by observed persons or personas, whereas negative affective dispositions motivate the disapproval of good fortunes and the approval of misfortunes. Such correspondence between affective disposition and the approval or disapproval of outcomes derives from appraisals that entail moral judgment. In turn, this presupposes that the conduct of persons or personas is monitored and judged as appropriate and good or inappropriate and bad.

Thus, it is argued that once persons or personas are liked, their benefaction seems appropriate and can be sanctioned; empathy with their positive emotions is free to unfold. In contrast, their victimization seems inappropriate and cannot be sanctioned; empathy with their negative emotions again is free to unfold. This situation reverses for negative sentiments toward entities. Once persons or personas are resented, their benefaction seems inappropriate and cannot be sanctioned; empathy with their positive emotions cannot materialize, and distress is likely. In contrast, their victimization seems appropriate and can be sanctioned; empathy with their negative emotions again cannot materialize, and euphoria is likely. We share, then, the emotions of happy occasions and threatening or tragic events with those we consider friends. However, our enemies' good fortunes distress us, and their misfortunes give us pleasure.

This reasoning extends to actively wishing or fearing particular outcomes. Positive affective dispositions toward persons or personas make us hope for good fortunes, and we share the emotions that the attainment of these good fortunes liberates. At the same time we fear misfortunes, and we suffer, in the experience of suspense, their prospect and, in tragedy, their occurrence. In contrast, negative affective dispositions toward persons or personas make us fear good fortunes, and we are disturbed by their occurrence. At the same time we hope for victimization, which we can freely enjoy in the name of justice.

Figure 11.1 summarizes the involvement of moral judgment in disposition formation, as well as the involvement of both moral judgment and active expectations in empathic reactivity. The indicated interdependencies among moral judgment, affective disposition, and empathy in the form of affect from both the anticipation of relevant events and the witnessing of outcomes have been established in numerous investigations (Jose & Brewer, 1984; Wilson, Cantor, Gordon, & Zillmann, 1986; Zillmann & Bryant, 1975; Zillmann & Cantor, 1977; Zillmann, Hay, & Bryant, 1975). The pertinent research has been discussed elsewhere in considerable detail (Zillmann, 1991b, 1994).

THE STRATEGIC EVOCATION OF EMOTIONS IN SUSPENSEFUL DRAMA

I am now in a position to articulate the validated principles that govern affective responding during suspenseful drama and on its conclusion.

For the effective creation of the experience of suspense, two components are indispensable.

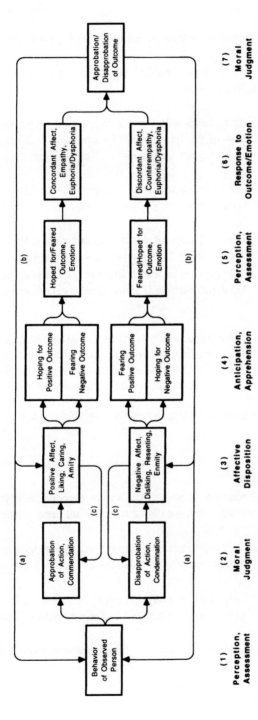

FIG. 11.1. A model of dispositional mediation of affect from witnessing the actions and experiences of others. Stages 2 and 7 indicate the involvement of moral considerations in the formation of affective dispositions, and Stages 3 and 4 indicate the resulting affective dispositions and their influence on anticipatory affects. Stages 5 and 6 specify affective reactions to pertinent outcomes, such as gratification or aversion, and to their expressive consequences, such as elation or distress. Feedback Loop c indicates the influence of formed dispositions on moral judgment, such as amity fostering tolerance and enmity fostering strictness. Loop b suggests a similar influence of witnessed outcomes through their impact on dispositions. For instance, punitive treatments deemed overly severe are likely to foster sympathy and promote liking, and gratifications deemed too generous might dismay and promote disliking. Feedback Loop a, finally, indicates that the process described in Stages 1 through 7 is recursive and can be chained to arbitrary length. The experience of suspense and the reaction to suspense resolution are specified in the upper half of the graph. Specifically, a protagonist's amiable conduct fosters liking and caring (Stages 2–3), negative outcomes are acutely feared and their prospect manifests itself in the suspense-defining experience of distress (Stage 4), and hoped-for positive outcomes, should they come about, are applauded (Stage 5) and prompt euphoric empathy (Stage 6).

1. Protagonists or substitute entities toward whom or which favorable affective dispositions are held.

2. Antagonists or conditions who or that can credibly threaten the welfare of the protagonists or substitute entities.

The narrative merger of these components will produce the noxious experience of suspense. The affective intensity of this experience of suspense is influenced by the following conditions, which may act in concert.

1. The intensity of experienced suspense increases with the magnitude of the respondents' positive affective dispositions toward protagonists or substitute entities.

2. The intensity of experienced suspense increases with the respondent-assessed magnitude of harm threatening protagonists or substitute entities.

3. The intensity of experienced suspense increases with the respondents' subjective certainty that the threatened harm will materialize, short of certainty about this outcome.

In addition to the experience of suspense, noxious affect is generated by witnessing antagonists or conditions victimizing third parties. Such victimization is necessary to establish credible threats to the welfare of protagonists. The witnessed victimization determines, of course, the magnitude of unfavorable affective dispositions toward antagonists.

Euphoric or dysphoric reactions manifest themselves on the resolution of suspense.

1. Euphoria is elicited when anticipated, feared harm to protagonists is averted either entirely or to a significant degree.

2. The intensity of euphoric reactions to averted harm to protagonists increases with the magnitude of favorable affective dispositions toward these protagonists.

3. The intensity of euphoric reactions to averted harm to protagonists increases with the magnitude of unfavorable affective dispositions toward the antagonists.

4. The intensity of euphoric reactions to averted harm to protagonists is the greater, the more this outcome can be attributed to the protagonists' own deliberate action.

5. The intensity of euphoric reactions to averted harm to protagonists is the greater, the greater the antagonists' perceived power to inflict harm.

6. The more the antagonists come to harm and the more the protagonists are benefited, the stronger the euphoric reactions.

The combination of Propositions 4, 5, and 6 points, of course, to the optimal resolution of suspense: the one in which the hero or heroine, by his or her own initiative, destroys "the forces of evil" and then is duly rewarded for the accomplishment.

The consideration of dysphoria on the resolution of suspense is of secondary importance, but relevant nonetheless. Dysphoria on the grand resolution of suspenseful drama would virtually demand a reclassification of a play under consideration. More or less by definition, suspenseful drama features a satisfying ending. Violation of this prescription converts such drama to tragedy, irrespective of suspenseful episodes that were presented prior to the concluding grand debacle in which the protagonists, although utterly undeserving of misfortunes, come to grievous harm.

Suspenseful drama may, however, feature suspenseful episodes with less than satisfying solutions, and do so rather frequently. For instance, heroes and heroines may emerge from an agonistic encounter bruised, beaten up, and even badly injured. Such outcomes tend to build up the antagonists' potency for malice, but offer little, if any, cause for euphoria. Getting away with life usually is deemed insufficient grounds for jubilation. If friends (i.e., secondary, expendable protagonists) are lost in the encounter, the episodic outcome is truly deplorable and tragic. For episode resolutions of this kind, dysphoric reactions, transitional as they may be, must be expected.

The prediction of these dysphoric reactions merely requires the inversion of the propositions concerning euphoria.

1. Dysphoria is elicited when anticipated, feared harm to protagonists actually materializes, either entirely or to a significant degree.
2. The intensity of dysphoric reactions to harm inflicted on protagonists increases with the magnitude of favorable affective dispositions toward these protagonists.
3. The intensity of dysphoric reactions to harm inflicted on protagonists increases with the magnitude of unfavorable affective dispositions toward the antagonists.
4. The intensity of dysphoric reactions to harm inflicted on protagonists is the greater, the more this outcome can be attributed to the antagonists' deliberate action.
5. The intensity of dysphoric reactions to harm inflicted on protagonists is the greater, the less the antagonists' perceived power to inflict harm.
6. The more the protagonists come to harm and the more the antagonists are benefited, the stronger the dysphoric reactions.

In this case, the combination of Propositions 4, 5, and 6 points to resolutions of episodic suspense that are utterly deplorable and that cannot be enjoyed.

THE PARADOX OF POSITIVE-AFFECT DOMINANCE
IN SUSPENSEFUL DRAMA

Given these determinants of negative and positive emotional reactions to dramatic events, on the one hand, and the characteristic flow of information in suspenseful drama, on the other, the fact that this genre of entertainment enjoys an extraordinarily strong following must seem puzzling. Even a cursory analysis of the amount of time dedicated to the elicitation of negative emotions, compared to that dedicated to the elicitation of positive emotions, should make it clear that substantially more time is given to negative emotions. Time dedicated to the induction of suspense is usually stretched to its limits. Additionally, the duration of time in which secondary protagonists fall by the wayside (so as to make later endangerments created by antagonists more credible and of greater, more severe consequence) and primary protagonists are less than triumphant (on the resolution of potentially many suspenseful episodes) tends to exceed, by a great margin, the duration of time in which protagonists dominate with ease and reap glory along with the attached social benefits. Focusing on the time course of emotional experience thus reveals that ample time is given to noxious empathic distress and equally noxious dissatisfying resolutions of suspenseful episodes, whereas comparatively little time is given to truly satisfying outcomes. Suspenseful drama apparently dwells on noxious affect (Zillmann, 1980).

Such disproportionality in favor of negative emotions poses problems for summative models of the enjoyment of suspenseful drama. If respondents suffer distress most of the time during exposure to dramatic exposition, and occasions for unmitigated pleasure are few and far between, the respondents' postconsumption assessment should be one of disappointment, contempt, and condemnation. The fact that this assessment generally yields enjoyment points to hidden sources of pleasure that are to be found and understood.

It might be argued, first of all, that the duration of affect is secondary, if not immaterial, and that the intensity of emotional reactions is crucial in determining enjoyment—immediate euphoric reactions as well as retroactive assessments of enjoyment following grand resolution. However, attempts to separate the stimuli that induce negative affect from those that induce positive affect in order to ascertain experiential intensity are unproductive. In fact, such separation is inconceivable. It would destroy the unique contiguity of negative and positive affect that characterizes fictional suspense and that potentially determines enjoyment on resolution. The actions of heroes and heroines would be next to meaningless if deprived of the endangerments that inspire them. The protagonists' triumph necessitates the preceding perpetration of something evil by antagonists who can be brought to justice or by conditions that can be brought under control. The indicated outcomes, in turn, are necessary for the elicitation of positive emotions in respondents. The suspense-resolution chain, therefore, must be left intact.

Acceptance of the inseparability of suspense and its resolution carries with it the acceptance of the dependence of the enjoyment experience on the resolution-preceding experience of suspense. This dependence can be construed as a simple semantic dependency: The suspenseful happenings are necessary to give meaning to the suspense-terminating, resolving actions. In such an interpretation, exposure to both the suspense treatment and the resolution creates independently unique affective reactions. Contiguity of these reactions is without further consequence.

The alternative view holds that the intensity of the preceding affective state, empathic distress, influences the intensity of the subsequent affective state, euphoria. More specifically, it posits that the affective intensity of a prior state is capable of increasing the intensity of the subsequent state. In the case of suspenseful drama, this would mean that the more distress is produced by a suspense treatment, the greater or more intense will be the enjoyment at suspense resolution. This expectation would not only apply to grand resolutions, but to all suspense resolutions in the microstructure of drama.

The notion that empathic distress may have a great payoff in enjoyment is not new. Numerous scholars entertained it, if only tacitly (Carroll, 1990; Marx, 1940; Smiley, 1971). In fact, one might consider the matter too obvious to bother with it. More intense distress comes, after all, with greater endangerments whose prompt abrogation gives heroes and heroines a chance to impress us more favorably and lets us more intensely enjoy the outcome. Research evidence actually shows that liking of protagonists and enjoyment of suspenseful drama increase with the magnitude of danger that the protagonists face and overcome (Zillmann, Hay, & Bryant, 1975).

However, enjoyment of suspenseful drama also has been shown to increase with the degree of the protagonists' vulnerability (Bergman, cited in Zillmann, 1980). The blind protagonist in *Wait Until Dark* might serve as an example. She fights off killers for sheer survival. In continual panic, not in self-confident fashion, she succeeds eventually, but other than providing relief from the torture of distress, the grand solution offers little cause for euphoria. Reportedly, the resolution prompted euphoric reactions of great intensity nonetheless.

As much suspenseful drama is built around the vulnerability of protagonists, the intensity of joy on resolutions that has them survive, but that provide little else to cheer about, seems incommensurate with the intensity of euphoria that may be expected on the basis of the outcome that the resolution presents. Perhaps not surprisingly, then, the search for an explanation of euphoria at suspense resolution has turned away from purely cognitive rationales and focused on psychophysiological mechanics.

EXCITATORY FACILITATION IN THE ENJOYMENT OF SUSPENSEFUL DRAMA

Berlyne (1960) offered an explanation for the apparent facilitation of the enjoyment following suspense by focusing on the waxing and waning of physiological arousal during suspense and its resolution. His model has become known as the *arousal jag.* Essentially, this model specifies that arousal increases during aversion and promptly decreases during relief. For suspense and its resolution, the presumed sequence of events is this: Suspenseful stimulation activates distress, which manifests itself in elevated noxious arousal; relief manifests itself in a sharp drop of the elevated noxious arousal; analogous to drive reduction, it is pleasantly experienced. Berlyne thus thought the mere reduction or termination of distress a sufficient condition for enjoyment.

Relief as Enjoyment

Berlyne's (1960) proposal that relief, manifest in a sudden drop of noxiously experienced arousal, is in itself enjoyable, is undoubtedly intriguing. It would explain, indeed, why suspense is retrospectively enjoyed, intensely so, although the postsuspense stimuli do not warrant such a reaction. Moreover, it would explain the positive relationship between the intensity of suspense-induced distress and the intensity of enjoyment of resolved suspense. This would be because higher levels of noxiously experienced arousal call for and allow a more pronounced drop that is more pleasurably experienced.

However, new research findings have made it clear that arousal reduction is not necessarily rewarding. Worse yet, they have established that arousal increments can be rewarding. In view of these findings, Berlyne (1967, 1971) modified his original model, allowing for the possibility that both arousal drops and arousal boosts may be rewarding and pleasantly experienced.[5] Unfortunately, the modified model no longer explains the distress to euphoria conversion. It fails, in fact, to explain distress as a noxious experience. Arousal boosts associated with distress are obviously not pleasantly experienced (Grings & Dawson, 1978). Additionally, the arousal jag reasoning suffers from imprecision in the conceptualization of arousal. What kind of arousal is supposed to be jagging? Studies in which autonomic arousal (the kind critically involved in affective reactions) has been measured have failed to show a sharp drop in arousal at suspense resolution (Zillmann, Hay, & Bryant, 1975).

In the face of these problems with the arousal jag, Berlyne's suggestions remain intriguing, but the mechanics of his model cannot be considered established. It would seem prudent, therefore, to return to conceiving relief as an experience that is cognitively determined, rather than determined by arousal changes. However, Berlyne's contention that the magnitude of experienced relief critically influences enjoyment in its wake appears to be worthy of further pursuit. To the extent that arousal levels are proportional with the intensity of experienced suspense, relief from the noxious experience of distress should be more intensely experienced, the higher the preceding arousal level. Although arousal is unlikely to drop sharply, its

---

[5]A more detailed discussion of Berlyne's proposals concerning the distress–relief–enjoyment chain can be found in Zillmann (1980).

noxiousness may be removed, possibly converted to positive affect, by an altered appraisal of the circumstances. If so, the experience of relief, despite persisting high levels of arousal, can be expected to invite a cognitive transition to euphoria—the more so, the more noxiousness is removed by the indicated appraisal.

Excitation Transfer in the Enjoyment of Suspense

A model of suspense enjoyment that gives equal recognition to cognitive and excitatory processes, and that focuses on the interaction between these processes, has been developed by Zillmann (1980, 1991b). This model is based on the excitation-transfer paradigm, which has been detailed elsewhere (Zillmann, 1978, 1983b, 1984). Suffice it here to present only those of its features that are essential to the explanation of the enjoyment of suspenseful drama.

It is proposed that individuals who anticipate or witness the victimization of agents toward which they are favorably disposed (a) experience an elevation of sympathetic excitation and (b) appraise their reactions as dysphoric. The intensity of these dysphoric reactions, defined as *empathic distress*, is determined by prevailing levels of sympathetic activity.

It is further proposed that, because of humoral mediation of excitatory processes, elevated sympathetic activity decays comparatively slowly. Portions of it persist for some time after the termination of the arousing stimulus condition. Such residual excitation tends to go unrecognized, mainly because of poor interoception. It is therefore capable of combining inseparably with the excitatory activity that is produced by subsequent stimuli.[6]

Finally, it is proposed that the experiential status of subsequent affective reactions is determined by the respondents' appraisal of the environmental circumstances that produce the reactions. The intensity of these affective reactions, however, is determined by the union of (a) excitation specifically produced by the subsequent stimulus condition and (b) residual excitation from preceding stimulation.

In general, then, the experiential status of any affective reaction is viewed as being cognitively determined. The intensity of affect, in contrast, is viewed as being determined by the prevailing level of sympathetic activity. To the extent that an emotional reaction is associated with sympathetic activity that derives in part from earlier stimulation, the intensity of the emotion will be higher than it should be on the basis of present stimuli alone.

This projection of an affective "overreaction" to subsequent stimuli is the key element in our approach to suspense. We conceptualize suspense and its resolution as a sequence of affective reactions in which residues of excitation from the antecedent condition intensify the reaction to the subsequent condition. The

---

[6]This conceptualization, it should be noticed, denies immediate excitatory changes (i.e., instantaneous arousal drops or boosts). In particular, it denies the excitatory determination of the sudden experience of relief on the removal of conditions that endanger protagonists.

experience of empathic distress during the suspense period should be acutely negative. Regarding excitatory residues from distress that enter the resolution period, the consideration of hedonic valence is not relevant, however. Residues from negative states are expected to intensify positive or negative subsequent states just as much as residues from positive states. Residues of sympathetic excitation are simply impartial to the hedonic quality of the experiences they come to intensify.

Satisfying Outcomes. It should be clear at this point that the transfer paradigm predicts the intensification of euphoria after empathic distress only if euphoria is cognitively achieved. Only if there is a happy turn of events in the resolution of suspense can this be expected. In line with earlier considerations, the mere removal of the threat that produced empathic distress may be regarded a minimal stimulus condition for the cognitive switch from dysphoria to euphoria. Satisfying, happy endings, however, usually offer more than relief alone. They tend to confound relief with a wealth of gratifications that await the protagonists who have faced danger (Zillmann, Johnson, & Hanrahan, 1973). As a rule, suspense resolutions provide ample cause for the hedonic turnabout from distress to positively toned affect.

Once the resolution of suspense accomplishes the discussed adjustment, the resultant feelings of euphoria should be enhanced by residual excitation from the distress response to suspense. The euphoric reaction to a satisfying resolution of suspense should be more intensely experienced, the greater the excitatory residues from the precipitating suspense-induced distress. Whether the microstructure or macrostructure of suspenseful drama is considered (i.e., episode resolutions or grand resolutions), the more suspense initially distresses, the more it is ultimately enjoyed. The better a suspense treatment takes effect, the more enjoyment will be liberated by its satisfying resolution. By the same token, the same satisfying resolution, when not precipitated by arousing events, can only produce flat drama—drama incapable of generating intensely felt enjoyment.

Dissatisfying Outcomes. It should be recognized that predictions for the appreciation of tragic events are quite different. A sad turn of events in drama is likely to produce dysphoric feelings. Analogous to our proposal regarding satisfying resolutions, it is to be expected that dysphoric reactions to dissatisfying resolutions of suspense will be more intensely experienced the greater the excitatory residues from the preceding suspense-induced distress. The more empathic distress is activated by the events preceding the resolutions, the sadder the tragic resolutions (Bergman, cited in Zillmann, 1980; Zillmann, Mody, & Cantor, 1974); and to the extent that the ultimate outcome is tragic, the sadder the tragedy. Consequently, if the creation of profound, deep feelings of sadness is accepted as the central objective of tragedy, distress from suspense (or more accurately, residual excitation from such distress) offers itself as a potent facilitator.

Excitement From Satisfying Outcomes. As suggested earlier, the two principal forms of truly satisfying resolutions (i.e., resolutions that accomplish more than mere stress relief) are the benefaction of good and liked protagonists and the just, punitive treatment of their transgressive and resented opponents. Drama usually features a combination of both. Even tragedy offers such satisfying outcomes in its microstructure (de Wied, Zillmann, & Ordman, 1994). The contribution of these "gratifiers" to the enjoyment of drama should not be underestimated. It must be acknowledged, in fact, that the display of gratifying happenings may foster excitatory reactions of nontrivial magnitude. Pronounced excitatory reactions are certainly not restricted to aversions, and they may well accompany joyous responses to hoped-for outcomes.

The possibility of appreciable to strong excitatory reactions to satisfying suspense resolutions is readily integrated into our theoretical model. It is proposed that the enjoyment of suspenseful drama that features satisfying resolutions of suspenseful episodes and at large will be greater (a) the more residual excitation from suspense treatments persists during the satisfying resolutions of these treatments, (b) the longer the excitatory residues in question persist, and (c) the more excitation the resolutions themselves contribute.

EPILOGUE ON THE ENJOYMENT EXPERIENCE

In our excursion into factors that influence the enjoyment of suspenseful drama we have concentrated, naturally, on suspense and its resolution. Such focus should not be interpreted as a claim that there are no other factors that appreciably contribute to the enjoyment of predominantly suspenseful drama. It should be understood that suspenseful drama is hardly ever purely that. It usually involves elements of mystery and even comedy (Zillmann, 1991b; Zillmann & Bryant, 1991). The likely contributions of these and other "alien" components must, of course, be considered. The contribution of aesthetic factors (e.g., originality and style of presentation, appeal of performers, quality of performance) also should not be underestimated.

Finally, the enjoyment of suspenseful drama should not be equated with pleasure at curtain fall. Immediately following the grand resolution, respondents' assessment of their enjoyment of a play is likely to be dominated by the final outcome. However, enjoyment of the final outcome does not necessarily reflect the enjoyment, in emotional terms, of a play up to this point or overall. Suspenseful drama may have featured numerous highly suspenseful episodes with greatly satisfying, enjoyable resolutions. The grand resolution may not do justice to the enjoyment following these episodes. Once the emotions elicited by the final outcome, or possibly prior to it, have dissipated, respondents should be in a better position to assess their enjoyment overall and pass a more balanced judgment. On the other hand, such a delay might shift attention away from emotional reactivity and ultimately favor consideration of alternative sources of enjoyment.

All this is to make the point that the conceptualization of drama enjoyment is plagued by a considerable degree of ambiguity, and that conceptual refinements of the enjoyment experience are worth pondering.

REFERENCES

Abrams, D., & Hogg, M. A. (Eds.). (1990). *Social identity theory: Constructive and critical advances.* New York: Springer-Verlag.

Altenbernd, L., & Lewis, L. L. (1969). *Introduction to literature: Stories* (2nd ed.). New York: Macmillan.

Aronfreed, J. (1970). The socialization of altruistic and sympathetic behavior: Some theoretical and experimental analyses. In J. Macaulay & L. Berkowitz (Eds.), *Altruism and helping behavior* (pp. 103–126). New York: Academic Press.

Baldwin, J. M. (1897). *Social and ethical interpretations in mental development.* New York: Macmillan.

Barthes, R. (1977). Introduction to the structural analysis of narratives. In R. Barthes (Ed.), *Image, music, text* (pp. 79–124). New York: Hill & Wang.

Berger, S. M. (1962). Conditioning through vicarious instigation. *Psychological Review, 29,* 450–466.

Berlyne, D. E. (1960). *Conflict, arousal and curiosity.* New York: McGraw-Hill.

Berlyne, D. E. (1967). Arousal and reinforcement. In D. Levine (Ed.), *Nebraska symposium on motivation* (Vol. 15, pp. 1–110). Lincoln: University of Nebraska Press.

Berlyne, D. E. (1971). *Aesthetics and psychobiology.* New York: Appleton-Century-Crofts.

Brentano, F. C. (1924). *Psychologie vom empirischen Standpunkt* [Psychology from an empirical standpoint]. Leipzig: F. Meiner. (Original work published 1874)

Carroll, N. (1984). Toward a theory of film suspense. *Persistence of Vision, 1,* 65–89.

Carroll, N. (1990). *The philosophy of horror or paradoxes of the heart.* New York: Routledge.

Comisky, P. W. (1978). *Degree of outcome-uncertainty and degree of positive disposition toward the protagonist as factors affecting the appreciation of suspenseful dramatic presentations.* Unpublished doctoral dissertation, University of Massachusetts, Amherst.

Comisky, P. W., & Bryant, J. (1982). Factors involved in generating suspense. *Human Communication Research, 9*(1), 49–58.

de Wied, M., Zillmann, D., & Ordman, V. (1994). The role of empathic distress in the enjoyment of cinematic tragedy. *Poetics, 23,* 91–106.

Freud, S. (1964a). The ego and the id. In J. Strachey (Ed. & Trans.), *The standard edition of the complete psychological works of Sigmund Freud* (Vol. 19, pp. 13–66). London: Hogarth. (Original work published 1923)

Freud, S. (1964b). Group psychology and the analysis of the ego. In J. Strachey (Ed. & Trans.), *The standard edition of the complete psychological works of Sigmund Freud* (Vol. 18, pp. 69–143). London: Hogarth. (Original work published 1921)

Freud, S. (1968). *Die Traumdeutung* [Interpretation of dreams]. Frankfurt: Fischer Verlag. (Original work published 1900)

Freud, S. (1987). Psychopathische Personen auf der Bühne [Psychopathological persons on stage]. In A. Richards (Ed.), *Sigmund Freud: Gesammelte Werke. Nachtragsband: Texte aus den Jahren 1885 bis 1938* (pp. 655–661). Frankfurt: Fischer Verlag. (Original work published 1905–1906)

Friedberg, A. (1990). A denial of difference: Theories of cinematic identification. In E. A. Kaplan (Ed.), *Psychoanalysis & cinema* (pp. 36–45). New York: Routledge.

Frijda, N. H. (1986). *The emotions.* Cambridge, UK: Cambridge University Press.

Gabbard, G. O. (1987). *Psychiatry and the cinema.* Chicago: University of Chicago Press.

Grings, W. W., & Dawson, M. E. (1978). *Emotions and bodily responses: A psychophysiological approach.* New York: Academic Press.

Hall, C. S. (1954). *A primer of Freudian psychology.* New York: Mentor Book.

Hitchcock, A. (1959, July 13). Interview by H. Brean. *Life,* p. 72.

Hoffman, M. L. (1973). *Empathy, role-taking, guilt and the development of altruistic motives* (Developmental Psychology Rep. No. 30). Ann Arbor: University of Michigan.

Hoffner, C., & Cantor, J. (1991). Perceiving and responding to mass media characters. In J. Bryant & D. Zillmann (Eds.), *Responding to the screen: Reception and reaction processes* (pp. 63–101). Hillsdale, NJ: Lawrence Erlbaum Associates.

Humphrey, G. (1922). The conditioned reflex and the elementary social reaction. *Journal of Abnormal and Social Psychology, 17,* 113–119.

Jose, P. E., & Brewer, W. F. (1984). Development of story liking: Character identification, suspense, and outcome resolution. *Developmental Psychology, 20*(5), 911–924.

Kaplan, E. A. (Ed.). (1990). *Psychoanalysis & cinema.* New York: Routledge.

King, S. (1981). *Danse macabre.* New York: Everest.

Kohlberg, L. (1964). Development of moral character and moral ideology. In M. L. Hoffman & L. W. Hoffman (Eds.), *Review of child development research* (Vol. 1, pp. 383–431). New York: Russell Sage Foundation.

Leventhal, H. (1979). A perceptual-motor processing model of emotion. In P. Pliner, K. R. Blankstein, & I. M. Spigel (Eds.), *Advances in the study of communication and affect: Vol. 5. Perception of the emotion in self and others* (pp. 1–46). New York: Plenum.

Lipps, T. (1903). *Ästhetik: Psychologie des Schönen und der Kunst: Vol. 1. Grundlegung der Ästhetik* [Aesthetics: The psychology of the beautiful and of the arts. Vol. 1]. Hamburg: Voss.

Lipps, T. (1906). *Ästhetik: Psychologie des Schönen und der Kunst: Vol. 2. Die ästhetische Betrachtung und die bildende Kunst* [Aesthetics: The psychology of the beautiful and of the arts. Vol. 2]. Hamburg: Voss.

Lipps, T. (1907). Das Wissen von fremden Ichen [Knowledge of foreign "I"s]. *Psychologische Untersuchungen, 1*(4), 694–722.

Marx, M. (1940). *The enjoyment of drama.* New York: F. S. Crofts.

McDougall, W. (1908). *An introduction to social psychology.* London: Methuen.

McDougall, W. (1922). A new theory of laughter. *Psyche, 2,* 292–303.

Mendelsohn, H. (1966). *Mass entertainment.* New Haven, CT: College & University Press.

Metz, C. (1982). *The imaginary signifier: Psychoanalysis and the cinema.* Bloomington: Indiana University Press.

Prandtl, A. (1910). *Die Einfühlung* [Empathy]. Leipzig: J. A. Barth.

Rabkin, E. (1973). *Narrative suspense.* Ann Arbor: University of Michigan Press.

Ribot, T. (1897). *The psychology of the emotions.* London: Walter Scott.

Rimmon-Kenan, S. (Ed.). (1976). *Discourse in psychoanalysis and literature.* London: Methuen.

Rogers, C. R. (1967). *Person to person.* Lafayette, CA: Real People Press.

Scheler, M. (1913). *Zur Phänomenologie und Theorie der Sympathiegefühle und von Liebe und Hass* [Contribution to the phenomenology and theory of feelings of sympathy, love and hate]. Halle: Niemeyer.

Skura, M. A. (1981). *The literary use of the psychoanalytic process.* New Haven, CT: Yale University Press.

Smiley, S. (1971). *Playwriting: The structure of action.* Englewood Cliffs, NJ: Prentice-Hall.

Smith, A. (1971). *The theory of moral sentiments.* New York: Garland. (Original work published 1759)

Spencer, H. (1870). *The principles of psychology* (2nd ed., Vol. 1). London: Williams & Norgate.

Spinoza, B. (1985). Ethics. In E. Curley (Ed. & Trans.), *The collected works of Spinoza* (Vol. 1, pp. 408–617). Princeton, NJ: Princeton University Press. (Original work published 1677)

Stotland, E. (1969). Exploratory investigations of empathy. In L. Berkowitz (Ed.), *Advances in experimental social psychology* (Vol. 4, pp. 271–314). New York: Academic Press.

Tajfel, H. (Ed.). (1982). *Social identity and intergroup relations.* Cambridge, UK: Cambridge University Press.

Titchener, E. (1915). *A beginner's psychology.* New York: Macmillan.

Turner, J. C. (1985). Social categorization and the self-concept: A social-cognitive theory of group behavior. In E. J. Lawler (Ed.), *Advances in group processes: A research annual* (Vol. 2, pp. 77–121). Greenwich, CT: JAI.

Wilson, B. J., Cantor, J., Gordon, L., & Zillmann, D. (1986). Affective response of nonretarded and retarded children to the emotions of a protagonist. *Child Study Journal, 16*(2), 77–93.

Wispe, L. (1987). History of the concept of empathy. In N. Eisenberg & J. Strayer (Eds.), *Empathy and its development* (pp. 17–37). Cambridge, UK: Cambridge University Press.

Worringer, W. (1959). *Abstraktion und Einfühlung: Ein Beitrag zur Stilpsychologie* [Abstraction and empathy: A contribution to the psychology of style]. München: Piper. (Original work published 1908)

Zillmann, D. (1978). Attribution and misattribution of excitatory reactions. In J. H. Harvey, W. J. Ickes, & R. F. Kidd (Eds.), *New directions in attribution research* (Vol. 2, pp. 335–368). Hillsdale, NJ: Lawrence Erlbaum Associates.

Zillmann, D. (1980). Anatomy of suspense. In P. H. Tannenbaum (Ed.), *The entertainment functions of television* (pp. 133–163). Hillsdale, NJ: Lawrence Erlbaum Associates.

Zillmann, D. (1983a). Disparagement humor. In P. E. McGhee & J. H. Goldstein (Eds.), *Handbook of humor research: Vol. 1. Basic issues* (pp. 85–107). New York: Springer-Verlag.

Zillmann, D. (1983b). Transfer of excitation in emotional behavior. In J. T. Cacioppo & R. E. Petty (Eds.), *Social psychophysiology: A sourcebook* (pp. 215–240). New York: Guilford.

Zillmann, D. (1984). *Connections between sex and aggression.* Hillsdale, NJ: Lawrence Erlbaum Associates.

Zillmann, D. (1990). Unterhaltende Ungewissheit [Entertaining uncertainty]. In E. Walther & U. Bayer (Eds.), *Zeichen von Zeichen für Zeichen: Festschrift für Max Bense* (pp. 68–75). Baden-Baden: Agis-Verlag.

Zillmann, D. (1991a). Empathy: Affect from bearing witness to the emotions of others. In J. Bryant & D. Zillmann (Eds.), *Responding to the screen: Reception and reaction processes* (pp. 135–167). Hillsdale, NJ: Lawrence Erlbaum Associates.

Zillmann, D. (1991b). The logic of suspense and mystery. In J. Bryant & D. Zillmann (Eds.), *Responding to the screen: Reception and reaction processes* (pp. 281–303). Hillsdale, NJ: Lawrence Erlbaum Associates.

Zillmann, D. (1994). Mechanisms of emotional involvement with drama. *Poetics, 23,* 33–51.

Zillmann, D., & Bhatia, A. (1989). Effects of associating with musical genres on heterosexual attraction. *Communication Research, 16*(2), 263–288.

Zillmann, D., & Bryant, J. (1975). Viewer's moral sanction of retribution in the appreciation of dramatic presentations. *Journal of Experimental Social Psychology, 11,* 572–582.

Zillmann, D., & Bryant, J. (1991). Responding to comedy: The sense and nonsense in humor. In J. Bryant & D. Zillmann (Eds.), *Responding to the screen: Reception and reaction processes* (pp. 261–279). Hillsdale, NJ: Lawrence Erlbaum Associates.

Zillmann, D., & Bryant, J. (1994). Entertainment as media effect. In J. Bryant & D. Zillmann (Eds.), *Media effects: Advances in theory and research* (pp. 437–461). Hillsdale, NJ: Lawrence Erlbaum Associates.

Zillmann, D., Bryant, J., & Sapolsky, B. S. (1989). Enjoyment from sports spectatorship. In J. H. Goldstein (Ed.), *Sports, games, and play: Social and psychological viewpoints* (2nd ed., pp. 241–278). Hillsdale, NJ: Lawrence Erlbaum Associates.

Zillmann, D., & Cantor, J. R. (1976). A disposition theory of humour and mirth. In A. J. Chapman & H. C. Foot (Eds.), *Humour and laughter: Theory, research, and applications* (pp. 93–115). London: Wiley.

Zillmann, D., & Cantor, J. R. (1977). Affective responses to the emotions of a protagonist. *Journal of Experimental Social Psychology, 13,* 155–165.

Zillmann, D., Hay, T. A., & Bryant, J. (1975). The effect of suspense and its resolution on the appreciation of dramatic presentations. *Journal of Research in Personality, 9*, 307–323.

Zillmann, D., Johnson, R. C., & Hanrahan, J. (1973). Pacifying effect of happy ending of communications involving aggression. *Psychological Reports, 32*, 967–970.

Zillmann, D., Mody, B., & Cantor, J. R. (1974). Empathetic perception of emotional displays in films as a function of hedonic and excitatory state prior to exposure. *Journal of Research in Personality, 8*, 335–349.

Zillmann, D., & Paulus, P. B. (1993). Spectators: Reactions to sports events and effects on athletic performance. In R. N. Singer, M. Murphey, & L. K. Tennant (Eds.), *Handbook on research in sport psychology* (pp. 600–619). New York: Macmillan.

Zillmann, D., & Zillmann, M. (in press). Psychoneuroendocrinology of social behavior. In E. T. Higgins & A. Kruglanski (Eds.), *Social psychology: Handbook of basic mechanisms and processes.* New York: Guilford.

12

▼▼▼▼▼▼▼

Toward a Psychological
Theory of Suspense

Peter Vorderer
University of Music and Theater, Hannover

This volume contains several analyses of suspense written from various perspectives, from numerous theoretical and methodological positions. The general goal—as emphasized in the introduction—is to somehow "encircle" the problem and thus achieve a conceptualization of suspense that would be as comprehensive as possible. Some authors gathered here present and discuss hypotheses based on an empirical, social-scientific approach, whereas others use philosophical, film-theoretical or semiotic theories. My aim is to formulate a psychological conceptualization, a description and explanation of suspense as a reception phenomenon. Of course, such a psychological conceptualization cannot and should not be attempted without recognizing the results of those works that primarily analyze the (suspense) text itself. However, I focus on the understanding and processing of texts, on the viewers' or readers' prerequisites of this processing, and on the effects this has on them.

As this volume demonstrates, there are already several, primarily theoretical contributions that focus on these problems. As is usually the case in relatively new fields of research, these contributions are suggestions rather than theories, able to describe and explain sufficiently what suspense is and how exactly it works. So far, I see three different possibilities for further developing the psychological study of suspense: (a) The reformulation and expansion of pre-existing conceptualizations by using new developments in psychological theory and methodology to gain a more detailed description and explanation of suspense (e.g., Ohler & Nieding, chap. 8, and Tan & Diteweg, chap. 9, both in this volume). (b) The discussion of specific problems that suspense research has revealed in the past. An example of this is the so-called "paradox of suspense," that is, the observation that the reading of a text already well known to a reader may still lead to the experience of suspense. This observation is a problem because it contradicts a hypothesis supported by most suspense researchers. According to this hypothesis, suspense can only develop if the viewer does not know the outcome of the narrative (e.g., Carroll, chap. 5, Gerrig, chap. 6, and Brewer, chap. 7, all in this volume). Finally (c) the expansion and differentiation of the object of study, which in the end is also meant to connect different analytical perspectives with one another. This is what I attempt to do in this chapter. The attempt is based on the assumption that the existing conceptualizations have often dealt with only one special (however prototypic) case of suspenseful reception. In the future, the description and explanation of this special case should be supplemented by a discussion of distinct variants of suspenseful reception. My aim, then, is to elaborate and differentiate the existent field of research in the hope of moving toward a psychological theory of suspense.

This is not possible without a concrete starting point. I therefore start with Zillmann's conception of suspense (cf. Zillmann, chap. 11, this volume), which seems to me to be the most highly developed on both the theoretical and the methodological level. On the basis of this conception, I explicate my suggestions along the following dimensions:

1. The dimension of the text, that is, with regard to the differences between various dramas.
2. The dimension of inter- as well as intraindividual variance, that is, with regard to the differences between the various users (readers, onlookers, etc.) of suspenseful texts as well as between various situations of reception.
3. The dimension of the affective prerequisites for suspense, that is, with regard to the importance of affective or emotional processes for the experience of suspense.

STARTING POINT: ZILLMANN'S CONCEPTION OF SUSPENSE

The most detailed psychological program available that investigates the conditions and effects of suspense can be found in the work of Zillmann and his collaborators, who have been publishing their results since the mid-1970s (Zillmann, 1980, 1991a, 1991b, chap. 11, this volume; Zillmann & Bryant, 1975; Zillmann & Cantor, 1977; Zillmann, Hay, & Bryant, 1975). It is probably the only research program in this field that has been able to identify not only different antecedent conditions for suspense on the reader's or viewer's side, but also to prove these effects experimentally in several studies. In Zillmann's (1991a) empathy theory, we have a plausible and empirically verifiable possibility that explains the emotional participation of viewers and readers psychologically. According to this theory, they experience suspense because in a sense they participate as witnesses in a narrative event shown by the media. During this process of observation, they feel—under certain specifiable conditions—empathy with protagonists who are threatened or in danger. Thus they experience empathetic distress. On the highest level of abstraction, the conditions that lead to this can be summarized as follows:

- Readers or viewers must feel sympathy for protagonists; at least they must not dislike them.
- The harming of the protagonists has to be likely but not (in the perception of the readers or onlookers) absolutely certain (for more detail, see Zillmann, chap. 11, this volume).

To a large extent, these conditions correspond to or are compatible with those also presented by other authors. For example, Carroll (1984, chap. 5, this volume) described the anticipation of a likely but not desired outcome and the anticipation of an unlikely but preferred outcome as inducing suspense. If one were to formulate Carroll's position in the form of experimentally verifiable hypotheses, the result would probably be a prognosis very similar to Zillmann's. Only when regarding the concrete operationalization of single variables (e.g., "hoping for" a specific outcome of the narrative), would differences be noticeable (cf. Vorderer, 1994b). In the cases where these hypotheses were actually tested (e.g., Comisky & Bryant, 1982; Zillmann & Cantor, 1977), it regularly proved possible to confirm this hypothesized causality. This led Zillmann, in the 1980s, to work out a general process model that described the connection between drama (e.g., a suspenseful film) and cognitive as well as emotional reactions (e.g., suspense; Zillmann, chap. 11, this volume; Zillmann & Bryant, 1994).

Following this model, the observation of media persons leads either to the onlookers' approbation or disapprobation of these persons' actions. This results— as can be inferred from the model—in specific dispositions of the viewers toward the protagonists, that is, either positive (liking, caring) or negative affects (disliking, resenting). From the positive affects toward the persons whose actions the viewers approve of, and from the negative affects toward those whose actions they disapprove of, arise certain expectations and emotions: the hope for a positive outcome and fear of a negative outcome for likable protagonists; and conversely, fear regarding a possible positive outcome and hope for a negative outcome for the disliked antagonists. According to Zillmann, empathy can be felt only for positive protagonists; toward antagonists, only counterempathy is possible (Zillmann, chap. 11, this volume).

The formulations in Zillmann's model show how much the text is seen as causal and relatively effective. Viewers, on the other hand, are conceptualized as more or less passive, reacting in a uniform manner to what they are exposed to. This reaction is based on predetermined dispositions, expectations, and affects (positive vs. negative). An active selection, understanding, and processing of a text by users—based on their actual preconditions and motives, but also dependent on the situation as well as on the concrete text–reader constellation—has not yet been taken into account. Certainly Zillmann does not think such active processes are nonexistent, nor does he conceive of their inclusion as inadequate. One can probably assume that he finds, specifically in the case of describing suspense (and possibly even generally in the case of describing entertainment), that they are unnecessary. I, therefore, think that Zillmann's conceptualization can be regarded as the description of a special case of entertaining or suspenseful reception. Because Zillmann gives numerous empirical confirmations for his hypotheses, I suggest this special case as the prototype of suspense reception. However—and this should definitely be kept in mind—his description implies not only a certain type of text but also very specific assessments of readers and their respective reception situations. However, suspense does not develop exclusively when precisely these conditions exist. In fact, if viewers, who actively generate meaning in respective situations, can understand (and this would now be a prototypic example of the opposite case) polyvalent texts and if they cannot possibly like the protagonists because they are portrayed and experienced in a much too complex way, viewers also experience suspense.

DIFFERENCES BETWEEN TEXTS

Zillmann arrives at the prototypical case of suspense reception quite correctly because he consequently implies (a reading of) those texts that are usually classified as entertainment or popular literature. These are texts that—according to literary criticism—are marked by a lack of variation, innovation, and ambiguity and do not demand that the readers be accomplished in actively generating meaning (Nusser, 1973, 1982; Westerbarkey, 1994). Let me give an example to clarify how this specific type of text leads to specific reading experiences that cannot be postulated for the reading of other types of text. For this purpose, I have chosen the very popular novels of John Grisham (*The Firm* [1991], *The Pelican Brief* [1992], *The Client* [1993]) that have also become international film successes. These texts are particularly suitable because audiences usually understand and judge them as suspenseful texts.

In each of these novels, only a few main characters play an important role and they are all exceptional in some way. In the case of *The Firm*, readers or onlookers witness the experiences of an exceptionally intelligent young man who enters professional life as a lawyer after completing a law degree with great success. In *The Pelican Brief*, the protagonist is an equally intelligent and exceptionally attractive female student. *The Client* presents a remarkably courageous child. All these characters face hostile forces: usually the Mafia, sometimes the FBI. With reference to Zillmann's process model, the reading can be described as follows: In the case of *The Client*, the actions of the young protagonist Marc presumably find the approval of the majority of readers. Those of the antagonists on the other hand are disapproved of. The reason for this is that young Marc becomes privy to certain secrets through no fault of his own, and the Mafia, whose secrets he now knows, represents a deadly threat. Marc is also exposed to danger by the FBI, which becomes interested in this secret in the course of a criminal investigation, because he represents, of course, a danger to the Mafia and thus provokes them to threaten Marc. This will—one can speculate along the lines of Zillmann's thesis—lead to positive affiliation with the protagonist Marc (he is liked by the reader) as well as to negative ones toward the representatives of the Mafia and even in part toward the FBI (the reader or the viewer regard these as unpleasant in the extreme). As a consequence, readers hope for a positive outcome for Marc, but they fear a possible negative outcome. Empathy is possible only in relation to Marc (and his allies) because empathy—in Zillmann's opinion—requires a positively affective (or at least neutrally affective) relationship with the target person. One can speculate that this is precisely the reason why Grisham's characters are so clearly portrayed. On the one hand, Marc is a weak, unfortunate victim, and the Mafia and the FBI are more or less unscrupulous organizations on the other.

I chose this example to show that texts such as Grisham's novels, which are the type of texts Zillmann uses in his studies, are notable for their quite definite and one-sided descriptions of characters. This nonambiguity permits the reader to just as definitely either approve or disapprove of the described characters' actions. It is very easy to imagine that such a description may indeed evoke the effects described in Zillmann's model. One must question, however, whether such effects can also be expected in the reading of other types of text. In other words, do different types of texts, those of varying complexity, for example, which imply or lead to different expectations, anticipations, hopes, fears, and so forth on the reader's side, lead to different types of reactions? Several theoretical studies indirectly answer this question affirmatively. These studies differentiate cognitive as well as emotional processes during the process of reading depending on how challenging the text is. Oatley (1994), for example, differentiated between texts that emphasize either assimilative or accommodative cognitive processes. As an example of assimilative reading material, he mentioned the reception of Grisham's *The Pelican Brief*, whereas a reading of Tolstoi's *Anna Karenina*, however, would demand accommodative processes (cf. Oatley, 1992). Cupchik (chap. 10, this volume) argues in a similar vein. In his opinion, the theater of the absurd demands an accommodative reading, whereas a classic suspense text may be understood assimilatively. This position thus represented by both authors comprises two theses: First, that the text's quality and its demands on readers (or onlookers) will determine the intensity of the cognitive effort needed to understand and process the text, and second, that suspense is a phenomenon linked to undemanding texts.

We can find confirmation for the first thesis within the empirical study of literature and reader psychology. The classic dichotomy between so-called "high" literature (as the literary canon) on the one hand and so-called "popular" or "light" literature on the other has been replaced with increasing frequency by a differentiation of various manners of reception. The assumption is that the text provides the reader with certain reception offers that the reader reacts to with acts of understanding that vary in complexity and creativity. Although readers are by no means determined by the text, one can hardly deny that the text does limit the readers' possibilities in certain ways (cf. for more detail, Groeben, 1980; Groeben & Landwehr, 1991; Groeben & Vorderer, 1988). Whereas in the 1970s, so-called dichotomy models ruled the discussion (as, e.g., the two prototypically differentiated manners of reception, "pleasure" vs. "understanding," which were seen as analogous to "popular" vs. "high" literature), today more differentiated, psychological models rule the field of research. According to these models, texts are in fact actively or constructively understood in various ways (Vorderer, 1994a) depending on a number of inter- and intraindividually different prerequisites and conditions. The text is still regarded as one of those conditions, although the position of the so-called "radical constructivists" differs with regard to this last-mentioned aspect (Schmidt, 1987). Whether the relation of these different cognitive acts with different sorts of texts can be proven empirically, however, remains in question.

The Reception of Action Versus Experience Texts

In all texts belonging to the genre of popular or light literature, not only in Grisham's novels, the focus is usually on the description of physical action; thus these texts can be called prototypic *action texts*. The presentation of the characters' experiences, thoughts, and emotions (as in so-called *experience texts*) is usually of lesser importance. Of course every text combines elements of action and experience, but the way they are combined will probably be very different depending on the text and genre. The prototypic suspense text described by Zillmann, for which the Grisham text constitutes a good example, will probably show a combination clearly favoring the action aspect. With regard to the understanding of texts categorized in this manner, Bruner (1986), for example, distinguished between the "landscape of action" and the "landscape of consciousness" (p. 14). Whereas in the first case the intentions, goals, and instruments of an agent are placed into the plot's foreground, the characters' knowledge, thoughts, and emotions form the focus in the second case. Bruner assumed that the demands made on readers by such differing texts in fact vary. To be understood, narrations that focus on physical action (action texts) demand causal explanations from readers; texts that create empathy with the protagonists' experiences, including inner ones (experience texts), primarily demand an interpretation of intentionality instead. This means that readers have to perform partially different cognitive acts to make use of a text's cues (e.g., the protagonists' facial expressions or the words describing their mental state) in order to understand it (Feldman, Bruner, Renderer, & Spitzer, 1990).

Cupchik and Laszlo (1994) even assumed that such different texts lead readers to various emotional reactions and thus to various forms of behavior. In the case of the action text, where the search for meaning is associated with causal analyses, the divergence between the readers' expectations concerning the narration and what actually happens leads to uncertainty or—as a physiological substratum— increased arousal. This increased arousal, Cupchik and Laszlo concluded, following Berlyne (1971), is the motive for further exploration, or, in concrete terms, for further reading of the text in order to reduce this increased arousal. They therefore expect that in this case, information processing will be quicker than when reading experience texts. In the latter, any cognitive and emotional acts on the part of the readers are largely due to *Einfühlung*, that is, to empathy with the protagonists' inner experiences. Cupchik and Laszlo (1994) showed that this also leads to a deeper understanding of the text and that it slows down information processing. Such texts or acts of reception are very interesting but, according to the authors, less suspenseful.

Cupchik and Laszlo (1994) as well as Vorderer, Cupchik, and Oatley (1994) checked the reading of literary texts in the context of an experimental design in which one of the independent variables represented the type of text (action vs. experience). The texts were excerpts from four different short stories by the Canadian authors Margaret Atwood (from "The Salt Garden" as an example of an action text and from "Hurricane Hazel" as an example of an experience text) and Alistair MacLeod (from "Grandmother" as an example of an experience text and from "Scott" as an example of an action text). In a preliminary test, these texts were found to be typical for the respective types of text. In the study by Cupchik and Laszlo (1994), the reading time was one of the important dependent variables. It was determined by letting the test persons read the excerpt sentence by sentence, and enabling them to call up new text on a monitor by touching the keyboard. Among other things it became clear that action stories were indeed read significantly faster than experience stories. The authors concluded that action texts were clearly considered more suspenseful than experience texts. In another experiment, Vorderer, Cupchik, and Oatley (1994) also examined how involving, complex, and meaningful these same texts were considered. Above all, the suspense the readers experienced was measured during and after the reading using a rating scale. In addition, the readers were asked whether they found the characters sympathetic and whether they would have liked to read on. In fact, significant differences were revealed on all dimensions between both types of texts; with only one exception, the action texts fell far behind the experience texts. This means that the experience texts were more involving, more complex, more meaningful, their characters were more likable, and the motivation to read on was higher. The question of suspense revealed the one exception: The action texts were considered more suspenseful than the experience texts. This was the case regardless of the point in time of the measurement. This does not, of course, mean that experience texts were not suspenseful at all, but rather that they were less suspenseful than action texts.

These results indirectly confirm the previously mentioned thesis that action texts such as those used in Zillmann's studies may be regarded as prototypic for suspense. The phenomenon of suspense, however, is illuminated only partially by these texts and the description of their understanding. Other types of texts (e.g., experience texts, more complex texts with less one-sided characters, etc.) also produce suspense, and the connection between their content and their understanding is presumably more complicated than described in Zillmann's process model. Examples of this are mentioned in studies by Brewer and his collaborators (Brewer, in press; Brewer & Lichtenstein, 1982; Brewer & Ohtsuka, 1988), Wulff (chap. 1, this volume), Wuss (chap. 4, this volume), Leonard (chap. 2, this volume), and Tan and Diteweg (chap. 9, this volume). The crucial difference between these studies and Zillmann's conceptualization is clearly the type of text the respective authors are working with. Whereas Zillmann proceeds from the reception of relatively prototypic entertainment or popular texts, these authors illustrate that suspense can also arise from the reception of so-called *polyvalent texts* (Groeben, 1980). To understand these texts, more complex cognitive operations are demanded of and produced by the reader.

If the thesis of the empirical study of literature proves true—namely that it is not the texts themselves that are polyvalent but that the reader understands and processes them in a polyvalent manner—it is likely that suspense may arise in these cases as well. To give another example: Obviously, suspense does arise when the distance between texts and readers is so high that they do not live within the narrative events or have the feeling of witnessing these events, as is assumed by Zillmann. In those cases the reader may not feel empathy with the protagonist, but instead think about the film from a rather aloof position and therefore lapse into an analyzing rather than an involved mode of reception (cf. Oatley, 1994; Vorderer, 1993). In this case, suspense would develop out of an interest in the progress of the story (qua story) and not out of an interest in the protagonist's well-being (the story as apparent reality). In my opinion, Ohler and Nieding (chap. 8, this volume) outline such a case when they discuss the film *Total Recall* (1990, Paul Verhoeven). The authors assume that suspense occurs when, during exposure, viewers develop the expectation that they will find an important clue in a particular scene that will help them solve a relevant question. This question focuses on an important plot outcome in a dual decision situation, and it causes especially high suspense if it emerges at a crucial point in the course of a narrative (plot point). That means that the director or the author controls the information available to viewers so that viewers know more than the protagonists but less than the director (Ohler & Nieding, chap. 8, this volume). In my opinion, what is most crucial here is that the onlookers remain in the role of viewer in so far as their primary interest is in the development of the film (for which the protagonists are, of course, important) and less in the well-being of the protagonists (whom the onlookers may like or not). In other words, viewers think more about the film and less "in" the film as would be typical for the involved reception mode (cf. for the concept of involvement, Brewer, chap. 7, this volume; Vorderer, 1992). Other readers or onlookers, however, might take the role of witnesses (i.e., be involved in the scene) and experience suspense in this sequence because they feel empathy with the threatened protagonist. Thus the same sequence may generate suspense for analyzing onlookers—as postulated by Ohler and Nieding—and involved viewers—whom Zillmann has in mind—and yet, one is dealing, psychologically speaking, with two different processes.

INTER- AND INTRAINDIVIDUAL DIFFERENCES

If one concedes that the understanding and processing of texts varies depending on the type of text, then one can and must also ask which factors, on the reader's side, have an impact on this process. The last example shown in the preceding section makes it clear that such an influence is most likely. To entirely deny or ignore it would be to adopt the stimulus-response model, which assumes that readers surrender totally to the text and its influences.

Interestingly enough, a comparable position to this stimulus-response model (at least regarding its implicit assumptions) can be found in a research area that uses the text itself as the starting point of its investigations. This is the so-called research of popular literature as developed in the 1970s in Germany. This research seems to me to be of some interest for the current discussion because the criticism it received from various perspectives and from psychology in particular illustrates clearly that the impact readers have on texts should not be underestimated.

On the basis of the already mentioned general development within literary criticism, which increasingly tried to involve readers in its analyses, this branch of research was particularly interested in the potentially ideological effects of literary texts (Bürger, 1973; Nusser, 1982; an overview: Groeben & Vorderer, 1988). Compared to the prevalent orientation of literary criticism toward so-called high literature, this development was a fruitful and generally broadening perspective. For the first time, attention was focused on those texts most commonly read, that is, popular or light literature. This type of text was alleged—with an ideologically critical impetus—to possibly have extremely unwelcome effects on the individual: to encourage an uncritical adjustment of the reader to traditional social values, to promote alienation, passivity, and so on. One deficit of this branch of research, however, was that a large portion of its analysis was not empirically verified. Usually a description of the texts was considered sufficient, sometimes even a mere subjective interpretation of ideological texts, from which conclusions concerning the effect on readers were drawn more or less directly. Of course, this procedure was repeatedly criticized from both a methodological as well as a theoretical perspective (Groeben, 1980, 1987). One of the most important arguments against these false conclusions was to point out the cognitive constructivity of readers: If these readers are understood as subjects who actively understand reality and do so in a constructive manner, one must also assume that they are competent enough to process ideological texts critically. In that case, they should at least be able to break the intended effects of such a text. This would mean that conclusions concerning the resulting effects texts can have on readers may not and should not be drawn from knowledge of the potential effects, which can be measured through content analyses (Groeben & Vorderer, 1988).

These arguments can also be applied to the understanding of suspenseful drama: It is likely that, besides the text, the readers or viewers, their preconditions (Schmidt, 1991), and the reading situation also have an impact on understanding and thus on the effect of a text. In other words, readers or viewers choose a certain text not only according to their current needs and interests, but, to a certain extent, they also process this text subjectively. During the act of reading, readers construct a text that is not identical with the text as it has been described objectively (e.g., by content analysis). To subscribe to this thesis, one certainly does not have to assume a radical constructivist position like, for example, the NIKOL group led by Schmidt (1987, 1991). A form of moderate constructivism (cf. Groeben & Vorderer, 1988) as it is also represented in communication research (cf. Früh, 1994; Früh & Schönbach, 1982; Schönbach & Früh, 1984) reaches the same conclusions.

The principal consequence of these moderate constructivist assumptions, which are currently disputed neither by psychology nor by communication research, is that one can expect interindividual differences. If the readers (or viewers) participate in the construction of the text, it is quite likely that different readers will arrive at different constructions. At the very least, it is much more difficult to infer what image a reader will have of a given text if one does not include information about this reader. This is certainly one of the reasons why these interindividual differences have already been thematized and empirically researched by media studies. Certain characteristics, such as age, gender, and especially the reader's or viewer's social situation, were repeatedly revealed as factors that have a significant impact on the choice, processing, and effect of texts.

This becomes especially clear in the field of reader psychology, to give another example, where the social specificity of literary reading has been empirically replicated many times (cf. Groeben & Vorderer, 1988). According to this line of study, there is a clearly recognizable empirical connection between the social situation of readers and their choice of reading material. The number of texts read and their difficulty correlate positively with an improved social situation. This empirical connection is usually explained by theories of socialization, that is, by a description of the specific reading or media environments of different social groups in which young people find different forms of access to literature (Dijkstra, 1994; Hurrelmann, Hammer, & Mieß, 1993).

Of course these results cannot be interpreted to mean that affiliation with certain social groups determines the selection of certain texts and their understanding. Reader psychology has shown that in fact people who belong to higher social classes (may) also read escapist literature. This means that the previously mentioned social differences between readers are by no means sufficient to account for the different acts of selection and understanding. Other characteristics, such as the age or proficiency of a reader, but also dispositions such as, for example, fearfulness (Vitouch, 1993) or the cognitive styles preferred by an individual, seem to be equally significant. One can ask, for example, whether viewers' responses to media as described by Zillmann are above all true for people who possess only a limited spectrum of social manners and processing possibilities due to their cognitive and/or emotional development, as is, to name an example, the case with children. Studies on the media behavior and processing competence of younger children suggest this (e.g., Cantor, 1994; Paus-Haase, 1994). At least it seems clear that children—much more than adults—use protagonists as *identification offers* (Best, 1994), which means that their understanding is more strongly and more often an involved one and less an analytical one. Presumably empathy, as described by Zillmann, plays a more important role in this group of viewers. The impact of proficiency is most likely quite similar; whether a viewer is more of an expert or more of a novice consumer of suspense texts presumably influences the amount, the type, and the complexity of expectations generated during the act of reception. Even if viewers choose and process texts under comparable prerequisites (regarding their competences), differences in how the text is understood can still be expected. These differences are influenced less by the respective person than by the concrete circumstances of reading, that is, the situation.

Differences Between Situations

It seems appropriate to assume intraindividual as well as interindividual variance. That means one expects that viewers can understand a certain text in various ways depending on situational characteristics, such as certain locations of reception, moods, current intentions, and so forth. When experiencing suspense, for example, it presumably makes a significant difference whether viewers watch a certain film at the cinema, that is, expecting to see a suspenseful film, or whether onlookers stay at home and get sucked into a film they found by coincidence when zapping between channels. To give a concrete example, whether the actions of the protagonist Marc in *The Client* are accepted or disapproved of, whether viewers respond with fear or hope, may also depend on what they generally expect to perceive and to experience in this concrete situation. Are onlookers in a stressful or rather boring situation and therefore ready or prepared to become involved (cf. for the impact of moods on the selection of films, Zillmann, 1988)? It is obvious that the question repeatedly asked by communication research, namely whether viewers are more active or simply passive users (e.g., Hasebrink

& Krotz, 1991), cannot be answered independently of the situation. It seems to be both unnecessary and unproductive to conceive of a general viewer or even of a person of a certain gender, age, or particular social situation as being either constructively active or helplessly passive. In view of the empirical facts, it is more appropriate to assume "processes of different activity, complexity and constructivity depending on various conditions" (Groeben & Vorderer, 1988, p. 341). That means that people understand and process media messages sometimes actively and critically and sometimes affirmatively and passively, depending on the situation. The thesis of the "activity flexibility" of the reader (Groeben & Vorderer, 1988, p. 341) covers this intraindividual variance.

If acts of understanding ensue not only as a result of the type of text but also as a result of readers' system of preconditions (Schmidt, 1991) and even as a consequence of specific situational characteristics, then the readers' or viewers' responses to suspenseful drama, as decribed by Zillmann, represent only one variant out of many. To demonstrate one more variant, I would like to use a specific perspective that has not yet led to recognizable consequences in the discussion of suspense. It is a perspective that allows one to see the understanding of supenseful drama and the response to it as a social situation.

Reception as Social Situation

To see acts of reading or understanding as a kind of quasi-social situation is not entirely new. The concept of the so-called *parasocial interaction* between media users and media persons (Horton & Wohl, 1956; Rosengren & Windahl, 1976) builds on this concept, as does Zillmann's assumption that viewers witness narrative events and thus have the illusion that the action presented on the screen is somehow real (Tan & van den Boom, 1992). It is all the more surprising, therefore, that this assumption has not led to any hypotheses about the social understanding of drama. For if the reception of a film or a book represents such a quasi-social situation in that readers or onlookers interact with the media persons, their perception and evaluation of these actors, in fact, even their own emotional response to them, is mediated by the social situation. This, however, would imply that to describe and explain these processes of perception, evaluation, and emotion, one should call on social-psychological approaches because only in this way can the social character of this situation be taken into account. Surely, one is not dealing with social processes here, but with individual ones that, however embedded in a certain social setting they are, in many ways run a different course than they would if there were no such social setting (Vorderer & Valsiner, in press).

I would like to make this clear by giving yet another example. Adolescent readers of *The Client* not only process information that leads to approval or disapproval depending on the description of the protagonist Marc. One can assume that these readers, during the act of understanding, compare themselves (in the sense of social comparison processes as described by Festinger, 1954) to the protagonist and then evaluate not only the protagonist but the whole text depending on how the comparison turns out for them (cf. for a most interesting example of these comparison processes influencing media selection, Mares & Cantor, 1992). It is equally possible that other readers (or the same readers in another situation) would use the given quasi-social situation to place themselves into a role they find attractive. Readers would then evaluate Marc depending on whether they enjoy these experiences or not. This could be because readers may (attempt to) complete themselves symbolically in the sense of the theory of symbolic self-completion, as decribed by Wicklund and Gollwitzer (1985) by experiencing Marc's adventures or by adopting his role (cf. on the use of social-psychological theories for the description of reading processes, Ritterfeld & Vorderer, 1993). The description of acts of understanding using social-psychological models or theories suggests itself if one takes the assumption that the reading of narrative texts in fact represents such a quasi-social situation seriously. On the basis of this assumption, it is only reasonable to expect such cognitive and emotional processes to occur during the reading of suspenseful texts. A dichotomous model (approval vs. disapproval, hope vs. fear, etc.) seems to be too limited here.

  The prevailing discussion should make it clear that the understanding of drama implies manifold and sometimes very complex mental processes and also that it is specified depending on the type of text, the individual reader or viewer, and the concrete reading or viewing situation. The examples mentioned here show that these different variants were indeed found or at least discussed in various fields of research. It is almost superfluous to point out that the previously mentioned complexity and variety of possible acts of understanding can vastly increase when all factors identified also interact with one another. Thus the validity of general statements (i.e., those that abstract from these specified conditions) is even more limited. Of course this does not call into question the theoretical models and empirical results presented by Zillmann and his collaborators. What is of interest for me here is to prove that these are special cases that should be expanded and completed by a description and explanation of further variants. The general direction promoted here is elaboration, differentiation, and thus substantiation.

SUSPENSE AND EMOTION

The (further) development of a psychological theory of suspense thus demands the inclusion of constructive cognitions of various forms and complexities. In this sense, it should follow the general development within psychology that has in recent decades developed from the description of mere mechanical stimulus-response relations (as in behaviorism) in the direction of the description and explanation of intervening cognitive processes (as in cognitive psychology). Such a development, however, is in danger of also adopting the one-sidedness and the simplifications symptomatic of recent developments in this field. I refer here to an exclusive or at least primary limiting of focus to the analysis of cognitive processes, neglecting emotional or affective aspects. This narrowing of perspective can already be noticed in the field of cognitively oriented suspense research. Some authors emphasize that a cognitive analysis should be the primary focus because cognitive processes are prior to any affective reaction. From the vantage point of cognitive psychology, emotional processes do indeed seem to be epiphenomena and are accordingly treated as subordinate to cognitive acts. However, if this leads to the consideration of emotional aspects of suspense only after the cognitive aspects have been described and explained satisfactorily, an analysis of the phenomenon of suspense cannot possibly succeed. I would like to show that suspense cannot be represented only by reference to cognitive structures and processes. Without the assumption that viewers not only perceive, anticipate, conclude, evaluate, and so on, but also always prefer, desire, or want something (and in particular a certain development or outcome of the narration), suspense cannot be psychologically understood or explained.

Interestingly enough, the desires or preferences of audiences are taken into account precisely by those authors who do not hold a position decidedly aligned with cognitive psychology. Zillmann's contribution (cf. chap. 11, this volume), and also those of Carroll (cf. chap. 5, this volume) or Brewer (cf. chap. 7, this volume) are good examples of this. According to these authors, a threatened protagonist must be liked by viewers (Zillmann), and the likely outcome must come into conflict with viewers' currently shared moral (Carroll) or with the readers' belief in a just world (Brewer) in order to produce suspense. Zillmann substantiates his thesis by pointing out that people can only be empathic with persons they like; Carroll assumes that viewers are usually "pro" (film) moral and "contra" evil. In most cases, both conceptions arrive at the same hypotheses, which can be made clear by a concrete example. That the adventures of the protagonist in *The Client* produce suspense can be explained by the fact that readers like the threatened protagonist, Marc, and that any injury he suffers would thus represent the triumph of evil over moral. In the less prototypic suspense texts, however, there are cases in which these hypotheses do not hold up. It is possible, for example, for a moral outcome to benefit an unpleasant protagonist. What would be necessary to produce suspense in this case?

To continue the previously mentioned differentiations of various types of texts, readers or viewers, and situations in a consistent manner, this question should, of course, be answered by pointing to the specific constellation between these variables. If one wanted, nonetheless, to make a prediction as general as possible, then this could, in my opinion, be done by pointing out readers' or viewers' current preferences: preference for a situation, for a person, or for a specific text. Suspense arises if an unpreferred outcome (or further development) seems likely (or if a preferred outcome seems unlikely). This may (and in the prototypic case, will) be because an unpleasant protagonist or, more simply, evil threatens to triumph. It causes viewers to link their fear (in the sense of an as-if-fear; cf. Oatley, 1994; Vorderer, 1994b; Walton, 1990) of this particular outcome to their hope for a different one. There might be other reasons, however, for readers' preferences; reasons not (only) dependent on whether the protagonist is sympathetic or represents good.

I have suggested elsewhere that one should replace Zillmann's sympathy variable with the variable of relationship (Vorderer, 1994b). The assumption that viewers prefer an outcome that benefits those protagonists whom they like better or whom they know better or with whom they have—in their own feeling—a (parasocial) relationship or with whom they would like to form such a relationship is wider than Zillmann's thesis and allows the inclusion of other such conditions. This is made necessary by the fact that there are innumerable examples in which protagonists are not portrayed in such unambiguously positive terms as the heroes of Grisham's texts. Tan and Diteweg (chap. 9, this volume) and Ohler and Nieding (chap. 8, this volume) furnish examples that show Zillmann's thesis of sympathy to be too narrow. None of the protagonists in the research film by Tan and Diteweg are sympathetic, yet the film is able to produce suspense to a certain degree. The viewers, in fact, do prefer a certain outcome (of the whole film or of individual sequences). Additionally, there are examples in which the characters of a novel or a film are not only portrayed in a much more complex manner, but in which the relationship between the readers and the character as well as the readers' attitude toward the character is more complex. Some aspects of the character might be liked by viewers, others are more or less clearly disapproved of. In such cases, it would probably not be as easy for readers or viewers to say whether they generally like or dislike one or the other character. This is, among other things, the difference between a prototypic suspense text and a more polyvalent text, which may also portray complex characters and even characters who develop in the course of the narrative (e.g., texts with a greater element of experience). Suspense, however, also arises when reading or viewing texts like the Canadian short stories showed in the studies by Cupchik and Laszlo (1994) and by Vorderer, Cupchik, and Oatley (1994). This suspense could be explained and predicted, I would argue, if one knew the readers' or viewers' preferences regarding the development or outcome of the narration.

Of course one problem that arises if we define suspense by referring to the preference of a reader is how to identify the conditions of it. To be able to predict these conditions, it is necessary to name factors that influence the viewers' biases ("for" a certain protagonist, "against" the antagonists). Zillmann takes recourse in sympathy, Carroll in morality. However, if one considers these conditions too narrow, it becomes necessary to use a theoretical model that allows one to take other factors into account, but that is nonetheless consistent with the already achieved empirical results (Vorderer, 1994c; Zillmann & Cantor, 1977).

I would like to conclude by suggesting such a model, by trying to explain and predict the bias (preference) that is, in my opinion, the crucial condition for the feeling of suspense. My hope is that this affective component will be investigated systematically in the future and that it will also become part of a psychological theory of suspense. I refer to studies conducted within social psychology that concern themselves with the problem of perspective taking. My central assumption is that the same factors that lead to taking the perspective of a target person can also be used to explain the bias (in the sense of a preference) of the observing person. On the basis of this assumption, the factors social psychologists identified as being most important for perspective taking can be applied to the problem of the conditions of suspense.

Conditions of Perspective Taking

The ability of individuals to take another person's perspective was first analyzed and empirically investigated in developmental psychology (Piaget & Inhelder, 1947). Today, this ability is considered an elementary step in the ontogenetic development of intelligence. In recent decades, this concept was strongly enhanced as well as differentiated so that in the meantime, psychologists have learned to distinguish between at least three different kinds of perspective taking: a visual-spatial one (in the sense of Piaget & Inhelder), an affective one (Borke, 1971), and finally a conceptual one (an overview give Steins & Wicklund, 1993; Taylor, 1988). However, a problem arose concerning these different theoretical conceptions: The named types of perspective taking hardly correlate with one another and even correlate negatively with other characteristics (such as intelligence; Steins & Wicklund, 1993). The relation between this concept and the concept of empathy, which is in fact interpreted quite differently by different authors, creates another problem. To furnish a multifaceted position, one can say that the affective perspective taking describes an understanding of the emotions of another person, whereas empathy signifies the actual experiencing of these emotions. This differentiation is interesting in this particular connection because it allows the thesis that suspense does not necessarily develop due to empathy. However, difficulties also arise in social psychology, when perspective taking is analyzed in adults. Whether the taking of another person's perspective primarily assumes proximity or distance to this target person, is controversial, for example. For both theses, there are numerous arguments and empirical results (Steins & Wicklund, 1993). Based on these problems, Steins and Wicklund (1993, 1994) suggested a concept of perspective taking that defines the conditions for this cognitive act, also taking into account the difference between perspective taking and empathy. According to this concept, perspective taking is influenced by two interacting variables: by, on the one hand, the intensity of the relationship with the target person (also in the sense of "press": Murray, 1938) that results from both, the type of relationship (is the target person subjectively important, interesting, etc.) and from an individual's disposition to emotionally react to other persons. One could say that the probability for perspective taking increases the nearer the target person is or the better the target person is known. This is immediately evident because, according to Steins and Wicklund (1993), it is more motivating to take the perspective of a person who is interesting and/or subjectively important and with whom it may even be possible to develop a longer relationship. The second variable on which perspective taking is dependent is the quality of the relationship between the observer and the target person (i.e., whether there is a conflict between these people). A relationship full of conflict, the authors argue, is marked by anger, distrust, and uncertainty and reduces the perspective of the observer to the problematic aspects of the relationship. Here one can say the greater the conflict, the less likely it is that an observer takes the perspective of another person.

Steins and Wicklund systematically varied both variables in several experiments and found the following. In nonconflict relationships, the perspective taking is indeed more likely if there is real proximity to the target person. The hypothesis that claims that intensity of the relationship motivates perspective taking could thus be confirmed. In the case of conflict, however, everything is reversed: If there is a conflict, one adopts the perspective of the target person more readily if one knows little about him or her (i.e., if intensity is limited). What Steins and Wicklund found is thus an interactive impact of intensity and conflict on perspective taking. As far as sympathy for a target person is concerned, the authors report no correlation between sympathy and perspective taking. They conclude that neither empathy nor sympathy represent prerequisites for perspective taking. Both reveal nothing about perspective taking if detached from the social situation.

It should be clear how this applies to the problem of suspense conditions. Whether readers or viewers take a certain protagonist's party and therefore feel suspense if the protagonist is threatened depends neither exclusively on themselves nor on the description of the character. It is rather the specific constellation between the readers or viewers and the characters that is decisive for the development of proximity and for the quality of the relationship between them. Again, proximity—as already explained—depends on the type of relationship (i.e., on intraindividual characteristics) as well as on the individual disposition of the reader to respond emotionally to other persons (which represents an interindividual characteristic). Whether the relationship is marked by conflict or not depends mostly on the actions and expressed attitudes of the protagonists. One can assume that the relationship is generally dynamic. In the same way as viewers or readers get to know a character in the course of watching a film or reading a book, proximity to this character and the possibility of conflict may change during exposure. This would mean that in a certain sequence of a book or film, a threat to the protagonist leads to suspense, whereas in another sequence it does not. It would depend on whether the relationship at this particular time is marked by proximity and/or conflict. One can also imagine viewers feeling suspense at the beginning of a film although they do not yet know the threatened person. The motivation to create proximity is influenced by the prospect of having a relationship with this character so that taking this character's side can occur although the relationship has not yet developed. Thus an application of Steins and Wicklund's (1993) model to suspense research allows an explanation of suspense as a phenomenon depending on:

- The type of text (are protagonists and antagonists presented in such a one-sided manner that conflicts can only arise with the antagonists or is the text more complex, thus allowing one to develop varying relationships with the characters?).
- The readers/viewers (do they usually react emotionally to other persons?).
- The situation (is the protagonist interesting or important for the reader? Do the character's attitudes and actions come into conflict with those of the reader?).

Another advantage of this model is that it allows us to represent (again inter- and intraindividually) different possibilities for the readers' or viewers' participation in narrative events. After all, one of the controversial subjects in reception research is whether viewer participation in the fate of various characters can be represented best as identification (as is argued by, e.g., Oatley, 1994) or as empathy (which is Zillmann's position, 1991a; cf. concerning this problem, Vorderer, 1994b). In my opinion, a crude decision in favor of one or the other variant is unnecessary. Again, we can assume that readers (may) realize different forms of participation depending on the actual text, on their own preconditions, habits, and motives, and on the specific situation. This can happen either in the sense of an empathic process, or at another point as an identification process. However, it can also be—and this is the advantage of the perspective-taking model—more detached than the empathy model would suggest. The perspective-taking model proceeds from the assumption that it is sufficient for readers to know the background of the protagonist to be on their side. In other words, readers do not have to share the protagonists' emotions, they do not even have to fear for them, but can develop very different emotions from their own personal perspective, using their knowledge of the protagonists' backgrounds. This could occur if, for instance, a protagonist's situation reminds readers of their own personal experiences and if these perceptions or memories evoke certain emotions of regret, grief, or joy (cf. Scheff, 1979).

In my opinion, the application of this social-psychological concept of perspective taking as suggested and systematized during recent years by, among others, Steins and Wicklund, allows us to specify the conditions responsible for readers' or viewers' preferences (regarding characters and being "for" or "against" concrete developments and outcomes of the narration). If this application and the hypotheses that can be derived from it could be confirmed, then the conditions for this preference would be broader than Zillmann's conception (in which, in my opinion, the prototypic case is again described). Both concepts, however, hold that suspense presumes not only cognitive processes, but always affective processes as well.

Suggestions for the further development of a psychological theory of suspense can thus be summarized as follows: expansion and differentiation of the inquiry by including varying forms of suspense where different types of text (i.e., their various reception offers), inter- as well as intraindividual differences, aspects of the (social) situation of reception, reception modes (involved vs. analytical), and last but not least preferences and biases of audiences regarding certain narrative developments (as a result of parasocial relationships between viewers and media figures) have to be systematically included and empirically examined. Of course the first steps have already been taken in the already completed description and explanation of prototypic cases in suspense reception. However, if one considers how all-encompassing such a systematic widening of the field is, then it becomes clear how much still remains to be done.

REFERENCES

Berlyne, D. E. (1971). *Aesthetics and psychobiology.* New York: Appleton-Century-Crofts.

Best, P. (1994). "MacGyver wollte ich immer mal sein." Identifikationsfiguren und Identifikationsbedürfnisse von Kindern ["I always wanted to be MacGyver." Children's needs of identification]. In Deutsches Jugendinstitut (Ed.), *Handbuch Medienerziehung im Kindergarten. Teil 1: Pädagogische Grundlagen* (pp. 257–263). Opladen, Germany: Leske und Budrich.

Borke, H. (1971). Interpersonal perception of young children: Egocentrism or empathy? *Developmental Psychology, 5,* 263–269.

Brewer, F. W. (in press). Good and bad story endings and story completeness. In R. J. Kreuz & M. S. MacNealy (Eds.), *Empirical approaches to literature and aesthetics.* Norwood, NJ: Ablex.

Brewer, F. W., & Lichtenstein, E. H. (1982). Stories are to entertain: A structural-affect theory of stories. *Journal of Pragmatics, 6,* 473–486.

Brewer, F. W., & Ohtsuka, K. (1988). Story structure, characterization, just world organization, and reader affect in American and Hungarian short stories. *Poetics, 17,* 385–415.

Bruner, J. (1986). *Actual minds, possible worlds.* Cambridge, MA: Harvard University Press.

Bürger, C. (1973). *Textanalyse als Ideologiekritik. Zur Rezeption zeitgenössischer Literatur* [Text analysis as critique on ideology. On the reception of contemporary literature]. Frankfurt, Germany: Fischer.

Cantor, J. (1994). Fright reactions to mass media. In J. Bryant & D. Zillmann (Eds.), *Media effects: Advances in theory and research* (pp. 213–245). Hillsdale, NJ: Lawrence Erlbaum Associates.

Carroll, N. (1984). Toward a theory of film suspense. *Persistence of Vision, 1,* 65–89.

Comisky, P., & Bryant, J. (1982). Factors involved in generating suspense. *Human Communication Research, 9*(1), 49–58.

Cupchik, G. C., & Laszlo, J. (1994). The landscape of time in literary reception: Character experience and narrative action. *Cognition and Emotion, 8*(4), 297–312.

Dijkstra, K. (1994). *Leseentscheidung und Lektürewahl: Empirische Untersuchungen über Einflußfaktoren auf das Leseverhalten* [Reading decision and the selection of reading material: Empirical studies on the factors influencing reading behavior]. Berlin, Germany: Edition Sigma.

Feldman, C. F., Bruner, J., Renderer, B., & Spitzer, S. (1990). Narrative comprehension. In B. K. Britton & A. D. Pellegrini (Eds.), *Narrative thought and narrative language* (pp. 1–78). Hillsdale, NJ: Lawrence Erlbaum Associates.

Festinger, L. (1954). A theory of social comparison process. *Human Relations, 7,* 114–140.

Früh, W. (1994). *Realitätsvermittlung durch Massenmedien. Die permanente Transformation der Wirklichkeit* [Mediating reality through mass media. The permanent transformation of reality]. Opladen, Germany: Westdeutscher Verlag.

Früh, W., & Schönbach, K. (1982). Der dynamisch-transaktionale Ansatz. Ein neues Paradigma der Medienwirkungen [The dynamic-transactional approach. A new paradigm of media effects]. *Publizistik, 27*, 74–88.

Grisham, J. (1991). *The firm.* New York: Dell.

Grisham, J. (1992). *The pelican brief.* New York: Dell.

Grisham, J. (1993). *The client.* New York: Dell.

Groeben, N. (1980). *Rezeptionsforschung als empirische Literaturwissenschaft* [Reception research as empirical study of research]. Tübingen, Germany: Gunter Narr Verlag.

Groeben, N. (1987). Möglichkeiten und Grenzen der Kognitionskritik durch Inhaltsanalyse von Texten [Possibilities and limitations of criticizing cognitions by content analysis of texts]. In P. Vorderer & N. Groeben (Eds.), *Textanalyse als Kognitionskritik? Möglichkeiten und Grenzen ideologiekritischer Inhaltsanalyse* (pp. 1–21). Tübingen, Germany: Gunter Narr Verlag.

Groeben, N., & Landwehr, J. (1991). Empirische Literaturpsychologie (1980–1990) und die Sozialgeschichte der Literatur: Ein problemstrukturierender Überblick [Empirical psychology of literature (1980–1990) and the social history of literature: An overview]. *Internationales Archiv für Sozialgeschichte der Deutschen Literatur, 16*(2), 143–235.

Groeben, N., & Vorderer, P. (1988). *Leserpsychologie: Lesemotivation—Lektüre* ..rkung [Reader's psychology: Reading motivation—reading effects]. Münster, Germany: Aschendorff.

Hasebrink, U., & Krotz, F. (1991). Das Konzept der Publikumsaktivität in der Kommunikationswissenschaft [The concept of the active audience in communication research]. *Siegener Periodicum zur Internationalen Empirischen Literaturwissenschaft, 1*, 115–139.

Horton, D., & Wohl, R. R. (1956). Mass communication and para-social interaction: Observations on intimacy at a distance. *Psychiatry, 19*, 215–219.

Hurrelmann, B., Hammer, M., & Mieß, F. (1993). *Lesesozialisation. Band 1: Leseklima in der Familie* [Reading socialization. Volume 1: The atmosphere for reading in the family]. Gütersloh, Germany: Verlag Bertelsmann Stiftung.

Mares, M.-L., & Cantor, J. (1992). Elderly viewers' responses to televised portrayals of old age. Empathy and mood-management versus social comparison. *Communication Research, 4*, 459–478.

Murray, H. A. (1938). *Explorations in personality.* New York: Oxford University Press.

Nusser, P. (1973). *Romane für die Unterschicht* [Novels for the lower class]. Stuttgart, Germany: Klett.

Nusser, P. (1982). Entwurf einer Theorie der Unterhaltungsliteratur [Draft of a theory of entertaining literature]. *Sprache im technischen Zeitalter, 81*, 28–58.

Oatley, K. (1992). *Best laid schemes. The psychology of emotions.* New York: Cambridge University Press.

Oatley, K. (1994). A taxonomy of the emotions of literary response and a theory of identification in fictional narrative. *Poetics, 23*, 53–74.

Paus-Haase, I. (1994). Die Helden der Kinder. Zur Attraktivität und Verarbeitung fiktionaler Geschichten und Figuren [The children's heroes. On the attractivity and the understanding of fictional narratives and persons]. In Deutsches Jugendinstitut (Ed.), *Handbuch Medienerziehung im Kindergarten. Teil 1: Pädagogische Grundlagen* (pp. 232–247). Opladen, Germany: Leske und Budrich.

Piaget, J., & Inhelder, B. (1947). *La représentation de l'espace chez l'enfant* [The representation of children's spacial thinking]. Paris: Presses Universitaires de France.

Ritterfeld, U., & Vorderer, P. (1993). Literatur als identitätsstiftendes Moment? Zum Einfluß sozialer Kontexte auf den Leser [Do literary texts help to construct identity? On the impact of social contexts on readers]. *Siegener Periodicum zur Internationalen Empirischen Literaturwissenschaft, 2*, 217–229.

Rosengren, K. E., & Windahl, S. (1976). Mass media consumption as a functional alternative. In D. McQuail (Ed.), *Sociology of mass communications* (pp. 166–194). Harmondsworth, UK: Penguin.

Scheff, T. J. (1979). *Catharsis in healing, ritual, and drama.* Berkeley: University of California Press.

Schmidt, S. J. (1987). Der Radikale Konstruktivismus: Ein neues Paradigma im interdisziplinären Diskurs [The radical constructivism: A new paradigm in the interdisciplinary discourse]. In S. J. Schmidt (Ed.), *Der Diskurs des Radikalen Konstruktivismus* (pp. 11–88). Frankfurt, Germany: Suhrkamp.

Schmidt, S. J. (1991). *Grundriß der Empirischen Literaturwissenschaft* [Empirical study of literature]. Frankfurt, Germany: Suhrkamp.

Schönbach, K., & Früh, W. (1984). Der dynamisch-transaktionale Ansatz II: Konsequenzen [The dynamic-transactional approach II: Consequences]. *Rundfunk und Fernsehen, 32,* 314–329.

Steins, G., & Wicklund, R. A. (1993). Zum Konzept der Perspektivenübernahme: Ein kritischer Überblick [On the concept of perspective taking: A critical overview]. *Psychologische Rundschau, 44,* 226–239.

Steins, G., & Wicklund, R. A. (1994). *Fifteen years later: Drawing an E on your forehead—Perspective-taking, conflict and press.* Manuscript submitted for publication.

Tan, E. S. H., & van den Boom, I. J. M. (1992). Explorations in the psychological affect structure of narrative film. In E. F. Nardocchio (Ed.), *Reader response to literature. The empirical dimension* (pp. 57–94). Berlin, Germany: Mouton de Gruyter.

Taylor, M. (1988). Conceptual perspective-taking: Children's ability to distinguish what they know from what they see. *Child Development, 59,* 703–718.

Vitouch, P. (1993). *Fernsehen und Angstbewältigung. Zur Typologie des Zuschauerverhaltens* [Television and coping with fear. On the typology of the viewer's behavior]. Opladen, Germany: Westdeutscher Verlag.

Vorderer, P. (1992). *Fernsehen als Handlung. Fernsehfilmrezeption aus motivationspsychologischer Perspektive* [Television as action. Watching TV movies from a motivational perspective]. Berlin, Germany: Edition Sigma.

Vorderer, P. (1993). Audience involvement and programme loyalty. *Poetics, 22,* 89–98.

Vorderer, P. (1994a). Lesen als Handlung [Reading as action]. In A. Barsch, G. Rusch, & R. Viehoff (Eds.), *Empirische Literaturwissenschaft* (pp. 206–222). Frankfurt, Germany: Suhrkamp.

Vorderer, P. (1994b). "Spannung ist, wenn's spannend ist." Zum Stand der (psychologischen) Spannungsforschung ["Suspense is when it's suspenseful." The state of (psychological) research on suspense]. *Rundfunk und Fernsehen, 3,* 323–339.

Vorderer, P. (1994c). Was macht die Rezeption von Filmen spannend? [What makes the reception of a film suspenseful?]. *Medienpsychologie, 2,* 103–109.

Vorderer, P., Cupchik, G. C., & Oatley, K. (1994). *The effect of perspective and story type on literary reception.* Unpublished manuscript, University of Toronto.

Vorderer, P., & Valsiner, J. (in press). (Sozial-)Psychologie und Soziologie—oder: Das Mikro-Makro-Problem(-Bewußtsein) [(Social-)psychology and sociology—or: The micro-macro-problem]. In N. Groeben (Ed.), *Zur Programmatik einer sozialwissenschaftlichen Psychologie.*

Walton, K. L. (1990). *Mimeses as make-believe. On the foundations of the representational arts.* Cambridge, MA: Harvard University Press.

Westerbarkey, J. (1994). Unterhaltungsliteratur: Das Triviale als hegemonialer Diskurs [Entertaining literature: The trivial as a hegemonial discourse]. *Communications: The European Journal of Communication, 1,* 23–31.

Wicklund, R. A., & Gollwitzer, P. M. (1985). Symbolische Selbstergänzung [Symbolic self-completion]. In D. Frey & M. Irle (Eds.), *Theorien der Sozialpsychologie. Band 3: Motivations- und Informationsverarbeitungstheorien* (pp. 31–55). Bern, Switzerland: Huber.

Zillmann, D. (1980). Anatomy of suspense. In P. H. Tannenbaum (Ed.), *The entertainment functions of television* (pp. 133–163). Hillsdale, NJ: Lawrence Erlbaum Associates.

Zillmann, D. (1988). Mood-management through communication choices. *American Behavioral Scientist, 31*(3), 327-339.

Zillmann, D. (1991a). Empathy: Affect from bearing witness to the emotions of others. In J. Bryant & D. Zillmann (Eds.), *Responding to the screen: Reception and reaction processes* (pp. 135-167). Hillsdale, NJ: Lawrence Erlbaum Associates.

Zillmann, D. (1991b). The logic of suspense and mystery. In J. Bryant & D. Zillmann (Eds.), *Responding to the screen: Reception and reaction processes* (pp. 281-303). Hillsdale, NJ: Lawrence Erlbaum Associates.

Zillmann, D., & Bryant, J. (1975). Viewer's moral sanction of retribution in the appreciation of dramatic presentations. *Journal of Experimental Social Psychology, 11*, 572-582.

Zillmann, D., & Bryant, J. (1994). Entertainment as media effect. In J. Bryant & D. Zillmann (Eds.), *Media effects: Advances in theory and research* (pp. 437-461). Hillsdale, NJ: Lawrence Erlbaum Associates.

Zillmann, D., & Cantor, J. R. (1977). Affective responses to the emotions of a protagonist. *Journal of Experimental Social Psychology, 13*, 155-165.

Zillmann, D., Hay, T. A., & Bryant, J. (1975). The effect of suspense and its resolution on the appreciation of dramatic presentations. *Journal of Research in Personality, 9*, 307-323.

13

The Utility of Various Research Approaches in the Empirical Exploration of Suspenseful Drama

Minet de Wied
NOS Audience Research, Amsterdam

Dolf Zillmann
University of Alabama

Brian de Palma's *The Untouchables* (1987) tells the story of a naive federal agent named Eliot Ness (played by Kevin Costner) and a seasoned street cop (played by Sean Connery) who join forces in their battle against both underworld crime and police corruption in prohibition-era Chicago. The film begins with an interview of Al Capone (played by Robert DeNiro) by newspaper reporters. After Capone states that he is not involved in violent coercion of store owners to buy his liquor, the scene changes to a local store where the owner tells Capone's men that he will not sell their alcohol. Assured that there is no problem with that, the storekeeper turns his attention to a little girl, a familiar customer and neighbor. Capone's sinister men depart, but leave behind a briefcase. Viewers expect malice. However, the innocent little girl sees the briefcase and, in an effort to help, picks it up and runs after the men. As she stands in the doorway, calling "Mister, ... Mister, ... you forgot your ... ," calamity is in the air: Yes, the briefcase explodes.

Scenes of this kind place viewers in a state of suspense, that is, in an emotional state that is brought on by the anticipation of events that endanger the welfare of liked protagonists. The frequent usage of such scenes characterizes and defines, in fact, the popular genre of the suspense film—or more generally, all of suspenseful drama. Viewers' fascination with this film genre, with chains of happenings of the described sort, has attracted considerable research attention since the 1970s (Brewer & Lichtenstein, 1982; Carroll, 1984; Comisky & Bryant,

1982; Gerrig, 1989; Jose & Brewer, 1984; Norden, 1980; Zillmann, 1980, 1991b; Zillmann, Hay, & Bryant, 1975). Many issues concerning suspense and its enjoyment have been clarified; however, many questions have remained and demand answers. These include questions such as: Exactly what are the content and time characteristics of suspenseful scenes or suspense films? Which psychological processes mediate the experience of suspense? What are the cognitive and excitatory properties of this experience? Which kind of person is particularly responsive to film suspense? Which personality traits are responsible for such sensitivity? Are there cognitive strategies that viewers can use to diminish the impact of film suspense—should the experience become overly intense and "unbearable"? Perhaps most fundamentally, why do viewers enjoy suspense, if they do, and return to torturous suspenseful drama time and again?

The way in which these and related questions are asked largely determines the way in which answers are pursued and found. In other words, it determines the methodologies that are used to investigate the various aspects of suspense. For instance, problem statements and research hypotheses that focus on questions of causality are likely to be investigated with experimental research designs. Research questions that focus on determining the direction and strength of relationships between relevant variables call for a correlational approach. Descriptive studies, such as content analyses, concentrate on identifying important features and characteristics of suspense treatments. Moreover, the investigation of aspects of the suspense experience often relies on survey techniques.

All these methods have their useful place in the empirical exploration of suspense. However, specific research questions call for specific research approaches. To answer particular questions, some research techniques are better suited than others. This circumstance assigns great importance to the choice of appropriate research methodologies—of techniques that have optimal utility in answering specific questions. In order to make these choices possible, it is necessary to have an overview of the available research methodologies. This chapter attempts to provide such an overview. Primarily by exemplifying research, and by discussing its productive features, we hope to furnish the know-how that is needed to make informed choices of techniques and procedures best suited for the investigation of the uncounted, yet unexplored facets of the suspense phenomenon.

CHARACTERISTICS OF SUSPENSEFUL DRAMA

Although suspense is usually associated with thrillers, the concept is not limited to a pure suspense genre (Gow, 1968). Suspense cuts across numerous genres (Zillmann, chap. 11, this volume). Thus, suspenseful scenes can be found in various dramatic presentations. In science fiction, for example, or action adventure, melodrama, or tragedy—even in comedy (e.g., the famous scene in *Safety Last*, 1923, in which Harold Lloyd is seen dangling from atop a skyscraper). What, then, typifies suspenseful drama?

Suspenseful drama may be described in terms of stylistic characteristics, narrative characteristics, or both. A description in terms of narrative characteristics, for example, comes from Zillmann (1980, 1991b), who defined suspenseful drama as drama that features liked protagonists in peril. Suspenseful drama typically portrays hostile encounters between good and evil forces (e.g., man vs. man, man vs. beast, or man vs. nature), with the evil forces being stronger and dominating the good forces for a certain period of time. Characteristically, the resolution provides a happy turn of events, with the hero-protagonists managing to escape the danger or succeeding in their attempt to eliminate the evil forces.

Regarding stylistic characteristics, cross-cutting, for example, is a familiar principle for peril-and-rescue sequences (Gow, 1968). On the other hand, the absence of cutting characterizes suspense scenes in which the subjective camera leads viewers into sinister, danger-laden environments (e.g., into a dilapidated building, down the steep staircase, into a dark cellar). Portions of the action (e.g., the killer's hands or feet, a doorknob slowly turning, murder weapons, or emotional reactions on the part of a potential victim) may be selected from the overall scene and shown full-screen in a close-up. Moreover, the action may be suspended just prior to the fighting or stabbing in hopes of facilitating the building up of suspense (Carroll, 1984; de Wied, 1991, 1995; Sternberg, 1978). These and other stylistic devices, such as rhythmic cutting, abrupt cutting, lighting, and sound effects, are all part of suspenseful drama.

Following these observations, it would be interesting to know what stylistic devices are typical of cinematic suspense, and how suspense techniques are typically related to the thematic flow of events. Questions abound: Exactly how is the endangerment of sympathetic protagonists accomplished in contemporary suspenseful drama? How is the vulnerability of the good forces created? How is the power of the evil forces established? What kinds of danger are employed in contemporary drama? Do resolutions typically feature a satisfying, happy turn of events? If so, what characterizes happy outcomes?

Questions such as these can be answered by systematic content analyses. Content analysis can help establish what is typical, prevalent, comparatively rare, scarce, or nonexistent. Its yield may confirm intuition-based or theoretically derived expectations. However, the generated finding may also help abolish erroneously held beliefs about the incidence of particular contents and stylistic features as well as about their specific manifestations. In this vein, content analyses may correct our views, refine expectations, and lead to new and intriguing hypotheses.

Consider, for example, the endangerment of sympathetic protagonists. The endangerment of sympathetic protagonists is thought to be a joint function of the degree of danger involved, and the protagonists' relative (in)ability to protect themselves against it (Zillmann, 1980). Accordingly, the endangerment of a protagonist produced by the confrontation with a hitman would depend on the protagonist's ability to avoid or avert the danger. The confrontation should constitute an enormous endangerment for an unarmed protagonist who is unaware of the presence of the hitman. For an experienced gunfighter, however, equipped with a gun and ready to shoot, it should prove far less endangering. In suspenseful drama, then, the helplessness of a potential victim is conceptually as important as the brute force of a villain. If we want to describe how, in suspenseful episodes, the vulnerability of the good forces typically relates to the power of the evil forces, we need to trace the development of the opposing forces up to and throughout suspenseful episodes. The following section discusses how content analysis could be used to trace the development of the opposing forces in contemporary suspenseful drama.

Content Analysis

The first task of any empirical research is to decide what is to be observed, recorded, and thereafter considered a datum. Unitizing demands the conceptualization and operationalization of these units. In content analysis, there are three functionally relevant units (Krippendorf, 1980). The selected content materials constitute *sampling units*. In our example, contemporary suspenseful drama accommodating the man versus man motif constitutes the sampling unit. *Recording units* are the separately analyzable parts of a sampling unit. As we are interested in the development of characters, the characters involved may constitute the recording units. It should be possible to describe each character individually, including traits (involving attitudes, skills, preferences, psychological desires, details of dress and appearance), the position he or she assumes in the network of interpersonal relations, the interactions he or she is involved in, and so forth. *Context units* delineate that portion of the material that needs to be examined in order to characterize a recording unit. Major encounters (within or across scenes), for example, may provide hints to traits and thus should be considered meaningful parts or context units that need to be examined.

Sampling of Material. If the body of relevant material turns out to be too large for analysis, we need to select a representative sample. For example, we can draw a *random sample* from a listing of all relevant films about which generalization are intended. To determine which units are to be included in the sample, we can use a random number table or draw numbers blindly from a hat. Alternatively, we can draw a sample *systematically* by selecting every nth unit of a list. *Stratified sampling* is called for when the population consists of distinct, differently sized subpopulations or strata. In our example, we could make a distinction between television productions and motion pictures, or a distinction between specific film genres. Random sampling can be carried out in each stratum separately, so that the resulting samples reflect distinctions presumed or known to exist in the population. In stratified sampling, however, weighing procedures are applied in combining the strata, according to their relative size, in order to obtain a sample that is representative of the population at large.

However, whatever procedure we elect to use, we need to draw a sample that is large enough to contain sufficient information for generalization, yet small enough to be manageable. Although there are no set solutions for sample size determination, some procedures have been suggested. For example, the so-called *split-half technique*, in which a sample is randomly divided into parts of equal size, may prove helpful. If the parts support the same statistical conclusions with similar levels of confidence, the whole can be accepted as an adequately sized sample. If the test fails, however, the sample size needs to be increased until the specified condition is met.

Content Categorization. Once we know what is to be observed, we need to decide what is to be recorded: the data proper. The *content categories* are to be defined. To determine these categories, it is useful to talk to film directors or editors, to consult textbooks on film production, to read up on suspense theory, and to review research on suspense. Knowing the subject thoroughly, however, suspense in this case, along with using sound common sense, may prove equally productive. Textbooks (e.g., Bordwell, 1985; Mascelli, 1965; Monaco, 1981) and psychological research on film perception and comprehension (Kraft, 1986, 1987) inform us that stylistic or formal elements may serve a rhetorical function by shaping the connotative meaning of the depicted characters. Low camera angles, for example, are said to connote strength, action, and superiority, whereas high camera angles are thought to connote weakness, passivity, and insignificance (Kraft, 1986, 1987). The relevant research is not entirely consistent, however (Zillmann, Harris, & Schweitzer, 1993). Close-ups or editing techniques, furthermore, may direct viewers' attention to character-relevant information and thereby influence their evaluation of the characters. Narrative elements provide another, yet more important source of information about characters. Hoffner and Cantor (1991) reviewed the different sources of information that viewers use in forming impressions about drama characters. Impressions are formed, for example, on the basis of the characters' physical appearance (including physical attractiveness, body type, facial characteristics, and manner of dress), their speech characteristics, their overt and covert behavior (including motives and consequences), their emotional states, and their nonverbal behavior (such as facial expressions and gestures). All these sources of information influence person perception and are likely to modify audience dispositions toward the characters.

Media research has revealed that heroes and villains are identified on the basis of this kind of information (Hoffner & Cantor, 1991). Manner of dress, for example, is a way to distinguish the so-called good guys from the so-called bad guys: The good guys are typically clean and well dressed, whereas the bad guys are dirty and scruffy looking. The characters' behavior is probably the most important informational source: Heroes typically engage in prosocial behavior (being kind, polite, helpful and generous), whereas villains engage in socially unacceptable behavior (e.g., drinking, fighting, gambling, or being cruel and unkind toward other characters). Furthermore, heroes and villains are distinguished on the basis of the motives for aggressive acts and the consequences of these acts for the victims. Bad motives for violent acts and bad consequences for victims are associated with negative character evaluations, whereas good motives (e.g., self-defense, rescue of others) and good consequences for others are associated with positive character evaluations. Portrayals of heroes and villains also provide ample information for the assessment of the vulnerability of the good forces and the power of evil ones. The vulnerability of protagonists and the power of antagonists may be coded, for example, in terms of physical strength, mental preparedness, fighting skills, emotional stability, and apparent intentions.

Coding and Reliability of Coding. Coding is the procedure by which the relevant information is converted to analyzable quantities. The conversion involves judgment on the part of the coders. Training of coders is a common preparatory task in content analysis. The research planner, as a rule, formulates recording instructions, and coders practice their application on a sample of material. As a result of the practice coding, the recording instructions are frequently revised. Such honing of the instrument should eventually yield intracoder consistency and agreement among coders, which is known as *intercoder reliability.* Various ways of computing coefficients of intercoder reliability exist (Krippendorf, 1980). By using these coefficients, acceptable levels of reliability must be established prior to conducting content classifications and alternative assessments of content features.

Data Processing. Once the information has been coded, the data can be subjected to statistical analysis. As most content assessments involve the classification of discrete events, tallied frequencies are commonly analyzed by the appropriate nonparametric statistical techniques. These techniques also apply to the analysis of category differences in cases where these categories can be ordinally arranged. They apply, moreover, to the analysis of ordinal measures. For example, they would apply to the comparative analysis of the amount of harm threatened in suspense scenes that is ranked as minimal, moderate, or severe in, say, thrillers versus horror films.

Although the assessment of specific content events in terms of frequency dominates content analysis, the technique is by no means limited to tallying discrete entities. Already the analysis of *content contingencies* breaks such a narrow frame. This type of analysis focuses on the contingent occurrence of two or more discrete content events. For example, rather than tallying violence threatened and violence performed independently, the contingency of threatened and performed violence, in relation to merely threatened violence and the performance of nonthreatened violence, could be ascertained in order to learn how much of suspense is built on "empty" threats (i.e., threats unlikely to be acted on).

Outlook. More important, however, content analysis may involve interval and ratio measurements within discrete categories. For cinematic presentations, time offers itself as a most meaningful, precise variable. Analogous to investigations outside suspenseful drama (Stocking, Sapolsky, & Zillmann, 1977), assessment of the time dedicated to developing the malice of an antagonist, to showing the fear and panic of threatened protagonists, and to the actual confrontation between the antagonistic forces, would seem to be most informative. The particular sequential structures of the events involved in building suspense would also be of great interest. Spatial manifestations of pertinent events could be similarly measured out. Owing to greater precision of such measures as well as the generally greater power of their parametric treatment, analyses of this sort hold great promise for elucidating the arrangements of events on the screen that are designed to place audiences into acute states of suspense.

THE EXPERIENCE OF SUSPENSE

The experience of suspense, as stated before, has been viewed as an emotional state that is brought on by dramatic presentations featuring liked protagonists in distressing situations (Brewer & Lichtenstein, 1981, 1982; Jose & Brewer, 1984; Zillmann, 1980, 1991b). Suspense arises through the anticipation of possible outcomes that endanger liked protagonists, and it terminates at the presentation of the outcome.

Emotional responses to suspenseful drama have been shown to be modified by a variety of factors, such as the degree of subjective uncertainty about outcomes that threaten liked protagonists (Comisky & Bryant, 1982), viewers' dispositions toward hero-protagonists (Comisky & Bryant, 1982; Jose & Brewer, 1984), the magnitude of danger threatening the protagonists (Zillmann, Hay, & Bryant, 1975), the duration of harm anticipation (de Wied, 1991; Nomikos, Opton, Averill, & Lazarus, 1968), and prior knowledge of the outcome (Cantor, Ziemke, & Sparks, 1984; Hoffner & Cantor, 1990). This list of factors is by no means exhaustive, however. Other presentational (e.g., emotional expressions displayed by the character, rate of cutting, framing, sound effects) or situational factors (e.g., watching a film at home or in the cinema, watching a film late at night or early in the morning, alone or in the company of others) may influence the experience of suspense as well.

Moreover, one might wonder how viewers react to different types of threat to others, what factors determine whether or not planted cues foster the perception of events as threatening, what kinds of people are most responsive to suspense produced by fiction, or which deliberate cognitive processes can be employed by viewers to reduce or enhance the impact of suspenseful scenes. It is beyond the scope of this excursion to consider all processes likely to influence the experience of suspense. We thus restrict ourselves to discussing the research methods that could be employed to examine viewers' cognitive and affective reactions to the apparent endangerment of others.

As viewers are witnesses to dramatic events involving others, and are thus neither directly threatened nor benefited by the dramatic events, the experience of *emphatic distress* is commonly thought to be the predominant determinant of the experience of suspense (Zillmann, 1980, 1991a, 1991b). The empathy-mediated suspense experience is nonetheless genuinely noxious and stressful, at times extremely so (Zillmann, 1994, chap. 11, this volume).

Stress-inducing suspense scenes can vary along many dimensions. They may feature the threat of different forms of coercive action or display threatened violence. Some suspense scenes may be devoid of violence (e.g., proceedings in courts of law), whereas others may graphically portray physical torture and bodily mutilation. In research on horror films, graphic violence has been identified as a presentational element capable of evoking significant reactions of stress, especially when the life of liked protagonists hangs in the balance (Cantor, 1991; Cantor et al., 1984; Hoffner & Cantor, 1990; Johnson, 1980; Mathai, 1983; Tamborini, 1991; Tamborini, Stiff, & Heidel, 1990).

The Focused Interview

Interviews in which the interviewer concentrates the respondents on specific phenomena are useful in probing beliefs concerning these phenomena.

Objectives. A focused interview may probe, for example, viewers' beliefs about their reactions to suspense; that is, about the causes, manifestations, and consequences of these reactions. Such beliefs may or may not be consistent with accepted theory or research findings. Accordingly, they may challenge some existing hypotheses and highlight the predictions from others. Challenge or support are in no way compelling, however. The interview is not designed to provide proof of any kind. It aims, instead, at useful insights and revelations. Productive focus interviews will yield new ideas and novel hypotheses that then can be subjected to more systematic analysis. Productive interviews, in short, generate potentially intriguing hypotheses that call for empirical testing. They inspire research rather than constituting the end of exploratory efforts.

Another use of the focused interview is in the development of measurement instruments. For example, once the range of responses to questions about fear-inducing thoughts is known (i.e., the various interpretations of the specific questions and the terminology used by respondents in their conceptualization), sensitive yet robust questions (in the sense of consistent interpretation) can be formulated. The proven questions then can be included in questionnaires or interviews for use in more systematic research.

Conducting the Interview. If we wanted to learn, for example, how the experience of victimization influences the experience of suspense in which the same kind of victimization is threatened in fiction, we could, by postinterview classification, select persons who suffered or did not suffer the victimization in question. More specifically, we could select women who suffered rape and women who did not. All women would be shown a suspense scene in which a liked female protagonist is acutely threatened with rape, and they could then be queried about their reaction to the portrayal.

The interviewer might start the interview asking general questions, such as: Was this scene suspenseful? How intensely suspenseful was it? Why (or why not) was it suspenseful? Eventually it would become more specific: What, if anything, irritated you about this scene? If it disturbed you, what was it that disturbed you? Why did it (or why did it not) disturb you? Although the respondents are entirely free to express their thoughts, the direction of the interview is clearly in the hands of the interviewer.

Data Processing. After data collection, the information needs to be reduced to manageable size. This is usually done by a content analysis that organizes it into a limited number of categories. The frequency of responses may then be tallied; for example, the number of articulations of moderate versus intense disturbances in response to the scene by women who did or who did not suffer rape.

The same technique could be used to learn how respondents deal with fiction-induced disturbances of other types that reach highly noxious intensity. Which strategies are used to prevent excitation from reaching such levels? Which strategies are used to curb them, should prevention have failed? The covering of eyes to prevent further stimulation is a common observation. However, respondents may employ numerous other strategies that carefully conducted focused interviews could bring to light.

Correlational Research Methods

Correlational techniques are used to explore and establish the direction and strength between measured variables of interest. Once the degree and the direction of a relationship between two or more variables are known, we can employ regression analyses to anticipate events on one or more variables on the basis of the variation in any number of other variables. The purpose of such analysis, then, is to predict data points on particular variables from knowledge of these variables' correspondence with other variables.

Research Objectives. Knowledge of the specific relationship between variables is informative in itself. It would be valuable to know, for example, to what extent empathic sensitivity (Tamborini & Mettler, 1990), sensation seeking (Zuckerman & Litle, 1986), trait anxiety (Spielberger, Gorsuch, & Lushene, 1970), and other personality characteristics correspond with the intensity of the suspense experience in response to seeing heroes and heroines in peril. Do highly empathic persons respond more intensely than comparatively nonempathic persons? Can this experiential intensity be predicted from knowledge of persons' empathic sensitivity? This is apparently so only in cases in which the two variables are related, and positively so (i.e., an increment on the one variable is associated with an increment on the other variable—not always, but clearly in a majority of cases). Does trait anxiety relate to the experience of suspense in a similar fashion? What might be the relationship between empathic sensitivity and trait anxiety? If both variables are positively correlated with the experience of suspense, and if both variables are not entirely redundant with one another, we are potentially in a better position to predict the experiential intensity of suspense more accurately than we could on the basis of either variable alone. What about sensation seeking? Could it be that persons high in this trait are comparatively unexcitable, and that they therefore respond less to suspense treatments than persons low in this trait? If such a correspondence existed, it would be negative in direction (i.e., increments in the trait would be associated with decrements in the intensity of the suspense experience).

Limitations. It is of the utmost importance to recognize that correlations neither establish nor imply causal relationships. The cause for the observed correspondence may lie outside the correlated variables altogether. This means that causal conclusions simply cannot be drawn from correlational information. Viable conclusions are limited to associations, their direction and strength, between one variable and another, one variable and a set of other variables, or sets of variables. For example, if empathic sensitivity and sensation seeking should be negatively correlated, it would neither follow that the former caused the latter nor that the latter caused the former. On the other hand, a positive correlation between empathic sensitivity and the intensity of the suspense experience may coincide with a causal relation: Empathy might create intense suspense. The correlation cannot be interpreted as any kind of proof of such a possible causal linkage, however.

Data Collection. In correlational research, the investigator may follow vastly different procedures in collecting data. Measured entities may be persons' physical characteristics, personality traits, moods, autonomic responding, endocrine activity, intelligence quotients, perceptions, or judgments of any kind. There is no need for compatibility of the measurements. Ratio and interval measures, ordinal measures, and even nominally different entities can be arbitrarily intermixed for the purpose of correlation and regression. As indicated, behavioral measures (e.g., physiological measures such as blood pressure or vasoconstriction, or specific locomotion such as restlessness and moving to the edge of a seat during suspenseful scenes) can be mixed with data from content analyses, interviews, questionnaires, or the census.

Data Processing. In correlational analyses, the strength and, if applicable, the direction of relationships between variables are jointly computed in correlation coefficients. If the variables involved are measured on interval scales, product-moment correlations (one variable vs. one variable), multiple correlations (numerous variables), or canonical correlations (numerous variables vs. numerous variables) can be computed. Rank-order correlation coefficients exist for the analysis of variables measured on an ordinal scale. Yet other correlation coefficients have been constructed to deal with situations involving assessments on nominal scales. In most cases, the coefficient's prefix tells us whether the relationship is positive (i.e., as one variable increases the other increases as well, although not necessarily to the same degree) or negative (i.e., as one variable increases, the other decreases). Coefficients are arranged such that values of zero or thereabouts indicate that the relationship is negligible and uninformative (i.e., useless for prediction purposes, as any predictive effort would not be superior to chance estimates). In fact, there are tests for the statistical significance of correlations to establish whether the relationship is above chance levels. In practical terms, such tests, when not significant, suggest that it is not worth one's while to ponder the relationship in question.

Correlational research also allows us to examine how two variables are related after the removal of the potential contribution of a third variable to the relationship of interest (partial correlation) or how a set of variables relates to one other variable (regression analysis). Suppose we suspected that the relationship between empathic sensitivity and the intensity of the suspense experience is partly due to trait anxiety, which may be correlated with empathic sensitivity. To obtain a less confounded measure of the strength of the relationship of interest, we can statistically *partial out* (i.e., extract by partial correlation) the involvement of trait anxiety. Suppose we wanted to learn how much various personality traits contribute to the suspense experience. We could enter a battery of traits (e.g., empathic sensitivity, extroversion, psychoticism, neuroticism, shyness, manifest anxiety, sensation seeking, etc.) into a regression analysis and see how much (or how little) the individual traits contribute to the prediction of the intensity of the suspense experience. In such an analysis, the measured traits constitute the predictor variables and the measured intensity of the suspense experience the so-called criterion or predicted variable. The regression coefficients, or beta weights in the regression equation, would indicate the relative contribution to the overall accuracy of prediction.

At a somewhat more sophisticated level of investigation, path analysis provides a means of exploring the viability of hypothetical causal structures. The value of such analyses lies in determining which presumed causal structures explain most of the variation in a criterion variable, such as experiential intensity of suspense or subsequent enjoyment.

Another useful correlational technique is factor analysis. This technique is applied to sets of variables in order to find redundancies such that the complexity of the data set can be substantially reduced. Essentially, highly intercorrelated variables are integrated to form factors, and the differences between factors is maximized, according to various criteria.

Suppose we were interested in learning about the nuances of emotional experience during suspense. We might construct an elaborate questionnaire for respondents to fill in after exposure to a suspense scene. More specifically, we decided to use adjectival scales labeled, say, calm, pleased, disturbed, euphoric, irritated, tense, terrified, and relaxed, among 30 other items. We would, of course, subject all 38 variables to simple correlational analysis and attempt to make sense of the 703 resulting correlation coefficients. Factor analysis offers an efficient way to do this for us. Redundant items, such as calm, disturbed, irritated, tense, terrified, and relaxed, are likely to form a factor. Coefficients, so-called *factor loadings*, would indicate the amount of contribution to a factor, as well as the direction in the item combination. In our example, calm and relaxed are bound to exhibit a prefix, plus or minus, opposite to the other items. The emerging factor might be labeled "noxious affect." The items pleased and euphoric might form another factor, which could be labeled "positive affect."

Such simplification of unmanageable data complexities is often used for exploratory purposes. In our context, factor analysis might be used to determine the affective composition of the suspense experience as an emotion. This composition might be compared with that of the response to horror. The research question would be: What, in terms of self-perceived semantic dimensions, is different in the experience of suspense and terror? Exploratory factor analysis is the technique best suited to tackle issues of this sort.

It should be mentioned that factor analysis is now routinely used in the construction of so-called composite measures. In measuring emotional reactions in the described fashion, for example, it is statistically inadvisable, if not illegitimate, to analyze 38 variables one at a time (because the error rate in making statistical decisions becomes intolerable, due to the sheer number of decisions). Factor analysis allows us to reduce this unacceptable complexity to a few measures: the factors. These factors combine the redundant assessments that are manifest in the ratings on scales. The integration of potentially many scales into a composite removes much nuisance variance in individual ratings and thus creates a more stable and robust measure. The described data reduction has become commonplace in experimentation, a research technique to which we turn after considering what survey research can do for us in exploring suspense.

Survey Research

Survey research is virtually synonymous with research using a carefully constructed questionnaire. The questionnaire items often come from focused interviews. They may, however, follow theoretical considerations (Rosengren, Wenner, & Palmgreen, 1985) or be dictated by practical informational needs (Babbie, 1989).

Objectives. The primary objective of surveys is the estimation of population parameters from sample data. The procedures of sampling have been indicated already in our discussion of sampling in content analysis. The obtrusive difference is, of course, that elements of content are sampled in content analysis, whereas respondents are sampled in conventional surveys. Nonetheless, the logic of sampling is identical. Every effort must be made to honor the premise that each and every person in a defined population whose parameters are to be estimated enjoys the same probability for inclusion in a sample. Pure random sampling ensures this. So do other, more economical forms of sampling, such as stratified sampling based on prior knowledge of the size of strata.

Survey research of this kind would aim, for example, at determining how many Americans are fascinated with thrillers, enjoy them greatly, like them a little, do not care for them, or abhor them. In terms of a proportion of Dutch teenagers, research might determine what percentage prefers thrillers over horror movies and what percentage despises both genres and lusts for romantic movie themes.

However, survey research does not always pursue population parameters. In uses and gratifications research (Palmgreen & Rayburn, 1985; Rubin, 1994), for example, the survey technique is used to determine dimensions of gratification. Applied to the suspense experience and any gratification derived from it, this approach would confront a nonrandom sample of respondents to highly structured questionnaires designed to assess why, in the respondents' perception, their reactions to suspenseful scenes are noxious and their postresolution experience is hedonically positive. This procedure obviously does not allow generalizations to a population, but focuses on attaining knowledge about persons' beliefs about their emotional reactions and the causes of their gratifications.

Limitations. The most apparent limitations of survey research, as used in communication studies, concern the respondent as an information source. Interviewees simply may not know the answers, at least not with confidence and the required accuracy. Retrospective assessments in response to questions such as "How many suspense films have you seen last month?" or "How did you feel when the detective (played by Michael Douglas) in *Basic Instinct*, while having sexual intercourse with a murder suspect (played by Sharon Stone), thought she appeared to grab for the ice pick—her murder weapon of choice?" are notoriously imprecise and unreliable. Moreover, respondents may distort answers in trying to make a good impression on the interviewer. For example, "Did you ever become sexually excited during particularly suspenseful murder scenes?" is unlikely to inspire honesty in young viewers.

In constructing a questionnaire for a survey, then, care must be taken to avoid questions that go beyond what respondents can be reasonably expected to know and questions that create evaluation apprehensions.

Data Collection. In survey research, the interview adheres to a carefully prepared questionnaire. This questionnaire may be administered by mail, which gives respondents privacy but prevents spontaneity in answering questions. Alternatively, it may be administered face-to-face or via telephone. Face-to-face aural interviewing is most likely to create evaluation apprehensions. If the interview is one-on-one, the interviewer fosters such apprehensions. If the interview is in groups, all persons present create them. The written interview (i.e., respondents anonymously fill in questionnaires) avoids the indicated problems, but invites some degree of nonspontaneity. Interviews by computer have gained acceptance in recent years. At present, they simulate the written interview. Aural forms may become available shortly, however. One of the great advantages of computerized interviews is the quasi-instantaneous availability of the results. The entered data can be immediately subjected to analysis.

Data Processing. In contrast to the focused interview, which favors open-ended questions that are difficult to convert to numerical values, survey research is partial to quantified judgments that are ready for statistical analysis. Data are usually prepared for parametric analysis that generates the population estimates of interest. However, the data may also be reduced by factor or cluster analyses, with response structures being of focal interest.

Experimental Research

Experiments are characterized by distinct conditions under which events of interest are observed. The analysis of differences in these events, due to the various conditions employed, constitutes the principal procedure of effect determination.

Not all arrangements of conditions of differing consequence are experiments, however. In true experimentation, the conditions are carefully created through the so-called *manipulation* of specific independent variables, and respondents are *randomized* across all manipulated conditions in order to control for extraneous influences. All this is done to implicate the condition differentiation with the causation of any observed differentiation of consequences as measured by the dependent variable or variables. Under these circumstances, alternative causes can be ruled out as highly improbable.

However, conditions are not always created by manipulation. They may be created by the selection or aggregation of entities that are already different in more than one regard. This situation renders the condition arrangement a pseudo-experiment with limited potential for drawing causal inferences.

We now examine the different paradigms more closely and in connection with suspense.

The Pseudoexperiment. Pseudoexperiments or differential research designs are used to explore differences between groups for which independent variables pre-exist and can be measured but not directly manipulated. For example, we might want to compare the emotional reactions of men and women to suspenseful scenes that dwell on the threat of rape. Men and women are obviously not manipulated in a controlled fashion. They potentially differ in many ways other than gender in genetic terms. They nonetheless would constitute the independent variable in the contemplated pseudoexperiment. We may want to compare the reactions of persons with low or high empathic sensitivity. Such sensitivity would be preassessed in order to assign respondents to one or the other condition. Notwithstanding this empirical determination, respondents again are only selected, and their empathic trait may be confounded with numerous other traits that could exert an influence on the reactions of interest. In a so-called *factorial design*, we could, moreover, cross-vary genre of respondent (female, male) with empathic sensitivity (low, high) and examine the combined effect of both variables (their interaction) in addition to their individual effects. Further factorial extensions are possible. They are limited only by practical considerations. The factorial extension also may involve any number of manipulated variables. Such involvement would make the design in part a pseudoexperiment and in part a true experiment. It is, obviously, the particular variation in each individual factor (selection vs. manipulation) that determines the factors' status as pseudoexperimental or truly experimental.

Because we do not manipulate pseudoexperimental variables, we cannot rule out all potential confoundings (i.e., variables that covary with the independent variables, and that may influence the dependent variables). The analysis of covariance provides some degree of statistical control and can help to minimize the confounded effect of a limited number of variables. However, because an unknown number of confoundings may remain, we cannot causally attribute any observed effects to specific aspects of independent variables that were created by selection, not manipulation.

The Experiment Proper. Whereas in correlational and differential research we seek to answer questions about the relationship among unmanipulated variables, in true experimentation the independent variables are purposely and systematically manipulated in order to implicate causal linkages. The prototypical experiment is a controlled laboratory study in which the effects of the independent variables (i.e., the variables we manipulate) on the dependent variables (i.e., the response measures) are assessed as confounding influences are ruled out. The experiment proper has the following characteristics (Graziano & Raulin, 1993): (a) a clearly stated research hypothesis about predicted causal effects of the independent variable on the dependent variable, (b) the independent variable includes at least two levels, (c) respondents are randomly assigned to conditions, (d) specific and systematic procedures are employed to test the hypotheses, and (e) specific controls are employed to reduce threats to internal validity. We return to these characteristics and exemplify them.

The Field Experiment. This research approach constitutes an interesting variant of experimentation. Essentially, it constitutes true experimentation without the respondents ever knowing that they served in an experiment. This feature is not unimportant. Respondents who know that they serve as respondents tend to ponder what the purpose of the experiment might be. At the very least, this may prove distracting and distort the effects of interest. More troublesome is the possibility that they form hypotheses about the purpose and then try either to be cooperative and help foster expected effects or to thwart the researchers by acting contrary to expectations. To prevent such guessing and its consequences, investigators often resort to deception and offer a plausible but innocuous explanation with the instructions.

The field experiment circumvents these problems and, hence, tends to have greater ecological validity. In suspense research, an investigator might, for instance, examine the effect of a companion viewer's behavior on the experience of suspense. Similar to a technique used by Zillmann, Weaver, Mundorf, and Aust (1986) in studying companion effects on the response to horror, companions could be planted next to persons taking a seat in a movie theater to watch a thriller. Following a random schedule, this companion then could express great distress, verbally ("Oh, my God!") and nonverbally (sliding about, covering eyes) in one condition or find matters amusing in another. In a control condition, the companion would be nonexpressive. A confederate would wait at the exit and, at the movie's conclusion, ask the departing target respondent to assist in a movie evaluation, part of which would be an assessment of the intensity of the respondent's suspense experience. Clearly, respondents need not learn that they took part in a controlled experiment. They might, however, be appraised of it after the fact. At any rate, the gain in ecological validity that the field experiment offers obviously comes at a rather forbidding price in efforts to create the independent variation and in respondent attrition. Respondents may, after all, refuse to volunteer the information that constitutes the dependent variable.

Research Objectives. As has been stated numerous times already, experimental research seeks to implicate cause-and-effect linkages. Ideally, conditions are manipulated to differ in one particular regard only. If the specific condition difference results in different outcomes, the outcome difference can be attributed to the condition difference. In other words, the outcome difference may be considered *caused* by the condition difference, or the independent, manipulated variation can be said to have caused the *effect* on the dependent variable.

For the consequences of pseudoexperimental variables, no such claim can be made, and essentially correlational interpretations must be applied.

Consider, for example, the simple experimental design used by Bryant (cited in Zillmann, 1980) to study various aspects of suspense. This investigator wanted to explore the effects of various levels of threat to a hero's welfare on the subjective perception of his endangerment, physiological reactions during the suspense experience, and the enjoyment on a satisfying resolution of the suspense. Bryant took a stock plot of a Western hero in peril and created successively lower levels of suspense by successively removing the various elements thought to foster suspense. The film segment featured a sympathetic pony express rider who lost his horse to a hostile environment, was injured in the process, and tried to make his way back to an outpost. He passed through barren territory populated by rattlesnakes and outlaws. In the condition of extreme suspense, this hero was severely wounded, outnumbered by outlaws who confronted him, threatened by a rattlesnake in a pit he entered for cover, and down to his last bullet. The hero eventually escaped his predicament, mostly through the cavalry's last-minute arrival. Bryant manipulated this footage by taking out the threatening elements, one by one. He removed, for example, the information about the last bullet, images of the rattler, shots indicating the severity of injury, several or all outlaws, and so on. In a minimal suspense condition, the hero, then, suffered no shortage of bullets, was not immediately threatened by the rattler, had a minor injury only, and was never threatened by outlaws. All other conditions were intermediate to the indicated extremes; that is, they incrementally involved threatening scenes. Bryant thus created an iterative differentiation consisting of five conditions, with threat increasing from minimal to maximal. Such an arrangement of conditions is referred to as a one-factor design with five levels.

Bryant had predicted that respondents' perception of doom would grow the more elements of threat to the protagonist were featured, and that their perception of doom would be positively correlated with sympathetic activity, which he measured in heart-rate acceleration. The findings confirmed these expectations. The greater the threat to the liked protagonist in the film, the more intense the experience of suspense as operationalized in the respondents' perception of doom and excitatory reactions. It was also found that, on resolution, enjoyment of the footage increased with the magnitude of threat. All findings were monotonic trends.

Such results may be interpreted as showing that the magnitude of threat to a protagonist in a story causes corresponding levels of perceptions of endangerment, of affective concomitants, and of postresolution enjoyment. Note that the independent variable is causally implicated with the creation of all dependent effects. The dependent variables, in contrast, are to be treated as correlated. No claim can be made about their causal interdependence. However, the cognitive and excitatory reaction to suspense can be considered to have influenced enjoyment as intervening variables, whereas influence in the reverse direction is ruled out by the fact that enjoyment was assessed at a later time and cannot have exerted its influence retroactively. Such suggested influences are usually examined more specifically in subsequent experimentation.

Bryant's manipulated experimental variable could, of course, have been crossvaried with nonmanipulated pseudoexperimental variables. For example, female and male respondents could have been separated on grounds that females tend to respond more empathically than males (Zillmann, 1991a). This would have made the design a 5×2 factorial one. Moreover, both gender groups could have been divided at their median on earlier ascertained psychoticism scores (Eysenck & Eysenck, 1976), as persons high in this trait can be expected to be callous and show minimal excitatory reactions during suspense. With this addition, the design would have grown to a $5 \times 2 \times 2$ factorial one: five levels of threat by two levels of respondent gender by two levels of respondent psychoticism, making for 20 experimental conditions. Such a design is capable of showing whether the four respondent groups react to the actual experimental treatment in a uniform fashion or differently; and if differently, in which particular way.

Let us consider a pure experimental design. Imagine that an investigator is fascinated with Hitchcock's (1959) model of the unsuspecting victim as a prescription for the utmost suspense experience, but also learned about empathy as a critical factor in the creation of suspense. How could he or she determine the relative merits of the two models? Easy! Film footage like that used by Bryant could be manipulated, say, to have the sympathetic protagonist, confronted by villains, seek shelter in a ditch. Hitchcock's scheme calls for editing such that a killer snake creeps up on the protagonist without him knowing. Suspense should be at a maximum as the camera shows close-ups of the snake's head, the tongue quivering, the fangs blinking, ready to strike the naked arm of the unsuspecting victim. Empathy considerations, on the other hand, lead to the expectation that the expression of apprehension is essential in creating intense suspense experiences (Zillmann, chap. 11, this volume). The show of apprehension presupposes, however, the threatened person's knowledge of the danger. Thus far, only two conditions are vital: The protagonist is appraised or not appraised of the immediate threat. However, suspense created on the basis of known danger usually involves more than a hint that the threatened person is cognizant of the threat. Such scenes tend to dwell on the expression of fear. Pearls of sweat are seen running down the endangered person's face, and images of the threat (i.e., the snake) and the reaction to it (i.e., the expression of fear) tend to be frequently intercut. In order to show the need for such exploitation of fear, our hypothetical experiment could cross-vary the hero's naiveté versus informedness with the expression of acute fear versus minimal fear expression. In the condition of naiveté and expressed fear, the hero's fear would, of course, be attributed to alternative dangers, not to the snake.

What can be expected in such a two by two design? If naiveté is essential, the two uninformed hero conditions should prove most suspenseful, more suspenseful than the informed hero conditions. This is tested by the main effect of informedness (no, yes). On the other hand, if the expression of fear is vital, the expressive conditions should create more suspense than the nonexpressive conditions. This would be tested by the main effect of expressiveness (low, high). It is also conceivable, however, that the hero's expression of fear that is attributed to causes other than the immediate danger posed by the snake (in the uninformed, high expressiveness condition) adds little to the suspense by naiveté, but that the meaningful attribution of much expressed fear greatly enhances the suspense experience. In this case we would obtain an interaction that calls for comparisons between individual means.

Our experiment might be expanded to include other sources of vulnerability, such as the hero's ability to defend against an immediate danger, and pseudoexperimental variables, such as empathic sensitivity. Measured nonmanipulated variables may also be used as covariates to help reduce the influence of variables that are extrinsic to the focal purpose of experimental investigations.

A rule of thumb for good experimentation is, nonetheless, to concentrate on an issue of theoretical relevance and to limit the complexity of the design to essential, necessary variables. Regarding the manipulation of variables, an old vestige urges to create only the slightest difference needed, and to hold everything else constant.

This should not deter investigators, who have sound reasons for using complex designs, from working with them. Experimentation with complex factorial designs allows, after all, the simultaneous determination of numerous causal influences in all their interactive manifestations.

Limitations. Experimentation is routinely criticized for its artificiality. In order to gain control over independent variations, freeing them from confoundings, research is often conducted with material and under conditions that poorly simulate ecologically predominant situations. In suspense research, it is the exception that respondents are exposed to a feature film sitting with their friends in a regular theater. They may sit, instead, in a chair in a laboratory with electrodes attached to them, looking at a highly edited snippet from a thriller. The artificiality of such situations may be greatly reduced, however, at least for suspense research. Suspense research can, after all, be conducted in theaters and with groups of friends. The solicitation of the respondents' views, their being disturbed by a suspenseful scene or their enjoyment of the outcome, is a tolerable artificiality. Even the measurement of physiological reactions, which now can be accomplished by unobtrusively placed sensors and wireless remote recording, is no longer an intolerable imposition.

Problems with artificiality are more likely to crop up in manipulatory efforts. Few experiments enjoyed the luxury of production according to specification (e.g., Bergman, cited in Zillmann, 1980; Zillmann et al., 1975). Almost all resorted to the editing of existing material. Such editing hardly ever creates only the needed variation. Confoundings had to be accepted and mar the rigor of experimentation. (Note the manipulatory freedom in studying written narratives. Brewer and Lichtenstein, 1982, exemplified the rigor that is possible in creating different written conditions for the exploration of suspense and its enjoyment.)

Seemingly more principal limitations of experimentation are content specificity (or context variance) and the associated evaluation of relative contributions to effects. Content specificity creates generalization problems. For example, the findings of an experiment in which suspense was induced by the threat of a snake bite are not necessarily generalizable to suspense induced by the threat of rape or bodily mutilation. There are, however, ways around this. Exposure to material that creates suspense in different contexts can be repeated (i.e., respondents are shown more than one film, potentially many) and such repetition treated as a random factor.

The assessment of relative contributions to effects hinges, of course, on the specific ways in which various factorially arranged variables were manipulated. Again, only many different-context repetitions of the explored effects, an enormously effortful undertaking, can bypass this problem.

One principal problem remains, however. It concerns the very arrangement of experimental conditions and the analysis of effects by central tendency in these conditions. The analysis of variance and the analysis of covariance are at the heart of experimentation. Yet they allow us to determine ordinally differentiated groupings only. Statistical comparisons allow us to rule out equality and to specify the direction of an inequality. The analysis is not sensitive to the magnitude of such inequality. Increasingly, regression models are being applied to complement the more basic analyses and to overcome the indicated deficiency. It should be emphasized, however, that the analysis of variance or covariance is well suited for theory testing. Theories in the suspense domain are hardly specific enough to make predictions of degrees and relative contributions. They tend to predict greater-than or less-than differences, and the available experimental paradigms are most capable of testing such predictions.

Experimental Designs.   In planning an experimental investigation, the most important consideration is the arrangement of conditions, the so-called *design.* If an experiment is to provide proof of a particular causal relation, conditions must be created such that an unambiguous attribution of the observed consequence to an inducing condition is possible. The principal conditional arrangements are absence versus presence of a presumed cause and different degrees of the manifestation of a presumed causal condition, such as minimal versus maximal or minimal versus intermediate versus maximal. A larger number of specific ordinal differences along the independent variable is desirable. Interval differentiation is preferable, but more difficult to achieve.

The factorial arrangement of conditions has been discussed already. Its principal advantage is the simultaneous evaluation of numerous causal factors and especially their interactions. The analysis of variance or covariance shows whether the combined effect of different variables is additive or deviates from additivity. The latter reveals interactive variables whose joint effect may be less or more than their summed individual effects.

To illustrate compelling condition arrangements, let us assume that someone doubts that suspense is caused by a liked protagonist's confrontation with danger. We could use the footage of the Western hero threatened by a rattler. To create a no-danger condition we would replace the snake shots with shots of a rabbit. After exposure of respondent groups to one or the other condition, we would ascertain the intensity of resulting suspense experiences. Such experiences should be nonexistent in the no-threat condition and pronounced in the threat condition. The outcome would prove that threat to a liked protagonist is causally involved in the creation of the suspense experience.

An investigation by Zillmann and Cantor (1977) provides an illustration of variation-by-degree effects. The research question was whether empathic distress depends on, or is a function of, favorable affective dispositions toward protagonists. Hence, a narrative was created that developed a character either as very likable, as somewhat likable, or as dislikable. The character eventually suffered an accident and displayed intense pain. As predicted from disposition theory (Zillmann, 1991b), empathic distress was found only when the suffering character was liked. It was absent when he was detestable. Disposition toward fictional characters thus has been shown to be causally involved in the mediation of empathic distress.

Dependent Variables. Once an experimental design has been determined, the dependent variable or variables, also referred to as dependent measures, must be selected. Clearly, in creating a design, effect assessments must have been considered in conceptual terms. Now such conceptualizations must be operationalized, that is, expressed in concrete measurement operations.

Considering the experience of suspense, measurement instruments or procedures can be classified as self-reports or behavioral measures. Investigators who are interested in viewer's conscious experience of aspects of suspense, or in their postexposure reflective assessments, must rely on the respondents' self-reports. The experimental questionnaire or response form is usually employed to obtain these reports. On the other hand, investigators who seek to understand the suspense experience independent of the respondents' introspection must devise behavioral assessments. Behavioral measures may focus on overt behavior, such as facial expressions or motor restlessness, as well as covert behavior, such as endocrine or autonomic reactions. Ideally, the reliability (i.e., the property of an instrument to measure whatever it measures with consistency) and validity (i.e., the property of an instrument to measure what it is supposed to measure) of these measures should be established prior to using them in research on suspense.

We briefly discuss measures likely to be used in the research domain under consideration.

Self-Report Measures. The type of self-report measure most frequently used in research on cinematic suspense is the rating scale—or more accurately, the rating-scale battery. Respondents are presented with mostly written questions, such as "How suspenseful was this segment?", "How much did you worry?", or "How anxious did you feel?" Scales for marking are displayed alongside the questions. Typical scales are unipolar, ranging from the absence of a property to its full manifestation. Scales may have any number of points for marking, but rarely exceed 11. An 11-point unipolar scale would start at 0 (*absence of*), iterate by integer, and end at 10 (*full manifestation of*). Bipolar scales are in use for ratings of diametrically opposite qualities, such as relaxed and tense or ugly and beautiful. Note that opposites are content specific (e.g., bright and stupid assumes different meanings for the evaluation of a person as compared to an apartment) and that there is ambiguity concerning the midpoint of scales (e.g., on a bipolar scale from −x to x, 0 might indicate the absence of either of the opposing properties or their equal manifestation resulting in cancellation). Ratings are mostly made following the presentation of experimental material, that is, suspenseful scenes and feature films. Given the need for multiple assessments during exposure, ratings may be solicited intermittently as well, however.

Ratings need not be made by pencil on paper. Questions can be presented aurally or in written form on a computer screen. In an experiment by Nomikos et al. (1968), for example, ratings were made repeatedly during film exposure by pressing one of several numbered keys on a keyboard. Another procedure, designed to obtain continuous recordings of subjective distress during film exposure (de Wied, 1991), required respondents to press a rubber bulb to express the amount of suspense experienced. They had been instructed to press harder the more intensely they experienced suspense. Measures of this kind have the advantage of automatic recording. Ideally, the measurements are entered in a format ready for data analysis. A common misconception should be pointed out, however. Although these measures bypass the pencil, they are not behavioral measures. They are self-reports because they necessitate the respondents' awareness of rendering judgments about aspects of their own behavior for the perusal and scrutiny by others.

Behavioral Measures. In research on suspenseful drama, measures of overt behavior have been used, for example, in studies with children (Zillmann & Cantor, 1977; Zillmann et al., 1975). In these studies, facial expressions were recorded and coded as nonverbal indices of distress. No other similarly overt behavioral indices have been used to measure suspense during film exposure. In view of much informal talk about spontaneous behavioral indicators of suspense experiences, this is surprising. Grabbing a fellow viewer, screaming, uttering dismay, shouting interjections, and looking away have all been observed on occasion. Perhaps it is feared that such expressiveness is limited to the theater or the home, and that respondents in laboratory situations are stifled to a point that renders the assessment of overt expressions insensitive. It should be possible, however, to devise less obtrusive yet overt behavioral measures, such as restless sitting, which could be mechanically recorded through pressure changes in portions of a seat.

Covert behavioral measures have been used sparingly in suspense research, presumably because of their relatively intrusive nature. However, measures of autonomic responding were employed in some investigations to index the intensity of experienced affect (Bryant, cited in Zillmann, 1980; Zillmann et al., 1975). Zillmann (1991c) reviewed the various conceptualizations and operationalizations of autonomic arousal and its components. The most commonly employed index of excitedness, sympathetic arousal, is measured in systolic and diastolic blood pressure, heart rate, blood pulse volume, vasoconstriction, and skin conductance. Endocrine indices of excitedness, such as the release of catecholamines that is measurable in plasma or urine, have been used in some film studies (Carruthers & Taggart, 1973; Levi, 1965, 1967), but have not yet found their way into suspense research.

Experimental Procedure. Whether the experimenter interacts with one respondent at a time or with respondent groups, whether he or she acts alone or collaborates with assistants and confederates, it is highly advisable that a detailed script be prepared for all interactions.

The experimental script specifies each and every action to be taken by experimenters. It usually starts with statements welcoming respondents and with the experimenter's self-introduction, along with the possible introduction of other partakers.

Next on the agenda must be a plausible, yet generally incomplete explanation of the purpose of the investigation. Clearly, the revelation of the actual research objective would compromise findings, and experimenters are forced to be vague or use deception. Deception is obviously undesirable and should be treated as a last resort. In suspense research, it should be almost always possible to be vague by indicating a roundabout research interest into how people respond to films. Neither the experimental manipulations nor the associated research objectives can be disclosed. However, the operations to be performed by respondents must be fully explained. For example, respondents must be appraised of the nature of materials to which they will be exposed (e.g., that they contain extreme forms of violence) and of measurements to which they will be subjected (e.g., that they are expected to indicate, in ratings, their emotional reactions, or that their blood pressure will be monitored). Prior to engaging respondents in the experimental procedures, their written consent must be obtained, and they must be given the opportunity to withdraw at this or any later time from the experiment for any reason and without penalty of any kind.

Consenting respondents then take part in the experiment proper. They may, for example, fill in initial questionnaires about entertainment habits or the consumption of different genres of drama in particular. Thereafter, they may be exposed to the manipulated materials, usually in only one of potentially many experimental conditions (because exposure repeated across manipulated conditions would lay open the manipulation). Measures might be taken during and following exposure.

Experimenters follow their scripts in administering these elements of procedure. They may read instructions or play them from a tape in order to ensure consistency. Much of the experimental procedure may be computerized. Instructions may come from a videotape (in written or spoken form), and responses may be entered on the computer keyboard. Computerized procedures grant respondents maximal privacy and minimize social influence. However, they also tend to make research impersonal in the respondents' mind.

At completion of all assignments, experimenters must debrief the research participants. Any deception must now be disclosed and justified. The research objectives should be explained as well. Only after all this is done may experimenters dismiss respondents by thanking them, or by remunerating them, for their participation.

Data Analysis. Experimentation involves all types of measurement: nominal, ordinal, interval, and ratio formats. The statistical treatment of the data depends, of course, on the type of measurement. For nominal and ordinal measures, nonparametric procedures are to be used. For interval and ratio measures, the analysis of variance and its variants are applicable.

Experimental research is exceedingly partial to interval and ratio measurements, however. The principal reason for this is the need for simultaneously testing numerous variables in all their potential interactions.

The reduction of complex data situations, such as batteries of ratings, has been discussed already in connection with factor analysis. Experimentation favors singular, composite, robust measures. Experimental research is nonetheless open to the employment of sets of dependent variables. Sets of measures can be readily analyzed with multivariate techniques, such as the multivariate analysis of variance.

THE ENJOYMENT OF SUSPENSEFUL DRAMA

As suspenseful drama produces considerable amounts of distress during much of exposure time (an experiential state that is hedonically negative), it seems puzzling and paradoxical that this type of entertainment is capable of generating great enjoyment. Why do we attend and enjoy suspenseful drama time and again? What exactly is it that fosters enjoyment?

The enjoyment of suspenseful drama has been explained from different theoretical perspectives. Berlyne's (1960, 1967) arousal jag model suggests that relief from distress constitutes the rewarding experience. Zuckerman's (1979) sensation seeking hypothesis holds that the experience of distress itself constitutes the rewarding experience, because it produces need-satisfying sensations. Zillmann (1980, 1983, 1991b) questioned both accounts and explained the phenomenon as an admixture of cognitively determined positive affect from resolutions and excitation from preceding noxious experiences of suspense. More specifically, he posited that suspense experiences are highly arousing, that such arousal lingers, that satisfying resolutions foster positive affect, and that the experience of this reaction of pleasure is greatly intensified by lingering arousal from suspense. In this approach, then, suspense and its resolution form a meaningful functional unit that must be kept intact for the enjoyment of suspenseful scenes and drama as a whole.

Findings obtained in various studies support the notion that the enjoyment of suspenseful drama featuring satisfying resolutions is largely determined by level of suspense, with high levels of suspense enhancing postresolution enjoyment. The predicted pattern of effects was observed by Bergman, by Bryant (both cited in Zillmann, 1980), and by Zillmann et al. (1975), among others. Correlational studies, conducted by Jose and Brewer (1984) and by Sparks (1991), give further evidence to the positive relationship between self-reports and autonomic measures of distress from suspense, on the one hand, and postresolution enjoyment, on the other. The techniques employed in the indicated research on the enjoyment of suspenseful drama are, of course, identical to those described for the exploration of the experience of suspense.

Taken together, the results suggest a positive linear relationship between amount of suspense and postresolution enjoyment. It would appear, however, that the pleasure enhancement by distress from cinematic presentations has its limits (Bozutto, 1975; Cantor & Reilly, 1982; Johnson, 1980; Mathai, 1983). Bozutto, for example, reported that viewers can tolerate distress only as long as they feel in control of their emotions. Such control failing, they may be emotionally overwhelmed and suffer persisting disturbance, unmanageable anxieties included. Depending on the emotional lability and vulnerability of viewers, then, suspense treatments may reach a point at which excessive experiential intensity prevents pleasure from materializing, even if satisfying endings are furnished.

Furthermore, the explanation of the enjoyment of suspenseful drama in terms of excitation transfer hinges on the provision of satisfying outcomes. In case of dissatisfying, unhappy resolutions, dysphoric feelings are to be expected. The intensification of these dysphoric feelings by residual excitation from prior suspense should then lead to diminished enjoyment. The findings from studies in which both the degree of suspense and the type of resolution (positive, negative) were varied show, in fact, that the enjoyment of suspenseful drama featuring a dissatisfying resolution tends to be impaired by intense antecedent distress (Bergman, Bryant, both cited in Zillmann, 1980). However, the enjoyment-facilitating effect of satisfying resolutions was generally stronger than the enjoyment-impairing effect of dissatisfying outcomes. This observation is puzzling in that it suggests that a negative affective state (i.e., distress) can more readily facilitate a hedonically discordant affective state (i.e., enjoyment) than by a hedonically concordant affective state (i.e., disappointment, sadness). Such findings may simply reflect the fact that respondents were reluctant to downgrade the quality of drama just because it failed to feature a happy ending. On the other hand, they could be interpreted as suggesting that there is something pleasurable in the suspense experience itself, as Zuckerman (1979) surmised (see also Tannenbaum, 1980), or in the termination of this experience, as Berlyne (1960, 1967) contended.

REMAINING CHALLENGES

Many conceptually significant and theoretically critical questions thus remain and call for definitive experimentation. Additionally, numerous somewhat more mundane questions await answers and beg for analysis and assessment by whatever technique best suited for the purpose. For example, how much does the enjoyment of suspenseful drama depend on the overall theme, on the density of thrilling plots with prompt joyous resolutions, on drawn-out titillation with threatening images, on the development of superheroes and supervillains, on the involvement of complex and contradictory personas, on special effects, on editing techniques, on camera perspectives, and on the soundtrack, including its music? Last but not least, how does the respondent figure in? What characterizes the thriller aficionado? Which traits are specific to those who detest being placed in suspense by fiction?

These and other questions constitute a profound challenge to the empirical exploration of the suspense phenomenon. The research methods for such exploration are in place, as we have tried to document with this review. It now is up to those who are intrigued with the intricacies of drama, of suspenseful drama in particular, to use them to best effect.

REFERENCES

Babbie, E. (1989). *The practice of social research* (5th ed.). Belmont, CA: Wadsworth.

Berlyne, D. E. (1960). *Conflict, arousal and curiosity.* New York: McGraw-Hill.

Berlyne, D. E. (1967). Arousal and reinforcement. In D. Levine (Ed.), *Nebraska Symposium on Motivation* (Vol. 15, pp. 1–110). Lincoln: University of Nebraska Press.

Bordwell, D. (1985). *Narration in the fiction film.* Madison: University of Wisconsin Press.

Bozutto, J. C. (1975). Cinematic neurosis following *The Exorcist. The Journal of Nervous and Mental Diseases, 161,* 43–48.

Brewer, W. F., & Lichtenstein, E. H. (1981). Event schemas, story schemas, and story grammars. In J. Long & A. Baddeley (Eds.), *Attention and performance IX* (pp. 363–379). Hillsdale, NJ: Lawrence Erlbaum Associates.

Brewer, W. F., & Lichtenstein, E. H. (1982). Stories are to entertain: A structural-affect theory of stories. *Journal of Pragmatics, 6,* 473–486.

Cantor, J. (1991). Fright responses to mass media productions. In J. Bryant & D. Zillmann (Eds.), *Responding to the screen: Reception and reaction processes* (pp. 169–197). Hillsdale, NJ: Lawrence Erlbaum Associates.

Cantor, J., & Reilly, S. (1982). Adolescents' fright reactions to television and films. *Journal of Communication, 32,* 87–99.

Cantor, J., Ziemke, D., & Sparks, G. G. (1984, Winter). Effect of forewarning on emotional responses to a horror film. *Journal of Broadcasting, 28*(1), 21–31.

Carroll, N. (1984). Toward a theory of film suspense. *Persistence of Vision, 1,* 65–89.

Carruthers, M., & Taggart, P. (1973). Vagotonicity of violence: Biochemical and cardiac responses to violent films and television programmes. *British Medical Journal, 3,* 384–389.

Comisky, P., & Bryant, J. (1982). Factors involved in generating suspense. *Human Communication Research, 9*(1), 49–58.

de Wied, M. (1991). *The role of time structures in the experience of film suspense and duration.* Unpublished doctoral dissertation, University of Amsterdam.

de Wied, M. (1995). The role of temporal expectancies in the production of film suspense. *Poetics, 23,* 107–123.

Eysenck, H. J., & Eysenck, S. B. G. (1976). *Psychoticism as a dimension of personality.* London: University of London Press.

Gerrig, R. J. (1989). Suspense in the absence of uncertainty. *Journal of Memory and Language, 28,* 633–648.

Gow, G. (1968). *Suspense in the cinema.* New York: Tantivity Press.

Graziano, A. M., & Raulin, M. L. (1993). *Research methods: A process of inquiry* (2nd ed.). New York: HarperCollins.

Hitchcock, A. (1959, July 13). Interview by H. Brean. *Life,* p. 72.

Hoffner, C., & Cantor, J. (1990). Forewarning of a threat and prior knowledge of outcome: Effects on children's emotional responses to a film sequence. *Human Communication Research, 16,* 323–354.

Hoffner, C., & Cantor, J. (1991). Perceiving and responding to mass media characters. In J. Bryant & D. Zillmann (Eds.), *Responding to the screen: Reception and reaction processes* (pp. 169–197). Hillsdale, NJ: Lawrence Erlbaum Associates.

Johnson, B. R. (1980). General occurrence of stressful reactions to commercial motion pictures and elements in films subjectively identified as stressors. *Psychological Records, 47,* 775–786.

Jose, P. E., & Brewer, W. F. (1984). Development of story liking: Character identification, suspense, and outcome resolution. *Developmental Psychology, 20*(5), 911–924.

Kraft, R. N. (1986). The role of cutting in the evaluation and retention of film. *Journal of Experimental Psychology: Learning, Memory, and Cognition, 12*(1), 155–163.

Kraft, R. N. (1987). Rules and strategies of visual narratives. *Perceptual and Motor Skills, 64,* 3–14.

Krippendorf, K. (1980). *Content analysis: An introduction to its methodology.* Beverly Hills, CA: Sage.

Levi, L. (1965). The urinary output of adrenalin and noradrenalin during pleasant and unpleasant emotional states: A preliminary report. *Psychosomatic Medicine, 27,* 80–85.

Levi, L. (1967). Sympatho-adrenomedullary responses to emotional stimuli: Methodologic, physiologic and pathologic considerations. In E. Bajusz (Ed.), *An introduction to clinical neuroendocrinology* (pp. 78–105). Basel, Switzerland: Karger.

Mascelli, J. V. (1965). *The five C's of cinematography.* Hollywood, CA: Cine/Graphic.

Mathai, J. (1983). An acute anxiety state in an adolescent precipitated by viewing a horror movie. *Journal of Adolescence, 6,* 197–200.

Monaco, J. (1981). *How to read a film.* New York: Oxford University Press.

Nomikos, M. S., Opton, E., Averill, J. R., & Lazarus, R. S. (1968). Surprise versus suspense in the production of stress reaction. *Journal of Personality and Social Psychology, 8,* 204–208.

Norden, M. (1980). Toward a theory of audience response to suspenseful films. *Journal of the University Film Association, 32*(1–2), 71–77.

Palmgreen, P., & Rayburn, J. D., II. (1985). A comparison of gratification models of media satisfaction. *Communication Monographs, 52,* 334–346.

Rosengren, K. E., Wenner, L. A., & Palmgreen, P. (Eds.). (1985). *Media gratifications research: Current perspectives.* Beverly Hills, CA: Sage.

Rubin, A. M. (1994). Media uses and effects: A uses-and-gratifications perspective. In J. Bryant & D. Zillmann (Eds.), *Media effects: Advances in theory and research* (pp. 417–436). Hillsdale, NJ: Lawrence Erlbaum Associates.

Sparks, G. G. (1991). The relationship between distress and delight in males' and females' reactions to frightening films. *Human Communication Research, 17*(4), 625–637.

Spielberger, C. D., Gorsuch, R. L., & Lushene, R. E. (1970). *Test manual for the state-trait anxiety inventory.* Palo Alto, CA: Consulting Psychologists Press.

Sternberg, M. (1978). *Expositional modes and temporal ordering in fiction*. Baltimore, MD: Johns Hopkins University Press.

Stocking, S. H., Sapolsky, B. S., & Zillmann, D. (1977). Sex discrimination in prime time humor. *Journal of Broadcasting, 21*, 447–457.

Tamborini, R. (1991). Responses to horror: Determinants of exposure and appeal. In J. Bryant & D. Zillmann (Eds.), *Responding to the screen: Reception and reaction processes* (pp. 305–328). Hillsdale, NJ: Lawrence Erlbaum Associates.

Tamborini, R., & Mettler, J. (1990, November). *Emotional reactions to film: A model of empathic processes*. Paper presented at the annual conference of the Speech Communication Association, Chicago, IL.

Tamborini, R., Stiff, J., & Heidel, C. (1990). Reacting to graphic horror: A model of empathy and emotional behavior. *Communication Research, 17*(5), 616–640.

Tannenbaum, P. H. (1980). Entertainment as vicarious emotional experience. In P. H. Tannenbaum (Ed.), *The entertainment functions of television* (pp. 107–131). Hillsdale, NJ: Lawrence Erlbaum Associates.

Zillmann, D. (1980). Anatomy of suspense. In P. H. Tannenbaum (Ed.), *The entertainment functions of television* (pp. 133–163). Hillsdale, NJ: Lawrence Erlbaum Associates.

Zillmann, D. (1983). Transfer of excitation in emotional behavior. In J. T. Cacioppo & R. E. Petty (Eds.), *Social psychophysiology: A sourcebook* (pp. 215–240). New York: Guilford Press.

Zillmann, D. (1991a). Empathy: Affect from bearing witness to the emotions of others. In J. Bryant & D. Zillmann (Eds.), *Responding to the screen: Reception and reaction processes* (pp. 135–167). Hillsdale, NJ: Lawrence Erlbaum Associates.

Zillmann, D. (1991b). The logic of suspense and mystery. In J. Bryant & D. Zillmann (Eds.), *Responding to the screen: Reception and reaction processes* (pp. 281–304). Hillsdale, NJ: Lawrence Erlbaum Associates.

Zillmann, D. (1991c). Television viewing and physiological arousal. In J. Bryant & D. Zillmann (Eds.), *Responding to the screen: Reception and reaction processes* (pp. 103–133). Hillsdale, NJ: Lawrence Erlbaum Associates.

Zillmann, D. (1994). Mechanisms of emotional involvement with drama. *Poetics, 23*, 33–51.

Zillmann, D., & Cantor, J. R. (1977). Affective responses to the emotions of a protagonist. *Journal of Experimental Social Psychology, 13*, 155–165.

Zillmann, D., Harris, C. R., & Schweitzer, K. (1993). Effects of perspective and angle manipulations in portrait photographs on the attribution of traits to depicted persons. *Medienpsychologie: Zeitschrift für Individual- und Massenkommunikation, 5*(2), 106–123, 154–155.

Zillmann, D., Hay, T. A., & Bryant, J. (1975). The effect of suspense and its resolution on the appreciation of dramatic presentation. *Journal of Research in Personality, 9*, 307–323.

Zillmann, D., Weaver, J. B., Mundorf, N., & Aust, C. F. (1986). Effects of an opposite-gender companion's affect to horror on distress, delight, and attraction. *Journal of Personality and Social Psychology, 51*, 586–594.

Zuckerman, M. (1979). *Sensation seeking: Beyond the optimal level of arousal*. Hillsdale, NJ: Lawrence Erlbaum Associates.

Zuckerman, M., & Litle, P. (1986). Personality and curiosity about morbid and sexual events. *Personality and Individual Differences, 7*, 49–56.

14

On the Methodology of Empirical Research on Suspense

Axel Mattenklott
Johannes Gutenberg-Universität, Mainz

To write about methodology of suspense without referring to at least one theory would presumably result in very general statements. I would have to inspect several related theories with the objective of detecting associations between the concepts discussed and the idea of suspense (perhaps these associations would not contain much more than what can be read in general textbooks on methodology). Fortunately, I found more than associations and therefore happily believed that I should not content myself with Alfred Hitchcock's frequently cited phrase: "The trouble with suspense is that few people know what it is."

AN EMPIRICAL THEORY OF SUSPENSE

Zillmann (1980, 1991) formulated an empirical theory of suspense in which he restricted suspense to a specific type of experience and stated that "respondents are witnesses to dramatic events involving others," and that "they are consequently neither directly threatened nor directly benefited by these events" (Zillmann, 1991, p. 282). These "others" are likable protagonists who are confronted with situations that threaten to have deplorable outcomes and often endanger their lives. As witnesses to these types of alarming events, the respondents experience a subjective emotion that is called *empathetic distress*. The more the events watched threaten the likable protagonists, the more intense the empathetic distress should become. Fortunately, the ultimate outcome is often positive (especially when a disliked protagonist, who according to the rules of classical

283

drama causes the threatening events, is punished). When this type of event happens, the respondents experience a subjective emotion that Zillmann (1991) called *euphoria*. Euphoria can be seen as a form of intense enjoyment that is characterized as an affective "overreaction" (Zillmann, 1991, p. 292). The more intense the empathetic distress, the more intense the enjoyment when the likable protagonist ultimately benefits.

There are two subjective emotions stated in Zillmann's (1980) theory of suspense. The specific subjective emotion is the empathetic distress respondents experience when watching events that threaten likable protagonists. This statement can be seen as the core of the theory. If the theory is valid, the subjective emotion of empathetic distress should be associated with the type of event just described. To prove this requires a demonstration in which respondents feel *empathetic distress* while watching a likable protagonist being threatened and that they do not (or, at least primarily do not) experience another type of emotion. A further requirement to prove the theory is to show that respondents will not feel empathetic distress or, at least, will not have it as the dominant emotion, if they are watching another type of event, such as a sport, mystery, or horror. These two requirements lead to the methodological question of whether empathetic distress as a specific subjective emotion can be measured and, if the answer is yes, how to do it. I discuss the two questions in the broader context of how to measure subjective emotions.

The second subjective emotion in Zillmann's (1980) theory of suspense is euphoria. It can be seen as a type of intense joy and is, presumably, not qualitatively different. He did not address whether euphoria and joy are different types of subjective emotions but rather concentrated on the relationship between empathetic distress and euphoria: The more intense the one, the more intense the other. This statement reflects Zillmann's (1971) principle of excitation transfer, the major premises of which are (a) autonomic arousal does not terminate abruptly, but dissipates slowly, and (b) individuals often fail to attribute autonomic arousal accurately to more than one cause. Therefore, respondents believe that the positive outcome for the likable protagonist causes their arousal and do not realize that a part of it comes from the prior situation in which they experienced empathetic distress. Because the specific subjective emotion of empathetic distress is more critical to the theory than the more general conception of excitation transfer, I focus the following discussion on the question of how to measure subjective emotions and, particularly, how to measure empathetic distress.

THE MEASUREMENT OF SUBJECTIVE EMOTION

I introduce this chapter with a preliminary note about the use of the terms *emotion, subjective emotion*, and *feeling*. Emotion will be used as the most general term. It denotes an inner state plus a behavioral and a physiological component. If one induces joy, for instance, one assumes that it will be felt (e.g., as a feeling of warmth), and that it has a behavioral counterpart (e.g., a smiling face) and a physiological response (e.g., a change of the skin conductance level). Subjective emotion will be conceived as a subjective experience of the individual. It can be represented by different indicators (e.g., by a communication about what the individual feels). Feeling will be used interchangeably with subjective emotion.

Emotions have been traditionally measured by three various methods, called the three-system approach to emotion (Lang, 1971): the registration of, respectively, the arousal of the autonomous or sympathetic nervous system, the recording of expressive behavior (most frequently facial expression), and self-report. It cannot be concluded that subjective emotions can be measured analogously by these three methods as respondents may feel something they express neither facially nor physiologically (e.g., change in the heart rate when coldness is experienced). So as not to make things more complicated, however, I assume that subjective emotions in principal can be measured in the same way as emotions.

Generally, the measurement of subjective emotion faces one with three questions. The first asks whether an indicator is specific to a particular subjective emotion, whether skin conductance, for instance, is a specific indicator for joy. An indicator for an emotion is defined as specific if it is present when the particular emotion is present and if it is absent when the particular emotion is absent (Cacioppo & Tassinary, 1990). In the example cited, skin conductance would have the property of specificity if it covaried only with the change of joy felt. The second question asks whether an indicator is independent of persons and situations. For example, if finger temperature were an indicator of empathetic distress, it would have the property of generality if it covaried with changes in empathetic distress across situations and individuals. These two questions can be assigned to the context of validity.

Clearly, it is the task of emotion theorists to conceive the type of relationship between feelings and their behavioral and physiological counterparts. The different emotion theories that I do not discuss here make inconsistent statements concerning the relationship between feelings and their behavioral or physiological responses. When citing the two extremes with respect to this type of relationship, one sees on the one side the cognition-arousal theory (Schachter & Singer, 1962) and, on the other side, the body reaction theory (James, 1890). According to the cognition-arousal theory, a subjective emotion is a product of an interaction between two components: physiological arousal (a heightened activation of the autonomous nervous system) and a cognition about the cause of that arousal. Arousal is conceived as emotionally nonspecific and it determines the intensity of the subjective emotion. Cognition determines its quality. If every physiological measure reflects only the intensity of the subjective emotion, the problem of specificity cannot be dealt with. The body reaction theory is based on the nativist assumption that a pattern of expressive behavior creates or reflects a specific subjective emotion. Even if one assumes an association between a subjective emotion and a behavioral or physiological response, this association can have various forms (Leventhal & Tomarken, 1986). First, both subjective emotion and its counterparts could be products of a process of the central nervous system. Second, they could be directly and causally connected, with either or both acting as a cause. Third, both could influence one another, but the degree of influence is mediated by an underlying mechanism of the central nervous system.

The third question asks whether the method used for measurement is sufficiently sensitive to register changes in the indicator. For example, if we rely on facial expression as an indicator of subjective emotion, we must ask whether judges who analyze the videotaped faces of subjects watching film scenes can reliably detect changes in their facial expressions.

In the following chapters, I address these three questions. First I ask if there are physiological variables that are specific and general indicators to subjective emotions and then demonstrate how these two questions have been dealt with. Then I question whether the methods used can reliably measure the supposed indicators. I apply these questions to empathetic distress by asking whether it is associated with a specific and general physiological indicator. I also continue this line of examination when I look at the second and the third approach: behavioral expression and self-report.

PHYSIOLOGICAL ACTIVITY AS AN INDICATOR OF SUBJECTIVE EMOTION

To address the question of whether a physiological variable is specific to a particular subjective emotion, a methodologically strict approach dictates to demonstrate that it is present when the assumed subjective emotion (e.g., distress) is present and that it is absent when the feeling is absent. In this latter case the individual may feel another type of emotion—fear, for instance—that should not be related to the physiological indicator of distress. The physiological indicator is not necessarily restricted to a single variable, for example, heart rate. What is more frequent is that a number of physiological variables are associated with one emotion. In this latter case, the physiological indicator is said to be a physiological pattern or profile (Cacioppo & Tassinary, 1990).

As already outlined, the main problem of this approach is that, at the moment, there is insufficient empirical evidence for emotion theorists to make valid statements about which physiological indicator is specific to which type of emotion. In the literature, one finds a series of studies that follow the approach of identifying specific physiological indicators. Several primary emotions like anger, fear, or joy are induced through the use of differing techniques. In one, for instance, individuals are instructed to imagine situations in which they experience positive feelings like joy. The supposed feelings are measured by various physiological variables and the analysis is directed to identify indicators, the discriminating power of which is highest with respect to the induced emotions.

Unfortunately, the studies that have addressed this approach do not use the same physiological variables and they do not compare the same emotions. An evaluation, therefore, must be restricted to comparable studies. I combine the studies that compare the same emotions and test at least three of the five supposed physiological indicators being used most frequently (cf. Schmidt-Atzert, 1993). These are heart rate, systolic and diastolic blood pressure, skin conductance, and hand or finger temperature. With this restriction, I may also get an answer to the question of generality when I check whether the physiological indicators identified covary with the psychological events across the various studies.

Positive Versus Negative Emotions: Joy, Fear, Anger, and Sadness

Some studies have compared joy with fear and anger (Stemmler, 1984, 1989), with sadness (Averill, 1969), or with fear, anger, and sadness (Ekman, Levenson, & Friesen, 1983; Levenson, Ekman, & Friesen, 1990; Schwartz, Weinberger, & Singer, 1981). The results can be summarized as follows:

1. The measures of both systolic and diastolic blood pressure, both Averill (1969) and Schwartz et al. (1981) used increased to a higher degree when sadness or fear compared to joy was induced.
2. Heart rate distinguished joy from fear and anger (and also from sadness in one study) with one insignificant exception. Compared to joy, heart rate increased to a higher degree when fear and anger were induced.
3. The negative emotions of fear, anger, and sadness led to greater increases of skin conductance than did joy in one study (Levenson et al., 1990) but the reverse was true in the two studies by Stemmler (1984, 1989).
4. Temperature did not seem to be a sufficiently sensitive indicator for differentiating joy from the negative emotions.
5. Stemmler (1989) reported that the physiological profiles of fear, anger, and joy could reliably be distinguished.

Distinctions Among Negative Emotions: Fear, Anger, and Sadness

More relevant to the identification of emotion-specific indicators is the differentiation of negative emotions. There are four studies that deal with fear and anger that can be compared (Ax, 1953; Engel, 1986; Stemmler, 1984, 1989) and four studies that deal with fear, anger, and sadness (Ekman et al., 1983; Levenson et al., 1990; Schwartz et al., 1981; Weerts & Roberts, 1976). The results can be summarized as follows:

1. Diastolic blood pressure consistently increased to a greater extent when anger, rather than fear was induced.
2. Likewise, finger temperature distinguished anger from fear.
3. In two studies, change of skin conductance was greater when anger, rather than fear, was induced (Stemmler, 1984, 1989), but the relation was reversed in another study (Ax, 1953). Ekman et al. (1983) showed skin conductance to increase to a greater extent for both anger and fear than it did for sadness.
4. On the other hand, heart rate and systolic blood pressure could not differentiate between fear, anger, and sadness.

The inconsistent results may be due to the fact that some of the physiological variables investigated lacked generality. Levenson et al. (1990), who addressed this question, found the results to be valid for both females and males. However, the results seem to be dependent on the different methods of inducing emotions. Engel (1986) used radio plays as a method of inducing fear and anger; he did not find significant differences between heart rate, skin conductance, and temperature. However, this may be because this method of inducing emotions was too weak to elicit physiological responses (see also Stemmler, 1989). Ekman et al. (1983) reported that the directed facial action task (muscle-by-muscle instruction) led to stronger results than did the instruction to relive past emotional experiences. Finally, the measurement methods may have been too insensitive to detect the supposed physiological changes. This interpretation may apply to heart rate with respect to distinguishing anger from fear. Because the three possible reasons for the inconsistent results may interact, the three interpretations are difficult to evaluate without further empirical evidence.

With the third potential reason for the inconsistent results I address the third question stated earlier: whether the measurement method is sufficiently sensitive to register the changes. Cacioppo and Tassinary (1990) reported a few examples of inference from psychophysiological research that turned out to be dependent on the measurement procedure. For example, considerable disagreement existed over how to measure skin resistance and skin conductance (Vossel, 1990). Clearly, ruling out the interpretation that a lack of differentiation between different emotions is due to the use of different methods of physiological measurement requires the establishment of standardized methods.

With the description of the approach aimed to identify specific and general physiological indicators of subjective emotions in mind, I now take a look at Zillmann's (1980) theory of suspense. To the best of my knowledge, only a few studies have addressed the task of testing the theory (Bryant, cited in Zillmann, 1980; Zillmann, Hay, & Bryant, 1975). Two common features of these studies are the variation of the degree and the resolution of suspense. For example, in the experimental study by Zillmann et al. (1975), 7- and 8-year-old subjects watched an adventure story showing two young boys on their first lion hunt in

Africa. The degree of suspense was created by depicting the lion as more or less dangerous, and its resolution was varied by having the story end with either the shooting and killing of the lion or with the failure to hit the lion. The measurement of skin temperature, the only physiological indicator used, failed to produce reliable results. Therefore, a second experiment was conducted with three levels of degree of suspense and heart rate was recorded as an additional physiological indicator. This indicator significantly covaried with degree of suspense, a result that is consistent with the theory that states that the higher the level of suspense, the stronger the supposed subjective emotion of empathetic distress. The greater the degree of suspense, the more pronounced the decline of heart rate was after the successful resolution of the adventure. In accordance with the results of the studies already outlined, more intensive feelings of joy were related to lower changes of heart rate. Again, the statement that the more intense the feeling of empathetic distress the more intense the feeling of joy (euphoria, respectively) is consistent with these results.

From the brief description of the experimental study by Zillmann et al. (1975), it should be clear that they did not prove heart rate to be a specific physiological indicator of either empathetic distress or joy. It can be assumed that the respondents felt empathetic distress while watching the two boys facing a dangerous lion but it cannot be safely inferred. Because they did not design the study to identify specific and general physiological indicators for the supposed subjective emotions, the authors cannot be blamed for not having done this task. Obviously, the main objective of the study was to test the two statements that postulate (a) a covariation between level of suspense and autonomic arousal, and (b) a covariation between the level of suspense and the intensity of joy if the watched event ends happily. The second statement is a variant of Zillmann's (1971) theory of excitation transfer. There may be a second reason why the study was not designed to identify a specific physiological indicator for the supposed feeling of empathetic distress. The authors refer to the cognition-arousal theory of emotion, according to which autonomic arousal is unspecific. Autonomic arousal reflects the intensity levels of a subjective emotion but not its quality. The quality of a subjective emotion can be discerned only if the context contains a salient cue that can be attributed as the cause for the perceived arousal. Consequently, indicators other than physiological ones should be chosen to prove that the emotion felt while watching suspenseful scenes is empathetic distress.

EXPRESSIVE BEHAVIOR

The second kind of potential specific and general indicators of subjective emotions is expressive behavior. Expressive reactions are perceived to be innate because they seem to be universal (Ekman, 1982), appear to be discriminable soon after birth in response to physical and social stimuli (Hiatt, Campos, &

Emde, 1979), and can be differentiated and elaborated on at nearly the same rate by both blind and sighted children (Goodenough, 1932).

The hypothesis that different expressive behaviors cause corresponding feelings has been called the *facial feedback hypothesis* (Izard, 1971; Tomkins, 1962). To show that feedback can elicit subjective emotions three different methods of manipulating expressive reactions have been used: (a) direct manipulation of facial muscles, (b) indirect manipulation of facial muscles, and (c) indirect manipulation through the instruction of the subject to display or hide expression. Contextual cues, such as canned laughter, have also been used as a method of indirect manipulation. Because this method is better suited to intensifying expressions than differentiating qualities of subjective emotion, I postpone the discussion of it until later in the chapter.

The most frequently used method of direct manipulation of facial muscles (Laird, 1974) is that of lightly touching specific facial muscles and instructing the subjects to contract them. There are three methods of indirect manipulation of facial muscles, one of which has the subjects control them by biofeedback. Subjects watch the signals from their electromyograms (EMG), which visually confirm whether they have contracted or relaxed the relevant facial muscles (McCanne & Anderson, 1987). When using the second procedure, the facial muscles are indirectly manipulated by having subjects hold a pen either in their teeth or in their lips (Strack, Martin, & Stepper, 1988). The first facial muscle position is similar to a smile, whereas the second position requires the tight contraction of the muscles. In the third method of indirectly manipulating the facial muscles, the subjects are instructed to hide or display a distinct emotional expression (Lanzetta, Cartwright-Smith, & Kleck, 1976). All three types of manipulation have been successful in varying the facial expression. A few seconds after the subjects take on the instructed expressions, they are faced with stimuli whose attributes are held constant (e.g., film scenes, cartoons, odors). These stimuli are evaluated with respect to their valence.

The search for specific facial indicators for subjective emotions leads to studies that investigate whether different facial expressions indicating feelings like joy or sadness create the corresponding subjective emotions. Few studies address this categorical perspective. Duclos et al. (1989) had subjects pose four facial expressions that were supposed to elicit corresponding negative subjective emotions. Indeed, the subjects reported the corresponding negative subjective emotions most frequently. Levenson et al. (1990), who instructed their subjects to display six different facial expressions, reported results similar to those reported by Duclos et al. (1989). Rutledge, Garvey, Johnson, and Sheldon (cited in Adelmann & Zajonc, 1989) instructed their subjects to contract isolated facial muscles. The reported results suggest that the subjects experienced qualitatively different feelings when they contracted different facial muscles. For example, a contraction of forehead muscles was associated with greater reported surprise. Two studies used techniques similar to Laird's (1974). McArthur, Solomon, and

Jaffe (1980) induced smiles, sad frowns, and neutral patterns by having subjects view positive, negative, or neutral slides. The subjects reported feeling less happy when frowning but not significantly happier when smiling than when neutral. Rutledge and Hupka (1985) had subjects pose joy and anger while viewing neutral slides, slides that portrayed high and low levels of anger, and slides that portrayed joy. Their subjects reported feeling more joyous and less angry when imitating joy, and more angry and less joyous when in a pose of anger. Unfortunately, these two studies do not report whether the feelings resulting from the facial expressions were actually the dominant ones. On the other hand, there is one study (Tourangeau & Ellsworth, 1979) that showed that effective manipulation of a fearful or joyous facial expression did not elicit corresponding feelings.

Although there is some empirical evidence that suggests that specific links exist between facial expressions and subjective emotions, the problem of generality remains to be resolved. The results of one study (McArthur et al., 1980) suggest that the facial expressions create corresponding feelings only within a subsample of subjects. According to Leventhal and Tomarken (1986), the negative results of Tourangeau and Ellsworth (1979) may have been due to a mismatch of the intensity of manipulated expressions with the intensity of feelings aroused by the stimulus. This mismatch may have disrupted the possible feedback effect. The results of several studies that indirectly manipulated facial expression by use of contextual cues point to further unresolved problems with the generality of expressive indicators. First, there appears to be a stronger association between expressive reactions and feelings under conditions that favor spontaneous rather than controlled or volitional response (e.g., Cupchik & Leventhal, 1974). Second, social context has been found to influence effects. Expressions may be more responsive to social cues than to states of internal feeling. In a study by Fridlund (1991), for example, subjects who viewed a funny film showed more activity of the zygomaticus, which is an indicator of smiling, when a friend was present than when they watched the film by themselves. Intriguingly, they also showed more zygomaticus activity when the friend viewed the same film in the next room. According to the literature on interpersonal communication, facial expression has an important function in controlling positive or negative affiliation (e.g., Wiemann & Giles, 1990) and related modes of interaction (Hops, Biglan, Sherman, Arthur, Friedman, & Osteen, 1987). Expressions may have little or no impact on experience if they occur during the course of conversation (Ekman, 1982).

The third question attempts to determine the kind of method that can reliably register facial expressions and can assign facial expressions correctly to corresponding emotional experience. In studies that address this question, subjects were presented with stimuli of differing valence (e.g., slides intended to elicit surprise, anger, sadness, joy, fear, disgust, or no emotion) and their expressive reactions were secretly recorded. The subjects rated their subjective emotional responses to the stimuli. There are three types of methods, for which I outline one application each. The first method uses judges who, while watching the faces being recorded, assign the facial expressions to subjective emotions and rate their intensity and valence. This method was applied by Wagner, MacDonald, and Manstead (1986), who investigated whether qualitatively different emotions can be diagnosed. The authors found that, among the six emotions already listed, joy, disgust, and anger were significantly better detected than it would have been predicted by chance. The ratings of valence by subjects and by judges correlated, $r = 0.36$, and the corresponding ratings of intensity correlated, $r = 0.05$. A second method consists of registering specific mimic reactions by judges. Ekman and Friesen (1978) constructed a coding system for this purpose, called the Facial Action Coding System (FACS). In applying this method, Ekman, Friesen, and Ancoli (1980) presented female subjects with one funny and one repulsive film and secretly recorded their faces. The women rated their feelings before and after having viewed the films. Frequency, duration, and intensity of smiling was analyzed by recording the activity of the zygomaticus. The indicator for negative emotions consisted of a combination of several facial activities. The correlations between ratings of subjects and ratings of judges ranged from $r = -0.08$ to $r = 0.60$ for the funny film and from $r = -0.10$ to $r = 0.35$ for the repulsive film. The third method registers facial activity by using an EMG. This method can detect changes in the facial activity that judges cannot discern. To compare results from studies that use this method it is necessary to agree to compare the muscles' activity within a standard set of facial parts. Fridlund and Cacioppo (1986) proposed a respective procedure. Fridlund and Izard (1983), who summarized the results of seven studies that use the electromyographic registration of induced emotions, inferred two robust effects: (a) a heightened activity of the zygomaticus when the positive emotions were induced, and (b) a heightened activity of the corrugator when the negative emotions were induced. Schmidt-Atzert (1993) summarized that, aside from the differentiation of positive and negative emotions by the activity of the zygomaticus and the corrugator, he did not find a further differentiation of electromyographically registered activity.

An examination of the study of Zillmann et al. (1975) with respect to the registration of facial activity reveals that they used the first method described here. Two judges analyzed the videotapes of the subjects' faces, which reflected the emotions they experienced while viewing the adventure film of the two boys at a lion hunt. The two judges rated the overall appreciation, the relief at resolution, and the fear reflected in the subjects' facial expression on scales ranging from 0 to 100. In addition, they assessed the duration of positive and negative feeling by pressing a correspondingly labeled button for as long as the perceived feeling went on. As the interjudge reliabilities demonstrate (0.56 vs. 0.96), it was more difficult to discern overall appreciation with facial display than with verbal expression. Similarly, in a study by Zillmann and Cantor (1977), judges could not reliably detect facial expressions indicating positive and negative feelings displayed by second- and third-grade students from an elementary school, who viewed an emotion stimulating episode experienced by a boy of approximately the same age as themselves. Nevertheless, the pattern of judged facial displays in the study of Zillmann et al. (1975) was consistent with the hypothesis that the degree of suspense covaries with the appreciation of the watched event. Likewise, the facially expressed fearful responses observed were consistent with the expectation that subjects experience a higher degree of response when they experience greater fear. (Curiously, the ratings of fearfulness were all below 10 on the scale from 0 to 100.) Zillmann et al. (1975) wrote that the judges "reported great difficulties in distinguishing between facially displayed appreciation and signs of relief" and that "with appreciation and relief thus confounded, the finding that facially expressed appreciation increased after the effective resolution of suspense may well reflect the fact that this resolution mainly relieved the viewer—without necessarily inducing euphoric feelings" (p. 316). What is obvious from this brief description is that the term *empathetic distress*, which according to Zillmann's (1980) research, is essential for the theory of suspense, did not emerge. Presumably, he defined empathetic distress as the specific feeling one experiences when exposed to suspenseful drama later.

SELF-REPORTS

Self-reports of subjective emotions seem to be indispensable in most of the studies on emotion. Emotion researchers frequently use self-reports as criteria for manipulation checks, which determine whether the methods used to induce emotions are effective. However, like autonomic and facial responses, self-reports are indicators as well. The subjects must transform the subjective emotion to be expressed as self-report into language. Because the language system primarily has the functions of communication and information processing (Lang, 1971, 1993), this process of transformation does not occur automatically. The main obstacle for a scientist using self-reports as indicators of emotional experience is that they are subject to volitional control and, therefore, may be biased by the individuals. A second argument against self-reports maintains that individuals lack the ability to perceive their inner states (Nisbett & Wilson, 1977).

A few studies have addressed the question of how laymen report their feelings. Subjects who participated in these studies were requested to unrestrictedly describe their feelings. Davitz (1969), for example, surveyed 1,000 individuals and found more than 500 terms being used as descriptions for feelings. He then had 50 subjects imagine emotional experiences and choose the corresponding descriptions. Finally, he condensed the descriptions chosen by a cluster analysis to 12 categories of descriptive statements. Among these statements, approximately 10% relate to bodily reactions and expressive behavior. There are two broad categories, one containing descriptions of activation states (e.g., tired, lively, dull), and the other consisting of behavioral intentions (e.g., to want to help somebody, to want to hurt somebody, to withdraw oneself). It is not easy to compare this study with others in which the subjects' responses were directed to preselected categories (e.g., Shaver, Schwartz, Kirson, & O'Connor, 1987).

Studies that use categories of bodily reactions and of expressive responses relate more directly to types of descriptions that are specific and general to different subjective emotions. For example, Wallbott and Scherer (1986) asked more than 2,000 students from 27 countries to choose from a list of 10 bodily reactions that they experienced when having felt joy, fear, anger, sadness, disgust, shame, and guilt. When listing the most frequent descriptions (according to the author's criterion of a 20% difference between the most and the next frequent symptom), the description "to have a lump in one's throat" was most specific to sadness. This result is consistent with the findings reported by Davitz (1969) and Scherer, Summerfield, and Wallbott (1983). Wallbott and Scherer (1986) found that sadness is further characterized by a lack of rapid heartbeats, trembling, feeling of warmth, and sweating. Fear was associated with the greatest number of bodily reactions, as 6 of the 10 symptoms reached a maximum. Respondents marked the descriptive "more rapid heartbeats" with a cross most frequently. Similarly, they chose muscle tension, trembling, sweating, and sweaty palms when they experienced fear. They strongly associated joy with sensations of warmth and, with less frequency, relaxed muscles. There were no comparably dominant bodily sensations for anger, disgust, guilt, and shame. The less frequent occurrence of the sensation of coldness distinguished anger from fear. Anger and shame are different from the other feelings investigated because of their association with the sensation of heat.

According to the results of the study by Wallbott and Scherer (1986), self-reported behavioral expressions are slightly less specific indicators than bodily reactions. This result may be partly due to the fact that behavioral expressions are under volitional control. For example, 28% of the individuals questioned by Shaver et al. (1987) reported that they did not display fear. On the other hand, joy is the feeling most often displayed when experienced. Joy is strongly related to laughing and smiling, and to a lesser degree, to movement to other individuals or objects. Sadness corresponds most frequently with crying. Anger does not have one dominant expression but is related to shouting, change of the voice, abrupt body movements, and movements against individuals or objects. Analogous expressions could not be identified for disgust, guilt, and shame. As the differences between the descriptions of individuals from different countries were small, the results support the hypothesis that self-reported bodily reactions and behavioral expressions turned out to be general.

When one evaluates the results of these studies, one should take into account the fact that the subjects retrospectively chose their bodily symptoms and expressive responses. Individuals know which expressions and which bodily reactions are stereotypically associated with feelings and this type of semantic knowledge will influence the reports of their own experience. For example, Rime, Philippot, and Cisamolo (1990) found that self-reports of physiological responses to four different emotions were nearly identical to descriptions of typical physi-ological responses. Nieuwenhuyse, Offenberg, and Frijda (1987) had their sub-jects locate subjective emotions experienced in the past to points on a body chart. When the same task was repeated 6 weeks later, the retest reliability was $r = 0.93$. Obviously, situational influences were negligible.

In the study of Zillmann et al. (1975), the 7- and 8-year-old subjects were asked five questions directed to measure the appreciation of the adventure story (a further two questions were asked to check the intended effects of the six stories being constructed). Two judges independently rated the interviews with respect to the overall appreciation and the appreciation of the story's resolution. Among the three indicators used, these ratings best corroborated the expectation that the subjects would prefer both the more suspenseful story and the successful reso-lution. Subjects were not asked if they felt fear. Its presence was judged from their facial displays. Again, empathetic distress was not mentioned with respect to self-report.

CONCLUSION: THE SEARCH FOR AN INDICATOR FOR EMPATHETIC DISTRESS

The methodological approaches described earlier that attempt to represent sub-jective emotions using the three indicators of autonomic activity, behavioral expression, and self-report, constitute the framework for an indicator that repre-sents empathetic distress. The fact that the three indicators do not necessarily covary positively should be taken into account (but see Adelmann & Zajonc, 1989, who argued that the type of covariation is dependent on between- and within-subject designs). For example, Lanzetta and Kleck (1970) assumed that individuals who are socialized to inhibit their expressive displays through the punishment or rebuke of free emotional expression show heightened autonomic response. This inverse relation between facial expressiveness and autonomic activation occurred particularly in stressful interpersonal contexts.

Empathetic distress as conceived by Zillmann (1980) is the very subjective emotion that distinguishes suspense from the related kinds of emotions people feel when they view other types of potentially suspenseful events (e.g., sporting events).

As very little is known about how to measure empathetic distress, I begin with the proposal that, as a first step in the search, self-reports on empathetic distress should be ascertained. Individuals should be exposed to scenes of sus-penseful drama, frightening films, mystery, sporting events, and also to stimuli that have been proven to elicit fear and sadness. Because more is known about which sensations relate to fear and sadness, these two emotions will function as control conditions. Respondents should unrestrictedly describe what they feel while watching these types of scenes. With this procedure, symptoms that might have otherwise been missed if the individuals' attention had been directed to the "classical" phenomena can be expressed. If it occurs that the free descriptions consist mainly of bodily reactions and behavioral expressions, categories of these feeling indicators should be constructed (cf. Wallbott & Scherer, 1986) and a second sample of subjects should be exposed to the same events and directed to choose the respective descriptions of their inner states.

It is necessary to identify potential indicators of empathetic distress by self-reports before proceeding to the measurement of behavioral expressions as responses to the types of scenes listed earlier. There is a tendency for individuals who report various feelings to not display corresponding facial expressions (Ekman et al., 1980). Even the children from elementary school, the subjects in the study by Zillmann and Cantor (1977), very rarely showed facial activity (as to use this indicator for testing the hypotheses). Similarly, Zillmann et al. (1975) reported that the two judges who evaluated the facial expressions of the infant subjects had great difficulty distinguishing appreciation from relief. If the self-reports of sensations induced by suspenseful drama and by mystery, for example, do not differ, or show negligible difference, it would be difficult to justify an expectation that facial expressions related to these two feelings are distinguishable. One could argue that more sensitive methods, like EMG recording techniques, would reliably detect different feelings in the facial expression, but before applying this type of method, a distinct notion of the facial expressions that related to the viewing of suspenseful drama and mystery should exist. According to construct validity (Campbell & Fiske, 1959) empathetic distress as a specific subjective emotion should be manifested as being different from both impatient curiosity (the subjective emotion supposed to be associated with viewing mystery; cf. Zillmann, 1991) and fear with respect to both self-report and facial expression.

Before turning to the third system of emotion and before trying to identify a pattern of physiological activity as an indicator for empathetic distress, it is necessary to decide on a theoretical approach to use as a reference. This is not meant to imply that one must embrace one or the other theory of emotion, because each provides its own valuable view. If one refers to the cognition-arousal theory, however, one finds that the theory's basic statements do not suggest a search for qualitatively different physiological indicators. If one restricts oneself to the measurement of physiological arousal, one would take a dimensional perspective that would lead to statements like: "The more frightening a film, the greater the increase of the autonomic arousal" (e.g., Sparks, 1991). Clearly, for an indicator to be specific, this type of statement is a necessary condition; but it is not a sufficient one. To accomplish the laborious task of identifying the specific physiological indicator for empathetic distress, one must conduct experiments analogous to those outlined earlier. Individuals would be exposed to scenes that are supposed to induce empathetic distress, impatient curiosity, excitement (when viewing sporting events), fear, and anger, and an indistinct mild feeling would be employed as a control. Different physiological indicators, like diastolic blood pressure or heart rate, should be used to measure the supposed feelings and to identify the specific indicator for empathetic distress.

After taking into account the results of studies that address the search for specific physiological indicators of primary emotions, I question whether the task of seeking a physiological indicator of empathetic distress would be worthwile today. Although diastolic blood pressure as an indicator of anger and heart rate as an indicator of joy seem to show attributes of specificity, further experiments are needed to establish their generality. The state of the art on the research of suspense and especially on empathetic distress as a specific subjective emotion, first requires theorists to ascertain the phenomena being experienced. They may bear more qualitative differences than the experientally less accessible bodily symptoms or, to cite Lang (1993): "The verbal behavior of a human being is capable of reflecting gradations of affect, to which the cruder autonomic system may be completely insensitive" (p. 23).

REFERENCES

Adelmann, P. K., & Zajonc, R. B. (1989). Facial efference and the experience of emotion. *Annual Review of Psychology, 40*, 249–280.

Averill, J. R. (1969). Autonomic response patterns during sadness and mirth. *Psychophysiology, 5*, 399–414.

Ax, A. F. (1953). The physiological differentiation between fear and anger in humans. *Psychosomatic Medicine, 15*, 433–442.

Cacioppo, J. T., & Tassinary, L. G. (1990). Inferring psychological significance from physiological signals. *American Psychologist, 45*, 16–28.

Campbell, D. T., & Fiske, D. W. (1959). Convergent and discriminant validation by the multitrait-multimethod matrix. *Psychological Bulletin, 56*, 81–105.

Cupchik, G. C., & Leventhal, H. (1974). Consistency between expressive behavior and the evaluation of humorous stimuli: The role of sex and self observation. *Journal of Personality and Social Psychology, 30*, 429–442.

Davitz, J. R. (1969). *The language of emotion.* New York: Academic Press.

Duclos, S. E., Laird, J. D., Schneider, E., Sexter, M., Stern, L., & Van Lighten, O. (1989). Emotion-specific effects of facial expressions and postures on emotional experience. *Journal of Personality and Social Psychology, 57*, 100–108.

Ekman, P. (1982). *Emotion in the human face.* New York: Cambridge University Press.

Ekman, P., & Friesen, W. V. (1978). *Facial action coding system.* Palo Alto, CA: Consulting Psychologist Press.

Ekman, P., Friesen, W. V., & Ancoli, S. (1980). Facial signs of emotional experience. *Journal of Personality and Social Psychology, 39*, 1125–1134.

Ekman, P., Levenson, R. W., & Friesen, W. V. (1983). Autonomous nervous system activity distinguishes among emotions. *Science, 221*, 1208–1210.

Engel, R. R. (1986). *Aktivierung und Emotion: Psychophysiologische Experimente zur Struktur physiologischer Reaktionsmuster unter psychischer Belastung* [Activation and emotion: Discerning the structure of physiological response patterns under psychological stress by psychophysiological experiments]. München: Minerva.

Fridlund, A. J. (1991). Sociality for solitary smiling: Potentiation by an implicit audience. *Journal of Personality and Social Psychology, 60*, 229–240.

Fridlund, A. J., & Cacioppo, J. T. (1986). Guidelines for human electromyographic research. *Psychophysiology, 23*, 567–589.

Fridlund, A. J., & Izard, C. E. (1983). Electromyographic studies of facial expressions of emotions and patterns of emotions. In J. T. Cacioppo & R. E. Petty (Eds.), *Social psychophysiology* (pp. 243–286). New York: Guilford.

Goodenough, F. L. (1932). Expression of the emotions in a blind-deaf child. *Journal of Abnormal and Social Psychology, 27*, 328–333.

Hiatt, S. W., Campos, J. J., & Emde, R. N. (1979). Facial patterning and infant emotional expression: Happiness, surprise, and fear. *Child Development, 50*, 1020–1035.

Hops, H., Biglan, A., Sherman, L., Arthur, J., Friedman, L., & Osteen, V. (1987). Home observations of family interactions of depressed women. *Journal of Consulting and Clinical Psychology, 55*, 341–346.

Izard, C. E. (1971). *The face of emotion*. New York: Appleton.

James, W. (1890). *The principles of psychology*. New York: Holt.

Laird, J. D. (1974). Self-attribution of emotion: The effects of expressive behavior on the quality of emotional experience. *Journal of Personality and Social Psychology, 29*, 475–486.

Lang, P. J. (1971). The application of psychophysiological methods to the study of psychotherapy and behavior modification. In A. Bergin & S. L. Garfield (Eds.), *Handbook of psychotherapy and behavior change: An empirical analysis* (pp. 45–125). New York: Wiley.

Lang, P. J. (1993). The three-system approach to emotion. In N. Birbaumer & A. Öhman (Eds.), *The structure of emotion* (pp. 18–30). Seattle, WA: Hogrefe & Huber.

Lanzetta, J. T., Cartwright-Smith, J., & Kleck, R. E. (1976). Effects of nonverbal dissimulation on emotional experience and autonomic arousal. *Journal of Personality and Social Psychology, 33*, 354–370.

Lanzetta, J. T., & Kleck, R. E. (1970). Encoding and decoding of non-verbal affect in humans. *Journal of Personality and Social Psychology, 16*, 12–19.

Levenson, R. W., Ekman, P., & Friesen, W. V. (1990). Voluntary facial action generates action-specific autonomic nervous system activity. *Psychophysiology, 27*, 363–384.

Leventhal, H., & Tomarken, A. J. (1986). Emotion: Today's problems. *Annual Review of Psychology, 37*, 565–610.

McArthur, L. Z., Solomon, M. R., & Jaffe, R. H. (1980). Weight differences in emotional responsiveness to proprioceptive and pictorial stimuli. *Journal of Personality and Social Psychology, 39*, 308–319.

McCanne, T. R., & Anderson, J. A. (1987). Emotional responding following experimental manipulation of facial electromyographic activity. *Journal of Personality and Social Psychology, 52*, 759–768.

Nieuwenhuyse, B., Offenberg, L., & Frijda, N. H. (1987). Subjective emotion and reported body experience. *Motivation and Emotion, 11*, 169–182.

Nisbett, R. E., & Wilson, T. D. (1977). Telling more than we can know: Verbal reports on mental processes. *Psychological Review, 84*, 231–259.

Rime, B., Philippot, B., & Cisamolo, D. (1990). Social schemata of peripheral changes in emotion. *Journal of Personality and Social Psychology, 59*, 38–49.

Rutledge, L. L., & Hupka, R. B. (1985). The facial feedback hypothesis: Methodological concerns and new supporting evidence. *Motivation and Emotion, 9*, 219–240.

Schachter, S., & Singer, J. (1962). Cognitive, social, and physiological determinants of emotional state. *Psychological Review, 69*, 379–399.

Scherer, K. R., Summerfield, A. B., & Wallbott, H. G. (1983). Cross-national research on antecedents and components of emotion: A progress report. *Social Science Information, 22*, 355–385.

Schmidt-Atzert, L. (1993). *Die Entstehung von Gefühlen* [The development of feelings]. Berlin: Springer.

Schwartz, G. E., Weinberger, D. A., & Singer, J. A. (1981). Cardiovascular differentiation of happiness, sadness, anger, and fear following imaging and exercise. *Psychosomatic Medicine*, *43*, 343–364.

Shaver, P., Schwartz, J., Kirson, D., & O'Connor, C. (1987). Emotion knowledge: Further exploration of a prototype approach. *Journal of Personality and Social Psychology*, *52*, 1061–1086.

Sparks, G. G. (1991). The relationship between distress and delight in males' and females' reactions to frightening films. *Human Communication Research*, *17*, 625–637.

Stemmler, G. (1984). *Psychophysiologische Emotionsmuster: Ein empirischer und methodischer Beitrag zur inter- und intraindividuellen Begründbarkeit spezifischer Profile bei Angst, Ärger und Freude* [Psychophysiological emotion patterns: Empirical and methodological contributions to the intra- and interindividual justifiability of specific profiles with fear, anger, and joy]. Frankfurt: Lang.

Stemmler, G. (1989). The autonomic differentiation of emotions revisited: Convergent and discriminant validation. *Psychophysiology*, *26*, 617–632.

Strack, F., Martin, L. L., & Stepper, S. (1988). Inhibiting and facilitating conditions of the human smile: A nonobtrusive test of the facial feedback hypothesis. *Journal of Personality and Social Psychology*, *54*, 768–777.

Tomkins, S. S. (1962). *Affect, imagery, consciousness I: The positive affects*. New York: Springer.

Tourangeau, R., & Ellsworth, P. C. (1979). The role of facial response in the experience of emotion. *Journal of Personality and Social Psychology*, *37*, 1519–1531.

Vossel, G. (1990). *Elektrodermale Labilität* [Electrodermal lability]. Göttingen, Germany: Hogrefe.

Wagner, H. L., MacDonald, C. J., & Manstead, A. S. R. (1986). Communication of individual emotions by spontaneous facial expressions. *Journal of Personality and Social Psychology*, *50*, 737–743.

Wallbott, H. G., & Scherer, K. R. (1986). How universal and specific is emotional experience? Evidence from 27 countries on five continents. *Social Science Information*, *25*, 763–795.

Weerts, T. C., & Roberts, R. (1976). The physiological effects of imaging anger-provoking and fear-provoking scenes. *Psychophysiology*, *13*, 174.

Wiemann, J. M., & Giles, H. (1990). Interpersonale Kommunikation [Interpersonal communication]. In W. Stroebe, M. Hewstone, J.-P. Codol, & G. M. Stephenson (Eds.), *Sozialpsychologie* (pp. 209–231). Berlin: Springer.

Zillmann, D. (1971). Excitation transfer in communication-mediated aggressive behavior. *Journal of Experimental Social Psychology*, *7*, 419–434.

Zillmann, D. (1980). Anatomy of suspense. In P. H. Tannenbaum (Ed.), *The entertainment functions of television* (pp. 133–163). Hillsdale, NJ: Lawrence Erlbaum Associates.

Zillmann, D. (1991). The logic of suspense and mystery. In J. Bryant & D. Zillmann (Eds.), *Responding to the screen: Reception and reaction processes* (pp. 281–303). Hillsdale, NJ: Lawrence Erlbaum Associates.

Zillmann, D., & Cantor, J. R. (1977). Affective responses to the emotions of a protagonist. *Journal of Experimental Social Psychology*, *13*, 155–165.

Zillmann, D., Hay, A., & Bryant, J. (1975). The effect on suspense and its resolution on the appreciation of dramatic presentations. *Research in Personality*, *9*, 307–323.

15

The Cognitive Development of Temporal Structures: How Do Children Make Inferences With Temporal Ellipses in Films?

Gerhild Nieding
Technical University of Berlin

Peter Ohler
University of Passau

Claudia Thußbas
Technical University of Berlin

In this chapter, a cognitive psychological approach to the processing of narrative films is adopted in which it is assumed that the viewers' specific information-processing mechanisms trigger suspense-inducing effects (see, e.g., Ohler & Nieding, chap. 8, this volume). Typical textual structures and strategies that induce cognitive processes and themselves result in the emotional experience of suspense are the creation of uncertainty in the viewer as to which of two possible outcomes for the protagonist will occur in a scene, the systematic transcendence of viewers' expectations horizons concerning the development of the plot, and the positioning of temporal omissions in the film narration so that viewers have to make uncertain inferences as to its course.

In this chapter, we concentrate on the third strategy for inducing suspense just mentioned: the temporal omission of elements from the film text and the cognitive processes viewers use to fill these omissions. The experience of suspense itself is a psychological process that is ontogenetically tied to the development of suitable cognitive processes, to text processing mechanisms in particular. In order to find a basis for the mechanisms through which suspense is caused by temporal omissions from film texts, it is first necessary to develop a cognitive model for the information processing of discontinuities in narrative text. This chapter is concerned with a particular aspect of the information processing of discontinuities, namely the acquisition of the relevant cognitive operations necessary for the processing of such discontinuities.

Cognitive psychological approaches in text processing are reviewed under a developmental perspective and then an experiment on children's processing of temporal omissions in film texts is subsequently reported.

TEMPORAL ELLIPSES IN FILM NARRATION

In linguistics an ellipsis may be defined at a sentence level as "the omission of sentence elements which are, according to the situation, superfluous for the purpose of the comprehension of a statement" (Ulrich, 1975, p. 37). Although Ulrich described the omission of elements in sentences, it is possible in larger texts, such as narrations, to leave out elements that are larger than a sentence. Möller-Naß (1986) defined the ellipsis in the context of film narration. A *temporal ellipsis* is a chronological discontinuity within a film narration.[1] The characteristic feature of an ellipsis is its dependence on the fundamental and salient event structure in the story (in comparison with the so-called *dialemma*[2]). Gaps within the central chain of relevant actions are labeled ellipses. An action is defined as being relevant when it makes a significant contribution to the coherence of the narration.

A further intrinsic characteristic of ellipses is their dispensability. If information that could be used to fill an ellipsis is made available by the film text before the ellipsis, then Möller-Naß (1986) would describe the ellipsis as weak. Strong ellipses, on the other hand, are characterized by the necessity to use information from subsequent situations or actions to fill the informational gap. In this case, according to Möller-Naß (1986), "at best, a *weak hypothesis* may be formed about that which has taken place in the interim period. Often this narrative strategy serves to build suspense, in that the omission leads the viewer to put questions which will not be answered for some time" (p. 277).

A more precise description of the relationship between the form of ellipses and the (hierarchically structured) narrative event structure in a film has not yet been developed in this semiotic text-related approach. The relevance of individual actions has to be given different weights depending on their function in narrative deep structure. It is still unclear on which level of text coherence an omission may still be described as elliptical, where the specific point when the course of a story becomes incoherent through the use of omissions is, and how this can be theoretically modeled. Is an omission only a particular form of dialemma (an omission of parts that are not necessary for the continuity of the action) or is it already an ellipsis?

---

[1]Ellipses can also be based on other dimensions, such as space (a so-called *spatial ellipsis*).
[2]Möller-Naß (1986) defined a "dialemma" as the omission of irrelevant actions or events.

TEXT-LINGUISTIC APPROACHES: THE FORMATION OF COGNITIVE INFERENCES DURING THE FILLING OF CONCEPTUAL GAPS IN TEXT

Approaches within a cognitive text-linguistic framework hypothesize internally structured mental representations of narrative texts or action sequences. Prominent advocates of this approach, such as Kintsch and van Dijk (1978; van Dijk & Kintsch, 1983), distinguished between local and global propositionally represented levels of text coherence in the episodic memory. The *local* coherence level consists of propositionalized sequences of sentence elements and relationships between sentence elements (e.g., the overlapping and embedding of successive arguments). The *global* level, on the other hand, combines elements on differing textual levels into so-called macropropositions, which are themselves linked to form macrostructures such as themes or topics (van Dijk & Kintsch, 1983).

Textual omissions may be bridged using inferences. A cognitive inference may be described as the activation of a knowledge element that is not explicitly stated in the text in relation to a text element. Inferences that are necessary to establish coherence between propositions are described as bridging, and inferences that are not necessary for the establishment of coherence are described as elaborative (cf. Long, Golding, & Graesser, 1992).

Models of text processing may be classified according to whether the formation of inferences on a global text coherence level takes place online during the information processing of the text (that is in parallel with the occurrence of textual hiati) or whether they are completed after textual hiati. Online generated global inferences tend to be seen, depending on the theoretical position of the authors, either as bridging or as elaborative. Global inferences tend to be seen as bridging in models of global coherence and as elaborative in the models of local coherence (cf. Long, Golding, & Graesser, 1992). The results of the following experiment could be used, among other things, as a guide when deciding which of these two models would be most relevant to children's processing of ellipses in audiovisual texts.

MODELS OF GLOBAL COHERENCE

There are three contemporary approaches to the online processing of text on a global coherence level: story grammars, mental models, and recursive transition networks.

The Story Grammar Approach

Story grammars (e.g., Mandler & Johnson, 1977; Rumelhart, 1975; Stein & Glenn, 1979; Thorndyke, 1977) are grammars for the description of narrative texts. So-called story schemata are hypothetical knowledge structures that are working rule-based and are used by recipients for the processing of narrative texts. The rule system underlying such a knowledge structure may be defined in the context of a story grammar. It consists of a set of rewrite rules that allow the constituents of a story to be defined on different hierarchical levels. Story grammars work analogously to procedures of the sentence grammar in Chomsky's (1957, 1965) standard theory. The main exception is that sentence-transcending layers of constituents are defined instead of constituents on the sentence level (for a critical comparison with sentence grammar, see Garnham, Oakhill, & Johnson-Laird, 1982; Wilensky, 1983).

Story schemata organize the encoding, storage, and retrieval of stories. Propositions that may be distant from one another on the textual surface are processed online with regard to their relationship to global constituents such as setting, theme, plot, and resolution (Thorndyke, 1977). Information from all available levels is brought together by the interaction of top-down and bottom-up processes.

One may question whether children are capable of such a flexible use of story schemata in the process of the online organization of mental representations of stories. On this basis, a second important question may be asked. Does the internalization of story schematic or related structures presuppose other necessary cognitive skills (operations) or are the skills acquired in the course of the internalization of narrative structures? Two positions may be discerned regarding processes that are necessary to comprehend narrative texts:

1. In the first position, the processing of stories is modeled as a competence, mainly built on operative processes, of a more or less general type. Here, the principle of cognitive reversibility, which was a characteristic feature of mental operations for Piaget (cf. Krafft & Piaget, 1925; Margairaz & Piaget, 1925), is a necessary precondition for the understanding of causal and logical relations within stories. In contrast with Piaget's theory of not-domain-specific general operations, the story processing operations can, in a similar manner, be of a specific nature. Thußbas (1994) showed that results in standardized tests for genuine linguistic operations were of high predictive power for the performance in the processing of stories with two parallel plot lines, whereas results in tests for general reversibility operations showed no predictive power.

According to the recursive transition network model of Trabasso and his collaborators (Trabasso & van den Broek, 1985; Trabasso, van den Broek, & Suh, 1989), inference processes use causal connections, which are specifically in force for narrative texts. Despite differences, each of the approaches described in this paragraph is characterized by the assumption that comprehension processes are supported and made feasible by operations, either through general or specific mental operations for example, in a linguistic medium.

2. In the second position, which is also held by the authors, story schemata or scripts are able to compensate and surrogate operative flexibility, and may even accelerate the acquisition of operative skills because of their inherent op-

erative functions. According to Fivush and Mandler (1985), the development of narrative competence does not depend solely on operative inference processes, "rather, what develops are organized event representations and the ability to manipulate these representations in increasingly flexible ways" (p. 1445).

Even 24-month-old children are able to imitate simple, familiar, sequences of events (O'Connell & Gerard, 1985). In the course of their cognitive development, young children appear to be able to create not only event schemata but story schemata as well (Nieding, 1989; Nieding & Ohler, 1990). Attention processes of children in the second class of primary school (about 8 years of age) are oriented online at global narrative structures.

Story schemata can be used to describe inference processes during the bridging of temporal hiati, and the building of vague hypotheses thereby formed, which will either be confirmed or rejected later on in the text processing. This story schema approach does, however, evoke problems: Only a very limited set of relationships between arguments is embraced (e.g., "then" and "causes"). Inferences are generated, however, with the help of a multiplicity of different narrative-causal relations. Further, precise classification rules have not been developed for the allocation of hierarchical levels within a narration, which would also allow a precise segmentation of the hierarchical structure for more complex stories.

There are problems stemming from the absence of an integrative theoretical framework that describes the general function of story schemata in cognitive text processing. There is a need for a model of the functional cognitive mechanisms in working memory that organize the activation of story schemata from long-term memory. Such a mechanism is necessary to generate retrospective and prospective inferences in the cognitive system. Alongside abstract narrative knowledge structures, general knowledge about the world plays a central role in the generation of (temporary) inferences (cf. Ohler, 1994). The question of how interaction between knowledge domains of different types takes place remains unanswered, however, within the framework of the story schema approach.

The mentioned problems are addressed in later sections on recursive transition networks and mental models.

The Mental Models Approach to Text Processing

The mental model construct as a description of the cognitive processing of (narrative) texts has recently drawn more and more attention. In this approach, it is assumed that, in the processing of stories, the meaning of the story is processed in differing representations. The representation that is responsible for the construction of mental models is characterized by its similarity to the state of affairs, that means to the objects, situations, and events that constitute the story. A different representation is characterized by its similarity to text (e.g., linguistic surface structure).

Mental models are seen as holistic representations of the state of affairs that lie behind texts (cf. Schnotz, 1988). Thereby, the construction of situational elements extends beyond the linguistic information. Newly thematized situations within the narration, more important persons and events, are represented. This is achieved using representations from information provided in the text and knowledge from long-term memory.

It is generally assumed that mental models describe the topical instantiation of the working memory (cf. Glenberg & Langston, 1992). The assumptions made regarding the representational form of mental models differ considerably, however. Some authors consider it possible that representations take the form of propositions (van Dijk & Kintsch, 1983). Others propose, as a direct alternative to discrete symbolic representational forms such as propositions, analogue representations. Examples are Johnson-Laird (1983) with his analogue structural descriptions or Franklin and Tversky (1990) with their perceptive spatial frameworks (with reference to an observer-object system). New approaches adopt Baddeley's (1986) representation in the form of a *visuo-spatial sketchpad* (Glenberg & Langston, 1992).

Mental models incorporate procedures and functions to simulate events and processes. In the case of a story with incomplete textual information, mental models that are activated during processing of the story allow the most probable inferences and hypotheses about the preceding and future course of stories to be generated. Coherence is thereby formed within the framework of the mental model and is not a characteristic of the text itself.

An important function for the generation of inferences is *updating*, the establishment of a momentary understanding of a story in the mental model through the addition of new elements and the deletion or modification of already existing elements. Moreover, specific knowledge elements may be emphasized within the mental model: New and relevant units of information may be *focused* (cf. Sidner, 1983), or elements may be brought to a position near functional related knowledge elements in the specific spatial analogue medium of mental models (e.g., the process of *noticing*, Glenberg & Langston, 1992).

All these approaches have the same online assumption in common: Mental models are developed and, if necessary, changed during the successive processing of text. Because of its extratextual representational form, the mental model is not bound to the linearity of the text (neither to its surface structure nor to the sequence of propositions). Access to relevant events, persons, and so on, is more or less independent of the specific point at which they are mentioned within the story.

Although mental models are well suited for the modeling of inference processes in the case of temporal hiati in stories, especially because they do not require linearity of information, they also evoke problems. The function of narrative topic information or other global organizing structures of stories remains more or less unsolved in this research tradition. Examples of this problem may be seen in the text processing models of Garnham et al. (1982) and Johnson-Laird

(1983), in which the difference in referential coherence between intra- and interepisodical structures is not made clear. Even newer models often concentrate too much on the role of everyday general knowledge in describing represented situations, neglect specific forms of narrative knowledge, and/or prefer spatially organized principles over the organizing influence of narrative deep structures (e.g., Franklin, Tversky, & Coon, 1992, with their "one place–one perspective rule"; Glenberg, Kruley, & Langston, in press).

In the opinion of the authors of this article, the model of van Dijk and Kintsch (1983) is still one of the most comprehensive for describing the different knowledge domains and processing levels involved in the formation of mental models. It can be taken as one of the most important points of their argument that structural narrative knowledge in the form of story schemata is an integrative component in text processing.

There is already some empirical evidence that implies that mental models are organized around (important) protagonists (e.g., Morrow, 1985; Morrow, Greenspan, & Bower, 1987; Wilson, Rinck, McNamara, Bower, & Morrow, 1993). Further research is necessary to extend the hypothesis that mental models are constructed on the level of macropropositions (Schnotz, 1988) and that story and event schemata also organize mental models.

The Recursive Transition Network Model

According to Trabasso (Trabasso & van den Broek, 1985; Trabasso et al., 1989), mentally represented recursive transition networks are formed during the cognitive processing of narrative texts. An important component of this approach is the assumption that inferences are generated, linking sentence elements, or propositions "operatively" according to causal relations. The relations so established are thereby more or less independent from their temporal distance within the surface structure of the text.

The following types of sentence elements or categories are included in the model: Setting (S), Initiating Event (IE), Reaction (R), Goal (G), Action (A) and Outcome (O). These categories are recursive; that is, a category may refer to another of the same type. Because of the recursive nature of these categories, this model, which is similar to story grammar approaches, represents a further development of the causal chain analysis approach of Trabasso and Sperry (1985). Unlike story grammars, however, the determining factor in their importance is not just membership of sentence elements to the constituent hierarchy of the story, but rather the number of causal relations an element has to other sentence elements (cf. van den Broek & Trabasso, 1986). The importance of a goal in a story is not determined exclusively through its relationships to other subordinate goals, but much more through the sum of the causal relations it has to propositions of different types within the story. The goals of the protagonists are the decisive propositions in the generation of hierarchies. Protagonists' subgoals are generated from superordinate goals when the latter do not directly lead to the desired outcome.

The type of category prescribes the relations through which it may be linked to other categories. The following relations are used in this approach: physical, motivational, psychological, and enabling. With the exception of enabling relations, these relations have a causal function "in the world of narrations." The concept of causality takes on a specific meaning for narrative texts according to a (weak) counterfactual criterion of necessity in the context of the story: an action or state, A, becomes a necessary condition or cause for B, when, with the omission of A, B would not take place (Mackie, 1980).

As already noted, the importance of a category is mainly defined through the number of its causal relations to other categories, and, in addition, through its membership to the prevailing chain of actions. In comparison with story grammars, there is no adequate criterion for assessing how far a story may be described as being of a canonical type. Deviation from the prototypical course of a story, given the same number of relations between sentence elements, leads to no differentiated prediction of the cognitive effort during text processing.

Further, it remains unclear how and if online expectations concerning the further course of a plot are realized. There is no analogy to the mechanism in story grammars that describes the expectation-generating functions of the membership of story elements to a constituent of the story grammar.

When seen from the standpoint of developmental psychology, the recursive transitional network model falls broadly into the category of models in which the processing of stories is seen as an operative competence. The operations are modeled as specifically narration dependent rather than general. As a global coherence model of story processing, Trabasso sees it as valid only for grown-ups (e.g., Trabasso, 1991). Primary school children (up to about 8 years of age), therefore, would be expected to understand stories only on an intraepisodical basis, that is in smaller units, without grasping the superordinate "gestalt" that spans episodes.

LOCAL COHERENCE MODELS: THE MINIMAL INFERENCE PROCESSING MODEL OF McKOON AND RATCLIFF

In contrast to the global coherence models already described, the McKoon and Ratcliff (1992) minimal processing hypothesis assumes that inferences generated during continuous online text processing are used only to establish a representation of local textual coherence in short-term memory. An exception, however, is the situation in which easily accessible knowledge elements in long-term memory favor the building of global coherences (e.g., highly available or well-known information, such as information with a high typicality and/or a high predictability). This extension of the core of the theory appears problematic to us because, typicality and high predictability, for example, are also central determining factors for information processing in the story schema approach.

McKoon and Ratcliff (1992) defined local textual coherence as follows: "We assume that a set of two or three sentences is locally coherent if it makes sense on its own or in combination with easily available general knowledge. It is not locally coherent if information from elsewhere in the discourse is required" (p. 444).

It is only when it is not possible to establish local coherence online that "higher" conscious processing mechanisms (e.g., problem-solving processes) are called on in addition to the automatic mechanisms already mentioned. McKoon and Ratcliff's (1992) approach does not deny that global inferences may be formed during tasks that imply conscious information processing.

The validity of the global and local coherence building models described could be empirically tested using an experimental design in which the effect of different types of conceptual gaps on cognitive processing is studied. In both versions of the film used in the following experiment, it should be possible for the viewers to complete ellipses using local coherence building. In one film version in which the viewers are offered sufficient additional organizing information to use additional topic-related structures in their text processing, the building of coherences on a global macrostructural level should be also possible. One of the aims of this study was to demonstrate that even children can process narrative texts on the basis of global inferences.

ASSUMPTIONS AND HYPOTHESES

We hypothezise that the inferential completion of temporal ellipses during the online processing of narrative films takes place on the level of macrostructural coherence, and we would thereby suggest that the model of minimal inference processes can be rejected. We further assume that this form of completion is valid for both adult and child viewers and that attention processes directed toward the audiovisual texts and their subsequent retrieval are influenced by the ease with which ellipses can be integrated into preceding events on a macrostructural level.

It is generally accepted that story schemata of children become more flexible in the course of their cognitive development. We would expect, in addition, that a more elaborate general knowledge will take on a successively larger compensatory role in the building of mental models; a function that could not be executed in earlier stages of cognitive development. The general, genre, and narrative knowledge of older children is more extended and more internally differentiated. Therefore, they could be expected to compensate more efficiently for departures from canonical narrative forms than younger, less developed children. In an experiment in which a version of a story is presented in a form in which successively more macrostructures could be used (as in the present experiment) a specific kind of confoundation is inevitable: The degree of canonicity is also varied. A story version with the successively enriched macrostructure would be expected to show a more canonical structure than a version without that.

The following hypotheses are proposed on the basis of the preceding assumptions.

Online Text Processing: Attention Processes

H_1: The search for information for the generation of a "bridging inference" on a global coherence level expands (in comparison to a search that is executed on a local coherence level) to include information lying further back in the mental model. Temporal ellipses, therefore, whose inferential closure could be conducted on a global coherence level would be expected to receive more pronounced attention than ellipses whose closure had to be completed on a local coherence level.

H_2: The difference in degree of attention hypothesized in H_1 would be expected to be less pronounced in more cognitively developed viewers. Whereas the search process in an experimental situation where macrostructural relations are available would be expected to be completed mostly after the updating of relevant goals, the search for explicit action-relevant goals in a situation without the macrostructural relations would not be expected to succeed. However, under this last condition, it would be expected that older children would execute the search for information needed to bridge an ellipsis using a greater degree of extratextual knowledge than younger children. This difference should lead to systematic differences in the pattern of attention processes in different age groups.

Retrieval Processes

In an experimental situation where extra macrostructural information is available (in comparison to a condition without), it would be expected that:

- (H_3) Ellipses (or the information thereby omitted from a text) will be remembered with a higher probability, and
- (H_4) Causal inferences from events just preceding an ellipsis to the omitted information have a higher probability of reproduction. For the different age levels of the children we hypothesize that:
- (H_5) The difference between the two experimental groups (with macrostructures/without macrostructures) in H_3 and H_4 should decrease with increasing cognitive development: Younger children would be expected to profit more from macrostructural information provided in the text than older ones.

METHOD

Overview and Participant Sample

A quasi-experimental design was implemented using 60 children. Half of the children were from the first class (16 boys, 14 girls: average age 7 years, 2 months) and half of them were from the fourth class (14 boys, 16 girls: average age 10 years, 2 months).

Subjects were tested individually, and were shown one of two versions of a children's detective film. Both versions told the same story with identical film material and both had temporal ellipses at identical points. In one version of the film, understanding of the entire content of the story was facilitated because viewers received additional, topic-related, macrostructural information prior to the start of the film.

The dependent variable used to measure allocation of attention was operationalized by the viewers' visual orientation to the stimulus material. The dependent variables used to measure retrieval of the story were operationalized by a free recall of the text, questions about the information "missing" in the ellipses, and questions about causal relations between ellipses and information provided in the text.

Independent and Dependent Variables

The following independent (IV) and dependent variables (DV) were realized:

- IV1: Macrostructural information for inferential completion of ellipses; experimentally varied with two discrete factor levels (with and without extra macrostructural information prior to film).
- IV2: Age/cognitive development: Quasi-experimental factor with two discrete factor levels (first and fourth class).
- DV1: Visual orientation toward the TV screen.
- DV2: Free recall of the story (not reported in this chapter).
- DV3: Reproduction of the ellipses: Direct questioning.
- DV4: Reproduction of causal relations between ellipses and preceding propositions: Direct questioning.

The experimental design is shown in Table 15.1.

Operationalization of the Variables

Independent Variable 1: Macrostructural Information Provision for Inferential Completion of Ellipses. The stimulus material was a modified version of the Danish children's detective film, *The Golden Rain* (1988, written

TABLE 15.1
Experimental Design

Class	Macrostructural Information	
	With	*Without*
Class 1	$N = 14$ Ss	$N = 14$ Ss
Class 4	$N = 15$ Ss	$N = 15$ Ss

and directed by Soren Kagh-Jacobson), shortened to 25 minutes. In the version without the topic information (i.e., without the macrostructural information), the sequence prior to the start of the film (3 minutes, 59 seconds) was not shown. The story can be summarized as described in the following. Note that in this summary, the start of the sequences common to both versions is indicated by a horizontal line, and temporal ellipses (the omitted information) are italicized and indicated by brackets. The content of ellipses and other text elements are divided into two parts, separated by a slash (/), which contain, respectively, first the possible completion of the ellipsis on a local coherence level, then the possible macrostructural completion.

Macrostructural Information Provision

Two men (Robber 1 and Robber 2) have robbed a post office. Robber 1 drives to the woods. At the same time, a girl, Nana, rides there on her bicycle. The man buries the loot there. Nana hears a car driving out of the woods (this is her only information).

Sequences Common to Both Film Versions

Nana rides over to her friends. *((1) The friends cycle to the woods)*. They find the loot. They decide to keep the money for the present, and to tell no-one. *((2) A/the post-office robbery is discovered)*. A culprit/Robber 2 is captured. The friends hear about the robbery. The police are looking for the loot. A man/Robber 1 sees the event. *((3) A man/Robber 1 travels to the woods)*. The man finds a library card with an address in the woods/Robber 1 discovers the loss of the loot in the woods, and finds a library card with an address. *((4) The man/Robber 1 travels to the address)*. There the man/Robber 1 meets one of the friends, Karen. He introduces himself as a police inspector in order to obtain information about the whereabouts of the loot,[3] and persuades Karen to accompany him to the "police station." *((5) They travel to a hideout)*. There, the man/Robber 1 asks Karen about the library card and the whereabouts of the loot. *((6) Karen runs home)* [It is not clear how she manages to escape]. She attempts to remember the way she took from the hideout. *((7) The friends meet up)*. The friends set off to find the man/Robber 1. Karen recognizes places along the way *((8) and they find the hideout)*. There they discover the man/Robber 1. *((9) The children go to the police)*. At the police station they hand over the loot. *((10) The police travel with the children to the hideout/robber's hideout)*. The police capture the robber and the children receive a reward.

The information contained in the film was transformed by experts, in a multiple-step procedure, into propositions that were themselves subsequently trans-

---

[3]It is improbable that viewers will infer this motive in the viewing process (above all for viewers of the film version without macrostructures). It is mentioned here for the understanding of the reader of this text.

formed into a network of causal relations according to the recursive transitional network theory of Trabasso et al. (1989).

The outcome of this analysis showed that it should be possible to infer the content of all ellipses (E) in both versions of the film at a local text coherence level (L); that is, for every ellipsis, there was at least one link to directly preceding propositions. In the version of the film with the macrostructural information, it was possible to make extra global inferences (G) on the basis of higher level goals. Here, there are extra links between the ellipses and the topic-related additional propositions. The differences between both versions of the film are illustrated schematically in Fig. 15.1. In order to further clarify the experimental variation of this independent variable, possible online formation of L and G inferences will be described for the fourth ellipsis. The closing scene before the start of the ellipsis is of a man (L)/the robber (G) who has found a library card in the woods with the address of a girl on it. In the next scene, the same man (L)/robber (G) is in a town, standing before the girl's house. It is possible to fill the ellipsis locally (L) with a goal–instrument relation: The man had changed his location in order to seek out the address (goal) noted on the library card. Using the information provided in the version with macrostructures, it is possible to make an additional global inference (G) on the basis of a superordinate goal of the robber distant in the film surface structure: The robber wants to recover the loot from his robbery, and the address is an indication as to the identity of the person that has taken his loot.

The film sequences common to both versions of the film were divided up into equispaced intervals of 8.03 seconds duration. Each time interval was taken to represent one observation in a time series, resulting in a series of 152 observations over the length of the film. A dummy coding was carried out to provide a formal description of the ellipses. Time intervals in which an ellipsis occurred were

Film **with** additional macrostructural information:

Topic

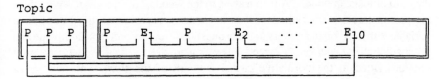

Film **without** additional macrostructural information:

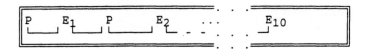

FIG. 15.1.   Schematic illustration of the experimental variation of the IVI. Key: P = proposition; E = ellipsis; ⌐ = causal relation.

assigned a code of 1 and all other intervals a 0. The resulting binary (0/1) time series contained 10 (the number of ellipses) times the number 1 and 142 zeros.

Dependent Variable 1: Visual Orientation. The eye and head movements of the children, and the picture being shown on the film screen were simultaneously recorded on a VHS video recorder using two hidden cameras. The precision of the observation of the movements was on the level of a single picture frame of the shown film. The distractors used to divert attention were slides with a content interesting for children projected next to the TV screen.

The children's visual orientation relative to the TV screen was measured by rating recorded head and eye movements with the aid of a computer. The duration of visual orientation of each subject toward the screen was then calculated for each time interval of the time series. Arithmetic means over all members of each of the four experimental groups (cf. the experimental plan shown in Table 15.1) were subsequently calculated for each time interval. This resulted in four visual orientation time series, each of 152 arithmetic means.

Dependent Variable 3: Reproduction of the Ellipses. Reproduction of the content of the ellipses was obtained from each subject using standardized questions with open answers. Propositions that occurred just before each of the temporal hiati were used as retrieval cues in each of the questions. Answers to the questions were tape recorded during the experiment. Protocols of the answers were transformed to propositions and compared with the normative "correct" propositions.

Dependent Variable 4: Reproduction of Causal Relations Between Ellipses and Preceding Propositions. Hypotheses H_4 and H_5 were tested using causal inferences between ellipses and preceding propositions. Subjects were questioned after the film viewing about the causal reasons for the propositions omitted by the ellipses and the justification for these inferences. For example, for the third ellipsis, in which "A man travels to the woods," the question, "Why does the person travel to the woods?" was introduced. As with the third dependent variable, subjects' open answers to these questions were recorded on audiotape and propositionalized later on. "Correct" answers were defined as those whose causal relations fitted to the normative causal network of the story. The number of concordant "correct" propositions was computed for all subjects of an experimental group and for each ellipsis.

PROCEDURE

The experiment took place in a laboratory at the Institute of Psychology at the Technical University of Berlin. A color monitor (with 0.68 m screen diagonal) was positioned in the laboratory (height of screen center was 1.5 m). Two white paper screens (0.60 m $\times$ 0.80 m, rectangular), positioned at an angle of $170°$ to each other, stood 0.5 m to the right of the monitor.

The subject sat in an armchair situated 2 m away from the monitor and the adjacent paper screens. The parents sat 3 m away from the children, out of the children's field of vision. The parents were asked not to exert any influence over their child's viewing.

During presentation of the films, slides were projected onto both paper screens at 10-second intervals and held for 20 seconds each. The synchronized exposition of the slides for all subjects was realized only during the course of the film sequences common to both versions of the film. The order in which individual slides were shown was randomly allocated to matched pairs of subjects (randomly paired subjects from a common age group who were shown different versions of the film). Equivalent matched pairs were formed for both age groups. The children were free to direct their attention toward the TV screen or the projection screens.

The children's retention of film content was tested after the end of the films. After a free recall of the film story, they were asked questions concerned with the content of each ellipsis in the film (DV3). The questions were ordered according to the appearance of the ellipses in the film. Each question about an ellipsis was directly followed by the corresponding question about the causal relations of the ellipsis (DV4).

ANALYSIS

Hypotheses H_1 and H_2 were tested using four analyses of the connection between the ellipses (IV1) and the visual orientation (DV1), carried out for each of the four cells of the experimental design (see Table 15.1). This took the form of four transfer function analyses between the visual orientation stochastic time series and the binary temporal series (0/1) indicating the occurrence of the ellipses.

The evaluation was carried out using the time-series analysis of Box and Jenkins (1976) for the following reasons:

1. In the use of classical regression and correlation procedures, it is presupposed that the individual variables are not autocorrelated. To fulfill this presupposition, the residuals from an ordinary least square estimation must be uncorrelated and identically distributed, with mean of zero and a constant variance σ_ϵ^2. However, the dynamic attention process (visual orientation) toward filmic stimulus materials is often autocorrelated. The measured values of attention at a particular point in time are influenced by previous values of the same variable, measured at an earlier point in time. It is, however, possible to correct data for such systematic inherent relationships, using a specific type of mathematical models in time-series analysis, the so-called ARIMA models.

2. Even when particular types of attributes of films are investigated in research literature for their correspondence with attention processes, experimenters operate assuming the simultaneous occurrence of both variables (Calvert, Huston, Watkins, & Wright, 1982, is an example of a variance-analytical procedure). The dynamic interplay between features in a film and attention, however, is still not taken into consideration in such investigations: The dependent variable measuring attention can also show a delayed reaction to the independent variable, and an external influence of the independent variable on the dependent variable at a point in time, Z_t, can conserve its effect on the dependent variable for later points in time (at the points in time Z_{t+1}, Z_{t+2}, etc.).

The Box and Jenkins method is described in relation to the interpretation of the findings of this study in the Appendix. A more extensive description in the context of film-related attention processes of children may be found in Nieding (1989) and in Ohler (1994). Empirical examples are presented in Nieding and Ohler (1990) and Ohler and Nieding (1993).

In the course of the time-series analysis conducted according to Box and Jenkins (1976), a so-called transfer function analysis was carried out. This allowed the modeling of the dynamic influence of an input series (the independent variable) on an output series (the dependent variable). In this chapter, we are concerned with the dynamic effect of the binary coded input series (ellipsis in text segment vs. no ellipsis) on stochastic processes of visual orientation. The value of the dependent variable, Z, at point in time, t (output series: course of visual attention) is within transfer models determined by the transfer function component (the modeling of the influence of the input variable, X, at point in time, t) and a noise component, N_t. The transfer function relates a dependent variable to an independent variable and describes the dynamics of a system in which the data points of the dependent variable results from a combination of its own history, a delay, and present and past data points of the independent variable.

RESULTS

Attention Processes: Results of the Time-Series Analyses

In testing hypotheses H_1 and H_2, four time-series analyses were computed in which the dynamic connection between the dummy-coded binary time-series ellipses with the macrostructural provision (E-Macro) and the visual orientation time-series (A—for attention), and between the dummy-coded binary time-series ellipses without the macrostructural provision (E) and the visual orientation time series (A; cf. IV1) is analyzed. These analyses were carried out twice: for subjects from the first and the fourth school classes (IV2). All four time series were standardized to provide a better comparison.

The time series were then compared as follows:

1. The dynamic connection between E and A was compared with the dynamic connection between E-Macro and A for the first class.
2. The dynamic connection between E and A was compared with the dynamic connection between E-Macro and A for the fourth class.
3. The differential characteristics of the models between 1 and 2 were compared.

Should the first hypothesis be verified (H_1), then the dynamic connection between E-Macro and A should be stronger for both school classes than the dynamic connection between E and A. The second hypothesis (H_2) would be confirmed should the difference between the dynamic connection between E-Macro and A in comparison to the dynamic connection between E and A for the fourth class be smaller than the same difference for the first school class.

The results of these analyses are presented in Table 15.2. The estimates of the parameters of the transfer models were calculated using the conditional least squares (CLS) method. The internal ARIMA model (the parameters denoted as AR) should not be interpreted. Meaningful transfer models only occur for the experimental groups with the macrostructural provision: Both these groups show significant Ω parameters (labeled UP in the table) with Lag 1. This means that, for these groups, in comparison with segments without ellipses, the occurrence of an ellipsis leads to a systematic increase in attention in the segment following that in which the ellipsis occurred. This is a confirmation of Hypothesis 1. That is to say that temporal ellipses, which may be filled on a global coherence level based on the additional topic information, are given more attention than ellipses that are not bridgeable on a macrostructural level. This result is independent of the age of the children. This systematic pattern of attention allocation for ellipses with macrostructure may imply that, during the online processing of narrative text, even younger children take not only local coherence information into consideration, but also salient topic-related information on a global level, when available. This would correspond with processes of a specific punctual allocation of attention.

There is no evidence in these results to confirm Hypothesis 2. Neither the type of transfer function (Ω parameter at Lag 1) nor the numerical values of the parameters differ substantially from one another. Even for the group of subjects from the fourth class, who were not supplied with macrostructural information, no significant dynamic connection could be found between the occurrence of ellipses and specific patterns of orientation to the TV screen.

Within the framework of this global type of analysis of all ellipses for the groups without topic-related preinformation, the change in the potential of previous knowledge to influence the bridging of ellipses in the course of the story cannot be tested. The global analysis shows the dynamic relationship between ellipses and attention allocation, but not the dynamic change in this relationship.

TABLE 15.2
Results for the Transfer Function Analyses Between the E and A, and Between the E-Macro and A Time Series, for the First and for the Fourth School Classes

Macrostructural Provision

Class	Parameter	With Factor	With Lag	With CLS Estimate	With T ratio	Without Parameter	Without Factor	Without Lag	Without CLS Estimate	Without T ratio
1	AR	1	1	.4736	6.34***	No statistically significant transfer model could be diagnosed.				
	AR	2	4	.2292	2.88**					
	UP	1	1	.6563	2.87**					
4	AR	1	1	.2013	2.27*	No statistically significant transfer model could be diagnosed.				
	AR	2	10	.2058	2.66**					
	UP	1	1	.6812	2.72**					

Note. UP = omega parameter. AR = autoregressive parameter.
*$p < .05$. **$p < .01$. ***$p < .001$.

It is possible that the children in the fourth class not provided with the macrostructural information were able to process the ellipses on a macrostructural level gradually through the course of the film. That is to say that ellipses become more bridgeable on a macrostructural level only in the course of the gradual development of a mental model.

This assumption was tested in a subsequent expost analysis. In the groups in which no transfer model could be diagnosed (i.e., those who were not provided with a macrostructural provision), the relationship between the occurrence of Ellipses 1 to 5 and the subjects' visual orientation and the relation between Ellipses 6 to 10 and visual orientation was investigated for both age groups. Apart from reasons of mathematical simplicity, this division of the ellipses into two equal-sized groups was motivated by the content of the film, as it is the information presented in the text between E5 and E6 which, for the first time, implies that the supposed detective was not genuine (he questions Karen in hiding). Table 15.3 shows the results of this second analysis. A significant transfer model with an Ω parameter at Lag 1 was only diagnosed for the data for Ellipses 6 to 10 for subjects from the fourth class; that is to say that these subjects showed a similar pattern of attentive behavior when viewing the ellipses in the second part of the film as subjects from both classes who were shown the film version with the macrostructural provision. However, children from the first class appear, presumably due to their reduced compensatory knowledge domains, to be bound more strongly to the canonicity of the story, which was constituted by the topic-related additional information. This was represented in these younger children by the absence of a systematic pattern of attention allocation toward film segments that follow ellipses.

This conclusion indicates that the difference in results for the different school classes does not occur because of a difference in general operative functionality: Children from the first class resort to global coherence information during online processing, just as the children from the fourth class. The younger children appear, however, to lack the flexible access to content-specific knowledge domains, which would appear to imply that their ability to use cognitive operations in interaction with the ability to use knowledge schemata is not as highly developed as that of the children of the fourth class.

These results speak clearly against the applicability of inference models based on local coherence to the processing of stories by children. It is clear and unambiguous that the preference for global inference building for the processing of stories retains its validity in the course of cognitive development, whereby the access to knowledge schemata used to build macrostructures becomes more flexible.

Retrieval Processes

The assertions made in the preceding section are based, however, only on the analysis of data regarding the orientation of the subjects' attention. To assess the wider suitability of these assertions as valid indicators for mechanisms of infor-

TABLE 15.3

Results of the Transfer Function Analysis Between the E and A Time Series, and Between the E-Macro and A Series for the First and for the Fourth Classes

Without Macrostructural Provision

	Ellipses 1–5					Ellipses 6–10			
Class	Parameter	Factor	Lag	CLS Estimate	T Ratio	Parameter	Factor	Lag	CLS Estimate	T Ratio
1	No transfer model					No transfer model				
4	No transfer model					AR	1	1	.1981	2.36*
						AR	2	9	.3014	4.24***
						UP	1	1	.6083	2.48*

Note. UP = omega parameter. AR = autoregressive parameter.
*p < .05. **p < .01. ***p < .001.

mation processing, it is necessary to seek supporting evidence in the form of patterns in the data collected concerning the subjects' retrieval processes. In the relevant hypotheses, it was assumed that the subject groups provided with the additional macrostructural information would remember the omitted content of ellipses better than the groups without the information (H_3), and that they could reproduce "correct" causal inferences concerning preceding events in the story more often (H_4).

H_3 and H_4 were tested using two-factor analyses of variance (ANOVAs) calculated using factors IV1 (macrostructural provision yes/no) and IV2 (school class 1 and 4), and, on the one hand, the frequency with which the content of ellipses were correctly reconstructed (DV3; H_3), and, on the other, the frequency of "correct" causal relationships for the ellipses (DV4; H_4).

The results of these ANOVAs confirm both hypotheses H_3 and H_4. Subjects from the groups provided with the macrostructural provision reproduced significantly more "correct" ellipses, $F(1, 52) = 4.57, p < .05$, and more correct causal relations for the ellipses, $F(1, 52) = 16.0, p < .001$. The older children produced significantly more "correct" answers than the younger (ellipses, $F(1, 52) = 45.84$, $p < .001$, and causal relationships, $F(1, 52) = 16.94, p < .001$). These results are congruent with the results based on the data collected for attention processes described in the previous section, where it was found that the attention of the groups provided with the macrostructural provision was drawn more strongly to the occurrence of ellipses than that of the groups without the provision (H_1).

Hypothesis 5, in which it was proposed that the differences within the two dependent variables for the groups with and without the macrostructural provision would reduce with increasing age of the subjects, was not verified.

In order to obtain differentiated results for the development of the story, the two-factor ANOVAs were extended by a third repeated measurement factor, ellipsis groups, with the two levels ellipses 1 to 5 and 6 to 10. However, a significant result was obtained here only for the differentiated analysis of DV4, the reproduction of causal relations. Beside the main effects of macrostructural provision and age, it was found that the reproduction rate for the first group of ellipses was less than that for the second group, $F = 5.23, df = 1, p < .05$. An examination of the numerical data gathered for this variable reveals that the main reason for this effect was a general increase in the number of correctly reproduced causal relations in the second ellipsis group (ellipses in the second half of the film), which were reported by the older children regardless of whether or not they had been provided with the macrostructural information. In contrast, such an increase in the proportion of correct answers was found only in the younger children who had been provided with the macrostructural information. The differentiated analysis of the DV3 variable, reproduction of the ellipses themselves, however, only narrowly missed the significance boundary ($p = .057$). Here it is important to note that this marginally meaningful result comes from a reduction in the number of correctly reproduced ellipses from the second ellipsis group.

The main effect of this differentiated analysis for the two groups of ellipses implies that causal relations connected with the ellipses in the second half of the film were reproduced better than those in the first half, regardless of the provision of the macrostructural information or the age of the subjects. Generally, it seems that viewers built up a successively elaborated mental model, which contains the causal relations between previous information and information omitted in an ellipsis. However, this does not appear to be because the ellipses in the second half of the film were easier to bridge, as this effect tends to be accentuated more strongly in the older children. Regardless of whether the auxiliary macrostructural information was provided or not, the older children were able to benefit from the filling in of ellipses from an internally formed mental model. Here, too, it appears that operations working in conjunction with flexible access to schematically organized content-specific knowledge domains are advantageous in the processing of information.

As previously mentioned, ellipses were defined in DV3 as correctly remembered when the components of the action that filled the temporal hiati (e.g., travel to hideout) could be reproduced. Such actions are very often paths the protagonists travel. The goals of the protagonists, however, are, in contrast, more important for the narrative deep structure, whereby the movements omitted in ellipses only represent the instrument through which goals are achieved. In the course of the construction of a situation model, the causal relations, which are connected with ellipses, become more precise, whereas the ellipses themselves take on a decreasingly meaningful role in the representational network of the story.

Subsequent expost multivariate analyses of the reproduction of the ellipses and the causal relations for the children in the first as well as in fourth classes who were not provided with the additional macrostructural information revealed, in the results for the fourth class, an apparent interaction effect between reproduced ellipses and reproduced causal relations in the two halves of the film. The older children reproduced more ellipses from the first ellipsis group (E1–5) than from the second (E6–10), whereas the opposite was true for the causal relations, $F = 14.2$, $df = 1$, $p < .01$. A similar, significant relationship was not found in the results for the children from the first class. In the version without macrostructural information, the reproduction rate for ellipses was lower for the second half of the film and the reproduction rate for causal relations was approximately equal for both film halves. This pattern of results supports the thesis that older children are able to resort to knowledge domains permanently stored in memory in a more flexible way in order to compensate for missing textual macroinformation. It also suggests that the mental model, which is constructed during online processing, primarily includes causal relations important for the course of the plot, whereas the type of information typically omitted in ellipses in narrative films, such as the way from one location to the next, tends to be excluded in the final postreceptive representation of the film. This shows that personal travel plays a less important role in the reception of texts with a narrative structure than it does in some results form the mental model approach (Morrow, 1985; Morrow et al., 1987; Wilson et al., 1993).

CONCLUDING REMARKS

The central hypotheses 1, 3, and 4 were confirmed. The hypotheses that postulated that differences in the online processing and the recall performance resulting from manipulation of the macrostructural variable (IV1) would be less for an older group of children, who would be expected to compensate for the missing macrostructural information through the flexible use of knowledge structures, were only partly verified. It was only after the formation of a mental model (operationalized in the experiment as the second group of ellipses) that the older children showed a systematic pattern in the direction of their attention after the occurrence of ellipses. It is only then that reproduction of ellipsis-related information acquires a significantly higher probability than for the younger children, whereby causal relations are shown to be more important than information about the ellipses themselves.

A text-processing mechanism, which is also constitutive of a particular type of experience of suspense (cf. Ohler & Nieding, chap. 8, this volume), is a change between global and local coherence building. This processing mechanism is often induced by temporal ellipses in narrative films. A prerequisite for this to be successful is a processing strategy of viewers that is aimed primarily at global coherence building. Suspense is created in viewers in a situation when the dominant global coherence building mode has to be left temporarily and coherence must be formed on a local level. The existing global schemata remain loaded, new macrostructures have a low probability at that point in time, and the viewers must switch to a local coherence-building mechanism in order to close the temporal hiati and reorientate themselves in the plot. If this type of experience of suspense is to work for small children, however, the preference of their cognitive system for global coherence-building mechanisms must be a precondition. The data presented here for the patterns of attention in relation to ellipses and the corresponding retrieval data imply that even children in the first class possess the necessary text-processing strategies. At this stage of development (about 7 years), however, the children must be adequately provided with macrostructural information throughout a text. The older children (fourth class; about 10 years), on the other hand, build mental models of a text, in which, by using their knowledge structures, they can generate sufficient macrostructural information so as to allow the tension-inducing forms of a text with temporal ellipses to unfold to full effect.

APPENDIX

The general transfer model is:[4]

---

[4]A notation used by Box and Jenkins (1976) simplifies the representation of the model components. The so-called "Backward-Shift Operator B" is defined by

(1) $Z_t = \dfrac{\Omega_s(B)B^b}{\delta_r(B)} X_t + N_t$

where

$\Omega_s(B)$ is a sth order polynominal operator
$\delta_r(B)$ is a rth order polynominal operator
B^b is a bth order "dead time" operator (representing a possible delay in the reaction of b periods)

with

(2) $N_t = \dfrac{\Theta_q(B)}{\Phi_p(B)} (1 - B)^d a_t$

where

$\Theta_q(B)$ is a qth order Moving Average (MA) operator
$\Phi_p(B)$ is a pth order autoregressive (AR) operator
$(1 - B)^d$ is a dth order difference operator
a_t is a normal random error variable; white noise

The first term after the equals sign in Formula 1 represents the transfer function component in which the dependence of the dependent (or output) series on the independent (or input) series is modeled. The term N_t in Formula 1, which is detailed in Formula 2, serves to model the noise component.

The dependency structure within a time series depends on the noise component N_t. This component consists of an unsystematic stochastic component a_t (white noise), usually assumed independent and normally distributed, with mean zero and constant variance, and a systematic stochastic component. The content of the systematic component is drawn partly from the visual orientation values, whose characteristics are not traceable back to the attributes of the film composition. This systematic component may be particularly observed and isolated from other external influencing factors. The Autoregressive Integrated Moving Average (ARIMA) process includes the systematic stochastic component and the unsystematic stochastic component. ARIMA (p, d, q) models provide a class of models and are characterized by the value of three parameters: p, the autoregressive

---

$$B^n Z_t = Z_{t-n}.$$

A random series Z_t is shifted backwards by B; n denotes by how many time points or lags an observed variable is "shifted" (e.g., $BZ_t = Z_{t-1}$, i.e., one lag).

order; d, the number of times the series has to be differenced to become stationary; and q, the moving average order.[5]

The transfer function $Z_t - N_t = Z'_t$ describes the reaction of Z_t on the external variable X_t. In our example, this function describes how the occurrence of ellipses is transferred to and how it continues to affect the attention process.

As with the ARIMA model, it is possible to differentiate in the transfer function between two model classes. The first model class contains only Ω parameters:

(3) $\quad Z'_t = \Omega_0 X_{t-b} - \Omega_1 X_{t-b-1} - \ldots - \Omega_s X_{t-b-s}.$

$S + 1$ indicates the number of Ω parameters. Ω parameters are described as input-lag parameters. These parameters characterize the dependence of the dependent variables on the independent variables, whereby this influence can be either direct (Ω_0) or delayed ($\Omega_1, \ldots, \Omega_s$). The aggregational level of the study influences the degree to which the effect of the delay b occurs. b can be either zero or a positive whole number.

The second model class, the δ (output-lag) parameter, contains only δ parameters alongside the term $\Omega_0 X_{t-b}$:

(4) $\quad Z'_t = \delta_1 Z'_{t-1} + \delta_2 Z'_{t-2} + \ldots + \delta_r Z'_{t-r} + \Omega_0 X_{t-b}.$

where the index r represents the number of δ parameters that characterize the inherent dependence of the output series, whereby an external influence ($\Omega_0 X_{t-b}$) is presupposed for the model class. Whereas the spontaneous effect of an input on an output is characterized through the Ω parameters, the δ parameters describe the duration and reaction pattern of the decay of the influencing effect within the output series. In this way, for example, a single input from one of the inde-

---

[5]An autoregressive model of order p, $AR(p)$, is of the form ($Z_t, Z_{t-1}, \ldots$ are deviations from the mean of the series, μ):

$$Z_t = \Phi_1 Z_{t-1} + \ldots + \Phi_p Z_{t-p} + a_t. \qquad E(a_t) = 0; \ \text{Var}(a_t) = \text{const}.$$

The measured value Z_t is the weighted sum of previous measured values $Z_{t-1}, Z_{t-2} \ldots$, plus the current white noise error term a_t.

A moving average model of the order q is of the form (again, $Z_t, Z_{t-1}, \ldots$ are deviations from the mean of the series, μ):

$$Z_t = a_t - \Theta_1 a_{t-1} - \ldots - \Theta_q a_{t-q}.$$

Where each data point Z_t is a weighted sum of previous errors, plus a current error term.

An ARIMA (p, q) model becomes an ARIMA (p, d, q) model when the data modeled are differenced to order d to reduce nonstationarity. As this component is of no consequence in the framework of the current results, it need not be described here.

pendent variables can influence a dependent variable over a longer period of time.

ACKNOWLEDGMENT

We would like to thank Mr. Alan Amos for translating the text into English.

REFERENCES

Baddeley, A. D. (1986). *Working memory.* Oxford, UK: Oxford University Press.
Box, G. E. P., & Jenkins, G. M. (1976). *Time-series analysis: Forecasting and control.* San Francisco: Holden-Day.
Calvert, S. L., Huston, A. C., Watkins, B. A., & Wright, J. C. (1982). The relation between selective attention to television form and children's comprehension of content. *Child Development, 53,* 601–610.
Chomsky, N. (1957). *Syntactic structures.* The Hague: Mouton.
Chomsky, N. (1965). *Aspects of the theory of syntax.* Cambridge, MA: MIT Press.
Fivush, R., & Mandler, J. M. (1985). Developmental changes in the understanding of temporal sequence. *Child Development, 56,* 1437–1446.
Franklin, N., & Tversky, B. (1990). Searching imagined environments. *Journal of Experimental Psychology: General, 119,* 63–76.
Franklin, N., Tversky, B., & Coon, V. (1992). Switching points of view in spatial mental models. *Memory and Cognition, 20,* 507–518.
Garnham, A., Oakhill, J., & Johnson-Laird, P. N. (1982). Referential continuity and the coherence of discourse. *Cognition, 11,* 29–46.
Glenberg, A. M., Kruley, P., & Langston, W. E. (in press). Analogical processes in comprehension: Simulation of a mental model. In M. A. Gernsbacher (Ed.), *Handbook of psycholinguistics.* Orlando, FL: Academic Press.
Glenberg, A. M., & Langston, W. E. (1992). Comprehension of illustrated text: Pictures help to build mental models. *Journal of Memory and Learning, 31,* 129–151.
Johnson-Laird, P. N. (1983). *Mental models.* Cambridge, MA: Harvard University Press.
Kintsch, W., & van Dijk, T. A. (1978). Toward a model of text comprehension and production. *Psychological Review, 85,* 363–394.
Krafft, H., & Piaget, J. (1925). La notion de l'ordre des événements et le test des images en désordre chez l'enfant de 6 à 10 ans [The sequence of events and tests with disrupted picture sequences with children between 6 and 10 years]. *Archives de Psychologie, 19,* 306–349.
Long, D., Golding, J. M., & Graesser, A. C. (1992). A test of the on-line status of goal-related inferences. *Journal of Memory and Language, 31,* 634–647.
Mackie, J. L. (1980). *The cement of the universe: A study in causation.* Oxford, UK: Clarendon.
Mandler, J. M., & Johnson, N. S. (1977). Remembrance of things parsed: Story structure and recall. *Cognitive Psychology, 9,* 111–151.
Margairaz, E., & Piaget, J. (1925). La structure des récits et l'interprétation des images de Dawid chez l'enfant [The structure of narrations and the interpretation of pictures of Dawid by children]. *Archives de Psychologie, 19,* 211–239.
McKoon, G., & Ratcliff, R. (1992). Inference during reading. *Psychological Review, 99,* 440–466.
Möller-Naß, K.-D. (1986). *Filmsprache. Eine kritische Theoriegeschichte* [The language of film: A critical history of film theory]. Münster, Germany: MAkS Publikationen.

Morrow, D. G. (1985). Prominent characters and events organize narrative understanding. *Journal of Memory and Language, 24*, 304–319.

Morrow, D. G., Greenspan, S. L., & Bower, G. H. (1987). Accessibility and situation models in narrative comprehension. *Journal of Memory and Language, 26*, 165–187.

Nieding, G. (1989). *Zeitreihenanalytische Evaluation von Modellen der Aufmerksamkeitslenkung: Ein Experiment zur kindlichen Informationsverarbeitung von TV-Programmen* [Evaluation of models of attention with time series analyses: An experiment of the human information processing of children when watching TV]. Unpublished diploma thesis, Institut für Psychologie, Technische Universität, Berlin.

Nieding, G., & Ohler, P. (1990). Ein kognitiver Ansatz zur kindlichen Filmverarbeitung: Bericht einer experimentellen Studie [A cognitive approach of children's TV perception: Report of an experimental study]. In G. Schumm & H. J. Wulff (Eds.), *Film und Psychologie 1. Kognition-Rezeption-Perzeption* (pp. 41–78). Münster, Germany: MAkS Publikationen.

O'Connell, B., & Gerard, T. (1985). Scripts and scraps: The development of sequential understanding. *Child Development, 56*, 671–681.

Ohler, P. (1994). *Kognitive Filmpsychologie. Verarbeitung und mentale Repräsentation narrativer Filme* [Cognitive film psychology: Information processing and mental representation of narrative films]. Münster, Germany: MAkS-Publikationen.

Ohler, P., & Nieding, G. (1993). Der Einfluß filmischer Montageformen auf kindliche Aufmerksamkeitsprozesse: Ansätze zur zeitreihenanalytischen Auswertung [The impact of film montage on the attention of children: Approaches for modeling with time series analysis]. In J. Felix & H.-B. Heller (Eds.), *3. Film- und Fernsehwissenschaftliches Kolloquium/Marburg '90* (pp. 55–64). Münster, Germany: MAkS Publikationen.

Rumelhart, D. E. (1975). Notes on a schema for stories. In D. G. Bobrow & A. Collins (Eds.), *Representation and understanding: Studies in cognitive science* (pp. 211–236). New York: Academic Press.

Schnotz, W. (1988). Textverstehen als Aufbau mentaler Modelle [Text comprehension as the construction of mental models]. In H. Mandl & H. Spada (Eds.), *Wissenspsychologie* (pp. 299–330). München: Psychologie-Verlags-Union.

Sidner, C. L. (1983). Focusing and discourse. *Discourse Processes, 6*, 107–130.

Stein, N. L., & Glenn, C. G. (1979). An analysis of story comprehension in elementary school children. In R. O. Freedle (Ed.), *New directions in discourse processing* (Vol. 2, pp. 53–120). Norwood, NJ: Ablex.

Thorndyke, P. W. (1977). Cognitive structure in comprehension and memory of narrative discourse. *Cognitive Psychology, 9*, 77–110.

Thußbas, C. (1994). *Die Entwicklung temporaler und kausaler Kognitionen bei Kindern. Zeitreihenanalytische Modellierung des Aufmerksamkeitsverlaufs bei synchron präsentierten narrativen Filmsequenzen* [The development of temporal and causal cognitions of children. Modeling the attention process toward synchronous presented narrative film sequences with time series analyses]. Unpublished diploma thesis, Institut für Psychologie, Technische Universität, Berlin.

Trabasso, T. (1991). The development of coherence in narratives by understanding intentional action. In G. Denière & J.-P. Rossi (Eds.), *Text and text processing* (pp. 297–314). Amsterdam: Elsevier Science.

Trabasso, T., & Sperry, L. L. (1985). Causal relatedness and importance of story events. *Journal of Memory and Language, 24*, 595–611.

Trabasso, T., & van den Broek, P. (1985). Causal thinking and the representation of narrative events. *Journal of Memory and Language, 24*, 612–630.

Trabasso, T., van den Broek, P., & Suh, S. Y. (1989). Logical necessity and transitivity of causal relations in stories. *Discourse Processes, 12*, 1–25.

Ulrich, W. (1975). *Wörterbuch. Linguistische Grundbegriffe* [Encyclopedia of linguistic concepts]. Kiel, Germany: Hirt.

van den Broek, P., & Trabasso, T. (1986). Causal networks versus goal hierarchies in summarizing text. *Discourse Processes, 9,* 1–15.

van Dijk, T. A., & Kintsch, W. (1983). *Strategies of discourse comprehension.* New York: Academic Press.

Wilensky, R. (1983). Story grammars versus story points. *The Behavioral and Brain Sciences, 6,* 579–623.

Wilson, S. G., Rinck, M., McNamara, T. P., Bower, G. H., & Morrow, D. G. (1993). Mental models and narrative comprehension: Some qualifications. *Journal of Memory and Language, 32,* 141–154.

16

▼▼▼▼▼▼▼

Problems of Measuring Suspense

Mike Friedrichsen
Free University of Berlin

The consideration of the phenomenon of suspense from a social-scientific point of view holds a considerable problem that may be phrased in one simple question: What is suspense anyway? To the present day, a clear, generally valid definition has not been submitted. The numerous attempts to define suspense do offer wide congruencies (Brewer, in press, chap. 4, this volume; Carroll, 1984, chap. 5, this volume; Vorderer, 1994a; Zillmann, 1980, 1991, chap. 11, this volume), frequently including the assumption of hypothesis by the viewer, but cannot be reduced to a common denominator. Consequently, substantial problems arise when measuring suspense by means of the techniques used in social science (de Wied & Zillmann, chap. 13, this volume) and when comparing the resulting conclusions.

Suspense is frequently defined by its conditions. This is the case, for instance, with Hitchcock: He assumes a danger unknown to his protagonist that the audience, on the other hand, is perfectly aware of (Hurley, 1993; Spoto, 1992). In this connection, the question of whether the conditions referred to in various definitory or theoretical approaches to suspense can be regarded as selective arises. Many a concept of those hitherto submitted are not in a position to name selective conditions. This is, for instance, true of the requirements for the development of suspense described by Zillmann (1991) and Carroll (1984). Even more frequent is the attempt to portray and outline suspense by using examples (or the genre of suspense film, which is a collection of examples in itself). This does not lead to a clear definition of the phenomenon of suspense, though.

A further distinction must be made between suspense on a textual basis and suspense felt by the viewers. Suspense on a textual basis (film basis) represents a stimulus, and its definition demands the accounting of stimuli conditions. To make matters more lucid, though, one should rather talk about suspense-evoking material. Content analysis ought to be the technique of choice, which in turn requires the development of clear categories based on the conditions already described (de Wied & Zillmann, chap. 13, this volume). To the reception theorists' knowledge, there has not been a serious attempt to context analyze suspenseful films until today. Suspense on the viewers' side portrays the audience's cognitive and physical tension, or actually the tension felt by individual spectators. Defining it demands making theoretical assumptions about human emotions and human behavior.

However suspense is defined, surveys tested in social science require indicators for its mensuration. Precisely because of the problems of measurement already mentioned, it seems crucially important to consider the existing criteria as to the quality of mensuration. All in all, a whole string of criteria on quality are conceivable. Psychological tests need to meet the demands of objectivity, comparability, economy, and utility as postulated, for instance, by Lienert (1969). Aside from the criteria referring to practical feasibility, two criteria on the quality of mensuration are of crucial significance: the reliability and validity of the measuring technique (Carmines & Zeller, 1979; Singletary, 1994; Wimmer & Dominick, 1994). Because causal relations are chiefly the subject of scrutiny in suspense research (e.g., certain scenes generate tension or they do not), the experience of tension is correlated to the respective protagonist, and so on—the following exposition is based generally on the method of experiment.

Threats to the validity and reliability of research apply to all kinds of research, not just experiments. However, experimental researchers are especially concerned with issues of validity because the strength of the method is in controlling for competing explanations of the research outcome. Researchers want to be able to rule out all but the explanation being studied. For example, experimentalists want to be able to rule out an outcome resulting from unexpected occurrences, maturation of research participants, and testing and instrumentation.

RESEARCH AND EXPERIMENTAL DESIGN

Given the variety of research questions in mass media, different research approaches are required. Some questions call for a survey methodology via telephone or mail; others are best answered through in-person interviews. Still other problems necessitate a controlled laboratory situation to eliminate extraneous variables. The approach selected by the researcher depends on the goals and purpose of the study and on how much money is available to conduct the analysis. Even projects that sound very simple may require a highly sophisticated and complex research approach (Anderson, 1987; Stacks & Hocking, 1992).

Research design and experimental design essentially provide blueprints, or sets of plans, for collecting information. The ideal design collects a maximum amount of information with a minimal expenditure of time and resources. Depending on the circumstances, a design may be brief or very complicated; there are no specific guidelines concerning the amount of detail required for a design. However, all designs incorporate the steps in the process of collecting and analyzing the data. Researchers must determine how the data will be collected and analyzed before beginning a research project. Attempting to force a study to follow a particular approach or statistic after the data has been gathered only invites error.

All research requires a design of some type, from very simple surveys of only a few people to nationwide studies covering complex issues. All procedures, including variables, samples, and measurement instruments, must be selected or designed in light of their appropriateness to the hypotheses or research questions, and all items must be planned in advance.

There are four characteristics of research design that should be noted if a study is to produce reliable and valid results (Haskins, 1968):[1]

1. Naturalistic setting. For the results of any project to have external validity, the study must be conducted under normally encountered environmental conditions. This means that subjects should be unaware of the research situation, if possible; that phenomena should not be analyzed in a single session; and that normal intervening variables, such as noise, should be included in the study. Also, long-term projects are more conducive to a naturalistic atmosphere than are short-term studies.

2. Clear cause-and-effect relationships. The researcher must make every effort to control intervening or spurious independent or dependent variable relationships. The results of a study can be interpreted with confidence if and only if all confounding effects are identified.

3. Valid measurements. There should be no perceptible connection between the communication presented to subjects and the measurement instruments used. Subjects tend to answer questions differently if they can identify the purpose of the study. Although this requirement fits laboratory experiments, it is not appropriate in all types of research. For example, there is no need to mask the nature of a music test conducted for a radio station. Also, the study should be designed to assess both immediate and long-term effects on the subjects.

To assure the validity of the measurements used, a sample should be large enough to allow detection of minor effects or changes, as with a greater sample

---

[1]Zetterberg (1965) named six criteria for the evaluation of empirical studies: "1. The validity (logical and/or empirical) of operational instructions; 2. the reliability (precision and objectivity) of operational instructions; 3. the correspondence between the trend in data and the trend predicted by the reviewed thesis; 4. the control of alternative hypotheses; 5. the representativity of sample selection and volume; 6. the extent, to which the reviewed thesis is a substantial part of the existing theory" (p. 143). Criteria 1, 2, and 5 are treated as criteria for the quality of empirical social research; Criterium 3 refers to the application of statistical models of evaluation and analysis.

size smaller effects are detectable (Bortz, 1993). Therefore, with the use of a large sample, one might be able to detect stimulus effects that are extremely small and completely negligible in a natural environment.

4. Realism. A research design must above all be realistic. This necessitates a careful consideration of the availability of time, money, personnel to conduct the study, and researchers who are competent in the proposed research methodology and statistical analysis.

Once the research design has been properly developed, researchers should pretest as many phases of the project as possible. A pretest of the questionnaire and a check for errors in the measurement instrument(s) and equipment will help determine whether significant problems are present. A trial run, or pilot study (a small-scale version of the planned research project) is recommended, but is not always necessary or possible. Researchers must determine through analysis whether their work is valid internally and externally.

Internal Validity

Control over research conditions is necessary to enable researchers to rule out all plausible rival explanations of results. Researchers are interested in verifying that y is a function of x, or $y = f(x)$. Control over the research conditions is necessary to eliminate the possibility of finding that $y = f(b)$, where b is an extraneous variable. Any such variable that creates a rival explanation of results is called an *artefact* (also referred to as an extraneous, or confounding, variable). The presence of an artefact indicates a lack of internal validity: The study has failed to investigate its hypothesis (Wimmer & Dominick, 1994).

In an experiment including with a control group the randomization of participants will ensure that all external influences (and all artefacts) will be equally distributed. However, this theoretical idea works only with a sufficient number of subjects. This means that, in an experiment with randomly assigned groups, artefacts should not influence a comparison across groups.

However, still other artefacts might be present. For example, if in an experiment suspense-evoking material that derives from different movies was used in order to examine the reaction to different suspense levels, or, even worse, if there is a comparison made between two complete, entirely different movies, these could work as artefacts if a comparison between groups is made. These different movies might contain not only different amounts of suspense-evoking material, but also different story settings and different actors—some famous, some not. They might also feature entirely different social relations. Therefore they should be controlled. The best solution to the problem would be to try to keep as much as possible similar in the different movie versions for the different experimental groups. For instance, this could mean editing just one movie into different suspenseful versions. This technique has been used in numerous suspense experiments (Comisky & Bryant, 1982; de Wied, 1991, 1995; Vorderer, 1994b; Zillmann, 1980; Zillmann, Hay, & Bryant, 1975).

Artefacts in research may arise from several sources. Those most frequently encountered are described in the following list (cf. Wimmer & Dominick, 1994). Researchers should be familiar with these sources if they wish to achieve internal validity in the experiments they conduct (Campbell & Stanley, 1963; Cook & Campbell, 1979; Wimmer & Dominick, 1994).

1. History. Various events that occur during a study may affect the subjects' attitudes, opinions, and behavior. The effects of history, for instance, are easily imagined if one attempts to compare, in a long-term study, today's reaction to Hitchcock's famous suspense thrillers *Psycho* or *North by Northwest* to the reaction and the suspense ratings of the early 1960s.

2. Maturation. Subjects' biological and psychological characteristics change during the course of a study. Growing hungry, growing tired, or aging may influence the manner in which subjects respond to a research study. An example of how maturation can affect a research project was seen in the early 1980s when radio stations around the country began to test their music playlist in auditorium sessions. Some unskilled research companies tested up to 500 or 600 songs in one session and wondered why the songs after about the 400th one tested dramatically different from the other songs. Without a great deal of investigation, researchers discovered that the respondents were physically and emotionally drained once they reached 400 songs (about 2 hours), and they merely wrote down any number just to complete the project (cf. Wimmer & Dominick, 1994).

3. Testing. Testing in itself may be an artefact, particularly when subjects are given similar pretests and posttests. A pretest may sensitize subjects to the material and improve their posttest scores regardless of the type of experimental treatment given to subjects. This is especially true when the same test is used for both situations. Subjects learn how to answer questions and to anticipate researchers demands. To guard against the effects of testing, different pretests and posttests are required. Or, instead of being given a pretest, subjects can be tested for similarity (homogeneity) by means of a variable or set of variables that differ from the experimental variable. The pretest is not the only way to establish a point of prior equivalency (the point at which the groups were equal before the experiment) between groups—this also can be done through sampling (randomization and matching). A more complex experimental design, like the solomon-four-group design, enables the reseacher to control the sensitizing effect of the pretest.

4. Instrumentation. Also known as instrument decay, this term refers to the deterioration of research instruments or methods over the course of a study. Equipment may wear out, observers may become more casual in recording their observations, and interviewers who memorize frequently asked questions may fail to present them in the proper order. Some college entrance tests, such as the

SAT and ACT, are targets of debate for many researchers and/or statisticians. The complaints mainly address the concern that the current tests do not adequately measure knowledge of today, but rather what was once considered necessary and important.

5. Statistical regression. Subjects who achieve either very high or very low scores on a test tend to regress to the sample or population mean during following testing sessions. Often outliers (subjects whose pretest scores are far from the mean) are selected for further testing or evaluation. Suppose, for example, that researchers develop a series of television programs designed to teach simple mathematical concepts, and they select only subjects who score very low on a mathematical aptitude pretest. An experimental treatment is designed to expose these subjects to the new television series, and a posttest is given to determine whether the program increased the subjects' knowledge of simple math concepts. The experimental study may show that indeed, after only one or two exposures to the new program, math scores increased. However, the higher scores on the posttest may not be due to the television programs; they may be a function of statistical regression. That is, regardless of whether the subjects viewed the program, the scores in the sample may have increased merely because of statistical regression to the mean. The programs should be tested with a variety of subjects, not just those who score low on a pretest.

6. Experimental mortality. All research studies face the possibility that subjects will drop out for one reason or another. This is especially true in long-term studies. Subjects may become ill, move away, drop out of school, or quit work. This mortality, or loss of subjects, is sure to have an effect on the results of a study, because most research methods and statistical analyses make assumptions about the number of subjects used. It is always better to select more subjects than are actually required, within the budget limits of the study.

7. Demand characteristics. The term *demand characteristics* is used to describe subjects' reactions to experimental conditions. Orne (1969) suggested that, under some circumstances, subjects' awareness of the experimental purpose may be the sole determinant of how they behave; that is, subjects who recognize the purpose of a study may produce only good data for researchers.

People who become involved in research quickly learn about the many variations of demand characteristics. For example, research studies that seek to investigate respondents' listening and viewing habits always find subjects who report high levels of listening to and viewing of PBS. However, when the same subjects are asked to name their favorite PBS program, many cannot recall a single one. (Their TV favorite is usually something like *Wheel of Fortune*, and their radio favorite is something like the *American Top 40 Countdown*.)

Cross-validating questions are often necessary to verify subjects responses; by giving subjects the opportunity to answer the same question phrased in different ways, the researcher can spot discrepant, potentially error-producing responses. In addition, researchers can help control demand characteristics by disguising the real purpose of the study. However, researchers should use caution when employing this technique.

In addition, most respondents who participate in research projects are eager to provide the information the researcher requests. They are flattered to be asked for their opinions. Unfortunately, this means that they will answer any type of question, even if the question is totally ambiguous, misleading, vague, or absolutely uninterpretable.

8. Experimenter bias. Rosenthal (1969) discussed a variety of ways in which a researcher may influence the results of a study. Bias can enter through mistakes made in observation, data recording, mathematical computations, and interpretation. Whether experimenter errors are intentional or unintentional, they usually support the researcher's hypothesis and are considered bias (Walizer & Wienir, 1978).

9. Evaluation apprehension. Rosenberg's (1965) concept of *evaluation apprehension* is similar to demand characteristics, but it emphasizes that subjects are essentially afraid of being measured or tested. They are interested in receiving only positive evaluations from the researcher and from the other subjects involved in the study. Most people are hesitant to exhibit behavior that differs from the norm and will tend to follow the group, although they may totally disagree with the others. The researcher's task is to try to eliminate this passiveness by letting subjects know that their individual responses are important.

10. Diffusion or imitation of treatments. In situations in which respondents participate at different times during one day or over several days, or where groups of respondents are studied one after another, respondents may have the opportunity to discuss the project with someone else and contaminate the research project. This is a special problem with focus groups where one group often leaves the focus room while a new group enters.

11. Compensation. Sometimes individuals who work with a control group may unknowingly treat the group differently because the group was deprived of something. In this case, the control group does not make sense any longer.

12. Demoralization. Control group subjects may literally lose interest in a project because they are not experimental subjects. These people may give up or fail to perform normally because they may feel demoralized or angry that they are not in the experimental group.

The sources of internal invalidity are complex and may arise in all phases of research. For this reason, it is easy to see why the results from a single study cannot be used to refute or support a theory or hypothesis. To try and control these artefacts, researchers use a variety of experimental designs and try to keep strict control over the research process so subjects and researchers will not intentionally or unintentionally influence the results. As Noelle-Neumann (1963) recognized: "All scientific inquiry is subject to error, and it is far better to be aware of this, to study the sources in an attempt to reduce it, and to estimate the magnitude of such errors in our findings, than to be ignorant of the errors concealed in our data" (p. 30).

External Validity

External validity refers to how well the results of a study can be generalized across populations, settings, and time (Cook & Campbell, 1979). The external validity of a study can be severely affected by the interaction in an analysis of variables such as subject selection, instrumentation, and experimental conditions (Campbell & Stanley, 1963). A study that lacks external validity cannot be projected onto other situations. The study is only valid for the sample tested.

Four factors that can influence this are pretesting, experimental arrangements, sampling, and multiple treatment effects. A pretest may increase or decrease a research participant's reaction to an experimental treatment. As noted earlier, the pretest sensitizes the person to the idea of change as the focus of the study. The experimental arrangements can affect external validity because a response to an independent variable in the relatively "artificial" environment of a laboratory may be different from how people respond to the variable in more naturalistic settings. For instance, music videos might have little impact on the liking of a song in a laboratory because people cannot relax as well as they do when watching music videos in the comfort of their living rooms. Thus, results of an experiment may be misleading. A solution is to gather more than one type of data. In addition to experimental data, evidence could be gathered from a survey or an interview. If several different types of data all point to the same conclusion, we can be more confident that the conclusion is valid.

Sampling is a major threat to the external validity in most social science research because of the predominant tendency to use an available, convenient sample rather than a true random sample. Thus, if a convenient sample differs from the population researchers want to measure, the results will not be generalizable. Of course, sampling is the controlling factor for the representativity of a study, also for an experimental study. However, many experimental studies in the field of media psychology are conducted with subjects of one special, well-defined and well-studied group: college students (Friedrichsen & Jenzowsky, 1995). This is also true for most of the suspense research conducted to date (Comisky & Bryant, 1982; de Wied, 1991; Vorderer, 1994b; Zillmann, 1980). As college students are in many ways (social position, level of education) nonrepresentative of the general society, it would seem desirable to use other groups of subjects for future experimental research.

Multiple treatment effects result when research participants are exposed to more than one experimental treatment: How they respond in one treatment affects how they respond in another. So, for example, each participant experienced one condition. However, learning becomes a problem. Having participated in one condition may influence someone's response to another condition. Suppose the researchers are interested in how familiarity with a rock group in a video affects the remembrance of the song. Research participants view a video of a familiar and an unfamiliar rock group. At the conclusion of each, the experimenter asks the participant to recite the lyrics. The problem here is that participants will do better for the second video. Because they know they will be expected to recite the lyrics, they will pay closer attention to them and probably practice subvocally during the second video.

Another way to increase external validity is to conduct research over a long period of time. Mass media research is often designed as short-term projects: Subjects are exposed to an experimental treatment and are immediately tested or measured. However, in many cases, the immediate effects of a treatment are negligible. In advertising, for example, research studies designed to measure brand awareness are generally based on only one exposure to a commercial or advertisement. It is well known that persuasion and attitude change rarely take place after only one exposure; they require multiple exposures over time. Logically, such measurements should be made over a period of weeks or months to take into account the sleeper effect; that attitude change may be minimal or nonexistent in the short run and still prove significant in the long run.

Reliability

A measure is reliable if it consistently gives the same answer. Reliability in measurement is the same as reliability in any other context. For example, a reliable person is one who is dependable, stable, and consistent over time. An unreliable person is unstable and unpredictable and may act one way today and another way tomorrow. Similarly, if measurements are consistent from one session to another, they are reliable and can be believed to some degree (Friedrichs, 1990; Singletary, 1994; Stacks & Hocking, 1992).

In understanding measurement reliability, it is helpful to think of a measure as containing two components. The first represents an individual's true score on the measuring instrument. The second represents random error and does not provide an accurate assessment of what is being measured. Error can slip into the measurement process from several sources. Perhaps a question has been ambiguously worded, or the pencil slipped as the individual was filling out a measuring instrument. Whatever the cause, all measurement is subject to some degree of random error (Stacks & Hocking, 1992).

A completely unreliable measurement measures nothing at all. If a measure is repeatedly given to individuals and their responses at a later session are unrelated to their earlier responses, the measure is useless. If the responses are identical or nearly identical each time the measure is given, the measure is reliable—it at least measures something—although not necessarily what the researcher intended.

The importance of reliability should be obvious now. Unreliable measures cannot be used to detect relationships between variables. When the measurement of a variable is unreliable, it is composed mainly of random error, and random error is seldom related to anything else. Reliability is not a unidimensional concept. It consists of three different components: stability, internal consistency, and equivalency (Singletary, 1994).

Stability is the easiest of the components to understand. It refers to the consistency of a result or of a measure at different points in time. Caution should be used whenever stability is used as a measure of reliability, because people and things can change over time.

Internal consistency involves the examination of the consistency of performance among the items composing a scale. If separate items on a scale assign the same values to the concept being measured, the scale possesses internal consistency. For instance, suppose a researcher designs a 20-item scale to measure attitudes toward television viewing. For the scale to be internally consistent, the total score on the first half of the test should highly correlate with the score on the second half of the test. This method of determining reliability is called the *split-half technique.* Only one administration of the measuring instrument is made, but the test is split into halves and scored separately. For example, if the test is in the form of a questionnaire, the even-numbered items might constitute one half, and the odd-numbered items the other half. A correlation coefficient is then computed between the two sets of scores.

A special case of the equivalency component occurs when two or more observers judge the same phenomenon, as is the case in content analysis. This type of reliability is called *intercoder reliability* and it is used to assess the degree to which a result can be achieved or reproduced by other observers. Ideally, two individuals using the same operational measure and the same measuring instrument should end up with the same results. For example, if two researchers try to identify acts of violence in television content based on a given operational definition of violence, the degree to which their results are consistent is a measure of intercoder reliability. Disagreements reflect a difference either in perception or in the way the original definition was interpreted.

MEASUREMENT OF DEPENDENT VARIABLES

One of the problems concerning the internal and external validity of suspense research arises from the fact that a tight definition of suspense is still missing. At first, this means that suspense-evoking stimulus materials cannot be theoretically classified with absolute accuracy. The second consequence may be more important. Researchers cannot be absolutely sure what they are measuring when they are trying to measure suspense. As the experience of suspense is a cognitive as well as physiological process, the different indicators of suspense can at least be divided into two groups: physiological indicators and cognitive indicators.

Physiological measures have been used as dependent variables in some suspense experiments (Zillmann, 1980; Zillmann, Hay, & Bryant, 1975). Although a broad range of physiological measures seem applicable in the context of suspense (heart rate, systolic and dialostic blood pressure, skin conductance, respiration, eye movement, etc.), it is still unclear what causal relation they have to the experience of suspense. Skin conductance, for instance, adresses the amount of sweat on the hand of a person. The reasons for sweating can be various: anxiety, fear, anger, and sexual arousal, to name a few. This does not mean that these physiological measures are useless; at least they are all measuring some kind of arousal. Under the assumption that the experience of suspense is always connected with an increase in arousal, the measures should be able to detect suspense.

Cognitive measures contain similar problems. As suspense as a term of our daily language is not clearly defined either, the concept might be understood multidimensionally by participants in a study. People tend to declare things suspenseful that scientifically can be labeled interesting or involving. Therefore, it also might be helpful to ask experimental participants if material was interesting. Also, involvement tests seem to be useful in suspense research, as the two concepts seem to be closely related. Involvement can be examined by the use of attention distractors (like nature slides) presented simultanously with the involving stimulus, as it is practiced in the work of the Children's Television Workshop (CTW) in the testing procedures for *Sesame Street* (Mielke, 1990).

The point in time is of crucial importance for questioning, too, especially if one is interested in the emotional experience of suspense itself. If questioning is done after a suspense-evoking stimulus has been presented entirely, the subject is usually not in suspense anymore. The dangerous situation in the stimulus material has already been resolved and so the emotion of suspense recedes. Following the theory of Zillmann (1980, 1991), this emotion has already been transferred into other emotions, like enjoyment (Zillmann, Hay, & Bryant, 1975). However, if the experimenter stops the presentation of the stimulus material at the moment of highest suspense (i.e., shortly before danger and suspense have been resolved), the emotions experienced during the suspense sequence might be more easily measurable, whereas the positive effects of the resolved suspense can hardly be measured. This leaves the researcher interested in both effects of suspense with a difficult decision. Vorderer (1994b) used incomplete (unresolved) suspense sequences for measuring suspense as well as enjoyment.

Which variables and measurement techniques are used by the suspense researchers in experimental designs? It seems to be necessary to present in a short form some specific experimental approaches.

1. Comisky and Bryant (1982): Systematic variation on conditions of the generation of suspense (protagonist likable or not likable, chances for positive ending good or bad). Measurement technique used in experiment: survey. Viewers: adults. Manipulation of material: past history of protagonist. Plot: policeman versus organized crime.

2. Zillmann and Cantor (1977): Systematic variation on conditions of the generation of suspense and of enjoyment of reception (ending of plot varied).

Measurement technique used in experiment: survey. Viewers: children. Manipulation of material: ending of film. Plot: children chase lion (cartoon).

3. Bryant (cited in Zillmann, 1980): Study 1: Systematic variation on one condition of the generation of suspense and of pleasure taken in reception (entire plot varied). Measurement technique used in experiment: survey and physiological measurement of rate of heartbeat. Manipulation of material: extent of danger. Plot: western hero versus bandits, snakes, and nature. Study 2: Systematic variation on one condition of the generation of suspense and of pleasure taken in reception (entire plot varied). Measurement technique used in experiment: survey. Manipulation of material: ending, extent of danger, and portrayal of female protagonist. Plot: woman is subject to surveillance and assault.

4. Zillmann, Hay, and Bryant (1975): Examination of effects (especially pleasure taken in reception) of suspense. Entire plot varied. Measurement technique used in experiment: survey. Viewers: children (age group: primary school or preschool). Manipulation of material: good or bad boy gets into danger and is rewarded or punished. Plot: boy drives around on bicycle (picture story).

5. de Wied (1991): Systematic variation on timing conditions of the generation of suspense. (Stretching and compressing of suspense-evoking sequences, especially compared with earlier film material and introductory sequences.) Measurement technique used in experiment: survey and mensuration of suspense extent by means of compressable rubber bellow (valid compared to survey method, highly reliable). Manipulation of material: organization of material regarding timing by cutting and omission. Plot: exciting western-style scene in family setting.

6. de Wied (1995): Systematic variation on timing conditions of the generation of suspense. (Stretching and compressing of films, keeping constant the timing of suspense-evoking sequences.) Measurement technique used in experiment: survey and mensuration of suspense extent by means of rotating indicators. Manipulation of material: organization of material regarding timing by cutting and omission. Plot: clips taken from *Falling in Love* (love story) and *Platoon* (war movie).

7. Vorderer (1994b): Systematic variation on conditions of the generation of suspense and of enjoyment of reception. Measurement technique used in the experiment: survey. Viewers: adults. Manipulation of the material: introductory story about the protagonists and plot varied. Plot: highway chase sequence, motorbikers versus couple in a car.

Given the different methods of measuring dependent variables, the conclusion can be drawn that more than one measure should be employed in a suspense experiment. On the other hand, the single question "Was the movie you just saw suspenseful?" can be a useful and fruitful measure if there is a sufficient consensus of the concept of suspense in the population questioned. How broad the concept of suspense and how similar the understanding of it in our daily life really is seem to be two important research questions for future suspense researchers to answer. An explorative study featuring several different movies and the measurement of the variance of the scaled answers to the question asked would be constructive. Moreover, this could lead to research on the interaction of personality variables and the suspense-evoking attributes of the text (movie).

Replication

One important point mentioned throughout this book is that the results of any single study are, by themselves, only indications of what might exist. A study provides information that says, in effect, this is what may be the case. To be relatively certain of the results of any study, the research must be replicated. Too often, researchers conduct one study and report the results as if they are providing the basis for a theory or law. The information presented in this and other chapters, and in other chapters that deal with internal and external validity, argue that this cannot be true.

A research question or hypothesis requires investigation from many different perspectives before any significance can be attributed to the results of one study. Research methods and designs must be altered to eliminate design-specific results, that is, results that are based on and hence specific to, the design used. Similarly, subjects with a variety of characteristics should be studied from many angles to eliminate sample-specific results; and statistical analyses need variation to eliminate method-specific results. In other words, all effort must be made to ensure that the results of any single study are not created by or dependent on a methodological factor; studies must be replicated. Researchers overwhelmingly advocate the use of replication to establish scientific fact. Lykken (1968) and Kelly, Chase, and Tucker (1979) identified four basic types of replication that can be used to help validate a scientific test.

- *Literal replication* involves the exact duplication of a previous analysis, including the sampling procedures, experimental conditions, measuring techniques, and methods of data analysis.
- *Operational replication* attempts to duplicate only the sampling and experimental procedures of a previous analysis to test whether the procedures will produce similar results.
- *Instrumental replication* attempts to duplicate the dependent measures used in a previous study and to vary the experimental conditions of the original study.
- *Constructive replication* tests the validity of methods used previously by deliberately avoiding the imitation of the earlier study; both the manipulations and the measures used in the first study are varied. The researcher simply begins with a statement of empirical fact uncovered in a previous study and attempts to find the same fact.

Despite the obvious need to conduct research replications, mass media researchers generally ignore this important step, probably because many feel that replications are not as glamorous or important as original research. Nothing is further from the truth than this belief.

This chapter stresses that the results of a single survey or other research approach only provide indications of what may or may not exist. Before the researcher can claim support for a research question or hypothesis, the study must be replicated a number of times to eliminate dependence on extraneous factors.

In conducting research studies, the investigator must be constantly aware of potential sources of error that may create spurious results. Phenomena that affect an experiment in this way are sources of breakdowns in internal validity. Researchers can validly say that the treatment was influential in creating differences between the experimental group and the control group if and only if differing and rival hypotheses are ruled out. A good explanation of research results rules out intervening variables; every plausible rival explanation should be considered. However, even when this is accomplished, the results of one study can be considered only as indications of what may or may not exist. Support for a theory or hypothesis can be made only after the completion of several studies that produce similar results.

In addition, for a study to have substantive worth for the understanding of mass media, results must be generalizable to subjects and groups other than those involved in the experiment. External validity can be best achieved through randomization of subject selection: There is no substitute for random sampling.

SUGGESTIONS FOR FUTURE SUSPENSE STUDIES

Having detailed the problems of measuring suspense, it would now seem appropriate to offer some suggestions regarding the future. These suggestions will take two forms: prescriptive and predictive. Let us consider first some prescriptive thoughts regarding a few things that ought to receive greater attention in future experimental studies of suspense research.

In order to increase the external validity of our studies, with only minimal costs in terms of internal validity, there should be greater emphasis on the creative use of field experiments. Furthermore, as an additional means of increasing the external generalizability of our findings with little or no noticeable cost, the researchers should make greater use of post hoc blocking variables in our analyses. Post hoc blocking variables are those measured variables such as age, gender, race, income, and religion, which may be used to assign subjects to fairly homogeneous analytical groups (blocks) after the experiment is completed. Each of these analytical groups can then be expected to contain subjects in each of the treatment conditions, thus transforming a simple single-factor experiment into a Treatment × Block design. This would enable the researcher, for example, to indicate specifically whether or not the experimental findings held regardless of the gender, age, race, or religion of the subject. In other words, the increased use of such blocking variables would allow greater confidence that experimental findings were not artefacts of what are often obviously unrepresentative subject pools. The greater use of post hoc blocking variables would have additional benefits in that they would likely increase the precision of experiments (Keppel, 1991) as well as force researchers to give greater attention to contextual variables. This would result in giving increased attention to the necessary and desirable task of specifying the contextual boundaries of the findings. In general, we should make every effort to utilize factorial designs. The use of such designs would result in increased attention to and analysis and discussion of interaction effects, thus adding to the richness of the theoretical understanding of the communication process.

The researchers should also make greater use of experiments as a tool for testing explicit theoretical predictions concerning communication outcomes. All too often the studies take the form of efforts that are guided by little more than educated common sense, a modicum of literature, and the question "Did X make any difference?" In this same vein, researchers should make greater use of the various causal modeling techniques in their analysis of generated data, such as the Blalock (1972) techniques or the use of structural equation models (Duncan, 1975). All too often the analytic procedures consist of little more than analysis of variance. Researchers should remember, however, that an F test is a significance test, and, as such, it does nothing more than indicate to them that they have a difference large enough to need explaining—it does not help to explain the difference.

On the other hand, the object of causal modeling techniques is to develop a theoretically sound and empirically justified model of the causal dynamics of the process under investigation—in this instance, the communication process. Merely knowing that an independent variable has some effect is only a part of the intellectual ball game. The more important part is to understand and to be able to explain the causal dynamics of the process by which the effect is produced (see Nieding, Ohler, & Thußbas, chap. 15, this volume).

Also important is the accentuation of the significance of a decision on a certain survey design in accordance with the logic of the experiment; for it is the potential of control, enabled by the survey design, that chiefly determines the meaningfulness of a study.

Against this background, triangulation has to be pointed out. Triangulation attempts to compensate by combining the use of different survey techniques, selection techniques, experiment design, and measurement techniques for the specific weaknesses of one strategy with the employment of a different one showing particular strength in that area. From the multitude of feasible triangulation possibilities, the "methodological-between-triangulation" will be pointed out, which puts different survey designs to use on the same respondents in order to scrutinize a theory. Consequently, the advantages of a correlative design (large amount of respondents examined, relatively distinct external validity) could be applied in a study combined with (numerous) experiments carried out in a laboratory setting (relatively high internal validity). In this way, it would be possible to expose a theory to a maximum of empirical testing, thus minimizing sources of technique-specific error.

Now for some predictions about areas of likely future growth in experimental studies of suspense. First, as indicated earlier, it would seem certain that increased attention will be given to the role played by the biological characteristics of audiences in communication outcomes. When one couples with this the idea that information processing theory will play a greater role in our theoretical explanations, it becomes likely that the biological characteristics of principal concern will be neurological states. This, of course, implies the likelihood of a massive importation of measurement technology from the medical sciences.

Further research should not only address the popular understanding of the concept of suspense, but also the consequences of the experience of suspense, like arousal-relief processes and enjoyment of suspense. The consequences of suspense have only been studied in a few experiments to date (e.g., Zillmann, Hay, & Bryant, 1975). As the beneficial consequences of the experience of suspense can be seen as gratifications, this research could lead to a better understanding of the motivations of and the exposure to suspenseful material. This is particularly interesting, as most of the verbal descriptions of the emotions connected to suspense seem to describe a rather unpleasant experience.

Also concerning motives and motivations of the exposure to (presumably) suspense-evoking materials, the influence of peer groups should not be underestimated. Peer groups seem to be especially important for the choice of texts (movies) collectively consumed, but its impact has not been studied extensively in connection with suspense. This leaves an open field for further research.

For the selection of cognitive dependent variables, it appears sensible to carry out further theoretically based measurements of potential participation in the plot (involvement) and expectation on the further course of action besides the simple question of whether the material has been experienced as exciting. The query as to the height of suspense lacks perspective. However, cognitive processes can be reflected in different ways as well. To mention a possible example, de Wied's (1991) study, which involves a compressable rubber bellows to gauge suspense may be cited here.

Quite another way of measuring suspense may arise due to the fact that possible tension felt during reception of light entertainment leads to diminished devotion to other things. This means that, among others, the extent of distraction shown while devoting attention to exciting stimuli could be used to measure suspense. The testing of distraction, long since familiar in connection with exploring the reception of childrens television in the United States (e.g., in the work of CTW), seems to be a useful supplement to the present techniques of measuring suspense.

Furthermore, it especially appears worth mentioning that the positive effects ensuing from the reception of suspense that have been postulated by Zillmann should not be tested by means of interrupted film sequences, because the pleasure of reception (according to the concept of Berlyne) is evoked by the resolving of suspense.

In many ways, the likely concerns of suspense scholars for the next decade will be both tremendously interesting and extremely challenging. The sources of interest inhere in the new questions that will be addressed. The sources of challenge, on the other hand, are not new. Devising appropriate measurement technologies is an old problem. Then too, scholars have always been faced with the difficulty of choosing a research strategy that will reliably provide answers to their questions. It is hoped that this discussion has shown the importance of reliability and validity for analyzing suspense and that it is necessary to heed these criteria to find the optimal strategy for dealing with questions of cause and effect in future suspense research.

ACKNOWLEDGMENT

Much of the theoretical work reported in this chapter was carried out in close collaboration with Stefan Jenzowsky. I would like to thank him for discussing some of the issues and for reading an earlier draft of this chapter.

REFERENCES

Anderson, J. A. (1987). *Communication research: Issue and methods.* New York: McGraw-Hill.

Blalock, H. M. (1972). *Causal inferences in nonexperimental research.* New York: Norton.

Bortz, J. (1993). *Statistik für Sozialwissenschaftler* [Statistics for social scientists]. Berlin: Springer.

Brewer, F. W. (in press). Good and bad story endings and story completeness. In R. J. Kreuz & M. S. MacNealy (Eds.), *Empirical approaches to literature and aesthetics.* Norwood, NJ: Ablex.

Campbell, D. T., & Stanley, J. C. (1963). *Experimental and quasi-experimental designs for research.* Skokie, IL: Rand McNally.

Carmines, E. G., & Zeller, R. A. (1979). *Reliability and validity assessment.* Newbury Park, CA: Sage.

Carroll, N. (1984). Toward a theory of film suspense. *Persistence of Vision, 1,* 65–89.

Comisky, P., & Bryant, J. (1982). Factors involved in generating suspense. *Human Communication Research, 9*(1), 49–58.

Cook, T. D., & Campbell, D. T. (1979). *Quasi-experimentation: Designs and analysis for field studies.* Skokie, IL: Rand McNally.

de Wied, M. (1991). *The role of time structures in the experience of film suspense and duration.* Unpublished doctoral dissertation, University of Amsterdam.

de Wied, M. (1995). The role of temporal expectancies in the production of film suspense. *Poetics, 23,* 107–123.

Duncan, O. D. (1975). *Introduction to structural equation models.* New York: Academic Press.

Friedrichs, J. (1990). *Methoden der empirischen Sozialforschung* [Methods of empirical social science]. Opladen, Germany: Westdeutscher Verlag.

Friedrichsen, M., & Jenzowsky, S. (1995). Methoden und Methodologie: Ein Vergleich ausgewählter Studien der 90er Jahre zur Gewalt in den Medien [Methods and methodology: A comparison of selected studies about violence in media]. In M. Friedrichsen & G. Vowe (Eds.), *Gewaltdarstel-

lungen in den Medien. Theorien, Fakten und Analysen (pp. 256–289). Opladen, Germany: Westdeutscher Verlag.

Haskins, J. B. (1968). *How to evaluate mass communication.* New York: Advertising Research Foundation.

Hurley, N. P. (1993). *Soul in suspense: Hitchcock's fright and delight.* Metuchen, NJ: Scarecrow Press.

Kelly, C. W., Chase, L. J., & Tucker, R. K. (1979). Replication in experimental communication research: An analysis. *Human Communication Research, 5,* 338–342.

Keppel, G. (1991). *Design and analysis: A researcher's handbook.* Englewood Cliffs, NJ: Prentice-Hall.

Lienert, G. A. (1969). *Testaufban und Testanalyse.* Weinheim: Beltz.

Lykken, D. T. (1968). Statistical significance in psychological research. *Psychological Bulletin, 21,* 151–159.

Mielke, K. (1990). Research and development at the Children's Television Workshop. In *Educational Technology Research and Development, 38* [Special Issue: Children's Learning from Television], 7–16.

Noelle-Neumann, E. (1963). *Umfragen in der Massengesellschaft* [Polls in faceless society]. Reinbek, Germany: Rowohlt.

Orne, M. T. (1969). Demand characteristics and the concept of quasi-controls. In R. Rosenthal & R. L. Rosnow (Eds.), *Artefact in behavioral research* (pp. 25–38). New York: Academic Press.

Rosenberg, M. J. (1965). When dissonance fails: On eliminating evaluation apprehension from attitude measurement. *Journal of Personality and Social Psychology, 1,* 28–42.

Rosenthal, R. (1969). *Experimenter effects in behavioral research.* New York: Appleton-Century-Crofts.

Singletary, M. (1994). *Mass communication research: Contemporary methods and applications.* New York: Longman.

Spoto, D. (1992). *The art of Alfred Hitchcock: Fifty years of his films.* New York: Hopkinson & Blake.

Stacks, D. W., & Hocking, J. E. (1992). *Essentials of communication research.* New York: HarperCollins.

Vorderer, P. (1994a). "Spannung ist, wenn's spannend ist". Zum Stand der (psychologischen) Spannungsforschung ["Suspense is when it's suspenseful." The state of (psychological) research on suspense]. *Rundfunk und Fernsehen, 3,* 323–339.

Vorderer, P. (1994b). Was macht die Rezeption von Filmen spannend? [What makes the reception of a film suspenseful?]. *Medienpsychologie, 2,* 103–109.

Walizer, M. H., & Wienir, P. L. (1978). *Research methods and analysis: Searching for relationships.* New York: Harper & Row.

Wimmer, R. D., & Dominick, J. R. (1994). *Mass media research: An introduction.* Belmont, CA: Wadsworth.

Zetterberg, H. L. (1965). *On theory and verification in sociology.* Totowa, NJ: Little, Field, & Adams.

Zillmann, D. (1980). Anatomy of suspense. In P. H. Tannenbaum (Ed.), *The entertainment functions of television* (pp. 133–163). Hillsdale, NJ: Lawrence Erlbaum Associates.

Zillmann, D. (1991). The logic of suspense and mystery. In J. Bryant & D. Zillmann (Eds.), *Responding to the screen: Reception and reaction processes* (pp. 281–303). Hillsdale, NJ: Lawrence Erlbaum Associates.

Zillmann, D., & Cantor, J. R. (1977). Affective responses to the emotions of a protagonist. *Journal of Experimental Social Psychology, 13,* 155–165.

Zillmann, D., Hay, T. A., & Bryant, J. (1975). The effect of suspense and its resolution on the appreciation of dramatic presentations. *Journal of Research in Personality, 9,* 307–323.

Author Index

Subject Index

Priming, 155, 172
Probability in a fictional world, 1–3, 81–82, 138
Problem solving, 5–6, 14, 54–55, 66, 95–104, 144–146, 160, 308
Psychoanalytic film theory, 23, 89

Q

Questionnaire, 262, 266–268, 275, 332

R

Radical constructivism, 238, 242
Randomization, 332–333
Reading situation, 242–243
Recall, 311, 323
Recursive transition network, 303–305, 307–308
Red herring, 14
Regression analysis, 274
Reliability, 267, 329–345, 337–338, 345
  intercoder, 260, 338
  intracoder, 260
  of physiological indicators, 295
  of registering facial expressions, 291–293, 295
Replication, 341–342
  constructive, 341
  instrumental, 341
  literal, 341
  operational, 341
Rereading, reviewing, 71–90, 107–125
Rescue scenes, 82
Resiliency, 93, 100–104
Resolution, 54, 118, 160, 175, 201
Response times, 102
Retaliation, 160, 163, 175
Retardation, 150, 159, 174
Retrieval, 319–323
Role model, 11

S

Sadness, 46, 207, 226, 279, 287–288, 290–291, 294–295
Salience, 302
Sample/sampling, 258–259, 266–267, 331–332, 336–337, 341

sample-specific results, 258–259
  stratified sample, 258–259, 267
Scene-by-scene analysis, 9
Schadenfreude, 176
Schema, 3, 55, 57, 61, 66, 131–132, 134–142, 145, 192, 319, 323
Science fiction, 256
Security of the spectator, 39, 41, 43
Self-report, 275–276, 279, 285, 293–295
Sensation-seeking, 263
Setting, 307, 336
Shame, 294
Shock, 42, 93
Showdown, 10
Situation model, 129, 322
Slapstick, 141
Socialization, 242
Solomon-four-group design, 333
Split-half technique, 338
Sport, Sporting events, 284, 295–296
Spy thriller, 29
Staging, 14, 46
Statistical analysis, 260, 264–265, 268, 274, 278, 320–322, 334, 341, 343
Statistical regression, 334
Stereotype, 56–57, 60, 66, 68
Stimulus-response model, 241, 245
Story Grammar, Story Schemata, 160, 303–305, 307–308
Story liking, 114, 117, 119
Storytelling, 4, 61
Stress, 151, 243, 262, 276, 278–279
Structural-affect theory, 107–125
Subjectivizing of the perspective,
    Point-of-view structures, 10, 167
  subjective camera, 10, 213, 257
Success, 160
Surprise, 32, 37, 110–111, 113, 124, 139, 150, 174–175, 192–193, 196, 291
Suspense
  anomalous, 71–90, 100–104, 234
  beneficial consequences, 107, 209, 339–341, 344–345
  conditions of, 73–74, 78, 81, 84, 98, 234, 247–249, 329–330, 338–341, 344
  degree of, 289
  definition of, 22, 74, 76, 78, 81, 89, 107–108, 114, 137–138, 151–152, 189–190, 194, 199–202, 204, 208–209, 246–247, 257, 283, 329–330, 340–341
  discourse structure, 110–114
  inner, 51, 60

Lightning Source UK Ltd.
Milton Keynes UK
28 October 2010

162048UK00007B/77/P